St. Louis Community College

Library

5801 Wilson Avenue
St. Louis, Missouri 63110

Shi'ism and Social Protest

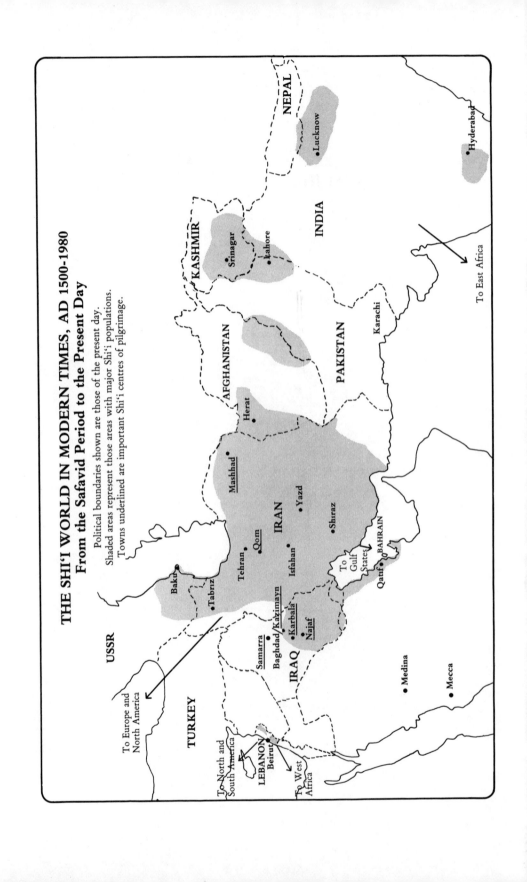

THE SHI'I WORLD IN MODERN TIMES, AD 1500–1980
From the Safavid Period to the Present Day

Political boundaries shown are those of the present day.
Shaded areas represent those areas with major Shi'i populations.
Towns underlined are important Shi'i centres of pilgrimage.

USSR

TURKEY

To Europe and
North America

To North and
South America

LEBANON
Beirut

To West
Africa

Samarra
Baghdad/Kazimayn
Karbala
Najaf
IRAQ

Medina

Mecca

Baku
Tabriz

Tehran
Qom
Isfahan
Yazd
Shiraz
IRAN

To
Gulf
States
Qatif
BAHRAIN

Mashhad

Herat

AFGHANISTAN

PAKISTAN

Karachi

To East Africa

KASHMIR
Srinagar
Lahore

NEPAL
Lucknow

INDIA

Hyderabad

Shi'ism and Social Protest

Edited by
JUAN R. I. COLE AND NIKKI R. KEDDIE

Yale University Press
New Haven and London

Designed by James J. Johnson
and set in Times Roman by
Brevis Press, Bethany, Connecticut.
Printed in the United States of America by
Vail-Ballou Press, Binghamton, New York.

Library of Congress Cataloging-in-Publication Data
Main entry under title:

Shi'ism and social protest.

   Includes index.
   1. Shī'ah—History—20th century—Addresses, essays,
lectures.   2. Islam and politics—Near East—Addresses,
essays, lectures.   3. Near East—Politics and government—
1945-   —Addresses, essays, lectures.   I. Cole,
Juan Ricardo.   II. Keddie, Nikki R.
BP192.7.N33S54   1986   322'.1   85–22780
ISBN 0–300–03550–0 (alk. paper)
ISBN 0–300–03553–5 (pbk.: alk. paper)

10 9 8 7 6 5 4 3 2 1

TO THE MEMORY OF
Malcolm Kerr, 1931–1984
SCHOLAR, TEACHER, FRIEND
Partisan of Peace and Justice in the Middle East

Contents

Preface

This volume originated in the editors' conviction that the widespread involvement of Shi'is in contemporary movements of social protest throughout the Islamic world needs closer investigation and explanation, especially since most academic books dealing with the subject confine their attention to one area, usually Iran. All but two of the essays in this book were specially commissioned for it, and they contain much new information and analysis not available elsewhere.

Suggestions regarding some of the essays were made by Rudi Matthee, David Gilmartin, Jerrold Green, and A. R. Norton, for which we are grateful. Both editors also commented on all essays.

The wide range of regions and languages covered in this book made consistent transliteration a problem. The editors' solution has been to adopt a simplified version of the systems of transliteration for Arabic and Persian employed in the *International Journal of Middle East Studies,* the official journal of the Middle East Studies Association of North America. Some Arabic and Persian consonants have been transliterated differently, when pronunciation demands it, without diacritics. Words that have entered English have been spelled according to the dictionary, and well-known names have been written in their habitual form. If an author expressed a strong preference for one of two legitimate transliterations of a foreign term, we have followed that preference.

An earlier version of the chapter by Hanna Batatu appeared in the *Middle East Journal,* and another version of Helena Cobban's essay was published by the American Institute on Islamic Affairs (Washington, D.C., 1985); we thank the editors of both for permission to reprint.

We also wish to thank Charles Grench, Nancy R. Woodington, and Cecile Watters of the editorial staff at Yale for their helpfulness, hard work, and kindness.

The editors and authors are dedicating this volume to the memory of Malcolm Kerr, whom most of them knew and all respected as a friend, teacher, scholar, and extraordinary human being, whose contribution to the understanding of the Middle East was probably unparalleled in his generation. His life was tragically cut short by an assassin's bullet in 1984 while he was president of the American University of Beirut. Our dedication of this volume to him reflects no opinion regarding the still-unresolved question of who his killer was, but expresses our admiration for his many scholarly and personal achievements.

NIKKI R. KEDDIE AND JUAN R. I. COLE

Introduction

Within a general trend toward a resurgence of Islamic political movements in the 1970s and 1980s, the Twelver Shi'i branch of Islam has produced more than its share of political activism, Islamic ideologies, and forceful movements comprising uprisings, assassinations, and the Iranian revolution of 1978–79.[1] In the Muslim lands, stretching across the southern half of the Old World from Morocco in the west to Indonesia in the east, two major branches of the Islamic religion predominate. Both had their origins in disputes within the early Muslim community over who should succeed the Prophet Muhammad as temporal and spiritual leader. The majority

1. Among books in English, see especially Ervand Abrahamian, *Iran between Two Revolutions* (Princeton: Princeton University Press, 1982); Shahrough Akhavi, *Religion and Politics in Contemporary Iran: Clergy-State Relations in the Pahlavi Period* (Albany: State University of New York Press, 1980); Shaul Bakhash, *The Reign of the Ayatollahs* (New York: Basic Books, 1984); Richard W. Cottam, *Nationalism in Iran: Updated through 1978* (Pittsburgh: Pittsburgh University Press, 1979); Nikki R. Keddie, *Roots of Revolution: An Interpretive History of Modern Iran,* with a section by Yann Richard (New Haven: Yale University Press, 1981); Nikki R. Keddie, ed., *Religion and Politics in Iran* (New Haven: Yale University Press, 1983); Nikki R. Keddie and Eric Hooglund, eds., *The Iranian Revolution and the Islamic Republic,* rev. ed. (Boulder, Colo.: Westview Press, 1985); Robert Graham, *Iran: The Illusion of Power,* rev. ed. (London: Croom Helm, 1979); Fred Halliday, *Iran: Dictatorship and Development* (New York: Penguin, 1979); and Eric Hooglund, *Reform and Revolution in Rural Iran* (Austin: University of Texas Press, 1982).

1

Sunni branch, with 90 percent of Muslims, holds that after the passing of Muhammad four rightly guided caliphs were elected by community leaders, after which less revered Muslim dynasties were established. At the opposite pole, Shi'is emerged as the partisans of 'Ali, the Prophet's cousin and son-in-law, holding that he and his descendants should rule the realms of Islam and serve as spiritual guides.

Shi'i religious and political movements, widespread in the Islamic world during its first five centuries, thereafter declined until the Safavid dynasty converted Iran to Shi'ism after 1501. At present, sizable Shi'i communities (excluding Lebanese and South Asian emigrants in Africa and Iranians in the West) exist only east of the Suez, mainly in the old heartlands of Islam, eastern Saudi Arabia and the Gulf, Iraq, Syria, Lebanon, Afghanistan, and, most numerously, Iran. Large but still minority Shi'i communities also exist in Pakistan and India.

Shi'i activism on a wide variety of fronts has caught the world unawares, and although a good deal of writing about contemporary Shi'ism in Iran has begun to appear, the role of Shi'ism in politics elsewhere in the Islamic world has attracted surprisingly little academic writing. The purpose of this volume is to help fill gaps in our knowledge about the various Shi'i communities who have recently shed quietism for political activism, from Lebanon in the west to Afghanistan in the east. The studies included here focus on Shi'ism as social protest, treating as well the perception of Shi'ism by, and its social and political uses for, the diverse communities covered. It is the common conviction of the editors and contributors that Shi'ism and its social protest can best be understood within specific historical and social contexts. Shi'ism is not now and never has been a monolithic movement, nor have either the ulama (religious scholars) or the followers of this branch of Islam always been activists or united in their views. The country studies presented here thus pay a great deal of attention to historical and social change.

This book does not wish to argue, as has become fashionable in some quarters, that fundamentalist Islam, including Shi'i social protest, has become a more important tool for understanding the contemporary Middle East than other factors such as modern nationalism. Indeed, one of the conclusions indicated by several contributors, which we discuss at more length below, is that nationalism has often proven stronger than obvious religious or sectarian allegiances, even in states with weak national identities. Shi'i activism, we argue, is different in Iraq or in Lebanon than in Iran, and most Iraqi and Lebanese Shi'is wish to achieve a more equal status within their own societies rather than to give up their national identities completely for religious ones.

To enumerate only some of the recent political activities mentioned above, Shi'is in Saudi Arabia and Iraq have held large demonstrations directed partly against discrimination toward their communities. Both governments suppressed these movements, but then changed their policies, pouring money into some Shi'i areas and showing greater respect and tolerance for Shi'i religious practices. In both countries the change of policy has had, for the past few years, considerable success in quieting the Shi'is. More violent moves have included an attempted Shi'i coup in Bahrain, bombings in Kuwait, and Shi'i participation in the Lebanese civil war, both in fighting Israelis and Americans, and in assassinations (to a degree that cannot be precisely determined) in Lebanon. Shi'is also mounted demonstrations in Pakistan against new religious taxation (*zakat*) and other laws that threatened the fiscal autonomy of their community.

Most important has been the Iranian Revolution of 1978–79, the leaders of which took a reinterpreted Islam as their ideology; they did not stress Shi'ism, partly because they hoped the Islamic revolution would embrace the whole Muslim world. Nevertheless, the revolutionary government favored Shi'is over Sunnis (who were mostly also ethnic minorities—a minority of Iran's Arabs, most Kurds, and all its Baluchis and Turkomans are Sunni). Outside Iran, although the influence of the Iranian Revolution spread beyond Shi'is to other Muslims and their movements, it was far stronger in Shi'i areas than in Sunni ones. Here we will try to sort out some of the main factors in the rise of Shi'i activism in the recent period.

Among these factors, the following may be noted as having widespread application: (1) certain aspects of Shi'i history and tradition that favor protest or alienation from the powers that be; (2) factors of economic and social change that are common to many Muslim, or sometimes even Third World, countries, but that, in combination with other forces, stimulate protest; (3) local grievances that, outside Iran, often center on the position of Shi'is as a discriminated-against minority (Saudi Arabia, Pakistan), plurality (Lebanon), or majority (Iraq, Bahrain) not having a proportionate share in the country's political, economic, or cultural life; and (4) very important, Iranian inspiration and/or direct help, which has been a factor in all non-Iranian countries. This listing only partially covers, under the general areas of local grievances, socioeconomic change, and history and traditions, the forces behind the Iranian Revolution, which have already been discussed at length by many writers. Clearly, neither Sunni discrimination nor Iranian influence entered into the Iranian Revolution itself.

As historians, we listed and will discuss history and tradition first, although this does not indicate a conviction that these are the most important factors in recent Shi'i activism. In fact, one conclusion that may be drawn in looking over the history of the various branches of Shi'ism in relation to social protest is the variability of activism among the branches, both in practice and in the theories they stress, according to time and circumstance. Although many of the particulars of the history of Shi'ism, and of its development into a widespread school with a variety of branches, are in dispute, even a general presentation, some of which may be subject to argument, shows how politically variable Shi'ism has been.

Shi'ism, it is true, began partly as a protest against those in power who had passed over what were believed by the Shi'is to be the legitimate rights of 'Ali, Muhammad's son-in-law and cousin, and later 'Ali's descendants to leadership of the community. The earliest politically active Shi'is engaged in movements of protest, including socioeconomic protest, which often heralded a messianic *mahdi* who would bring back justice and equity after the current reign of injustice and oppression. In later centuries, however, there were remarkable transformations within Shi'ism. The divisions among Shi'is came to center in part on which *imam* (leader) descended from 'Ali each sect considered especially important. Zaidi, or Fiver Shi'ism began with active revolts but then settled down to become generally quietist. From the first close to Sunnism in its law and doctrine, its acceptance of *elected* imams in the Alid line led to frequent, generally dynastic rather than ideological, uprisings in favor of rival candidates to the imamate (in North Yemen, the only area where it dominated for long).

Even more dramatic have been the transformations in Isma'ili, or Sevener Shi'ism, which in its early centuries had a strong ideologically rebellious and even socially radical component, as indicated in the Fatimids, who ruled in medieval Egypt, the so-called Assassins, who fought and often assassinated Sunni leaders, and especially the radical Qarmatians, all of whom succeeded in conquering territory in the name of their ideology. Even the Isma'ilis, like more recent revolutionaries, often compromised with their former radical extremism when in power. The non-Assassin branch of the Isma'ilis, which spread to India and elsewhere, as well as the "Assassin" Nizari branch, after its thirteenth-century suppression by the Mongol invaders, became increasingly quietist politically. Both branches, found chiefly in India but also in Africa and the Middle East, have remained generally nonrebellious until now. The change may be symbolized by the Nizari leaders, the Agha Khans, for over a century wealthy and conservative leaders of the South Asian Muslim establishment. Yet the Agha Khans, descended from the often rebellious leaders of the "Assassins," came to British-ruled India in the middle of the nineteenth century after an abortive revolt against the Iranian government from their southern base in that country. As recently as ten years ago many scholars treated the Isma'ilis as radicals and the Imami Twelvers as moderate or middle of the road, but clearly this typology is false for the twentieth century and in many instances for some centuries before that.

Indeed, it is only the largest Shi'i community, the Imamis or Twelvers, whose rebellious political activity is now important and generally noted, and hence in a book on contemporary Shi'ism and social protest only Twelver Shi'i movements require our attention. Although the history of Twelver Shi'ism in relation to politics has become a controversial subject in recent years, an outline of this history may still be essayed.

Twelver Shi'ism developed out of a broader movement of Imami Shi'ism in the ninth century. Under the Umayyad Empire in the first century of Islam, the Alid imams were either openly rebellious like Husain (martyred in an uprising in A.D. 680) or, even if quietist, were a subtle threat to the dynasty's legitimacy by virtue of their descent from the Prophet and their charisma. The Abbasid Revolution against the Umayyads contained important Shi'i elements, though its leaders did not allow the imams to come to power. The success of the Abbasids from the middle of the eighth century meant that little chance remained for an Alid leader to come to power. The fifth imam, Muhammad Baqir, and his successor Ja'far al-Sadiq, initiated a trend toward quietism and cooperation with the ruling dynasty that reached its peak under the eighth imam, 'Ali al-Rida.

One cannot speak of Twelver Shi'ism before the doctrine developed of the disappearance of the infant twelfth imam, who is believed by Twelvers to be in supernatural hiding, but will return as the messianic mahdi to institute a reign of justice and equity on earth. This creed emerged in the wake of a still obscure crisis of succession that occurred when the eleventh imam, Hasan al-'Askari, died around A.D. 874. W. Montgomery Watt has argued convincingly that it became established Imami doctrine only some time after the death of the eleventh imam, and that for a time there were rival doctrines circulating in the Imami community. He shows that the belief that won out was favored by the Naubakhti family, prominent at the Abbasid court. In the early Islamic period it was a doctrine that favored temporal rulers (specifically the Abbasids), because by declaring the succession of imams ended and transporting the twelfth imam into a supernatural realm, it removed from influence imams, who in theory had prior claims to rule.[2] It culminated in a trend toward separation of religion from politics and political quietism.

Shi'is of the Twelver line existed as pastoral nomads and peasants, as well as in urban communities. Some cities, mainly in Iraq and Syria, served as centers of a literate, formally established Twelver Shi'ism, producing learned men, or ulama, in the tenth through fifteenth centuries who remained predominantly quietist politically. After the supposed disappearance of the infant twelfth imam, the Twelver Shi'i community had depended briefly for its leadership on a series of four agents who claimed to be in contact with the imam. Thereafter the community evolved a leadership of men learned in the oral reports (*akhbar*) passed down from the imams, which served as a basis for Twelver Shi'i law. In the tenth through thirteenth centuries most Twelver ulama adopted a strict-constructionist approach to this corpus of oral reports, denying the validity of Greek rationalism in legal reasoning. This early majority grouping became known as Akhbaris. They believed that no individual jurisprudent should be emulated, but that all believers, including religious experts, should emulate the imams. Most Twelver ulama from the tenth through thirteenth centuries likewise held that in the absence of the imam, such central duties of the Islamic state as the holding of Friday congregational prayers, holy war (*jihad*), and the collection of certain kinds of religious taxes could not be undertaken. Such conservative views had the twin effect of removing any strong motivations for political activism until the imam returned and yet of also questioning the justice of any existing government until that time.

Radical movements among Shi'is in this period tended to take sectarian shape, such as the Hurufis among urban artisans in Iran and Anatolia, or the tribal Musha'sha' movement among pastoralists in Iraq. Thus, when politically important rebellious movements with a Twelver ideology arose, it was not among learned or "orthodox" urban Twelvers but rather among unruly, largely pastoral nomadic, peoples of eastern Anatolia and neighboring Syria then being displaced eastward toward Iran by the rise of the Sunni Ottomans.

In the late fifteenth century many of these Twelver tribes adopted as their leaders the heads of the formerly Sunni Safavid Sufi order, who had been based in Iran near Anatolia. Although the Safavids are, rightly,

2. See W. Montgomery Watt, *The Formative Period of Islamic Thought* (Edinburgh: Edinburgh University Press, 1973), and idem, "The Significance of the Early States of Imami Shi'ism," in Keddie, ed., *Religion and Politics in Iran*, 21–32.

known as Twelvers, many of their early ideas, apparently adopt
their new pastoral nomadic followers, seem closer to rebellious 𝔰ᵤᵣᵣ
and other sectarian extremists—as is shown, among other ways, by religiously extremist and unorthodox poetry of the first, early sixteenth-century, Safavid shah of Iran, Isma'il. When the nomadic Safavid cavalry
conquered Iran and established a Safavid monarch on the throne in 1501,
the new government determined to convert Iran forcibly from Sunnism to
Shi'ism, a program carried out with some brutality. But the folk Shi'ism
of the Turkoman tribespeople ill lent itself to systematic propagation as
a state religion or legal system, and so the Safavids turned to the literate,
urban tradition of Twelver Shi'ism for support in their endeavor. They
imported some Shi'i ulama from what is now Lebanon, Iraq, and later
Bahrain, along with books of the Shi'i great tradition, an action that points
to the scarceness of these resources in the Iran of that time. One contemporary historian wrote that when the Safavids took the Iranian capital,
Tabriz, they sent out for Shi'i books and could find only one. This is
probably hyperbole, but it seems clear that the Safavids and their first
followers had little idea of learned Shi'ism.

Once in power, much like the Fatimid and Abbasid caliphates before
them, the Safavids wished to move away from extremist or revolutionary
ideas and to support a religious establishment, which they increasingly
did. The Shi'i ulama were not just docile followers of the shahs, however.
Developments within Shi'ism strengthened the independent position of
the Shi'i ulama. Most important, the Safavid monarchs granted land to
immigrant Arab ulama whom they thus attracted to Iran to help with the
work of converting the population. The government also increasingly
alienated land in the form of pious endowments put under ulama control.
By the seventeenth century the more powerful ulama had a secure economic base of their own, a feature that continued in Iran into the present.

Second, clerical ideology came to support an independent role for
the Safavid-era ulama. Although there were some early ulama who supported a stronger role for Greek rationalism in Imami theology than did
the Akhbaris, it was not until the late thirteenth and the fourteenth centuries that prominent Twelver ulama emerged to challenge the Akhbari
predominance with a rationalist jurisprudence. These held that certain
tools of Greek logic could be applied to the task of deriving legal judgments from the oral reports of the imams and the Qur'an. This rationalist
approach was called "endeavor," or *ijtihad,* and its practitioners were
mujtahids. In time proponents of this new *Mujtahidi* or *Usuli* school came
to argue that Twelver ulama could stand proxy for the imam in legiti-

mating Friday prayers, the collection of land taxes, and other state-related functions, even during the time of the imam's occultation. They also held that all laypersons were obliged to emulate a mujtahid.

In early Safavid times, the Usulis allied themselves forcefully with the shahs, receiving in return powerful appointments as prayer leaders. Arab Akhbaris, until then probably the majority, often opposed the alliance between the court and the high mujtahids, as research by Andrew Newman has indicated.[3] Since Friday congregational prayers were places where large numbers gathered, and the concluding sermon formula (khutba) included blessings on the Safavid monarch, Usuli ulama became important agents in legitimizing Safavid rule throughout Iran. In later times, however, Usuli-Mujtahidi arguments were used to stress the independence of the ulama in relation to the shahs. The doctrine of the need for laymen to emulate mujtahids had the potential of putting the claims of the mujtahids to determine how people should be ruled higher than those of the shah, and such claims are recorded in the late Safavid period. Few, if any, Shi'i mujtahids before Khomeini seriously proposed that the ulama should actually rule, but in some ways this stance is a logical (though not inevitable) development from the Usuli school of jurisprudence, which sees the ulama as the general representatives of the twelfth imam.

The Safavid Empire fell in 1722 to Afghan Sunni invaders, initiating a period of Sunni influence in Iran that temporarily disestablished the Twelver ulama establishment. Many ulama families suffered downward mobility, and numbers were forced to seek a new relationship with the bazaar classes to replace the patronage they had lost from the shahs. This period saw an increased prominence of the Akhbari-dominated Shi'i shrine cities of Iraq, under Sunni Ottoman rule, and a relative decline of Usuli centers such as Isfahan in Iran. Many Iranian Usuli families emigrated to Iraq as refugees after 1722, often adopting the Akhbarism of their Arab Shi'i hosts there. But a generation later, during the Zand period in Iran, these Iranian immigrants in the shrine cities conducted a successful revival of the Usuli school. With the rise of the Shi'i Qajar state in Iran (1785–1925), the newly Usuli shrine cities served as important

3. Andrew Newman (Ph.D. diss., University of California at Los Angeles, in progress). On the development of Shi'i doctrine in pre-Safavid and Safavid times, see Norman Calder, "The Structure of Authority in Imami Shi'i Jurisprudence" (Ph.D. diss., University of London, 1979). For religion in Safavid Iran, see Said Amir Arjomand, The Shadow of God and the Hidden Imam (Chicago: University of Chicago Press, 1984), and for a survey, see Moojan Momen, An Introduction to Shi'ism (New Haven: Yale University Press, 1985).

recruiting grounds for clerical personnel, ensuring the final triumph of Usulism as the predominant school of Twelver Shi'ism. From the middle of the nineteenth century a convention developed that the leading mujtahid in the Iraqi shrine city of Najaf was the chief (*ra'is*) of all the Shi'is. This position was buttressed by his control of huge sums in charitable and religious contributions that flowed in from notables, governments, and bazaar classes throughout the Shi'i world, as well as by Usuli doctrine, which preferred that laymen choose the single most learned mujtahid to emulate. Residing under Ottoman rule, he was less subject to political control by the shahs than were Qajar religious officials inside Iran.[4]

Although the Iranian ulama supported the shahs most of the time, they sometimes acted independently. Ulama pressured the government into the second Irano-Russian war in 1826 and incited the killing of the Russian envoy, Griboyedov, in 1829. The late nineteenth century witnessed the beginnings of a serious and long-term breach between ulama and state, as the weak Qajars increasingly acquiesced to foreign economic and diplomatic influences. Ulama protested the Reuter concession in 1873 and the tobacco concession of 1891–92, and participated in the constitutional revolution of 1905–11. There are disputes about the relative weight of oppositional and pro-shah forces among the ulama, with the latter being emphasized especially by Said Arjomand and by anticlerical scholars in Iran. But it cannot be denied that, even though they were pushed by merchants and intellectuals, some ulama played a key role in leading and getting popular support for the tobacco movement and the constitutional revolution, although many ulama turned against that revolution once its secularist implications, harmful to their power and influence, became clear.[5]

Later movements in which Shi'i ideology played a role in Iran included those in Gilan and Azerbaijan after World War I; ulama protests

4. This reinterpretation of Shi'ism in the eighteenth and nineteenth centuries rests primarily on soon-to-appear articles by Juan R. I. Cole, including "Shi'i Clerics in Iraq and Iran, 1722–1780: The Akhbari-Usuli Controversy Reconsidered," *Iranian Studies* 18, no. 1 (1985); " 'Indian Money' and the Shi'i Shrine Cities of Iraq 1786–1850," *Middle Eastern Studies*, forthcoming; and J. Cole and Moojan Momen, "Mafia, Mob and Shi'ism in Iraq: The Rebellion of Ottoman Karbala 1824–1843," *Past and Present*, forthcoming.

5. Downplaying the ulama's role is Said Amir Arjomand, "The Ulama's Traditionalist Opposition to Parliamentarianism: 1907–1909," *Middle Eastern Studies* 17, no. 2 (1981): 174–90. A different view is found in Nikki R. Keddie, "Religion and Irreligion in Early Iranian Nationalism," in Nikki R. Keddie, ed., *Iran: Religion, Politics and Society* (London: Frank Cass, 1980), and in A. K. S. Lambton, "The Persian Ulama and Constitutional Reform," in *Le Shi'isme imamite* (Paris: PUF, 1970).

against Reza Shah's reforms, especially forcible unveiling of women; the post–World War II Fida'iyan-i Islam, who assassinated politicians and intellectuals; Ayatullah Kashani's anti-imperialist movement culminating in a temporary alliance with nationalist prime minister Muhammad Musaddiq in the early 1950s; participation of conservative ulama in the U.S.-sponsored overthrow of Musaddiq; and major demonstrations in 1963 against the shah's reforms and complaisance toward the United States and Israel, in which Khomeini emerged as the main leader, after which he was exiled in 1964.

Although some recent authors have stressed, with some justice, that the Iranian ulama have been, over time, predominantly royalist and complaisant to the powers that be, on a comparative scale with other Muslim countries, one must note that there is no other country where the ulama have entered into nearly the amount of protest one finds in Iranian history from the late nineteenth century and throughout the twentieth. Reasons for this have been discussed in other works, but here we will say briefly that ulama independence and power in Iran was supported by ulama (rather than state) receipt and distribution of religious taxes, by long-standing residence of the top ulama leadership outside Iranian state control in Iraq, and by a doctrine that said that all believers must follow the rulings of living ulama. Moreover, Iran's decentralized form of government, with a state too weak to enforce controls over the ulama (unlike the governments of the nineteenth-century Ottoman Empire and Egypt, and twentieth-century Tunisia, where ulama were deprived of endowments and put on a state payroll), resulted in ulama who could take independent positions and lead independent movements. Very few of the ulama were or are "progressive" as some Iranians called them before and during the 1978–79 revolution; they were and are fighting largely for their own power and prerogatives and for what they see as an Islamic way of life, the conception of which has varied over time; but this fight has at times led them into alliances with oppositional secularists. During the 1905–11 revolution secularists perhaps gained more than did the ulama; in the Musaddiq period in the early 1950s the secularists were on top from beginning to end, and in both these periods key ulama broke with the movement. Only since 1978 have the ulama, for the present, come out on top in a joint movement that took governmental power. (See the chapter by Cottam in this volume.)

These are the main outlines of the development of religion and state relations in Shi'i Iran. Unfortunately, tracing developments among Twelver Shi'is elsewhere presents many greater difficulties, since little scholarly work has been published on the political history of Twelver Shi'is outside Iran in recent centuries. In Iraq, where Shi'is form a slight majority and predominate in the south of the country, the Shi'i Arab pastoral nomads and the inhabitants of the shrine cities of Karbala, Najaf, Kazimain, and Samarra often demonstrated great independence from the Sunni Ottoman government and more than once in the nineteenth century had to be subdued by Sunni armies from Baghdad. Shi'i ulama also played a part in some popular movements in modern Iraq, as in the anti-British agitation after World War I.

Political and ideological developments in Iran and Iraq, the demographic centers of the Shi'i world from the sixteenth century, had great impact elsewhere. In India in the wake of the eighteenth-century fragmentation of the Mughal Empire, a Shi'i-ruled state called Awadh (Oudh), whose dynasty governed from 1722 until the British annexation of 1856, emerged northwest of Bengal and southeast of Delhi. There, a Shi'i notable class grew up that served as patron for an increasing number of Shi'i ulama, though Shi'ism remained a minority religion in a region where Hindus predominated and most Muslims were Sunni. Although northern India's Shi'is were largely Akhbaris before the late eighteenth century, developments in Iraq and Iran had an almost immediate impact in Shi'i-ruled Awadh. Especially after the triumph of Usulism in the shrine cities of Iraq in the latter half of the eighteenth century, young Indian ulama who went to Iraq and Iran for study or visitation at shrines brought back with them Usuli ideas. Usuli doctrines were also spread by Iranian immigrants to Awadh in search of patronage. These ideas appealed both to the rising class of Shi'i ulama in Awadh and to the Awadh government. Akhbaris in Awadh opposed Friday congregational prayers, whereas Usulis permitted them, and since the leaders in the emerging Awadh state favored holding the prayers as a statement of their legitimacy, they tended to bestow their patronage on Usulis.[6] Similar ideological influences emanated from the Iraqi shrine cities and from Iran to Arab Shi'i centers in what is now Lebanon and in Bahrain and East Arabia, as well as to Afghanistan, Pakistan, and Kashmir. Of course, the traffic in ideas and practices was two-way, with scholars from these peripheries making an impact also on the center. Significantly, Usulism does not appear to have triumphed in the peripheries until after it did so in Iraq, which points to

6. J. R. I. Cole, *Roots of North Indian Shi'ism in Iran and Iraq: Religion and State in Nishapuri Awadh, 1722–1859* (Berkeley and Los Angeles: University of California Press, forthcoming).

the centrality of the shrine cities for networks among Shi'i scholars throughout Asia.

Although many of the leading Shi'is in the shrine cities were ethnic Iranians, they were not all so, and Iraqis sometimes had top positions. Some Iranians (including the late shah) wished to recognize an Iraqi mujtahid as the top "source for emulation" (*marja'-i taqlid*) after the 1961 death of Ayatullah Burujirdi. In the Arab world, however, as in India and Pakistan, the primary contender with Khomeini for top leadership of the Shi'i community remains Abu'l-Qasim al-Khu'i, an Iranian based in Najaf in Iraq. The interplay of nationalities among leading Shi'is is suggested in the present volume by the mobility of ulama among Shi'i countries; by the influence in Iran of the writings of Ayatullah Muhammad Baqir al-Sadr, an Iraqi of Lebanese origin; by the leading role of the Iranian Musa al-Sadr (of Lebanese descent) among Lebanese Shi'is; and by the mixed Iranian, Iraqi, and Lebanese nature of some prominent clerical families. In the absence of badly needed research on the history of most non-Iranian Shi'i communities, what we now see suggests that their evolution has not diverged radically from those in Iran, and that the development of doctrine by ulama of Iranian and Iraqi origin came to be followed by Shi'is from Lebanon to India. One major similarity, and a contrast with nearly all Sunni areas, is that the ulama have been important in Shi'i political ideology and movements outside Iran, the two ulama mentioned in Lebanon and Iraq being the most striking examples. In Sunni areas Islamic political movements, by contrast, tend to be led by laypersons. It is true that Shi'i ulama outside Iran often lacked the Iranian ulama's bazaar ties and political strength until recently.[7]

The all-Islamic or Third World factors of economic and social change behind many Shi'i protests may be dealt with more briefly, as they are familiar, however much individual writers may differ about their relative weight. The differential impact of capitalism, or of modernization, on various groups and classes, usually involving growing gaps in income distribution and life-styles, often brings forth protest, especially in a context of rapid social change. This has been a factor in protest among Saudi Shi'is who, even though, or rather, perhaps, because, they worked in a region of oil production, felt with some justice that their economic needs were not being met and that their Shi'i culture was suppressed by intol-

7. For a contrast between Lebanese and Iranian ulama in these respects, see Michael Gilsenan, *Recognizing Islam* (London: Croom Helm, 1982), a book analyzing complex interactions among social, economic, religious, and political changes.

erant Wahhabi Sunnis. As noted earlier, their protest brought some redress. (See the chapters by Goldberg and Ramazani.) Similarly, economic development in Iraq and Lebanon did not proportionately benefit Shi'is, who remained predominantly proletarians and subproletarians or peasants. Again in these cases local protests have brought some improvements. (See the chapters by Batatu, Cobban, and Norton.) It should be added that although a group with a clear identity, ethnic or sectarian, may be discriminated against, such groups may also be in an advantageous position to mobilize around their own cultural identity and gain redress; Arab Sunni workers are at a disadvantage in this respect. It is sometimes said, regarding such protests, that what appears to be an ethnic or religious dispute is *really* a class dispute; this, however, is oversimplified revisionism or vulgar Marxism; it is *really* both an ethnic and a class struggle, and, in recent decades at least, ethnic appeals have usually proved stronger than straight class appeals.

Another factor common to the Third World is that of anti-imperialism, in the Middle East directed especially at the United States and Israel. The nationalist rulers who have dominated the Middle East in recent decades similarly speak in anti-imperialist terms for the most part, but they are often seen as having failed to carry out their socioeconomic programs, as well as having failed to accomplish anything regarding Israel or the Palestinians. This perceived failure directs many protesters both against the formerly popular nationalist ideologies, which are seen as inadequate for either domestic or foreign policy goals, and against what is perceived as subservience by their governments to the United States and impotence regarding Israel. Shi'is, like many other people, have legitimate grievances against the foreigners who have operated and are still operating to achieve their own foreign policy and economic goals in their countries. Many militant Shi'is, as indicated especially by Khomeinist rhetoric, share a Third Worldist tendency to blame nearly everything on the United States and Israel, and on those of their own rulers who are seen as puppets of, or collaborators with, the two countries. (Examples of such views expressed by Egyptian Sunni admirers of the Iranian Revolution are found in Matthee's chapter.)

Under the heading of anti-imperialism comes a series of truck-bombings and hijackings carried out by various Shi'i groups, especially in Kuwait (where Shi'is make up 19 percent of the population) and Lebanon (where they are over a third). In Kuwait, suicide bomb attacks by Shi'i activists against the U.S. embassy and the French consulate on December 12, 1983, resulted in extensive destruction. Seventeen conspirators were arrested and three sentenced to death. They were reportedly members of the originally Iraqi Shi'i organization al-Da'wah, and their deed was apparently inspired by Khomeini's radicalism and by anti-Israeli sentiments. A year later, on December 5, 1984, a group of Shi'i fighters, apparently from Lebanon's Party of God, hijacked a Kuwaiti Airlines jet to Tehran and killed two Americans; they were demanding the release of the radical Shi'i prisoners in Kuwait. The hijackers eventually surrendered to Iranian authorities without having their demands met (*New York Times*, December 5–10, 1984). The release of the imprisoned Shi'i fighters in Kuwait was also one of the demands of Lebanese Shi'i radicals who hijacked a Trans-World Airlines jet full of American passengers from Athens to Beirut in June of 1985, along with the release of Lebanese Shi'is held in Israeli detention facilities. (For al-Da'wah, see Batatu's chapter; for Shi'ism in the Gulf, Ramazani's; and for the TWA hijacking to Beirut, see the chapters by Norton and Cobban.)

Regarding what appears to be a great rise of religious as against national or nationalist identity in the Middle East, one should not, relying on published writings and rhetoric, exaggerate its extent. An example of the strength of loyalty to existing territorial lines, despite a lack of published rhetoric by the involved groups defending them, is found in the Iran-Iraq War, where many foreign observers followed local ones in thinking that Iraq's Shi'is would rally in great numbers to Iran, but they did not do so (as discussed in Batatu's chapter). As noted earlier, both Iraqi and Saudi Shi'is have experienced decreased militance after concessions.

Among Shi'is, revivalism accompanied rapid modernization and the growth of capitalist relations tied to the West, not only in Iran, but also in Saudi Arabia, the Gulf, Iraq, Lebanon, and Pakistan. Preindustrial Twelver Shi'i peasants, dwelling for the most part in arid regions where villages were far apart and horizontal organization proved difficult, were relatively quiescent. As new bourgeois, Western-tied relations have developed, Twelver Shi'is have been increasingly rebellious and oriented toward revivalism. A related factor in Middle Eastern instability, reflected among Shi'is, is the sudden rise and recent fall in oil income, which has sped social changes like urban migration and agricultural decline, increased income distribution gaps while raising average incomes, and, largely via Saudi expenditures, spread Sunni institutions and propaganda and, in reaction, Shi'i response.

The third factor in Shi'i protest—specific grievances—has been alluded to in the discussion above. To elaborate slightly: In Iraq, where

Shi'is are often estimated at 55 to 60 percent of the population, though some say they are fewer, they have been grossly underrepresented in government and in bureaucratic and business positions. Although not nearly as rebellious as the Kurds, they have in recent decades developed both underground militant movements and a more far-reaching community sense of grievance. Since their demonstrations the government has applied a strong carrot-and-stick policy—hanging Muhammad Baqir al-Sadr, his sister, and others, but making concessions to help meet the Shi'is' economic, political, and cultural differences. For now their protest movement has decreased. The situation in Saudi Arabia where Shi'is are a small minority, but strategically concentrated in the oil-producing eastern area, is similar. Protests and their leaders have been suppressed, but economic concessions and an end to the main restrictions on the Shi'is' observance of their beliefs and ceremonies have led to a quiet situation and even to complaints by Sunnis that the Shi'is are favored (see Ramazani's chapter).

Lebanon is clearly more complicated in this as in other matters, with the main Shi'i political differentiation being between the rather moderate and secular Amal led by Nabih Berri and the more radical or break-off groups that are sometimes associated with assassinations and kidnappings. In Lebanon, too, however, the political influence of Shi'is has grown with their protest, and as the plurality religious group in their country they may emerge with commensurate political power. Shi'is in Sunni Afghanistan, traditionally discriminated against, have emerged as an important element in the struggle against the Soviet Union, such that often Sunnis have fought side by side with them. (These developments are discussed further in the chapters by Batatu, Goldberg, Ramazani, Cobban, Norton, and Edwards.) Some concessions after protest have also been made to the Shi'i majority in Bahrain.

The Shi'i minority in Pakistan also waged a successful fight against a Sunni government for more autonomy and recognition. Since no individual chapter in this volume treats Pakistan, it is worth considering its Shi'is in some detail here. West Pakistan, a modern creation dating from 1947, comprises the provinces of Punjab (with the majority of the population), Sindh, and Baluchistan, the Northwest Frontier Province, and part of Kashmir (all of largely Muslim Kashmir is claimed, but despite several wars almost all of it remains with India). Abutting Iran and Afghanistan, and accessible from the Persian Gulf, parts of Pakistan have been involved in Islam since the religion's earliest expansion. Moreover, Shi'i movements have been important. In the late tenth to early twelfth centuries A.D., an Isma'ili state arose in Multan and Sindh. Seveners still exist in the northern area of Baltistan and are commercially prominent in Karachi.

From the early sixteenth century the Sunni Mughal Empire ruled today's Pakistan and most of central and northern India, reinforcing Sunni orthodoxy. But the sixteenth-century conversion of Iran to Twelver Shi'ism under the Safavids had an impact on Iran's neighbors to the east, and under its influence most Punjabi Shi'is converted to the Twelver branch. Iranian emigration to the wealthy Mughal Empire was so sizable that one seventeenth-century European traveler said it contributed to underpopulation in Iran.[8] Many Iranian notables and merchants settled in Kashmir, Sindh, and the Punjab, bringing their Shi'ism with them. Some Iranians, valued for their knowledge of Persian, the Mughal state language, successfully climbed the Mughal Empire's bureaucratic ladder and were rewarded with high positions and lands in the Punjab and elsewhere. Indigenous developments also sometimes favored Shi'ism. A Twelver Shi'i Sufi order, the Jalali Suhrawardi, has been based in Multan for centuries. A cult of the family of the Prophet, and of the martyred Imam Husain, also played a large part in Sindhi and Punjabi folk culture. In the sixteenth century a Twelver Shi'i dynasty briefly ruled Kashmir. It attempted to convert the population forcibly to Imami Shi'ism, before a Sunni restoration.[9] In Baluchistan and the Northwest Frontier, dominated by fiercely Sunni Baluchi and Pukhtun pastoralists, Shi'is gained few footholds. Even in Sindh, Punjab, and Kashmir, Sunnis remained the vast majority of the population, but Shi'is existed and may have grown in number in the eighteenth and nineteenth centuries after the fall of the Sunni Mughal Empire and its replacement by Sikh and then British regimes, which had no interest in maintaining Sunni orthodoxy.

The way in which major Shi'i centers such as Iraq, Iran, and Awadh/Oudh (in North India) affected what is now Pakistan is demonstrated by the life of Sayyid Abu'l-Qasim Rizavi (d. 1906).[10] Born in a town south of Delhi, he studied first with the Shi'i mujtahids of Awadh's capital city, Lucknow. He then set off to train in Shi'i sciences at Najaf in Iraq. On

---

8. Sir John Chardin, *Travels in Persia* (London: Argonaut Press, 1927), pp. 130, 139. Members of some tribal peoples such as the Qizilbash appear to have emigrated from Iran to India, but Chardin was probably most struck by notable-class emigration, which would have been demographically much less significant. Such immigration probably did not actually contribute to Iran's underpopulation, but Chardin's comments underscore how remarkable it was in the seventeenth century.

9. For these developments, see John Norman Hollister, *The Shi'a of India* (London: Luzac & Co., 1953).

10. Cole, *Roots of North Indian Shi'ism.*

his way to Iraq he stopped in the Punjab at Lahore, where the influential local notable Nawab 'Ali Riza Khan Qizilbash insisted that he settle. Qizilbash, a wealthy Shi'i of Iranian origins, prospered under British rule. Sayyid Abu'l-Qasim agreed to stay, but he did make a trip to Iraq, where he studied in Najaf with the great source for emulation, Murtaza Ansari (d. 1864). Back in Lahore, Sayyid Abu'l-Qasim vigorously promoted Usuli Shi'ism in the second half of the nineteenth century, founding Friday congregational prayer mosques in that city and in Peshawar farther north, having edifices built for commemorating the martyrdom of Imam Husain, and establishing an Imami seminary in Lahore with stipends paid for by the Qizilbash nawab.

The change from living under British rule to being part of an Islamic republic greatly affected Punjabi and Sindhi Shi'is. Modern Pakistan came into being in 1947 as the result of several political processes. First, mass agitation for independence in the period between the wars made it increasingly apparent that British India was destined to become an independent country dominated by the Congress party. The scattered Muslims in the Hindu heartland of British India began yearning for a secure base in the overwhelmingly Hindu subcontinent, which was, with Mahatma Gandhi's movement, entering the era of mass politics. This program for a Muslim state enunciated originally by the Muslims of the Hindi belt and some urban Muslims in Punjab was adopted only very late by rural religious Sufi leaders and big landlord politicians in the solidly Muslim western Punjab. These processes resulted in a Muslim West Pakistan being carved out of British India, originally in union with a Bengali Muslim wing in the east (the union ended with the civil war of 1971, leaving Pakistan in the west and Bangladesh in the east as separate states).

Some of the Indian Muslim immigrants into West Pakistan, who settled mainly in Karachi, were Shi'is from Bombay and the old centers of Awadh (now the Indian state of Uttar Pradesh), joining the minority of Sindhis and Punjabis who were Shi'is. Most of the politically influential Shi'is, like their Sunni counterparts, held a secular outlook. Still, small Sunni revivalist sects sought to reestablish a Muslim state on the pattern of the early Islamic caliphal empire, and among the Shi'is, activists excoriated the Sunni caliphs as usurpers and saw the example of the twelve imams as the only just pattern for government.

But Pakistan's long struggle with Hindu India, including three wars, served to unite Sunnis and the 17 percent (or more) of the population who were Shi'is for most of the country's first thirty years. Moreover, although Pakistan became an Islamic republic, the ideology bequeathed it by its founders, such as Muhammad 'Ali Jinnah (himself a nominal Isma'ili convert to Twelver Shi'ism), contained a large dose of secularism. Frequent bouts of secular military rule in Pakistan during the late 1950s and throughout the 1960s lessened the impact of sectarianism. The brief return of democracy under Zulfiqar 'Ali Bhutto and the Pakistan People's party in the 1970s did not threaten minority Shi'i interests because of the secular thrust of the party and the influence of prominent Shi'is (including Bhutto's ethnically Iranian wife, a Shi'i). Indeed, Sunni fundamentalism never posed much of a threat to secularists or to Shi'is in times of democracy, since with a few exceptions the Sunni fundamentalists have never done well in Pakistani elections outside the cities. Still, Sunni-Shi'i violence, endemic in the subcontinent for centuries, broke out with some frequency. The Islamic month of Muharram, when Shi'is mourn the martyred Imam Husain and ritually curse the early caliphs revered by Sunnis, always presents opportunities for mob violence, as the Shi'is take out public processions during the first ten days of that month, often parading through Sunni neighborhoods.

The institution of a policy of Islamization by Gen. Muhammad Zia al-Haqq after his 1977 coup against the secularizing, left-leaning Pakistan People's party raised dramatic issues for the minority Shi'is. Zia al-Haqq, representing large landlord and industrialist interests, sought to use an Islamic ideology to create a national unity program that would have legitimacy among the urban middle and working classes, as well as among peasants. But his conception of Islamization derived from strongly Sunni models and involved the greater entry of the government into religious administration. The general made the paying of Islamic religious taxes compulsory, so that they were deducted directly from bank accounts at 2.5 percent per annum; the money was put in the hands of a government-administered zakat distribution program. This move threatened the autonomy of the Shi'is and meant that Shi'i religious taxes would often be collected and administered by the majority Sunnis.

In early July 1980, the third anniversary of Zia's coup, Shi'i leaders called a huge conference of 100,000 Shi'is in the capital, Islamabad, where they harangued those attending with what the government called "objectionable and provocative speeches." On July 5 about 25,000 Shi'is mounted a violent protest demonstration in Islamabad, forcing the Zia al-Haqq government to back down and allow Shi'is to continue to pay religious taxes on a voluntary basis to their own ulama. On July 6 Zia met with a Shi'i delegation headed by Mufti Ja'far Husain, leader of the Movement for the Implementation of Ja'fari [Shi'i] Law, assuring them that exemption clauses would be written into the law to be promulgated on September 15, 1980. To mollify Sunni fundamentalists, the government also inserted a clause into the law forbidding the cursing of the Sunni caliphs, traditionally part of Shi'i mourning sessions. One side effect of the immunity from compulsory payment of the poor tax for Shi'is has been that a few wealthy Sunnis have declared themselves Shi'is to avoid deductions from their bank accounts. Allowing Shi'is some autonomy is clearly a stopgap measure and has not resolved the problems posed by a Sunni Islamization policy for Pakistan's diverse Muslim community.[11]

The Iranian Revolution of 1978–79 also had the effect of inspiring Pakistan's Shi'is to greater mobilization and collective action. Soon after the revolution Khomeini himself attempted to intervene with the Zia government on behalf of Pakistan's Shi'is who felt threatened by the Sunni Islamization measures. Because of their frequent mourning processions for martyred imams, mounted on a neighborhood basis, Shi'is have traditionally had exceptionally good organization and firm networks. Many Shi'is in India and Pakistan are divided over whether to support Khomeini. Those in Lahore appear rather solidly to back the Iranian Revolution; they hand out leaflets during their processions asking Pakistanis to pray for Khomeini. The Iranian embassy in Islamabad and the consulate in Karachi have also been active in promoting Shi'i militance. This new visibility of the Shi'is has provoked opposition from hard-line Sunnis.

On April 12, 1983, in the Karachi suburb of Liaquatabad, thousands of newly militant Shi'is clashed with Sunnis in a long-running conflict over ownership of a religious edifice. Police moved in and arrested 135 persons over the next few days. At least 44 were convicted and sentenced to a year of rigorous imprisonment and ten to fifteen lashes. A few days later on April 15 further violence broke out in another Karachi locale when 350 angry Shi'is gathered at a building devoted to mourning Imam Husain and attempted, contrary to martial law prohibitions, to take out a protest

11. For the 1980 Shi'i demonstrations against their inclusion in the Pakistan zakat law, see *Dawn* (Karachi), July 6, 1980, and July 7, 1980; and *Foreign Broadcast Information Service,* Daily Report: South Asia, July 14, 1980, E2; the estimates of numbers of Shi'is involved derives from the *New York Times,* July 6, 1980, and July 7, 1980. For the promulgation of the zakat ordinance in a form approved by Shi'i leaders Mufti Ja'far Husain, Shabir Husain Naqvi, and Kazim 'Ali Shah, see *Dawn,* September 16, 1980; for the context, see Lawrence Ziring, "From Islamic Republic to Islamic State in Pakistan," *Asian Survey* 24, no. 9 (1984): 931–46, esp. 942.

march.[12] The disturbances in Karachi seem likely to continue. In October 1984, Karachi Sunnis conducted a general strike to protest Shi'i practices. Whatever the local grievances involved, this communal violence at least in part reflects tensions caused by the increasing assertiveness of Pakistani Shi'is in the wake of the Iranian Revolution. The experience of the Shi'is in Pakistan thus parallels that of Iraqi and Saudi Arabian Shi'is. Local grievances deriving from minority status in a Sunni-dominated state, combined with greater Shi'i activism in the wake of the Iranian Revolution, brought about a clerically led mass mobilization of Shi'is, with strikes, demonstrations, and marches, causing the Sunni government to accommodate some demands even while it dealt with the protests harshly.

It seems probable that Iranian events, aid, and inspiration constitute the most important factor in a variety of Shi'i protests in the first years after the Iranian Revolution.[13] (See Halliday's chapter in this volume.) This is true even though Khomeini and most of his followers did not speak in specifically Shi'i terms, but rather of Islam, and hoped to spread the revolution throughout the Islamic world (and then beyond). Nonetheless, there remained specifically Shi'i elements in the ideology and practices of the revolutionary government that alienated Sunnis even in Iran and especially abroad. The Sunnis most attracted to Khomeini's ideas were militant revivalists who, outside the Shi'i world, were overwhelmingly led by laypersons, many of whom had little or no specialized religious education. The ulama in most Sunni countries did not have a militant history to match that of the Iranian ulama, and in many countries they were rather tame followers of their own governments on religious matters. These ulama did

12. For the 1983 violence between Sunnis and Shi'is (and then between Shi'is and the police) in Karachi, see the *New York Times,* April 13, 1983, and *Dawn,* April 13, 14, and 16, 1983; and Hasan-Askari Rizvi, "The Paradox of Military Rule in Pakistan," *Asian Survey* 24, no. 5 (1984): 534–55, esp. 546. Some of the above is based on personal observations by J. R. I. Cole in Lahore, Pakistan, in the fall of 1981 and the spring of 1983, and in Lucknow and New Delhi, January 1982 through March 1983. Thanks are owed to David Gilmartin, also, for his comments in a personal communication.

13. For comparative purposes, it is worth pointing out that our categories of causation, including mobilization to express specific grievances and the influence of a foreign revolution, were also found important in European movements of collective violence by the Tillys. Likewise, among Shi'is there has recently begun a transition from reactive forms of protest (petitions, demonstrations, strikes) to more active ones (including a demand, as in Lebanon, for greater formal political power in their national government), paralleling similar developments that occurred earlier in Europe. See, among other works, Charles Tilly, Louise Tilly, and Richard Tilly, *The Rebellious Century 1830–1930* (Cambridge, Mass.: Harvard University Press, 1975) and Charles Tilly, *From Mobilization to Revolution* (Reading, Mass.: Addison-Wesley Publishing Co., 1978).

not see the extremist groups as allies in a common cause. And in most Sunni countries neither the fundamentalists nor the average pious Muslim wanted to be ruled by the ulama, as Khomeini's formula demanded. In addition, Sunnis, like many Iranians, became in time largely disillusioned with Khomeinism in practice, although some Islamic revivalists continue to follow him. As Matthee's chapter on Egypt shows, even politically activist Muslims lost much of their initial enthusiasm for the Iranian Revolution. Among Shi'is Khomeini's appeal was much greater, partly because of a common tradition and pride in a Shi'i accomplishment. In addition, Shi'is outside Iran were more likely to see their own (Sunni or Sunni plus Christian) governments as illegitimate and tyrannical than were Sunnis, and, partly owing to discrimination against Shi'is, their ulama had not been discredited and neutralized by being tools or passive followers of the government as had, in large degree, the Sunni ulama of various countries. In fact, the Shi'i ulama could not, by their very beliefs and identity, be complete followers of Sunni or (as in Lebanon) mixed governments. This meant that even if these Shi'i ulama had not been rebellious in the past they did not form a caste of government supporters. In many Sunni countries the ulama formed a rather closed hierarchy, tied to the government. The fluid hierarchy of Shi'ism allowed for the rapid rise of radicals or protesters like Musa al-Sadr in Lebanon and Muhammad Baqir al-Sadr in Iraq. Their movements began well before 1978 and hence were not caused by Iran's revolution, but Musa al-Sadr was an Iranian, influenced by Iranian radical Shi'ism.

Iranian revolutionary ideology and aid were important in Iraq, in Lebanese Shi'i fundamentalism, in the failed Bahrain coup, and in protest movements by Saudi Shi'is. Even where, as in Iraq and Lebanon, organized Shi'i politically oriented movements existed before the Iranian Revolution (reflecting both Shi'i grievances and ideology and also factors common to Islamic, ethnic, and Third World movements), the influence of the revolution's success and of its Khomeinist ideology, with its successful stress on populist Islam, was strongly felt. Most of the major protest movements by Shi'is came after the Iranian Revolution. The success of many of them in getting concessions that improved the position of Shi'is from the governments is in part attributable to those governments' fear of what Shi'i political movements might accomplish if their grievances, and support from Iran, continued. This fear was based on the Iranian example and on Iranian aid, both real and imagined, to the local movements.

The foreign impact of the Iranian Revolution was not limited to Shi'i countries or even to Islamic militant movements. Although the latter were the most enthusiastic (though with decreased enthusiasm over time), many ordinary Muslims welcomed, to one degree or another, the example given by Iran of Muslims standing up as Muslims and effectively saying no to the Western powers. On the level of militant Muslims, the examples given by Matthee in his chapter on Egypt could be multiplied to range as far as militant Muslims in Malaysia, not to mention such Muslims in the Soviet Union and in the United States, where the main Muslim mosque in Washington, D.C., was long controlled by Khomeinists. Some fundamentalist men and women, from West Africa to Malaysia, insist, for example, that the position of women has improved under the Islamic Republic.[14] On the other hand, the typical assessment of Khomeini and the Islamic revolution among the world's Muslims does not seem to be high today in most cases. This is not primarily because Iranians are Shi'i rather than Sunni, but more because of what are seen as dictatorial excesses in human rights, the Iran-Iraq War, the treatment of women and some ethnic and religious minorities, and the like. Most governments of Muslim countries understandably dislike the revolution because of the real or ideological threat it poses. Fundamentalism and Khomeinism seem stronger in places that have undergone disruptive modernization, such as Iran, Egypt, and Malaysia, than in less modernized countries, such as Yemen and Indonesia.

The negative reaction of Western, and today also the Soviet, governments to revolutionary Iran has even less to do with its Shi'ism; it is based more on the threat it poses as an important country that has broken many of its former ties and all of its former subservience to the Western (and Eastern) blocs, and has influenced other movements and nations to follow in its footsteps. In both the United States and the Soviet Union, not to mention such countries as France and Germany, the revolution moved governments or major parties, directly or via organizations and foundations they funded, to sponsor research and seminars on Iran and on Shi'ism. (Among many examples: two international conferences on contemporary Iran were sponsored by the German Social Democratic party's foundation in 1980 and 1981;[15] and in Japan by 1984 a greatly disproportionate number of Japanese scholars holding government-funded research

14. Talk and discussion by Nikki R. Keddie with university women belonging to an (ideologically mixed) Malaysian women's association, September 1984, near Kuala Lumpur, and with Nigerian women, Kano, April 1985.

15. See, as one result of these conferences, the fine volume *Iran in der Krise* (Bonn: Verlag Neue Gesellschaft, 1981), which includes eight articles in English, mostly by participants from the United States and Great Britain.

posts were doing research on Iran.) In part, the attitude of the powers, especially the United States, reflected the dread usually aroused in status quo powers in the face of any major revolution—the French, Russian, and Chinese revolutions come to mind. Although Iran was a smaller country, its strategic position, its role as the world's second largest oil exporter, and the part it might play as an exporter of revolution to the large Muslim world, especially to the strategic Middle East, all entered into Western reaction. Some differentiation must be made in early reactions among different Western governments, however. Actions of French and German leaders made it clear that, for a time at least, many of them hoped to move economically and politically into Iran where the United States had been pushed out. To some extent countries like Italy and Germany succeeded in maintaining or increasing economic and technological ties to Iran, although the French have since 1981 opted for the anti-Iranian Iraqi side. The Japanese, who depend overwhelmingly on Iranian and Gulf oil, continue to push their exports and to be friendly and complaisant toward Iran. (This was reflected in the scholarly papers they delivered at the Congress of Human Studies in the Countries of Asia and North Africa, Tokyo and Kyoto, 1984, which were quite positive in their assessment of the Khomeini regime and its ideology.)

Shi'ism and social protest is but one of many themes in the spate of endowed and nonendowed studies of Iran and the Muslim world undertaken outside that world, but Iran and Shi'ism get vastly more attention than they used to. Even in countries where scholarship is not overwhelmingly government controlled, much money is poured into these subjects by governments. In the United States, in addition to in-house studies funded by various government agencies, which often bring in university scholars, there has been direct and indirect governmental funding of projects on Iran, Shi'ism, and the Islamic revival. Similar trends are found in Western Europe and Japan, where universities and most funding agencies are government supported, directly or indirectly. Clearly many scholars in all countries were led to an interest in Iran and in Shi'ism by dramatic events, but the sudden availability of funds and official and press interest sped up the movement of scholars into such fields. Journalistic books and articles have multiplied, some with serious intent, but others reinforcing biases about Shi'ism, Iran, and Islam.

It is partly within this context that one may assess the lesser known shifting Soviet attitudes toward Shi'ism and politics discussed by Atkin in this volume. Although Soviet scholarship responds more directly to government attitudes and pressures than does Western scholarship, it does have, as Atkin notes, its internal disagreements, and scholars sometimes voice views contrary to the current party line. In a general way, however, the Soviets have gone from a pre–Iranian Revolution negative attitude toward Shi'ism and Islam as reactionary to an emphasis on their positive populist features after the revolution and then, with the deterioration of Soviet-Iranian relations, to a more negative view. Scholarly as well as other approaches, however, are still open to a possible reconciliation between the Soviet Union and Iran. The firm Iranian attitude against the United States helped make the Soviets forgive a multitude of other sins.

The Iranian Revolution in power, like many revolutions, has evolved substantially from a ruling coalition of differing groups and forces to one in which pro-Khomeini clerics hold most of the top posts. There are some political splits among them, however, and lower, less political posts are often held by more liberal technocrats who may influence pragmatic policies. The revolution still has many adherents, but it has alienated not only large numbers of foreign Muslims, including many Shi'is, but also millions of Iranians. Many alienated Iranians have been able to escape, usually to the West, especially if they had enough money, but others remain in Iran. Although the intensity of persecution has varied according to circumstances, the regime has continued to jail and execute opponents on a large scale.

The main target group has been the left-Islamic Mujahidin-i Khalq, considered responsible for the wave of largely successful assassinations of government leaders in 1981. From the viewpoint of Shi'ism and protest, the sharp split between these Mujahidin and the Iranian government is important, as both claimed to represent true Shi'ism and both had an influence abroad. As the struggle of the Mujahidin with the clerically dominated Islamic Republican party progressed, the Mujahidin took increasingly anticlerical and prolaity positions that are strangely reminiscent of aspects of the long dormant Akhbari school. In practical terms the Mujahidin were seen as the most serious threat to the regime because of their large numbers, good organization, and ability to carry out assassinations. Those associated with them were for a time jailed, and often executed, almost indiscriminately. It was in part this treatment of the Mujahidin that dampened the enthusiasm of Muslim and other leftists outside Iran for the Iranian Revolution. Leftist Muslims outside Iran were often closer to the Mujahidin interpretation of Islam as quasi Socialist than they were to Khomeini's views. On the other hand, some non-Iranian Muslims with leftward leanings still see themselves as partisans both of Khomeini and of the progressive ideologue, Ali Shariati (d. 1977).

Whereas the earliest postrevolution jailings and executions concentrated on those with ties to the Pahlavi regime, later ones included many categories, among which the Mujahidin were a great majority, and those following the Baha'i religion were disproportionately present. No Iranian government has ever formally recognized the Baha'is, seen as an illegitimate break-off from Islam (breaking with Islam to join another religion is not permissible by Muslim law). But Pakistan has formally recognized the Baha'is as a non-Muslim community, and they are informally tolerated in many other Muslim lands. Iran's active persecution and executions of Baha'is, who are distinguished from the Mujahidin and most other targets by their political quietism, far exceed anything previously seen from any government of a modern Muslim country.

A different form of discrimination, seen by Khomeinists and similarly minded Shi'i and Sunni Muslims as a fulfillment of Islam, concerns the legal, ideological, and de facto treatment of women. The early patriarchal development of Islamic law and practice was influenced by Arab tribal patriarchy and by Byzantine and Iranian elite veiling practices to become more restrictive for women than was prescribed by the Qur'an. The treatment of women, however, remained variable by class, region, and period. Twentieth-century reforms in personal status law in practice helped primarily middle- and upper-class women. Popular-class women, as well as men, tended to associate their relative or absolute distress with those classes and Westerners who did not adhere to traditional Islamic practices. Hence the Third Worldist reaction against the West and its ways came to encompass "Western" ideas on women (associated with the privileged Westernized classes) and to call for a return to "Islamic" ways.

As in many spheres of life, the reaction regarding women was strongest in countries like Iran where social change and Westernization had been the most rapid and disruptive. Although women fought in unprecedented numbers in the Iranian Revolution, few of them were organized or fighting for women's rights. Those who were so fighting were primarily educated middle- and upper-class women, or women working in the modern sphere, and it was mainly these women who demonstrated against Khomeini's original abortive attempt to enforce veiling in the workplace. Feminist strength declined via emigration and intimidation, however, so that now veiling in the public sphere is enforced. The reformist Family Protection Law of 1967–75 was early suspended and replaced by Islamic law via Islamic courts, which affects women's lives in many ways. Even village women are reported to be more segregated than before. Without discussing all the issues behind the revival in Iran (as in Sunni countries with

"Islamic" governments) of strict practices that affect more women than ever before, one may note that the increased modern power of government makes it possible to *enforce* rulings on matters like veiling and segregation throughout a country. In the past such practices were less universal, were more centered in major cities and in the middle and upper classes, and were enforced more by informal means, such as the power of public opinion, than by government decree. Traditionalist governments use modern means to enforce their writ nationwide and in this and many other ways are not really traditional.

The revival of veiling and sex segregation, like other "Islamic" measures, is in part a reaction against Western power in the Muslim world, of which Israel is seen as an important part. The West is blamed, among other things, for a breakdown in morality via its free social practices. Many women in Iran and elsewhere, particularly among students or the popular classes, accept or promote this version of Islam. (At a discussion among Malaysian women in 1984 all the students wore Islamic dress and defended revivalist positions, whereas most of their teachers did not;[16] and this type of generation gap is far from unique.)

The imposition of "Islamic" rules on women (in quotation marks because Islamic practice has in fact varied considerably) is thus not entirely parallel to the other forms of persecution discussed, as many women, even some quite sophisticated ones, accept or promote it. And, on the other hand, some Muslim leftist organizations like the Mujahidin-i Khalq speak and act in favor of greater, not lesser, equality between men and women, oppose segregation, and insist that their use of a nonrestraining head covering for women does not mean inequality in other areas.[17] (For a discussion on women, see the chapter by Yeganeh and Keddie.)

In sum, although both Shi'is and Sunnis have had grounds and ideological instruments for social protest (which on some points, like Western interference in local politics, economics, and social mores, were quite similar), the Shi'is had some advantages in mounting *effective* protests. They have, as this book indicates, been effective not only in Iran but, to a large degree, in Iraq, Saudi Arabia, Lebanon, and Pakistan. One ad-

---

16. Personal observations by Nikki R. Keddie in Malaysia (see n. 14).

17. On women and the Iranian Revolution, see especially Guity Nashat, ed., *Women and Revolution in Iran* (Boulder, Colo.: Westview Press, 1983), and Azar Tabari and Nahid Yeganeh, eds., *In the Shadow of Islam: The Women's Movement in Iran* (London: Zed Press, 1982).

vantage derived from the modern history (especially since the nineteenth century) of independent political action by Shi'i ulama—first in Iran and more recently in Iraq and Lebanon. Ulama leaders often had contact with the masses and spoke a language they understood; neither of these things was generally true of Westernized intellectuals. The Sunni ulama have long been largely subservient to secular governments and are rarely important in political protest movements. A second advantage was that protest and rebellion, dissociation from secular rulers and financial independence of them, and belief in changing interpretations of Islam either by mujtahids or by believers have been stronger in Shi'ism than in Sunnism, even though most Shi'is over time have accepted their own governments. Such elements are emphasized at times of social discontent. Third, discrimination against Shi'is in several countries gave them a basis for a kind of ethnic cohesion, which may be roughly compared to that of the Sunni Kurds, and a will to fight for equal treatment. Their struggles were largely effective, owing to their own efforts, to newfound ideological and political cohesion, and to the fear instilled in their governments by the Iranian Revolution and some direct or indirect Iranian aid to their movements.

It seems most improbable that an Iranian-type revolution can spread with a similar pattern of clerical participation and rule. In Sunni countries "Islamic" governments either are traditional ones or have been installed from above by military dictators. The lack of a strong, oppositional, and organized ulama cadre outside Iran appears to preclude a repetition of the Iranian pattern. When it comes to Islamic measures imposed from above, however, Shi'is are, if anything, at a disadvantage outside Iran, as they are minorities both in the current ruling classes and in the military officer classes that tend to produce coups. When it is realized, however, that Khomeini and his followers have called not for Shi'i rule but for Islamic revolutions, one may appreciate that their influence is far from spent. (Some say it increases with the distance from Iran, as in parts of Africa and in Malaysia, where the Islamic revivalist party is growing in strength and influence and Khomeini is admired by many.) At the same time, the social egalitarian aspects of Islam find some of their strongest statements in organizations made up of Shi'is, especially Iran's Mujahidin-i Khalq and the late ideologist Ali Shariati, and their influence continues to be felt among students and activists around the Muslim world (Shariati's works are very popular in Indonesia, for example).

Muslim intellectuals and activists have increasingly in the past century tried to overcome the Shi'i-Sunni split in order especially to present a united Islamic front against imperialism. Our finding that Shi'is have, in recent years, been generally more successful in social protest than have Sunnis does not mean that the Shi'i-Sunni division will continue to be as important in assessing social protest movements as it has been in the past two decades. One might equally surmise that now that Shi'is have forced Sunni or Sunni-Christian governments to deal with some of their grievances, they may continue to be less oppositional in countries like Iraq and Saudi Arabia, or they may increasingly unite with non-Shi'is to work or fight for the same causes. This result is not inevitable, but it could occur.[18]

One final note. This book is not intended to reinforce an unfortunate stereotype that has emerged recently in the West. In the past several years the word *Shi'i* has often, especially in the United States, taken on the connotation of "fanatic" or "terrorist," and we are often told that Shi'is have a "martyr complex" that makes them welcome death in pursuit of their cause. In fact, the majority of the world's assassins in the past century have been Europeans of Christian background, and with the exception of the medieval "Assassin" sect, which belonged to a different line than today's politicized Shi'is, Shi'is were not known until very recently for either terrorism or special devotion to offensive holy wars (which most Twelver ulama have held were forbidden during the occultation). Shi'i veneration for martyrs has in the past been used far more as an incitement to mourning ceremonies and an identification with suffering leaders than it has been for political purposes. The recent activist political use of martyrdom traditions is more an example of a worldwide trend to use deeply believed religious, nationalist, and other themes for political purposes, including self-sacrifice, than it is proof that Shi'is intrinsically tend to sacrifice themselves for political and religious causes.

For many centuries, in fact, most Shi'is took special measures to avoid martyrdom. The practice of *taqiyah,* or "precautionary dissimulation," was particularly characteristic of Shi'is, although some other Muslims also followed it. This doctrine taught that it was permissible, or even obliga-

18. The notes for this chapter provide some bibliography for Iran and countries farther east. For bibliographical guidance regarding the Arab countries and the Soviet Union, see the notes to the relevant chapters in this volume. See also Nikki R. Keddie, "Shi'ism and Revolution," in Bruce Lincoln, ed., *Religion, Rebellion, Revolution* (London: Macmillan, 1985). In order to limit this book to ideologically parallel groups, the editors and authors have omitted "unorthodox" groups, which include elements of Twelver Shi'ism, such as the Turkish Alevis, the predominantly Syrian 'Alawis, and the so-called 'Ali Ilahis or Ahl-i Haqq, found mostly among the Iranian Kurds. It is worth noting, however, that these sects, at least when out of power, have generally been to the left politically of Sunnis and have been involved in social protest.

tory, for Shi'is to dissemble their religious identity and also to hide their true beliefs when they were in Sunni or other hostile territory and felt their lives were in danger. The main aim of this was for Shi'is to save their lives or well-being from those ideologically hostile to them. Live Shi'is were preferred to martyrs, unlike the situation in Christianity and some other religions. Only recently has such use of taqiyah begun to be denounced by Shi'i activists and stress put on martyrdom for the sake of true Islam. Here, as in many matters, different aspects of Shi'i and other traditions are stressed, suppressed, or reinterpreted in accord with a variety of social, political, and ideological needs.

There is no reason to think that because of Shi'i doctrine Shi'is will remain politicized in the same way as they have been in recent years. Circumstances change, and doctrines along with them. Twelver Shi'is, having traveled a centuries-long complex path from quietism to revolt, have not by any means reached a final point in their political orientations and activities. Shi'is have now entered the era of mass politics, and their political future depends largely on the degree to which the demands and desires of their masses are met.

R. K. RAMAZANI

Chapter One # Shi'ism in the Persian Gulf

The world's oil heartland also happens to be the Shi'i heartland. Out of an estimated 750 million Muslims in the world, about 11 percent are Shi'is. More than half of them are Twelver or Imami Shi'is who live in the Persian Gulf region, as majorities of the citizen populations in Bahrain, Iran, and Iraq, and as minorities in Kuwait, Oman, Qatar, Saudi Arabia, and the United Arab Emirates (UAE). Iran is the single largest Shi'i Muslim–inhabited country in the world as well as in the Gulf region; 95 percent of its 40 million citizens are Shi'is. Iran also happens to be the single most populous state, the most strategically located country—abutting at once the Soviet Union and the Strait of Hormuz—and putatively still the most powerful state of the region despite the recent material toll that the revolution and the war with Iraq have exacted.

Shi'ism in the Persian Gulf region may be viewed from different perspectives. It may be seen from the wider perspective of the resurgence of Islam in general and from Khomeini's perspective of what I call "Islam of the Oppressed" in particular. It may be studied as a Third World phenomenon since, despite the oil wealth, the Gulf societies are essentially underdeveloped. And finally, it may be examined as a specimen of a worldwide surge of "fundamentalism" that encompasses Judaism and Christianity as well as Islam. Who could fail to notice the intriguing parallel behavior among "fundamentalists" in all three monotheistic religious traditions in the face of the existence of such radical groups as the Egyptian al-Takfir wa al-Hijra, the Shi'i Hizbullahi, some of the followers of evangelist Jerry Falwell, and the Jewish Gush Emunim?

Such exercises in speculative thought, however, cannot aid the study of Shi'ism in the Gulf region. Empirical research, both documentary and in the field, forms the basis of the conception of Shi'ism in the Gulf in this chapter,[1] although the broader relevance of this conception to the Middle East area as a whole will also be considered at the end. As conceived here, Shi'ism is both an ideological and a sociopolitical movement. It is the official creed of the Iranian state, a major determinant of its policies, and a major force that influences the behavior of Shi'i groups and individuals outside as well as within the Iranian society, whether a given Shi'i group constitutes a minority or the majority of the population of a given Gulf society. The ideology involved in this definition is based primarily on the interpretation of Islam by the Shi'i leader Ayatullah Ruhullah Khomeini, an interpretation that is today the official Iranian creed, embodied in the Constitution of the Islamic Republic of Iran, and the primary ideological force among his followers. Among the Shi'i populations in the other Gulf states, Khomeinism is, to be sure, an influential force for certain, but not all, groups, just as it is not for all Iranian Shi'i Muslims either.

As a sociopolitical movement, Shi'ism today is simultaneously both a negative and a positive force. It was more quietist than activist in the historical past. Negatively, it is a widespread movement of social and political protest against perceived domestic "tyranny" (*zulm*) and foreign domination (*tahmil*), a movement supported yesterday by a wide variety of groups as well as the followers of Khomeini against the shah's regime and supported today primarily by diverse Shi'i groups within the other Gulf societies, although not exclusively by them. Positively, it is a widely shared social and political aspiration for a better life, especially for justice and equity, an aspiration that was shared yesterday by various lay and religious forces in Iran and is shared today primarily by the Sunni-dominated Shi'i groups in the other Gulf societies.

1. The research materials on which I have drawn for this chapter have been collected since 1979 from documentary sources and extensive interviews during repeated visits to the Middle East in connection with two book projects, one on Iran's revolution and the Middle East, and the other on the foreign policy of revolutionary Iran. Nevertheless, I have provided a number of references here pending the publication of these works. I would like to acknowledge the support of the University of Virginia's Energy Policy Studies Center, and the Center for Advanced Studies for their generous support of these two research projects.

Most important of all, the conception of Shi'ism as both an ideological and a sociopolitical movement in this study is informed by a complex legacy of emotional and spiritual frustration and hope, a mix of sentiments that is deeply rooted in the experience and eschatology of the Shi'i cultural tradition. The frustration stems largely from the repeated failure of Shi'i leaders in actual historical circumstances over the centuries to realize an ideally just society for their community. And the hope springs from an abiding chiliastic faith that ultimately the just society will be established by the messianic *mahdi* who will appear (*zuhur*) before the Day of Resurrection (*qiyamah* or *ruz-i qiyamat* as the Iranians popularly call it). Neither Khomeini's ideology—especially as it relates to his conceptions of government and international politics—nor the social and political protest and aspirations of the Shi'i people can be fully comprehended without bearing in mind this profound ethos of the Shi'i cultural tradition.

Essential for an understanding of Shi'ism as an ideological movement in the Persian Gulf today is first an analysis of Khomeini's conception of security in the Gulf within the context of his basic ideas about government and international politics. Then Shi'ism as a sociopolitical movement will be analyzed by selecting three case studies of the Shi'a in Iraq, Saudi Arabia, and Bahrain. At the end, the broader relevance of this study to the question of Shi'ism in the Middle East as a whole will be considered with a view to its policy implications.

KHOMEINI'S CONCEPTION OF SECURITY
IN THE PERSIAN GULF

Khomeini's conception of security in the Persian Gulf requires three conditions. First, all states of the area should establish for themselves "true Islamic governments." What should these governments be like? The answer partly lies in understanding the centrality of the idea of the guardianship of the jurisprudent—*vilayat-i faqih,* "rule of the leading cleric"—in Khomeini's political thought. Regardless of the scholarly controversy about the compatability of that idea with the Shi'i tradition, Khomeini's interpretation requires that all spiritual and temporal authority be vested in a supreme jurisprudent (*faqih*) or, in the absence of consensus on one person, in a group of supreme jurisprudents (*fuqaha*). Does this mean that all Gulf states should establish governments that are identical with the Iranian government? In Khomeini's view the answer is no; it would suffice for their new governments to be similar to, if not identical with, the Iranian model. What does that similarity imply? The answer is not wholly clear, but it is evident that besides clerical rule—instead of "shameful and reactionary" monarchies—true Islamic government must also be supported by all strata of the people, especially by the disinherited (*mustaz'afin*).

The second prerequisite of Gulf security is "true independence." This condition requires complete severance of all "links and associations" between the littoral states of the Gulf and the superpowers. This requirement should be examined in the light of Khomeini's view of the international system as a whole. His conception of that system rejects the primacy of the territorial state as the basis of the modern international system because the ephemeral idea of the territorial state is the creation of mortal man. In place of such a system, he desires what I call an "Islamic world order."[2] He believes that such an order will be eventually established as a result of the formation of an "Islamic world government," and that such a government in turn will be realized ultimately with the appearance (zuhur) of the absent twelfth imam as the messianic mahdi, or Master of the Age (*Sahib-i Zaman*). In his absence (*ghaibah*), however, the ground should be prepared for the coming of the mahdi by creating the rule of the faqih to whom all legitimate temporal and spiritual authority belongs during the waiting period.

The policies of the state of the faqih, aiming as they do at the eventual creation of such an Islamic world order, will inevitably entail confrontation between that state and the superpowers. Such a conflict is inevitable because the superpowers have arrogated all power (*qudrat*) to themselves. In Khomeini's own words, "we must settle our accounts with great and superpowers, and show them that we can take on the whole world ideologically, despite all the painful problems that face us."[3] It is in the context of these basic ideas that the Iranian slogan "neither East, nor West, only the Islamic republic" (*nah sharq, nah gharb, faqat jumhuri-i Islami*) should be understood, not the irrelevant notions of equidistance or nonalignment as these terms are ordinarily understood. Khomeini's view differs from Musaddiq's idea of negative equilibrium (*muvazinih-yi manfi*), and especially from the shah's so-called positive nationalism. These ideas in effect accept the Western notion of power politics, whereas Khomeini's religious, millenarian, and idealistic view rejects the global role of both

2. For details, see R. K. Ramazani, "Khumaini's Islam in Iran's Foreign Policy," in Adeed Dawisha, ed., *Islam in Foreign Policy* (Cambridge: Cambridge University Press, 1983), 9–32.

3. *Sukhan-raniha-yi Imam Khumaini Dar Shish Mahi-yi Avval-i 1359* (Tehran: Nur, 1359), 8.

superpowers; they are both considered to be illegitimate players in the international system they dominate.

Any country, including the Gulf states, that has close and necessarily dependent relations with the superpowers is also considered to be an illegitimate player in the world arena, simply by association. The United States is the Great Satan (*shaitan-i buzurg*) and its Gulf associates are mini-Satans (*shaitanha-yi kuchik*). The Soviet Union is regarded as a lesser Satan, but it is satanic nevertheless. Both superpowers belong to the camp of oppressors (*mustakbarin*) that dominates the camp of the oppressed peoples (mustaz'afin). In Khomeini's Qur'anic-inspired sentence, "the oppressed or the meek must triumph over the dominant powers" (*bayad mustaz'afin bar mustakbarin ghalabih kunand*).

The key notion that underlies the denunciation of the current role of the superpowers and their associates is domination (*tahmil*). It is a notion closely related to the historical Shi'i concern with tyranny (zulm). Not only the "capitalist imperialists" and "socialist imperialists," but also their "Zionist, Fascist, Phalangist, and Communist instruments" as well belong to the oppressors' camp, whereas the economically poor, the socially disadvantaged, and the culturally deprived individuals, groups, and masses of people belong to the camp of the meek. In such a context, no state can claim true independence so long as it establishes and maintains intimate relations with super or lesser powers within the oppressors' camp.

The third ideological prerequisite for Gulf security is Arab acknowledgment of Iran's spiritual propriety and political primacy. To understand this requirement in its wider context, once again we have to relate it to Khomeini's more general ideas about government and international politics in the context of Shi'i cultural tradition. The key Shi'i notion here is salvation (*najah*). The ultimate establishment of the Islamic world order by means of the creation of the world government of the faqih has already been advanced one major step by the establishment of the first and only government of God on earth in Iran. In Khomeini's own words, "Islam is a sacred trust from God to ourselves, and the Iranian nation must grow in power and resolution until it has vouchsafed Islam to the entire world." In such a context, the liberation of mankind is a divine obligation of the Iranian people, an obligation that makes Iran in Khomeini's view what I call the Redeemer Nation. In pointing out this notion of special leadership qualification of Iran for the creation of the virtuous political order everywhere, one of Khomeini's disciples states, for example, that if the Muslims want the establishment of Muhammad's Islam, they should entrust the political leadership of their countries to a religious leader, and "this magnificent fact has only come to reality in the Islamic country of Iran, and Imam Khomeini . . . has accepted the responsibility for the political leadership, formation of the Islamic Government as well as the Commander-in-Chief of the Armed Forces."[4]

For the sake of Gulf security, other Gulf states should acknowledge not only Iran's spiritual propriety but also its political primacy. In Khomeini's view, all power is a divine gift. But from a historical perspective his perception of Iran's political primacy in the Gulf region resembles significantly the view of all past Iranian secular rulers as well. The shah used to talk about Iran's security perimeter (*harim-i amniyyat*), and Iranian leaders today speak of its security umbrella (*chatr-i amniyyat*). In the words of Hujjat al-Islam Hashemi Rafsanjani, speaker of the Majlis, "we declare once again that the security of the Persian Gulf is more important to us than to any other party, and we will strive to maintain the Gulf's [security] as much as we can. If one day we should despair as a result of the enemy's [Iraqi] madness and recklessness and are compelled to make the Gulf unsafe, then no one will be able to prevent us."[5] This means that although the revolutionary regime has rejected the shah's notion of Iran as the policeman of the Gulf *on behalf of the United States* it has by no means abandoned the idea of Iran's political primacy in the entire Gulf region. This also means that although revolutionary Iran, like prerevolutionary Iran, accepts the general notion of Gulf security by Gulf states, it continues to consider itself as primus inter pares.

It ought to be obvious from the foregoing analysis that Khomeini's views about government and international politics in general and his conception of the requirements of security in the Persian Gulf in particular make it mandatory for Iran to export its Islamic revolution. But the significance of the subject makes it necessary to examine it in greater detail. Does Khomeini's ideology specifically require such an export? If it does, what means are considered permissible? Can force be used as a legitimate means? And what kind of peaceful means are considered to be most desirable?

Clearly, in Khomeini's view export of the Islamic revolution is obligatory. In his own words, for example, "We should export our revolution to the world," and "Today we need to strengthen and export Islam everywhere. You need to export Islam to other places, and the same version of Islam which is currently in power in our country." The source of this

4. *Tehran Journal,* November 4, 1981.
5. U.S. Foreign Broadcast Information Service (hereafter FBIS), Daily Report, South Asia, October 24, 1983, vol. 8, no. 206.

obligation is the view that only in Iran has the government of God been established, and as the Redeemer Nation, Iran must aim at the liberation of mankind from the yoke of the superpowers and their allies who dominate the structure of the international system.

What is not so clear in Khomeini's ideology, however, is the kind of means that he considers legitimate for exporting the revolution. On numerous occasions, he has declared categorically that "swords" should not be used. For example, on one occasion he said, "It does not take swords to export this ideology. The export of ideas by force is not export"; on another occasion he said, "When we say we want to export our revolution, we do not want to do it with swords." But what does this mean? Does it mean that the use of force is prohibited? No clear answer has been given so far on the specific meaning of such a prohibition, and hence I shall explore this question further within the context of Khomeini's view of war rather than export of revolution.

His idea of war follows the traditional Shi'i legal theory. He considers resorting to holy war (*jihad*) as the prerogative of only the infallible imam, and in his absence the faqih is estopped from waging an offensive war. But defensive war (*jang-i difa'i*) is another matter since it is in self-defense and hence the faqih is duty-bound to resort to it by all means. Generally, this conception of use of force appears to be compatible with the modern principles of international law. Article 51 of the Charter of the United Nations embodies such a principle, although it is well known how troublesome this Charter principle has always been. Given the primacy of states in the existing international system, governments do not ordinarily submit to an impartial forum the question of what constitutes self-defense; they usually act as judges in their own cause, especially if they expect an impartial judgment to go against them.

The problem of what constitutes self-defense, however, raises even more difficult questions in the case of Khomeini's international legal thought. The fundamental reason for this is his rejection of the primacy of the territorial state, as explained before. In his view the defense of what he calls "the homeland" appears time and again after "the defense of Islam." If this implies that defending Islam rather than Iran is a higher value in theory, then the problem arises seriously in practice since the abode of Islam transcends the boundaries of the Iranian state. To cite an important example, when Iran carried the war into Iraqi territory on July 13, 1982, it justified its action largely in terms of the defense of Islam. My view that the defense of Islam rather than Iran is the primary principle in Khomeini's theory of self-defense is evidenced also by his statement to the representatives of the Islamic Conference Organization. He told them categorically that their mediation efforts were contrary to the Qur'anic precept that requires that "if one tribe invades the other then all others are obliged to defend the latter in war, until they obey God. Once they obey God, then make peace with them." This sounds like what I call an Islamic conception of collective security. It shows that the value of Islamic faith is accorded a higher priority than that of the territorial state in Khomeini's theory of individual and collective self-defense.

Assuming that only defensive war is permissible, what about the use of force short of war? For example, does Khomeini's ideology allow acts of terrorism and subversion in exporting revolution? The question has obviously far-reaching practical implications in the light of the charges leveled against Iran for its alleged involvement in all kinds of terrorist acts in the Middle East, including the Gulf region. Again since no answer can be constructed on the basis of statements specifically on the subject of export of revolution, we should look elsewhere. The Iranian Constitution as well as Khomeini's own statements indicate that revolutionary Iran should observe the principle of noninterference ('*adam-i dikhalat*) in the affairs of other states. In admonishing the Gulf Arab leaders for supporting Iraq, for example, he declares, "We have neither ambition in, nor right to, any country, and God Almighty has granted us no permission to interfere in any country, unless it is solely a matter of self-defense." But what constitutes self-defense is as ambiguous here with respect to interference as in the case of war.

Is it any more clear what peaceful means are preferable in Khomeini's ideology? Without attempting to enumerate all kinds of acts short of use of military force, two major instruments in particular are highly valued for export of revolution. One is the example of Iranian Islamic behavior, and the other is publicity or propaganda. Khomeini urges Iranian diplomatic and consular as well as other officials and individuals and groups of private citizens to observe Islamic ethics in their behavior as the best means of exporting revolution. He also places a great deal of emphasis on the value of propaganda by private as well as official individuals and institutions for export of revolution. Given the great importance of the sermon in the Shi'i cultural tradition, it is considered to be one of the most powerful instruments for promoting Islamic revolution at home and abroad.

The prominent role of the Iranian clerics in this respect is widely known, but the importance that Khomeini and his disciples attach to the role that foreign Muslim clerics should play in importing revolution into their own societies has been little noticed. Quite apart from receiving streams of individual clerics (*ulama*) from other Muslim countries since the revolution, the Iranian clerics, most particularly Khomeini and Muntaziri, have been very keen in gathering together foreign ulama in Iran for the purpose of export of revolution. For example, Khomeini told some five hundred clerics during the final session of "the second global congress of the world Friday prayers leaders" on May 13, 1984: "You should discuss the situation in Iran. You should call on people to rebel like Iran" (*da'vat kunid mardum-ra bih-inkih nazir-i Iran qiyam kunand*). He also said, "Friday imams, congregational imams, ulama of Islam all over the world, you should note that all the powers today have risen against Islam, and not against Iran. You should note that we all have great duties at this time. If they find the opportunity and if you do not pay attention, Islam will be uprooted."[6] They surely did pay attention. In closing their meeting, the congress members declared that they "accept Ayatullah al-'Uzma [the great sign of god] Imam Khomeini as having the necessary qualifications for the imamat [*sic*] [leadership] of Muslims, and we will invite Muslims to follow his call." That, of course, includes Khomeini's most repeated call of all, the export of revolution.

Khomeini's call on the ulama to incite rebellion parallels his own repeated direct and indirect sermonizing to Gulf leaders; sometimes he has even condemned them for their alleged servility to foreign powers. For example, on one occasion he said:

> It is hoped that the heads of these governments, some of whom are indulged in sensuality, some preoccupied with their debaucheries, some embroiled in clashes with their brethren, and some emasculated by their fear of the United States, will be awakened [by my warnings] into an Islamic humanitarian consciousness, thus putting an end to their sordid governments and rejecting all superpowers, just as our heroic nation has done.[7]

SHI'ISM: CONTAINMENT AND CONTAGION

As seen by the Gulf Arab leaders, revolutionary Iran presents a far more formidable threat than did the shah's Iran. The degree of threat perceived differs from state to state, but what frightens them all is this addition of Khomeini's Shi'ism to Iran's putative political power. To be sure, the

6. For the text, see *Kayhan Hava'i,* May 23, 1984. In English, see *FBIS,* Daily Report, South Asia, May 14, 1984, vol. 8, no. 094.

7. Ibid., September 23, 1983, vol. 8, no. 186.

Gulf Arab leaders regarded the shah's Iran as a hegemonic state, but this perception never concerned them the way Khomeini's Shi'ism does today. Paradoxically, at a time when the raw *military* power of the state in Iran, as opposed to the shah's days, has declined and that of the Gulf Arab states relative to revolutionary Iran's has increased, the Gulf Arab leaders feel all the more threatened. The fundamental reason for this is the Arab fear of Shi'ism on two closely related levels.

On one level, Gulf Arab leaders fear Khomeini's hostile ideology backed by the power of the Iranian state. From the perspective of that ideology, their governmental systems are seen as basically illegitimate and their states as completely subservient to alien powers, and both conditions must be changed by the revolutionary establishment of truly Islamic government and truly independent states. As also seen in this perspective, there can be no true security and stability in the Persian Gulf until such revolutionary changes are accompanied by the Arab acknowledgment of Iran's spiritual propriety and political primacy.

On the other level, the Gulf Arab leaders fear Khomeini's Shi'ism for its potentially adverse effects on the Shi'i communities in their own countries. To be sure, Khomeini never tires of warning against division between the Sunni and the Shi'i Muslims, although, contrary to the general view, pan-Islamism is *not* the ultimate goal of his Islam; it is merely a way station to the establishment of the Islamic world order. Yet, the fact that Khomeini's ideology is nonsectarian, or ecumenical, is no real source of comfort to Gulf Arab leaders; the susceptibility of their Shi'i communities to the Khomeini appeal is considered to be a constant and dangerous source of potential threat to the political stability of their conservative regimes. In other words, to them Khomeini's Shi'ism poses a twofold external and internal threat, and the urgent question is how to contain simultaneously the threat of the powerful revolutionary state of Iran and the potential contagion of Khomeini-type Shi'ism within their own societies.

Iraq

In absolute terms, Iraq has the most Shi'is of any Arab country numbering over eight million Shi'i Muslims; they are 60 percent of Iraq's population. Furthermore, Iraq happens to be the site of the holiest Shi'i shrines in Karbala, Najaf, and Kazimain, names that are powerful symbols of faith for millions of Shi'i Muslims in the world. Finally, the Sunni-dominated, secular, and Baathist regime of Saddam Husain rules the only

Arab country in the Persian Gulf that abuts the Shi'i-dominated and po-
pulated state of Iran over a stretch of hundreas of miles of land and river
boundaries.

These concrete circumstances influence Saddam Husain's perceptions
of the threat of Shi'ism and his regime's response to it. As opposed to
the historical past, Iran-Iraq relations in the few years between 1975 and
1979 were characterized by an unprecedented degree of cooperation; Saddam Husain and the shah even consulted each other on the security of
the Gulf region as a whole. Even after the revolution, the Bazargan government got along rather well with the Iraqi regime, but its fall on
November 6, 1979, reversed all that. The relations have been marked ever
since by an unprecedented degree of hostility, epitomized by the Iraq-
Iran War, which started in September 1980 and has been the longest,
bloodiest, and costliest war in contemporary Middle East history.

The underlying conflict between Iran and Iraq involves both dimensions of Shi'ism. First, the Khomeini religious Islamic ideology backed by
the power of the Iranian state clashes with Husain's secular Baathist ideology, which is also backed by state power. Khomeini is perceived to
believe in the continuing primacy of Iranian power and the new spiritual
priority of Iran in the Gulf region, a belief that no other state has the
right to challenge. From this perspective, only Saddam "the infidel" (ka-
fir) had the gall to do so by invading Iran. As we have seen, Khomeini
also believes that it is the sacred duty of Iran to project and export its
power and ideology abroad, and yet Saddam Husain "arrogantly" sets
himself up to contain the Islamic revolution. On the other side, Saddam
Husain believes that the Iranian Revolution simultaneously presents an
opportunity and a threat. It was seen as an opportunity for him to project
the long-desired Iraqi power into the Gulf region at a time when internal
and external problems besetting the revolutionary regime appeared to
weaken the Iranian power position; it was seen as a threat because the
new Iranian ideology is intrinsically opposed to that of his regime. Saddam
Husain believes that Khomeini's religiously based ideology is antithetical
to the Baathist secular ideology in which Arabism, not Islam, is the core
value. Long before the outbreak of the war, when Khomeini was char-
acterizing the Baathist ideology as an imported amalgam of such alien
ideas as socialism and nationalism as opposed to the "authentic" Islamic
ideology of Iran, Husain vehemently rejected Khomeini's dogma. Any
Islamic ideology of Iran, Husain argued dogmatically, that contradicts
Arabism is "not Islamic at all."

Second, the Iran-Iraq conflict also involves Shi'ism at the grass-roots level of the people. Saddam Husain fears the potential threat of Iraqi Shi'i dissidents to his regime. The Shi'i Muslims in Iraq have always considered themselves the underdogs, or to use their own characterization, the deprived (*mahrumin*), despite their overwhelming majority in Iraqi society. They have seldom perceived their share of power and prosperity as fair or just whether ruled by the Ottomans, the British, and the monarchy in the past or by the minority Sunni-Baathist regime of the Takriti clan at the present time.

Yet not all the Iraqi Shi'i Muslims who predominate geographically in the southern parts of Iraq and hail socioeconomically from the rural areas and such poor urban localities as the slums of the township of al-Thaurah, for example, want a Khomeini-type Islamic government. Nor have they all joined the underground Shi'i movements that have been ably discussed by Batatu.[8] As he points out, the Islamic Call (al-Da'wah al-Islamiyah) is older than the Muslim Warriors (al-Mujahidin), the other major Iraqi Shi'i party, but Ayatullah Sayyid Mahdi al-Hakim, son of the founder of the party, the late Muhsin al-Hakim, dates the beginnings of the Da'wah to "after the 'revolution' of 1958" rather than "in the late 1960's" as Batatu first suggested.[9] Batatu himself now favors an earlier date. "The main objective of this party," according to Mahdi al-Hakim, "is to establish an Islamic state. . . . The leaders of the Da'wah party," he continues, "had also consulted the leaders of al-Ikhwan al-Muslimun who broadly agreed that the objective of establishing an Islamic state constituted the best program of cooperation between the Shi'i and Sunni Muslims."[10] As Batatu points out, the al-Mujahidin party, which was established in 1979, was "strongly affected by Iran's popular upheaval," but as the Iranian Revolution has in fact developed over the years, especially under the impact of the Iraq-Iran War, it has been, I should add, the Ikhwan-inspired Da'wah rather than the Khomeini-inspired al-Mujahidin that has cooperated most closely with the revolutionary regime in Iran. The leading figure in this cooperation has been Hujjat al-Islam (Khomeini uses this title for him; Batatu calls him Ayatullah) Muhammad Baqir al-Hakim, another son of the founder of the Da'wah mentioned before.

Although the late Ayatullah Sayyid Muhammad Baqir al-Sadr—the

8. See H. Batatu, "Iraq's Underground Shi'a Movements: Characteristics, Causes and Prospects," *Middle East Journal*, Autumn 1981, 578–94, and his chapter in this book.

9. For the text of his interview in English, see *Impact International*, April 25–May 8, 1980. In Batatu's chapter in this book, although not in his *MEJ* article, he summarizes al-Hakim's and other recently available accounts, and concludes that Da'wah was founded in 1960 or soon after.

10. Ibid.

most respected Iraqi *'alim* (learned religious leader) who was executed by the Baathist regime in April 1980—had not been associated with the Da'wah, his martyrdom to date inspires all Shi'i dissidents in the Gulf region, including particularly the Iraqis living in Iran. There are over 350,000 Shi'is from Iraq in Iran today, including those Iranian residents of Iraq who were expelled by the Iraqi regime at the outset of the war, Iraqi refugees from various countries, and Iraqi prisoners of war. The organization of the Iraqi activist Shi'i Muslims in Iran is called the Supreme Assembly of the Islamic Revolution in Iraq (SAIRI) and is led by Hujjat al-Islam Muhammad Baqir al-Hakim. The Hakim family has paid dearly for its embrace by the Iranian government. On June 17, 1983, al-Hakim made public that the Baathist regime had executed six members of his family, and other sources indicated that three of them may have been his brothers. The assembly publishes a bulletin, reporting on the activities of the Shi'i dissidents in Iraq. It also has training camps in Iran and dispatches Iraqi warriors (mujahidin) to the war front to fight on the side of Iran against Iraq, as evidenced, for example, by their large-scale participation in the Iranian advance to Hajj 'Umran at the northern front. Should Iran's war of attrition against Iraq succeed, in all probability the Iraqi Shi'i dissidents will be aided by the Iranian government to advance into Iraq for the establishment of an Islamic republic, perhaps headed by al-Hakim.

It is well-known that Iran's stickiest peace condition is the removal and punishment of Saddam Husain for his "war crime." But it is seldom noted that the Iraqi Shi'i dissidents in Iran are in fact being groomed for the postwar establishment of an Islamic republic in Iraq. In addressing the SAIRI on September 20, 1983, for example, Khomeini told the Iraqi Shi'i dissidents in Iran: "You should aim to form an Islamic government and to implement God's commands." "God willing," he said, in concluding his address, "you will be successful in your efforts to be a mujahid along the path of God. God willing, you will return to Iraq, *where we too will join you in the shrine of Imam Husain,* peace upon him. God bless you all."[11]

The Iraqi underground Da'wah party clearly supports the Iranian-based SAIRI. For example, when in March 1984 President Khomeini called on all Iraqi militant forces to rally around the SAIRI in its efforts to overthrow the Iraqi regime, the party responded immediately that it regarded "its religious duty" to uphold and further activate the assembly so that

11. See FBIS, September 21, 1983, vol. 8, no. 184.

the party's members could take "pride in defending Islam and in liberating suppressed masses in Iraq who are denied their civil rights under the Baathists' rule [*sic*] in that country." Although both the SAIRI and the Da'wah represent Shi'i dissidents of Iraq, Iranian leaders constantly encourage cooperation and unity between them and Sunni dissidents. In practice, the Iraqi underground opposition to the regime has at times involved collaboration between Shi'i and Sunni dissidents, and this is no mere Iranian wishful thinking. For example, the bombing of the Iraqi government-controlled television stations and the air force headquarters in the spring of 1983 was done by the Sunni as well as pro-Khomeini Shi'i Muslims in Baghdad.

Saudi Arabia

Only superficially would it appear that the rise of an Islamic state should have improved rather than aggravated the relations of Saudi Arabia and Iran, considering that Saudi Arabia is a renowned Islamic country. But, in fact, the conflict between Khomeini's Shi'ism and Saudi Islam underpins what I call a cold war between the two largest states of the Persian Gulf today. The shah's relations with King Faisal and with Crown Prince Fahd did not always fare well, but the potential power rivalry between Saudi Arabia and prerevolutionary Iran was muted by the common interests of the two basically conservative regimes in opposition to communism, in a special relationship with the United States, in opposition to Iraqi Baathist-sponsored subversion, especially in smaller Gulf states, and in resistance to the potential threat of the Soviet Union. The House of Saud tolerated the overbearing posture of the shah so long as this unpalatable attitude seemed to be balanced by his welcome efforts to preserve the status quo in the region, particularly at a time when the Saudis themselves seemed to prefer an insular, indirect, and limited kind of diplomacy to a more comprehensive, active, and forward policy before the Camp David Accords and the Egyptian-Israeli peace treaty, which subsequently isolated Egypt and propelled the Saudis into the forefront of Arab diplomacy.

For these reasons in particular, when the Iranian Revolution erupted, Saudi leaders firmly stood by the beleaguered shah. In 1978–79 Prince Sultan and Prince Fahd urged the other Arab governments to support the shah, and even after the seizure of power by the Iranian revolutionary forces (February 11, 1979), the devout King Khalid prayed, in his personal message to Khomeini, for God to guide him "to the forefront of those who strive for upholding Islam and Muslims." The king's prayer was answered, but Khomeini did not emerge in the forefront of the kind of Islam that the king would have preferred. The Saudis, like the Iraqis, hoped to maintain a semblance of correct relations with the Bazargan government. But once the Khomeini followers snatched the reins of power from the less doctrinaire elements after the fall of Bazargan, the conflict between Tehran and Riyadh became almost inevitable. Until then the Saudi leaders had feared, above all, the potential seizure of power by the communist elements within the chaotic revolutionary politics in Iran. To their surprise, the Khomeini disciples monopolized power step by step to the exclusion of all other forces, including the communists. The ensuing domination of Iranian politics by the followers of the Khomeini line spelled unexpected trouble for the House of Saud. Shi'ism of any kind had always been antithetical to Wahhabism, let alone the kind that Khomeini now adopted as the official creed of the revolutionary state. For the Saudis, as for the Iraqis, the challenge of Shi'ism has been twofold.

On the diplomatic level, Saudi Arabia and Iran clash both ideologically and politically. For the sake of clarity, on the basis of Khomeini's ideology, I characterize this overall conflict as one between Iran's official Islam of the Oppressed (mustaz'afin) and Saudi Arabia's official Islam of the Oppressors (mustakbarin). The former denotes Khomeini's revolutionary, populist, and millenarian Islam, and the latter describes the official Saudi conservative, unitarian, and elitist Islam. This basic conflict may be broken down into its four principal ingredients as follows: republicanism versus monarchism, populism versus elitism, universalism versus insularism, and anti-Westernism versus pro-Westernism.

Saudi Arabia's originally popular, not populist, Islam has over time become a conservative legitimizing force for the House of Saud. The eighteenth-century coalition between the religious reformer Muhammad ibn 'Abd al-Wahhab and the local ruler Muhammad ibn Sa'ud formed the basis of not only an Islamic state but also an essentially royal political system. In other words, Islam was transformed from an initially revivalist force to a conservative formula for legitimacy in Saudi Arabia. On the other side, Khomeini's Islam, which initially accepted the concept of a limited monarchy, has been transformed into an antimonarchical revolutionary force.[12] Second, Saudi official Islam is endorsed by the conservative religious establishment as well as the House of Saud, whereas Khomeini's Islam presumably embraces all strata of the society in which

12. Ramazani, "Khumaini's Islam."

the uplifting of the underdog, or the oppressed (mustaz'afin) is the hall-mark of its revolutionary mission. Third, although Saudi official Islam is the traditional guardian of Islam's holiest sites at Mecca and Medina on behalf of the Muslim world, it is still comparatively insular as opposed to Khomeini's Islam which, it is thought, aims to ultimately establish Islamic world order everywhere. Fourth and finally, Saudi official Islam enjoys a special relationship with the United States and the West in general, whereas Khomeini's Islam is irreconcilably opposed to both superpowers and their allies as a matter of ideological as well as political preference. In this context, the Saudi government becomes the agent of the Great Satan, and the Saudi allies in the Gulf become mini-Satans, and all of them, like Israel, belong to the "oppressors' camp." If Iraqi Baathist ideology is regarded as atheistic, Saudi Muwahhid Islam is considered blasphemous.

On the sociopolitical level, Saudi Shi'i Muslims, as contrasted with the Iraqi, constitute a minority. Some estimates put them at 115,000 and others at 200,000 to 300,000. In any event, they probably number about 5 percent of the citizen population. Their relatively insignificant number is far outweighed by their demographic concentration, strategic location, and crucial profession. They are concentrated in the oil-rich Hasa Province where they constitute between 40 and 60 percent of the work force in the oil industry. In Saudi Arabia not only are such statistics considered highly sensitive, and hence not always reliable, but also the conditions and activities of the Shi'i community are shrouded in great secrecy. Not a single Saudi official I have talked to during my visits to the kingdom has ever denied past mistreatment of the Shi'i minority and the persistence of anti-Shi'i attitudes among the Saudi Sunni Muslims. But in all fairness, the Saudi Shi'is have also been prejudiced against what they pejoratively call the "Wahhabi" faithful (they prefer to be called unitarians or Mu-wahhidun). In any event, the Shi'is of the Eastern Province continue to resent especially the perceived discriminatory acts of the Juluwis, the provincial governors. One of my Shi'i respondents, for example, told me that the Wahhabis believe that "you must keep the dog hungry so that it will follow you," and another told me that the "Shi'i suffers not so much from an empty stomach as from a sense of injured dignity."

It is no wonder that the cry for justice ('adl) symbolized the two major recent Shi'i uprisings in Saudi Arabia like so many throughout Islamic history. The first Shi'i disturbance in the Eastern Province in late November 1979 was, no doubt, inspired by the Iranian revolutionary up-heaval. Some ninety thousand demonstrators carrying portraits of Khomeini defied the government ban on the religious commemoration of the martyrdom of Imam Husain on Ashura, the tenth of the month of Muharram. During the riots a number of people were killed, and the National Guard soldiers, who are perceived symbolically as the agents of Saudi repression, were among them. The second Shi'i unrest took place also in the Eastern Province in February 1980 when the demonstrators demanded among other things that oil should remain in the ground since the revenues from its sale did not help alleviate the sufferings of the oil workers.

One of my most reliable Saudi Sunni respondents recounted the two Shi'i disturbances as follows:

> The revolution in Iran which was led by a religious leader stirred up emotions and struck a responsive chord in Qatif. The religious factor, however, was not the only reason for the disturbances. Until ten years ago, all villages in the Kingdom suffered from a lack of basic services. Basic services were not getting to them. The situation in the cities and urban centers was far better than it was in the villages. This created a climate—a fertile soil for disgruntlement, contributing to the response in Qatif to the events in Iran. Note that no disturbances occurred in al-Hasa, because it is more of an urban area. But in the villages, the situation was different. Villagers felt they were deprived of benefits [mahrumin].

Regardless of the accuracy of the details, one can hardly find better evidence for the proposition that the perceived threat of Shi'ism to the House of Saud is not simply an external matter of the Shi'i ideology as expounded by Khomeini and backed by the power of the Iranian state; more important, it is one of susceptibility of alienated elements within the Saudi Shi'i community to the Iranian appeal. All my official Saudi respondents invariably pointed out the recent expenditure of billions of dollars by the Saudi government for the betterment of the standard of living among Shi'i Muslims. Even many of my private respondents were keenly aware of government efforts for the betterment of Shi'i living conditions ever since King Khalid met with Shi'i leaders in Qatif in the wake of the above-mentioned disturbances. One private respondent optimistically told me in 1984 that the Shi'i in Qatif were now "immune to the Iranian influence" because of the government extension of social services to them, and also because of the increasingly better attitude of Saudi officials toward the Shi'i minority. Another respondent pointed out that perhaps the government had overdone a good thing! He said, and I quote him verbatim:

There are now people [in Saudi Arabia] who believe that attention to Qatif [by the Saudi government] far exceeds that given to other villages. Yesterday [March 7, 1984], the cabinet decided to build six hundred villas in Qatif, but only four hundred in al-Hasa, although al-Hasa is bigger and larger. In fact Qatif now ranks fourth in the government's priorities—after Riyadh, Jidda, Damman, and al-Qasim which is being overlooked despite its half a million people. All this is congruent with the need to eliminate any climate which would be conducive to injustice.

The Saudi Shi'i problem is potentially susceptible annually to the catalyst of the Iranian pilgrims to Mecca. Ever since the revolution, the pilgrims from Iran have tried to use the Hajj ceremonies for the purpose of proselytizing the Khomeini brand of Islam. The Iranian pilgrims constitute the single largest, most cohesive, and most politicized group of Shi'i pilgrims from any Muslim country in the world. In recent years they have numbered about 100,000 each year. They have taken posters of Khomeini and revolutionary tracts to Mecca, staged political demonstrations, and shouted slogans against the United States, Israel, and Iraq. These have been reported by the Western press, although the facts of each crisis have been disputed by Tehran and Riyadh.

What is less known, however, is the underlying conflict between Khomeinist and Saudi official Islam as it relates specifically to the opposing conceptions of the Hajj itself. At the height of the dispute between Saudi Arabia and Iran over the behavior of the Iranian pilgrims in 1981, King Khalid wrote Ayatullah Khomeini, complaining that the Iranian pilgrims had in his name acted in ways "contrary to the aims of pilgrimage and the honor of holy places," and their behavior not only "disturbed and disgusted other pilgrims" but no doubt would also "damage Iran's credibility and prestige."[13] Khomeini not only rejected the king's version of events but, more important, contested his view that the purpose of pilgrimage was religious worship only. He contended categorically that under all prophets, especially the prophet of Islam, pilgrimage had been "completely linked to politics," and their separation was the idea of the superpowers.

What is important from a practical standpoint, however, is that, despite the recurrence of the problem, Saudi authorities do not allow themselves to be provoked; they bend over backwards not to give any offense to Shi'is. One of the leading Saudi officials dealing with the problem told me that they try to pursue a two-pronged strategy. First, they continue to maintain a dialogue with the Iranian authorities about the logistical prob-

13. Ibid., 27.

lems associated with the travel and stay of such a large group of pilgrims from Iran, regardless of doctrinal differences. Second, they handle the troublemaking pilgrims with utmost care, seeing to it that they leave Saudi Arabia with the least possible disturbance. So far, this cautious and pragmatic policy seems to have paid off rather well.

Bahrain

Our last case study of Shi'ism in the Persian Gulf focuses on the only archipelago state of the region. Bahraini Shi'i Muslims constitute 71 to 98 percent of the citizen population of 238,420. This means that, although percentage-wise Bahrain has the largest group of Shi'i Muslim citizens of any Gulf Arab country, in absolute terms it ranks third after Iraq and Saudi Arabia. But the Bahraini like the Iraqi and Saudi Shi'i Muslims are found predominantly in the rural areas and Sunni Muslims in the urban centers, and they, like the other Arab Shi'i Muslims, live under the rule of an indigenous Sunni minority. But, unlike both Iraq and Saudi Arabia, this tiny state carries the burden of an ancient Iranian claim to its territory, which was for all practical purposes settled in 1971 when the shah relinquished the claim of sovereignty to the island state; his government was the first to recognize its independence.

The Iranian Revolution, however, revived the ancient claim in a new form. Unlike Iraq and Saudi Arabia, Bahrain felt the brunt of the impact of the revolution even before the fall of the Bazargan government. A leading Iranian cleric, Ayatullah Ruhani, announced in 1979 that he would lead a revolutionary movement for the annexation of Bahrain, unless its rulers adopted "an Islamic form of government similar to the one established in Iran." The claim was qualitatively different from the old Iranian claim; previously it had always been a claim based on the "uncontested Iranian sovereignty" over the territory of Bahrain. But the Ruhani claim reflected the earliest clerical bid for export of the Islamic revolution to other Gulf states, in this case through the threat of physical annexation.

The threat caused the Bazargan government considerable embarrassment. It was trying to maintain equitable relations with all states, most particularly with the neighboring Gulf states. Bazargan in effect tried to blame Ruhani's "unauthorized" claim to Bahrain on the revolutionary chaos in Iran, which, he repeatedly complained, had a "thousand chiefs." Bahraini officials, however, would not let the matter rest at that; they embarked on a feverish diplomatic exchange with other Arab leaders who joined them in a chorus of sympathetic support. Bazargan's ambassador to Riyadh, Muhammad Javad Rizavi, declared, "We respect other nations' sovereignty and Iran has no claim or ambitions of any sort on any part of the Gulf." Bazargan's deputy Sadiq Tabataba'i went to Bahrain to ease the mounting tensions between Tehran and Manama, where he assured Bahrain that Ruhani's statement did not represent the official position of the Iranian government, and also told the correspondent of the Kuwaiti newspaper *al-Qabas* that the whole thing had been a "misunderstanding."

What really shocked the Bahraini and other Gulf Arab leaders was the discovery of an alleged Iranian-supported coup plot two years later in December 1981. The whole region seemed to be gripped by this essentially quixotic plot, the facts of which are still debated, but the Arab view of it may be related on the basis of documentary research and on-site interviews. Briefly, the Bahraini government announced on December 13 that it had arrested a group of "saboteurs," allegedly trained by Iran. Subsequently, the Bahraini interior minister charged that the group planned to assassinate Bahraini officials; it belonged to the Islamic Front for the Liberation of Bahrain with headquarters in Tehran; and all its sixty members were Shi'i Muslim. Actually the group turned out to have had seventy-three members, including sixty Bahraini and eleven Saudi as well as an Omani and a Kuwaiti national; there were no Iranians among them by anyone's account. But at the time five unidentified armed men reportedly presented a written memorandum to the Bahraini embassy in Tehran in which they claimed responsibility for the group arrested in Bahrain. At the time also Bahrain asked Iran to recall its chargé d'affaires. After a long drawn-out investigation and trial, the plotters were finally sentenced in May 1982, receiving jail sentences ranging from seven years to life imprisonment.

The results of my interviews on this plot in Bahrain and Saudi Arabia may be summarized as follows: Arab officials seem absolutely convinced that the Shi'i dissidents arrested had been both trained and equipped by Iran; the Saudi officials seem to have been closely involved in the whole process of investigation through consultation and exchange of intelligence information. Also, every official I talked to in the region seemed to confirm what the secretary-general of the Gulf Cooperation Council (GCC)— Majlis al-Ta'awun li Duwal al-Khalij al-Arabiyah—Abdullah Bisharah, had said in February 1982: "What happened in Bahrain was not directed against one part of this body but against the whole body." This was an enigmatic way of saying what the Arab press had already reported, that

is, that besides Bahrain, Saudi Arabia and other Gulf Arab countries had
been the targets of the plot. Finally, private Bahraini Shi'i respondents
told me that the plotters had been trained in paramilitary camps in Iran's
holy city of Qom by a certain "Hadi Mudarrisi," presumably an Iraqi
Shi'i Muslim who carries a Bahraini passport. Others believe that they
were trained by Hujjat al-Islam Mudarrisi, who had lived in Bahrain in
exile from Iran during the shah's regime. The latter information is cor-
roborated by more reliable private sources. Bahraini respondents also told
me that the plotters got such "light sentences" either because Iran threatened revenge if they were executed or because the Liberation Front for
Bahrain and the Arabian Peninsula threatened to punish members of the
Bahraini royal family if the court handed down death sentences. I suspect
these are perhaps more rumors than accurate reports, but that is also part
of the Gulf political scene.

No single incident attributed to Shi'i radicals until December 1981
had threatened the Gulf Arab leaders so much. The Saudis behaved as if
they were even more threatened than the Bahrainis themselves. The Saudi
interior minister Prince Nayif minced no words about the alleged Iranian
involvement in the plot to overthrow the al-Khalifah regime. He called
on Iran to stop supporting "sabotage activities" in the Gulf, reminded
the Iranian leaders that they had said earlier that they would not be "the
policeman of the Gulf," and charged that today "they have unfortunately
become the terrorists of the Gulf." More important, Saudi Arabia rushed
to sign four bilateral security agreements with Bahrain, Qatar, the United
Arab Emirates (UAE), and Oman, but Kuwait has held back ever since,
resisting also Saudi pressure for a single collective internal security agreement among all the GCC members. During my last visit to Saudi Arabia,
I found the Saudi officials still hopeful about the prospects of such an
agreement perhaps during the organization's fifth summit meeting in November 1984. Meanwhile, however, the GCC interior ministers, with an eye
to the alleged Iranian support of the Shi'i coup plot, have agreed in
principle that "intervention by any country in the internal affairs of one
of the member states is considered to be intervention in the internal affairs
of the GCC states."

The panicky reaction of the GCC leaders to the Shi'i coup plot at the
diplomatic level tends to blur the older and deeper sociopolitical problem
of Shi'i dissidence in Bahrain. From such a perspective, the more important facts of the Shi'i coup plot are almost universally overlooked. To
mention just a few, about 30 percent of the members of the coup plot
group were disaffected Arab students, about 17 percent were unemployed
workers, and the overwhelming majority were young alienated indigenous

Shi'i nationals of the Gulf Arab states. To be sure, the catalyst of the Iranian Revolution, with all that it has entailed ideologically and politically, exacerbates the problem of Shi'i dissidence—as in fact the Sunni dissidence as well—in Bahrain as well as other Gulf Arab states, but the problem long predates the advent of the revolution. Certainly the Bahraini Shi'i Muslims seem to believe that their most active organization, the Islamic Guidance Society (IGC), was established, they told me, in 1972 and began activities in earnest in 1976, before the revolution in Iran. Today IGC is considered by the Bahraini authorities to be "an illegal political organization," the Central and Ideological Committee (CIC) of which receives its orders from "foreign quarters."

The president of the IGC, Ibrahim Mansur Ibrahim, who is better known as Ibrahim al-Jufairi, was arrested in February 1984, eleven days after the arrest of another member of the IGC, Muhammad Abdullah Muhammad Husain. He reportedly "confessed to possessing pistols, ammunition and a rocket-propelled grenade." I was told in Bahrain that Muhammad Husain was arrested at the nearby village of al-Markh where he had hidden arms and ammunitions, perhaps left over from the coup plot of December 1981. The coup plot has certainly made for tighter security measures against suspected Shi'i dissidents, particularly those of Iranian origin or with Iranian connections.

To go back to earlier years, the first major Shi'i unrest in Bahrain occurred in the wake of the Iranian Revolution in 1979 when a Shi'i leader by the name of Muhammad 'Ali al-'Akri was arrested and incarcerated. But the second major Shi'i unrest was triggered by the arrest of Ayatullah Sayyid Muhammad Baqir al-Sadr in Iraq in January 1980 before he and his sister, Bint al-Huda, were executed in April. I was also told that the Shi'i demonstrations at the time had been directed against the Iraqi embassy and bank in Manama and not the regime, but a Shi'i leader named Jamil 'Ali, better known among the Bahrainis as al-Thaur, was arrested and "beaten to death" subsequently; the Bahraini police, however, claimed that he had "died in custody." In November of 1980 when I happened to be in Bahrain during Ashura, I learned that the Shi'i mourners commemorating the martyrdom of Imam Husain carried the picture of "the mutilated Body" of al-Thaur with the inscription "Martyred by the Pharaonic Regime."

In answer to my questions about Iran, one of my Bahraini Shi'i respondents enthusiastically offered the following observations without ever suggesting that Bahrain should have an Iranian-type Islamic government:

1. The only Muslim country in the world that dares to successfully

defy both the East and the West and maintain its independence is Iran.

2. The Iranian government is the only oil-rich government in the Arabian Gulf that distributes wealth among the people equitably.
3. It is only the wealthy, the privileged, and the upper-class individual in Iran who does not like Ayatullah Khomeini.
4. Who says freedom is squashed in Iran? Even Sunnis and Christians can talk and act freely!
5. Should Iran win the war against the Aflaqite regime in Iraq, the Bahraini Shi'i Muslims, like all others, will be delighted.

When I asked another Shi'i respondent if he could list the views of the Shi'i Bahrainis about their own government, he replied as follows:

1. We don't say the ruler of Bahrain should be a Shi'i because the majority of the people are, but we want to have more say in our government; the present Shi'i membership in the cabinet does not include important ministries; it is a kind of tokenism.
2. We want freedom of the newspapers. We also want a parliament; you know we used to have one, but we don't have one now. On the whole we want more participation.
3. An Islamic government could help all this. It could give our children more Islamic education.

Only a gullible analyst would jump to the conclusion that the Shi'is are really asking for "democracy"—far from it. When I pressed the same respondent about what he meant by "freedom," "participation," or "parliament," and how an "Islamic government" could help all that, he simply replied that such a government would follow "the right path" (*sirat al-mustaqim*). We should remember, I might add, that in Iran "the right path" has become the "Khomeini line" (*khatt-i imam*), and that any deviation from it cannot be tolerated. Instead of reading our own wishes into such terms, they should be understood in the context of the Shi'i cultural tradition. In this context, such terms as "participation" most often turn out to be an inchoate way of expressing the Shi'i sense of having been unjustly treated in the historical past, and the belief that justice will prevail if only the "right government" is established by "the right people."

PROPOSITIONS

Given the underdeveloped state of the study of Shi'ism in the Persian Gulf region, there can be no firm conclusions here. Rather, I will present two major propositions intended (1) to integrate the main findings of the foregoing empirical analysis based on documentary and field research, and (2) to point out their central policy implications.

1. Shi'ism is a major force in both the foreign policy and the domestic political process of all the states of the Persian Gulf in varying degrees as an international ideological and sociopolitical movement that cuts across state boundaries. In Iran, it is the official ideology of the state, a major determinant of its foreign and domestic policies, and a particular interpretation of Islam by Ayatullah Ruhullah Khomeini (khatt-i imam) that is supported by various groups. Khomeini's basically revolutionary, millenarian, and populist Islam clashes with the ideological orientation of all other Gulf states, particularly with the conservative Saudi Islam and the revolutionary Iraqi Baathism. In war, however, as with Iraq, and in cold war, as with Saudi Arabia—which briefly warmed up on June 5, 1984, when the Saudis shot down an Iranian F-4 aircraft—Khomeini's Islam is perceived by the Gulf Arab leaders as not just an external ideological threat backed by the power of the Iranian state. Rather, it is seen as an internal revolutionary force, either potentially, as evidenced by Shi'i dissident groups in Bahrain and Saudi Arabia, or actively, as shown by the underground existence of the Da'wah in Iraq, which is supported by the Iranian-based Iraqi SAIRI led by Hujjat al-Islam Muhammad Baqir al-Hakim.

2. The policy implications of Shi'ism in the Middle East as an ideological and sociopolitical movement involve both regional and external powers. The United States, for example, poorly estimated the situation in Lebanon largely because of misperceiving Shi'ism, and paid dearly as a result in both human life and credibility by subjecting hundreds of American Marines to the terrorist acts of angry Shi'i activists who are by no means representative of the Shi'i Muslims today, as the extremists (*ghulat*) were not in the historical past. The United States would suffer all the more in the Persian Gulf region—the world heartland of Shi'ism as well as its oil heartland—should it intervene militarily in the area by deploying ground forces. Sociopolitical and ideological Shi'i movements do not call for military solutions, and Henry Kissinger, who simplistically advocates the containment of Shi'ism as well as communism in the region, has yet to say how he proposes to do that. The external powers, the United States or any country, have failed to understand that despite sociopolitical and ideological fragmentation, Shi'ism today is emotionally and spiritually united, as in the historical past, in opposing foreign and domestic tyranny (zulm), and in demanding justice ('adl).

Regional, no less than external, powers have difficulty in understanding Shi'ism. On the Mediterranean side of the Middle East, the Israelis do not seem to appreciate that all their persistent efforts for cooptation, manipulation, and recruitment of Shi'is cannot possibly provide any real solution for their dilemma in southern Lebanon. Despite all factional divisions and incessant jockeying for power, the Shi'is—moderate and radical, armed and unarmed—are united in their opposition to the perceived tyranny of Israeli occupation. Those Israelis who view their own destiny in terms of foreign persecution and the suffering of the Jews throughout history and also in terms of religious hope for the Promised Land do not seem to appreciate the Shi'is' sense of historical suffering (*masa'ib*) and the emotional and spiritual hope for the establishment of justice by the promised mahdi.

Fellow Muslims do not seem to show much better understanding of their Shi'i brethren either. The Iraqi, the Bahraini, the Saudi, and other regimes have yet to realize that neither resort to war, as by Iraq, nor diplomacy, nor a mix of military deterrence and diplomacy by all other Gulf Arab states alone can contain the perceived threat to their security. Nor do they seem to realize that no degree of religious pretense, socioeconomic cooptation, and political manipulation will resolve their Shi'i majority or minority problem whether or not their Shi'i citizens are susceptible to the appeal of Khomeini's Islamic ideology. The Shi'is perceive their accumulated grievances in terms of their historical experience as the most deprived group (mahrumin), and also in terms of the emotional and spiritual promise of salvation (najah), and the establishment of justice by the mahdi before the Day of Resurrection (qiyamah). This is, in my view, the fundamental force that underlies Shi'ism and no regional leader can afford to ignore it. Khomeini himself is no exception. His Islamic revolution will no doubt suffer grievously from a failure to heed *in practice* this ancient and inexorable Shi'i quest for justice. The "government of the oppressed," as he characterizes the Iranian government, will help the masses "to inherit the earth," he repeatedly promises. But that government will, instead, look increasingly more like the government of the oppressors if the Iranian leaders continue to fail to bring their millenarian revolutionary goals within mundane, realistic means.

RICHARD W. COTTAM

Chapter Two The Iranian Revolution

There is no generally accepted definition of revolution and hence no agreement as to the criteria that must be met if an event is to be classified as
a revolution. Thus there can be, and are, individuals who deny that what
has occurred in Iran since 1978 is a revolution. Yet it would be perverse
for anyone to deny that radical change has occurred in Iran along a number of dimensions.

One dimension of change that could serve as a criterion for revolution
is the extent to which the ruling elite has been replaced. In this respect,
change in Iran since 1979 is surely comparable to that in Russia after
1917. The old sociopolitical elite has been ousted and many of its members
now live in exile. Those who remain are excluded from positions of influence, although a good number of them continue to prosper economically.
Power redistribution is a major aspect of the radical change that has occurred. Also, the process of recruiting and training a new elite is gaining
momentum—a trend that is essential if the new elite is to consolidate its
position.

Paralleling this change is a major alteration in the focus of identity.
Before the revolution the focus was the national community of which the
modern business and professional class was the core societal element. Now
the focus of identity for supporters of the revolution is the Islamic com-

55

munity of which the urban lower middle class is the core element. Furthermore, because of the persecution and exclusion of secular nationalists, the two communities are sharply polarized. Indeed, the distinctiveness in behavioral terms of each of the two communities is so great that Iran appears to have two cultures cohabiting the same territory. In some ways the resemblance again to the Soviet Union is striking, although the excluded community there was the religious one.

A third parallel with the Bolshevik Revolution and also with the French Revolution is the universalism of the pretensions of the Iranian Revolution. Khomeini sees his divinely ordained rule to have as its objectives the liberation of oppressed peoples from their oppressors and the demonstration to all humanity of the way to the blessings of living in accordance with God's law. The utopia in Khomeini's vision is no less real than was that of Lenin. Living within God's community and accepting the advice of his guides is the path not only to material and spiritual satisfaction but also to true freedom and incorporates the only real potential for individual self-realization.[1]

Those who deny that the Iranian phenomenon is a true revolution can make their best point in terms of its institutionalization. Programmatic implementation of the holy law is not an easy task. Those who sincerely, even fervently, embrace Islam vary tremendously in their views. Some see Islam as egalitarian and favor a radical economic redistribution program. Others see Islam as protecting private property and being in accord with a system of landowning and the commercial institutions of the bazaar. Similarly, the distinction between Islamic and secular higher education is difficult to define for most of the curriculum. Distinctions seem to be more symbolic than substantial. Also, as the revolution ages, the institutional distinctiveness of its early months seems to be fading. The Islamic Republican party, for example, looks increasingly like other authoritarian single parties. Governmental agencies that earlier had to compete with parallel revolutionary institutions are steadily gaining full jurisdictional control. Still unique but rapidly evolving toward a more familiar routinization are the Revolutionary Guards, the judicial and prosecutory system, and the construction jihad (an organization designed to mobilize resources to plan and execute public works projects in areas of particular social need).

The trend away from institutional distinctiveness even embraces the

1. For a persuasive picture of Khomeini's worldview, see Farhang Rajaee, *Islamic Values and World View: Khomeyni on Man, the State and International Politics* (New York: University Press of America, 1983).

institution that appeared at one time to give primary definition to the Islamic Republic, the Vilayat-i Faqih. As initially formulated this institution seemed capable of being the institutional base for the most total one-man control of government the world has yet seen. But Khomeini by his actions had to give definition to the Vilayat-i Faqih. Far from developing it into a vehicle for totalitarian control, Khomeini has used his powers so sparingly that dispassionate observers cannot describe his control as dictatorial. This permits a broader decisional scope for Khomeini's lieutenants. They, in particular the speaker of parliament and the president of the republic, have broadened considerably the power the constitution appeared to grant them. Indeed, this devolution of authority has been broad enough that no individual or even collective in Iran can be said to possess dictatorial control. The Iranian system is totalitarian but lacks a dictator. In this sense it is truly anomalous. Nor can one predict a successor to Khomeini as faqih who would exercise more control than does Khomeini.

If, as asserted, Iran is totalitarian but lacks a dictator, what is the basis of control?[2] In my view the two most defining characteristics of the Iranian movement are its focus on one of the world's few genuinely charismatic figures and the intensity of its appeal to a large core support group. The control system in Iran therefore rests on two factors: the ability of those with authority to mobilize intense support from large numbers of people essentially through symbol manipulation and their possession of coercive instruments, including large, intimidating mobs of supporters to convince the dissatisfied of the regime's invulnerability. The revolutionary regime in Iran thus can be characterized as authoritarian and populist, a type of regime associated with the era of mass politics. Iran under the shah had been described as rapidly modernizing but still categorized as a developing society, and such societies are presumed to be in a pre–mass politics stage. Obviously the growth in political participation in Iran had been much faster than observers, both Iranian and foreign, had expected.

If we are to understand the Iranian Revolution, it would be helpful to compare it with other great revolutionary movements concerning which we have a historical record. Analysts most commonly turn to the French Revolution and the Bolshevik Revolution for this purpose. However, neither is a particularly useful referent for the Iranian Revolution. The Bolshevik Revolution was authoritarian but certainly not populist. Its leaders

2. A particularly useful development of control system as analytic construct is found in Amitai Etzioni, *A Comparative Analysis of Complex Organizations* (New York: Free Press, 1961).

appealed to workers and peasants by offering major economic incentives, but they were never able to attract widespread, intense, and unquestioning support through the manipulation of appealing symbols. The French Revolution did have populist features, and symbol manipulation was a major aspect of control. However, the percentage of the French population that was politically participant could not compare with that of Iran at the time of its revolution. There was nothing comparable to the mass demonstrations of December 1978 in Iran when as many as one-fourth of Iran's population took to the streets against a regime still capable of brutal repression.

There have been a number of regimes that can be categorized as authoritarian populist and as manifestations of mass politics. Comparing the Iranian regime to others that have had like systems of control should help in our understanding and assessment of the significance of the Iranian Revolution. Unfortunately analysts have yet to develop authoritarian populism as a regime type for comparative analytic purposes. One reason for the failure to do so is that the phenomenon will have a wide variety of manifestations. The particular symbols that will be attractive will vary with the culture and with the social base of the core support group appealed to. But probably the most important reason for the failure is historical. European fascism clearly meets the control system definition of authoritarian populism and as such should be a major comparative referent. However, negative judgments of that phenomenon are so strong that placing another movement in the same category appears to be name-calling. In addition, fascism has been conceptualized inductively, abstracting features primarily from the German, Italian, and French movements.[3] Since populist movements will be culturally idiosyncratic, those appearing in Third World states such as Iran will differ in important specific regards from these abstractions from the European experience.

There is much about the Iranian Revolution and the Khomeini regime that is unique. But many of the conditions that gave rise to it can be found in much of the Third World. It is probable that many future regimes there will be populist and authoritarian. However wide the cultural variance, there are general patterns associated with authoritarian populism that can be identified and can be helpful in comparative analysis.[4]

Authoritarian populism occurs typically when a radical elite asso-

3. Ernst Nolte, *Three Faces of Fascism* (New York: Holt Rinehart & Winston, 1963). This is an excellent discussion of the European variant of authoritarian populism.

4. William Kornhauser, *The Politics of Mass Society* (New York: Free Press, 1959). Kornhauser's discussion is an early, highly suggestive essay on the subject of mass politics.

ciated with a charismatic figure is able to bypass the established political and social elite structure and gain access to a large mass public; then, with this mass support, it overturns the established elite and the system within which it has operated. The mass public that supports the new regime need not be, and generally is not, the majority. It is controlled by its benefiting from a radical redistribution of power and wealth and by the manipulation of highly attractive symbols. Those symbols are usually associated with the community with which the affected mass public identifies most intensely—most commonly, the national community. For Iran today the community is religious and hence the symbolic representation has an added force. It refers both to basic identity and to divine sanction. The old elite and those not strongly attracted to the symbols manipulated by the regime are subject to a system of terror control. That system consists of both the governmental coercive instruments and the ability of regime supporters to brutalize those who have the temerity to oppose the regime. Awareness of the brutalizing potential of the devoted core element is sufficient to intimidate even a majority of the population.

The number of authoritarian populist regimes that have appeared in this century is not large. Those that have appeared have manifested a striking vulnerability. In fact such regimes have not survived for long the passing of the charismatic leader. Peronism survived Perón in Argentina and even returned to power briefly with the late charismatic leader represented by his wife. Furthermore, when they have lost control, there has been a strong tendency for the old ousted elite to return in part and restore the previous normative system. Extreme examples of this were Mussolini's fascist regime and Hitler's Nazi regime. When overturned, the supporting elite and the new normative system disappeared, leaving hardly a trace. To be sure, in these cases, both regimes were destroyed by external forces. But given the apparent popularity of the two dictators, one might have expected to see a far greater manifestation of persisting popular support for the fascist or Nazi elite.

There are two obvious reasons for this vulnerability. First, the new governing elite will be narrow and will lack the necessary depth to find occupants for many decisional posts, especially those requiring technical expertise. Recruiting and training a new elite is a slow process, and in the interim the regime must rely on cooperating elements of the old elite or suffer breakdown in the economy and in social services. The problem is particularly serious with regard to security forces. Having to rely on officers who despise the regime that employs them is not conducive to a sense of security.

The second basis for vulnerability arises from the extent of regime reliance on the charismatic leader for its survival. His ability to articulate the core support group's anguish, fears, and aspirations is the likely basis of his charisma. Finding a successor for him is a most difficult task. The leader is unlikely to want to share top billing and is most unlikely to groom a successor who has a competing personal appeal. Thus, when the leader passes from the scene, the regime will be confronted with a serious crisis. Having relied on symbol manipulation as a control device, it must turn to some other form of control when its ability to manipulate symbols suddenly declines. In the short term the only real additional control option is an increased use of coercion. At this point regime survival is likely to depend on the extent to which a new elite has been recruited and has replaced the old—especially in the security forces.

The Islamic Republic clearly has the vulnerability of the classical authoritarian populist model. It has only begun to recruit a new, technologically proficient elite that will serve it faithfully. The Revolutionary Guard is the institutional replacement for the old military, and it appears to be increasingly effective. The process of replacement, however, is far from complete. Coercion is decentralized and as yet lacks a unified leadership. This is true of the Revolutionary Guard but even more so of the Komitehs that provide local security in jurisdictional areas that often embrace only a few square blocks of cities. Also, because of the Iran-Iraq War, the regime must rely on a military of dubious loyalty and, given Iran's isolation, must continue to do so for some time. Khomeini's apparent choice as successor, Ayatullah Husain Ali Muntaziri, also fits the model. He is loyal and supportive and no doubt a source of security for Khomeini. But it is hard to see any charismatic potential in him. When Khomeini passes from the scene, a real test of the institutional development of the Revolutionary Guard and the other security forces will quickly occur.

The Iranian Revolution continues to be a source of great bewilderment in the Western world. It is described as "rightist," "reactionary," "fanatic," and "irrational." A reason for the appeal of these descriptions and for the bewilderment may be the failure of Iran to change in a direction we have come to expect of Third World countries. We saw Iran as a developing state that should follow expected developmental patterns. The very term *development* suggests that there is a change process underway and that we know both the beginning and the end. Samuel Huntington discussed the possibility that the expected end of development might not be achieved. In this event, he concluded, the good developmental end would be replaced by "decay," obviously a very bad end.[5] What the good end would be was made clear by symbol usage. The process would go from the "traditional" to the "modern" and from "undeveloped" to "developed"; this was called "nation-building." The model for the good end was obviously the Western nation state.

What can one say about the Iranian Revolution in this context? Khomeini could not be more emphatic in rejecting the implicit model. He offered in its stead another model, one consistent with his interpretation of Islam. The radical change he wanted was in directions entirely different from those implicit in the Western notion of development. Khomeini's model is highly abstract. In order to reach it, a society must be willing to follow the lead of those few guides, like Khomeini, able to comprehend its arcane heights. After several years of revolution there is still no accepted developmental strategy for achieving this esoteric end. Indeed, programmatic translation of Khomeini's version of Islam is proving to be extraordinarily difficult and controversial.

The Iranian Revolution, then, has followed a course of change that conforms very little to the direction Western developmental models suggest. The task here is to describe and to some extent explain the patterns of change that ultimately were to find expression in that revolution. To approach this task I will focus particularly on two especially critical areas of sociopolitical change. The first of these is a change in attitude toward political participation.[6] A century ago direct participation in the Iranian political process was limited to the traditional elite and its associated employees. The overwhelming majority of the population was deferential to established authority and passively acquiescent in the decisions made. Today a predisposition to participate in the political process is at a level approaching that of the Western democracies. No dimension of change has been more important than this in the transformation of the Iranian political system.

Paralleling change in participation and of comparable importance has been change in the relevant political community with which an individual identifies at a primary level of intensity. The trend here has been away from parochial communities, such as the extended family or clan, and toward a large community focus. The large communities with which in-

<hr />

5. Samuel Huntington, "Political Development and Political Decay," *World Politics* 17 (April 1965): 386–430.

6. Marion J. Levy, Jr., *Modernization and the Structure of Society* (Princeton: Princeton University Press, 1966). Levy presents the classic statement of value change in the developing process.

dividuals tend to identify are four: religious, racial, ethnic, and national. The national community may coincide with one or more of the other three or may be entirely separate. In Japan, for example, the national community coincides with the other three. The American national community, in contrast, is multireligious, multiethnic, and multiracial but a focus of intense identity nonetheless. When an identity shift is made by a majority of the population to a single large community, behavior we describe as nationalistic is likely to occur. There will be a concern for community dignity, grandeur, and welfare. There also will be a strong drive for full independence, and the legitimacy of a regime will depend on its ability to appear to its people as exercising full control over the national destiny. In Iran over the past century a fundamental identity shift has occurred, but there is considerable uncertainty whether the Iranian national community and the Islamic religious community, both foci of identity, generally coincide.

As change occurs in the two dimensions, as a people moves in the direction of mass participation and identity shifts from the familial toward large groups, there will be inevitably an alteration in the governing elite. The traditional governing elite in Iran was well suited for a society that was largely nonparticipant and concerned with familial matters. But it had to change as society changed. However, the directions of alteration of the governing elite and the speed with which these alterations occurred varied a great deal. It will be instructive to note the patterns in elite alterations that accompanied change in other dimensions.

In conjunction with looking at governing elite adjustments to deal with rapid change, another analytic focus will be that of the kinds of control strategies the various elites followed in order to produce regime stability. First, how important has coercion been in the attempt to maintain stability and what kinds of coercive instruments were created for the purpose? Second, how effectively has the governing elite dealt with the problem of providing at least an essential minimum of material satisfaction? Third, has the governing elite been seriously concerned with and successful in providing institutions that accommodate the growing demand for participation in the political process?

Iran entered the era of rapid change in the late 1800s. It was centuries behind Western Europe, a century behind Russia, a half century behind Turkey, but a half century ahead of Africa. These are only moments of difference in human history, but they help account for some very different rhythms in the change process. The discussion to follow will sketch the patterns of change in Iran in terms of the dimensions just outlined. One theme that will emerge is that the rhythm was deeply influenced in contradictory ways by encounters with peoples who were far ahead of Iran in terms of change—especially the British, Americans, and Russians. The case will be made in fact that the Khomeini phenomenon is to an important extent a product of the alteration of natural change patterns in Iran by the interference of external powers.

By 1906 the process of change had reached a point at which the control strategy of the traditional elite was no longer capable of maintaining regime stability. An insistence on participating more actively in the political process had begun to pervade intellectual, commercial, and clerical elements. All three groups were beginning to manifest nationalistic attitudes reflecting an altered identity and were demanding that Iran be freed from almost constant intervention by Britain and Russia. These groups were not large, surely not more than 1 percent of the population. Although their numbers were small, these individuals were centrally located in the regime structure. The ruling elite lacked the flexibility to adapt its control strategy to the needs of the changed situation. Coercive institutions developed to deal with old-style conflict patterns were completely inadequate for dealing with sizable urban mobs led frequently by sons of the social elite. Similarly, existing institutions were in no way adequate to satisfy the participation demands of the increased numbers of individuals voicing them. Nor were there institutions to satisfy sharply altered demands for governmental concern with education, health, transportation—all the elements of the minimal infrastructural and social welfare base that the newly participant would insist on. Nor were there institutions that could provide a comfortable environment for a rapid expansion of domestic commerce.

The traditional regime, then, was overturned in 1906 and a constitutional government established.[7] Progressive members of the traditional elite entered into alliance with pro-change elements, and a new governing elite began to emerge that incorporated the liberal intelligentsia, commercial leaders, and clerical activists. Ideologically opposed to coercion, the new leaders groped for a noncoercive control strategy that would permit the stabilizing of the regime. Participatory institutions satisfied the demands of those seeking a role in the political process. But the new regime had little success in gaining control over rural Iran and the pro-

---

7. For the best account of the revolution and Iranian society at the time by a contemporary observer, see Edward G. Browne, *The Persian Revolution: 1905–1909* (London: T. F. Unwin, 1910).

vincial centers where traditional elements continued to prevail. The result was a floundering economy and an inability to satisfy the material demands of the people. The old control formula had failed and could not be restored; what was needed was a new formula that could allow for an accommodation of both the old and the new plus a means for adjusting to a continuing, even escalating, change process.

However, Iran was not to be allowed the luxury of a time period in which a new formula could be found. The chaos associated with the constitutional regime was highly disruptive of the modus vivendi British and Russian imperialism sought in Iran, and they cooperated in terminating the regime in 1911–12.

The European political response was paradoxical in the extreme. Contact with Europeans, especially Russians and Britons, had helped set in motion the forces of fundamental change in Iran. Economic interaction with European merchants disrupted the traditional economic system and altered forever individual aspirational levels. Political manifestations followed naturally. Merchants, attracted by the expanded horizons of commerce, bitterly resented governmental grants of economic concessions to foreigners. Religious intellectuals sought to revitalize and reform Islam and thereby to create a force able to accept the challenge of technological change and to counter the inroads of Christian powers. Secular intellectuals were attracted to European ideologies but were quickly repelled by European affronts to their own developing nationalism.

But having played a major catalytic role in the appearance of demands for rapid change in Iran through their economic interactions, the European powers also played an active role in encouraging rulers in Iran who opposed rapid change.[8] The appearance of a radical elite that would inaugurate a policy of rapid change in Iran was thus a development to be avoided. It would mean this arena of delicate balance would be upset and the two powers would lose control.[9] Since their interest was an urgent one, the Russians and British adopted a formula that was expensive but in the short term effective. A British-supported Russian ultimatum backed by Russian military intervention brought down the constitutional regime and restored the traditional ruling class. This was made possible by the Russians and the British providing the essential coercive instruments to

8. An excellent picture of Egypt that points to similar patterns there as in Iran can be found in Afaf Lutfi al-Sayyid, *Egypt and Cromer* (New York: Praeger, 1968).
9. See Great Britain, *State Papers, 1909, Persia No. 2,* for evidence of similarities of British and Russian views, esp. 1, 3, 43, 90, 100.

suppress and control what can be described as a change-oriented counter-elite.

Two additional patterns important for understanding revolution in Iran crystallized at this point. How could the British, proud of their own liberal nationalist system, explain their role in overturning elites in Iran who advocated for their country the same normative system? The answer was that the British refused to see the Iranian constitutionalists in this light. Rather they described them as self-serving agitators who irresponsibly stirred mobs of ignorant, uncomprehending people. The conservative elite, on the other hand, consisted of limited but responsible individuals who had the courage to stand against demagoguery.[10] This essentially contemptuous view was with only euphemistic modifications the one that all interfering governments, including the American, would adopt toward Iran. It was a natural rationalization of imperial interests.

The other attitudinal pattern that crystallized at this time continues to pervade change-oriented elements of the Iranian population. They saw those Iranians whom the interfering Europeans described as "responsible" and "moderate" as agents of imperial interests. They saw the European and later American modus operandi as one of working through the conservative elites to ensure that Iran and other Third World countries continued to produce raw material and to provide markets for European finished products. Later dependency theory modified this picture to fit changed circumstances in the capitalist system, but in essence it was the same view. The anomaly in Iran was that the United States prior to World War II was seen as an exception to this European rule.

The Bolshevik Revolution produced a momentary hiatus in the rhythm of imperial rivalry that was so determining of change patterns in Iran. Weakened as it was and not yet prepared to resume the rivalry with Western—now seen as capitalist—imperial interests, the Russians temporarily ceased being a major threat to British interests in Iran. This afforded the British an opportunity to maintain their influence in Iran but at a lower price. They suggested a formula that again has proved to be a natural one for the United States in its dealings in the Third World. They did this via the Anglo-Persian Agreement of 1919. Seen in terms of the conceptual frame advanced earlier, the implicit formula was ingenious. It amounted to an acceptance of the fact of change and a means for controlling and channeling that change so that it could be protective rather than destructive of British interests—and all at a much reduced price for

10. Great Britain, *State Papers, Persia No. 4*, 102.

the British. The formal British role would be tutorial, and the governing elite would continue to be Anglophilic conservatives.[11] The plan was that the Iranians would contract with the British for experts to train Iranians to provide the coercive instruments and institutions necessary to develop a stable and expanding commercial environment. The British plan if successful would have resulted in a ruling elite of "responsible" conservatives, a new internal security force capable of providing order, the beginnings of a competent technocratic force, and an improved environment for economic expansion.

This elite formula, naturally attractive for external powers exercising preeminent influence in Third World countries in the era of rapid change, lends itself to maximum influence at low costs. This is because the conservative elite recognizes the danger to its survival from rapid-change counterelites and thus wishes to promote an alliance with the external power. Both the conservative elite and the external power wish to control and channel change, and this commonality of interest makes it fairly easy to agree on policy matters.

The British and their conservative allies, however, were unable to cajole and purchase sufficient support for their plan to get it ratified. The explanation for this failure rests on three factors. First, the percentage of people participating in politics and seeking rapid change was growing. But the coercive force necessary to control their behavior was decreasingly effective. The Russians had withdrawn and the British wanted to leave Iran. Since the tutorial formula had no appeal to the growing pro-change element of the population, it could be applied only by force.

Second, neither the conservative elite nor the British were willing to deal with the insistence of this growing element for a positive role in decision making. Their only institutional access was through parliament, and in only a few districts could elections be described as reasonably free.

Third, and by far the most fundamental, the perception that the conservative elite elements in Iran were functionally agents of the British made support for the agreement extremely unlikely. Collaborating Iranians lacked nationalist legitimacy and any real ability to attract broad public support. Recognizing this, conservatives turned even more to the British for support and in doing so underlined and reconfirmed their image as traitors.

Unable to gain acceptance for this formula and unwilling to pay the price for a reinforced coercive instrument, the British reached an impasse.

11. On the Anglo-Persian Agreement, see Harold Nicolson, *Curzon: The Last Phase, 1919–1925* (New York: Houghton Mifflin, 1934).

But political paralysis in Tehran had developed to the point that a coup d'etat was almost an inevitability. The one that was successful in 1921 was led by Sayyid Zia al-Din Tabataba'i, a journalist whose newspaper was willing to endorse the Anglo-Persian Agreement and as a result was regarded by nationalists as serving British interests. The man selected to provide coercive support of and protection for the new regime was Col. Reza Khan, soon to be Reza Shah Pahlavi. Following the coup, Reza Khan began the long and difficult task of creating a truly effective security force capable of providing the means for coercing support or acquiescence from the public.

The extent of British involvement in this coup is a matter of persistent speculation. Documentary evidence is lacking to support the thesis of their active collaboration.[12] But even if there was involvement it is unlikely that it was more than an ad hoc response to a difficult situation. Iranian observers, however, drew a very different conclusion. They saw a well-orchestrated conspiracy reflecting a long-term strategy for inexpensive and indirect control of Iran. Within three months Sayyid Zia was dropped by Reza Khan and left Iran. Reza Khan's ascendancy to the premiership and ultimately to the throne of Iran was a prolonged process. It involved a long series of clashes not only with the liberal nationalist intelligentsia but also with conservative elites with whom the British had cooperated—allies the British could betray without a twinge of regret. Iranian nationalists believed that his rise to power, with all its vicissitudes, was part of a British master plan.[13]

The British clearly recognized that Reza Khan (soon Reza Shah) could serve their interests very well. He could provide the order and stability their commercial interests needed, particularly in oil production, and he could control difficult tribal groups whom the British otherwise would have had to subsidize. Reza Khan moved too rapidly at one point for the religious leaders and provoked a difficult confrontation with them, but he survived the encounter and mollified them. When he had consolidated control he began to treat religious leaders differentially, exiling or incarcerating the more obstreperous of them. He treated the landowning elite similarly—brutal with some, accommodating with others. But the societal base of support he appealed to was more change oriented. He developed a strong military elite and rewarded them handsomely. He en-

12. On the British role, see Richard Ullman, *Anglo Soviet Relations, 1917–21: The Anglo Soviet Accord,* vol. 3 (Princeton: Princeton University Press, 1972).

13. For the Iranian interpretation, see Husain Makki, *Tarikh Bist Salih Iran,* 3 vols. (Tehran, 1945–47; reprint, Amir Kabir, 1978–79).

couraged the training and recruitment of a technocratic element and provided a good environment for the growth of an Iranian commercial middle class.

Thus we have a second elite formula—authoritarian leader, military, technocratic, and bourgeois—for dealing with rapid change in Iran. It was not the preferred formula for the British but they quickly accepted it. Furthermore, it appeared to be well suited to the needs of adjusting to rapid change. It paralleled closely the formula that was working well in Turkey. But there was a critical difference between Ataturk's and Reza Shah's positions as leaders. Ataturk had led the forces of Turkish nationalism in an epic battle to rid Turkey of the imperialists and their agents. Reza Shah had begun his rise to power in an imperialist-supported if not inaugurated coup and did so in league with Sayyid Zia who was known as an agent of British imperialism. Furthermore, the first victims of his rise to power were men with impeccable nationalist credentials. Reza Shah was almost surely an intense Iranian nationalist, but the history of his rise to power made it difficult for him to achieve nationalist legitimacy. Moreover, the religious leaders he later exiled or otherwise disposed of were the very ones who spoke most effectively for change-oriented elements who identified primarily with the religious community. Ataturk had dealt even more harshly with religious leaders, but he could offer to the newly participant identification with the Turkish nation. Reza Shah tried to do the same with the Iranian nation, but his success was only partial. Military officers, large merchants, and others who profited from the regime could give enthusiastic support. But very few intellectuals could support him, and intellectuals constituted an important segment of the pro-change element.

In the 1930s Reza Shah carried out many policies that should have distanced him from the British. He forced a renegotiation of the oil agreement, but one of only modest proportions. His real declaration of independence came with his policy toward Hitler's Germany. Commercially and politically the shift toward Germany was important. Because of the seriousness of the threat Hitler posed, the British could not accept this degree of independence from Reza Shah. In 1941 an Anglo-Soviet invasion of Iran took place, and Reza Shah was exiled to South Africa. The Iranian press applauded his departure but the message, that Reza Shah had tried to take more rein than the British could allow one of their men, was clear. Reza Shah's young son and successor, Muhammad Reza Shah, caused the Allies little trouble.

The comparison of Reza Shah with Ataturk is instructive. The governing elites they established were parallel and so were the control strategies. The two dictators were nationalists with similar aspirations for their peoples. Both worked for radical transformation of their societies. They differed most sharply in terms of the image their people held of them. Ataturk came to symbolize the achievement of true independence and dignity for the Turkish nation. Reza Shah was perceived by important opinion-formulating elements in Iran as an instrument for British imperialism. External intervention in Iran as perceived thus had denied legitimacy to cooperating conservative elites and to the most important modernizing authoritarian leader Iran had produced. Neither the conservatives nor the Pahlavis would be able to mobilize the support of the awakening Iranian masses.

The superficial quality of Iranian acceptance of Reza Shah and his failure to socialize the newly participant into his normative system became quickly apparent after his abdication. The officer corps on which he had relied for coercive control disintegrated. In fact, many officers sold their arms to the very tribal elements Reza Shah had tried so hard to bring under central government control. His other institutions, with the exception of the dynasty itself which was supported by the external invaders, either disappeared or transferred their loyalty to the new regime which had accommodated to imperial occupation. The old conservative elite returned and reasserted its leadership. This was possible during the occupation since the Allies provided the coercive force. But now the pro-change element was numerically large though still small in percentage— probably around 10 to 15 percent—and it was clear that whatever new elite formula emerged, this element had to be taken into account.

The pro-change element consisted of students, professionals, intellectuals, including many in the bureaucracy, religious leaders, including both liberal reformists and nascent populists, much of the bazaar-oriented old middle class, the new middle class, and a number of sons and daughters of the conservative upper class. It was strongly fractionated into often highly ideological groupings. These included a vigorous leftist Tudeh party, which attracted many of Iran's most outstanding intellectuals. In the relatively free elections in Tehran in 1952, the Tudeh party received about a fifth of the popular vote. There were commonalities among the pro-change element. Except for Marxist literalists, the attraction of the Iranian national community and/or the Islamic community was intense. And all were opposed to imperial control of Iran, although here again

Marxists were inclined not to include Soviet policy in that category. What was required was a galvanizing force capable of producing some unity of action under a common umbrella. That galvanizing force appeared in the form of the charismatic appeal of Dr. Muhammad Musaddiq. In 1951, ten years after the Allied invasion, Musaddiq was named prime minister of Iran and a new ruling coalition was established that challenged Muhammad Reza Shah's control.

Prior to this, the external actors had made clear their own preference for a ruling elite formula. The British appeared to be reliving the post–World War I years. Sayyid Zia returned to Iran and organized the National Will party. The virtually universal assumption in Iran was that this was a British exercise. The British probably would have been happy with a number of other leaders, but all would be members of the conservative elite who understood that Iran had to accommodate minimally the forces of change. Allied with them would be the court, what remained of the officer corps, and members of the new middle class who had supported Reza Shah. Conservative clerics, including several spellbinding orators, and mob leaders who could bring out large crowds for a reasonable price would provide what the British saw as sufficient popular support. There is little evidence that the British policymakers were aware of an Iranian public opinion that had to be taken into account.

The Soviets in Iran during World War II behaved opportunistically. At first, in their area of occupation they dealt mainly with established conservative elites. As it became clear that Germany would be defeated, Soviet policy began to take on a more activist flavor, embracing two autonomy movements—Kurdish and Azerbaijani—and concentrating most fully on relations with the pro-Moscow Tudeh party. This opportunism proved costly. Kurdish nationalist leaders saw a major opportunity and sought to use Soviet support to wrest functional independence for Iranian Kurdistan. When broader strategic interests led the Soviets to drop support for the Kurds, however, they did so with no apparent reluctance. Iranian nationalists were far more worried about Soviet activity in the extremely important Azerbaijan. By supporting an autonomist movement in Azerbaijan, the Soviets did a great deal to delegitimize any Iranian group sympathetic with them. Some of the most important figures of the left intelligentsia broke with the Tudeh because of this. The Azerbaijani response to the Soviet effort was instructive. Progressive social and economic programs were appreciated but evidence of an Azerbaijani nationalism simply did not appear—in sharp contrast to the Kurds. When Soviet interest was seen to be better served by allowing the collapse of their surrogate regime in Azerbaijan, the populace disposed of the pro-Soviet leadership with apparent enthusiasm.[14]

The importance of this Soviet behavior is to be seen in its impact on change-oriented Iranians. Given British policy, which seemed in tune with Iran of two generations previous, and given the Iranian conviction that external intervention in Iranian politics was a critical aspect of the domestic political process, the Soviets had the opportunity to attract pro-change Iranians as allies. But Soviet policy in fact reduced their base of appeal. This left only the United States, an external power of rapidly growing consequence, as a potential ally of pro-change Iranians. Furthermore, as official American diplomatic correspondence makes clear, American officials concerned with Iran at the close of World War II were sympathetic to the aspirations of these people.[15] Yet within a very few years the American government embraced the old British formula.

The Musaddiq government in 1951 was supported by an amalgam of forces that reached from the progressive wing of the conservative upper class to nationalistic socialists and included both those who looked to the Iranian national community and those who looked to the Muslim community as the natural community base of support for the state. It included individuals devoted to enlightenment values and others who believed Iran needed tough, authoritarian leadership. In fact, of the now substantial change-oriented populace, only two significant groups stood outside the support group of the new regime. These were typified by the Tudeh and the bitterly antisecular Fida'iyan-i Islam. That such a conglomerate with all its internal contradictions should have persisted for months and years was possible only because of Musaddiq's charismatic appeal.

The elite formula that the Musaddiq government represented was typologically close to that of the 1906–12 period. The percentage of the politically participant population that supported the new regime was very high, several times that of 1906. The base of support for the regime, in other words, was broad enough to give some real promise of growing stability. Furthermore the Musaddiq movement would serve as a mobilizing catalyst accelerating the growth in numbers of those predisposed to become participants in the process. And it would socialize the newly participant in the prevailing normative system—which included national, religious, liberal, and humanitarian norms.

14. The best account of this episode in English thus far is in Bruce R. Kuniholm, *The Origins of the Cold War in the Near East* (Princeton: Princeton University Press, 1980).

15. See, for example, United States, Department of State, *Foreign Relations of the United States* (Washington, D.C.: Government Printing Office, 1945), 6:501.

The internal contradictions of the amalgam inevitably led to critical confrontations, but Musaddiq consistently prevailed as long as the external powers remained aloof and even—as in July 1952—when those powers tried to maneuver Musaddiq out of office.[16] Many of the early supporters from the old conservative ruling elite turned away from the regime. So did several leaders who saw the opportunity to supplant Musaddiq and to use the symbolic appeals of nationalism to establish an authoritarian movement led by them—men such as Dr. Muzaffar Baqa'i and Husain Makki. But the confrontation of fundamental importance for the future of Iran was that with Ayatullah Abu'l-Qasim Kashani.[17] Musaddiq's National Front included a great many religiopolitical leaders. But from a political point of view they can be placed roughly in two categories. The first consisted of men such as Ayatullah Mahmud Taliqani who could be at peace with a movement that rested on both the national and religious communities and would work to produce a formula that would balance the two. The second consisted of men such as Kashani who saw an alliance with secularists as a temporary convenience. Ayatullah Ruhullah Khomeini was already middle-aged at this time, and his refusal to participate in the political life of the Musaddiq era reflected his deep conviction that political leaders of Iran must look to the great religious scholars for guidance and understanding. He wanted nothing to do with a movement such as the National Front that appeared to be primarily secular in focus. Kashani's disagreement with Khomeini was tactical. Their objectives were the same.

Seen in terms of the change process, this conflict was a critical one. As the disposition to become politically participant moved with accelerating force into the urban lower and lower middle classes and eventually into the peasantry, would the newly participant look to a secular liberal like Musaddiq or to a religious leader? Would they see themselves more as members of the Iranian national community or as members of the Islamic community? This conflict was never fully resolved, but in 1953 Musaddiq clearly had the upper hand. Clerical figures such as Taliqani and lay leaders such as Mihdi Bazargan went with Musaddiq. Kashani and his supporters were isolated and lost influence.

16. Hasan Aranjani detailed his role as intermediary between the American and British ambassadors and Iranians interested in ousting Musaddiq in a pamphlet entitled *Si-i Tir,* which is almost impossible to find. He confirmed his role to the author in several interviews in 1956–57.

17. Concerning Ayatullah Kashani, see Yann Richard, "Ayatollah Kashani: Precursor of the Islamic Republic," in Nikki Keddie, ed., *Religion and Politics in Iran* (New Haven: Yale University Press, 1983).

Given Iran's long experience with interventionism by external powers, it was inevitable that those bested by Musaddiq would turn to those powers in order to reverse their fortunes. Fazlullah Zahidi, Baqa'i, and Kashani all did so, and they looked both to the British and to the Americans. Musaddiq did his best to convince the Americans in particular that his regime served American national interests. Not only was the regime philosophically close to the United States; it was fiercely independent and sufficiently popular to be able to oppose any effort by an external power— read the Soviet Union—to subvert it. Indeed there were highly placed Americans such as Ambassador Henry Grady who accepted this position. But America's position had changed dramatically in ten years. By 1953 the United States was a superpower, the leader of a bloc of states opposed to what they saw as a Soviet aggressive purpose.[18] Because of nuclear weaponry, the Soviet-American conflict could not be resolved by an all-out exercise of violence. Rather the conflict was to be fought on many fronts, including that of strategically placed Third World states. Of these none was more important than Iran.

The parallel with the earlier modus operandi of the British and Russians in Iran was striking. Now as then the struggle was one for influence and preeminence in Iranian affairs; and now as then, neither of the great competitors dared risk the development of an uncontrolled situation. At best that could lead to domination of Iran by the other power. At worst it could lead to violence that could escalate to the nuclear level.

The governing elite under Musaddiq—liberal intellectual, technocratic, and bourgeois—was viewed by the Eisenhower administration as undesirable. It was in their eyes unstable, chaotic, and fanatical. Far from viewing Musaddiq as a Western-educated son of the Enlightenment, they saw a man given to weeping, fainting, and receiving foreign dignitaries in his pajamas. He was an absurd figure who allowed communist mobs to roam Tehran shouting "Yankee go home" and was creating an ideal climate for Soviet subversive purposes. The administration therefore was receptive to British suggestions that he be removed.[19] The Allies agreed that the successor regime in Iran should be one led by a no-nonsense dictator, Zahidi, who would rule in cooperation with the shah and the court. The elite formula they had in mind was familiar: conservative lead-

---

18. A book-length manuscript on Operation Ajax, the code name for the CIA coup plan, is near completion by Leonard Bushkoff. It will be a detailed account based on documents and extensive interviews of participants.

19. For a view of Iran by one of the main actors in the 1953 coup, see Kermit Roosevelt, *Countercoup: The Bloody Struggle for Control of Iran* (New York: McGraw Hill, 1979).

ers aware of the necessity for controlled change, a strong military and internal security officer corps, strictly professional technocrats, and an entrepreneurial and industrial element largely independent of the old bazaar-related middle class. As formerly, conservative clergy and mob leaders could provide the crowds to support the regime when needed. Also true to form, the British, now joined by the Americans, evinced no awareness of the lack of nationalist or religious legitimacy of their Iranian collaborators.

This formula was one that did recognize that change had to be accommodated; but it was premised on the assumption that a conservative, collaborating elite supported by a sufficient coercive force and able to provide minimal material satisfaction could control and regulate the pace and direction of change. There was no evident acceptance of any need on the part of the regime to be able to manipulate symbols relating to the national or religious community nor of the need for institutions that would provide an outlet for a demand for participation in the political process.

On August 19, 1953, Musaddiq was overthrown by a coup that received direction, financing, and logistic support from the CIA in high-level collaboration with the British MI-6. The coup overturned an elite that was responsive to rapid change in Iran and that reflected very well the middle-class and intelligentsia base of the participant public in Iran. We cannot know whether the Musaddiq regime could have served to mobilize and socialize the lower-middle- and lower-class elements that were only beginning to become politically participant. Had it been successful in doing so, the polarization of secular and religious elements that characterized the Iranian Revolution would not have occurred. The conclusion is defensible that had Musaddiq not been overturned by a foreign-sponsored coup, the Khomeini regime would never have appeared. But it would be difficult to defend the conclusion that once Musaddiq was overturned a Khomeini-type phenomenon in Iran was inevitable.

In 1955 there came the first major elite adjustment in post-Musaddiq Iran. Fazlullah Zahidi had failed to live up to the expectations of his external sponsors. His leadership was marked by gross corruption and aimlessness, and he had lost his personal base of support—narrow though it had been. Recognizing this, the shah dismissed him, and from 1955 until 1960 the shah continued to rely on the same elite elements as had Zahidi to provide support for the regime. By 1960, however, the shah believed he could dispense with the support of his conservative allies. His coercive force by this time was large, relatively competent, and apparently loyal. He was willing therefore to risk a major shift in his alliance system—

away from the conservative elite and toward the peasantry and urban working class. His move amounted as well to an effort to relate more closely with mass elements that were on the verge of becoming participant in the political process. His gamble was an audacious one and came close to failing. In the ensuing period of crisis, 1960–63, a great deal was revealed about the change process in Iran.

The old Musaddiq coalition was still a potent one. Individuals who had been close to Musaddiq and his regime demonstrated that they could still rally professional elements, students, and much of the middle class. The National Front proved it was still regarded as the locus of nationalist legitimacy and that the shah had yet to establish any credible claim to that legitimacy. However the National Front support base was clearly not expanding despite the huge increase in numbers of the politically participant. Significantly, the more religious wing of the Musaddiq coalition, the Freedom Front, which was led by Mihdi Bazargan and Ayatullah Taliqani, had benefited from this change. In January 1963 the shah, feeling renewed confidence after an upturn in the economy, suppressed with some brutality the National Front leaders and proclaimed his White Revolution. In April 1963 in a referendum he received support in excess of 99 percent and thereby revealed his ability to conduct a referendum totalitarian style. But two months later riots took place in Tehran and several other cities of Iran that were so serious the regime stood in danger of collapse.[20]

The episode forecast better than contemporaries could possibly have understood the successful revolution of 1979 and the rhythm of its development. The June 1963 rioting was in response to the treatment of Ayatullah Ruhullah Khomeini, now a major, soon to be preeminent, political leader. The National Front leadership was as unprepared for this event as was the government itself. What it foretold was that newly participant Iranians were looking to the clerics for political leadership. Khomeini's time was approaching. Whatever the theory behind his White Revolution, the shah was not attracting the broadening mass of potential participants in the political process. Neither was the National Front nor the left socialist opposition of which the Fida'iyan-i Khalq was to become the most important organization. The newly participant tended to be highly religious and respectful of clerical leaders such as Khomeini who spoke their language and understood their anger, bitterness, and aspirations. The 1963 demonstrations protested lack of political freedoms, and American influence. In identity terms their attraction was to the Islamic community more

20. For a brief account of the episode, see Marvin Zonis, *The Political Elite of Iran* (Princeton: Princeton University Press, 1971).

than to the Iranian national community. Lacking sophistication or even basic understanding of the political process, they were naturally attracted to a leader whom they could trust to look to their aspirations. In June 1963 Khomeini's charismatic potential was already apparent.

The shah survived the demonstrations of June 1963, thanks to the quality of his coercive forces, and for the next thirteen years Iran had the appearance of unprecedented stability.[21] It was a period of sometimes extraordinary economic growth, commercialization, and physical change. There were only occasional surface manifestations of regime vulnerability and these were generally disregarded. The truly fundamental change occurring in Iran and the basis of fundamental vulnerability was not easily apparent. This was, as the events of 1963 indicated, the rapid extension into the lower middle and lower classes of a predisposition to be politically participant. This element of the population, as it became politically aware, identified with the Islamic community rather than the Iranian national community and looked to clerical rather than to secular nationalists or the shah for leadership.

A common wisdom is that the Iranian Revolution was in part the consequence of the shah's "modernizing" too rapidly. Those arguing this case are really saying that the shah was inducing far too rapid change for the comfort of his traditional and conservative population. The analysis here argues a different case. Change in the fundamental dimensions indicated above was following a strong, probably irreversible momentum. Prosperity in those thirteen years may have accelerated it but was not responsible for it. The shah's failure was a consequence of working with an elite institutional base that was inadequate for dealing with a society that was rushing into the era of mass politics.

The elite structure of the regime rested first of all on one of the most, if not the most, absolute dictators of his era and surely the most vainglorious—Muhammad Reza Pahlavi, King of Kings, Light of the Aryans, One Possessing Great Powers. Measured in terms of decisional latitude, the range of freedom to make decisions for his polity, the shah was rivaled only by a few individuals such as Castro. Indeed, the shah's attitude toward his own countrymen, including especially those in his government, was essentially contemptuous.[22] He acted through a large officer corps and

21. For a good indication of just how stable Iran appeared to scholars right on the eve of the revolution, see George Lenczowki, ed., *Iran under the Pahlavis* (Stanford: Hoover Institution Press, 1978).

22. See the Oriana Fallaci interview, "The Shah of Iran," *New Republic* 1969 (December 1975): 16–21.

a professional technocracy which could manage governmental institutions and maintain security. The economic and social elite included members of the old conservative elite, who had adjusted to changed circumstances, and a much larger newly rich element, often non-Muslim. This elite was in no way equipped to comprehend the needs and aspirations of those seeking to enter the system. Accepting the shah as the decision maker and hence caring little about national policy, members of this ruling elite were concerned primarily with advancing their own personal interests.

How then did the shah achieve such remarkable stability for more than a decade? A satisfactory explanation of the Iranian Revolution must first answer this question and then point to the fatal vulnerability in the shah's system of control that events proved existed.

The shah's control strategy rested essentially on two factors, a strong and effective institutional base for coercion and the ability to satisfy the basic material demands of a critically significant sector of the population.[23] The need to rely on coercion as a primary means for controlling one's population is in itself an admission of vulnerability. A coercive force is expensive to construct and difficult to control. But it was an essential aspect of the shah's control system, and until 1977 it functioned at a level close to the optimal. The shah was confronted throughout his dictatorial period with a revolutionary core that could not be reconciled to his rule and had to be controlled by force or the threat of force. The shah recognized that were he to allow that core access to the mass of Iranians he could be overthrown. There was therefore always an implicit understanding on his part that this core group had legitimacy and that he did not.

The core consisted first of all of individuals who had been associated with the Musaddiq regime or who looked to that brief period in Iran's history as one to be emulated. The Musaddiqists can be classified into two groups, secular-minded liberal nationalists and religious liberals.[24] Following the events of 1963 the secular nationalists declined rapidly as a significant group. The new generation that might have looked to them for leadership did not do so. Sons and daughters of secular liberals who found the system intolerable saw their elders as hopelessly ineffectual. They were more likely to be attracted to the revolutionary secular left. But for the most part the young middle class and professional element who viewed Musaddiq favorably and were the natural support base for

23. The shah's mode of control is nicely outlined in Robert Graham, *Iran: The Illusion of Power* (New York: St. Martin's Press, 1978).

24. This revolutionary core is described with particular clarity in Homa Katouzian, *The Political Economy of Modern Iran, 1926–1979* (New York: New York University Press, 1981).

secular liberals saw the shah's regime as invulnerable and allowed themselves to be coopted into a system about which they had strong reservations but no hope of altering.

The religious liberals were loosely united in the Freedom Front. They too had difficulty retaining the support of a younger generation that either accepted cooptation or turned to the activist guerrilla force, the Mujahidin-i Khalq. Both the coopted and the revolutionary found considerable inspiration in the lectures and writings of Dr. Ali Shariati, a sociologist who was much concerned with the revitalization of Islam. Shariati's great appeal should have been recognized more than it was as an indication of regime vulnerability.

Most antiregime, activist clerics were to some degree associated with the Freedom Front, and this included Ayatullah Ruhullah Khomeini in his years in exile. The Freedom Front and especially Bazargan recognized the exceptional appeal of Khomeini in 1963 and maintained close contact with him right up to the moment of his return.

The revolutionary left was badly damaged by the good to excellent relations that existed between the shah and virtually all communist regimes—Eastern European, Soviet, and Chinese. Pro-Moscow or pro-Peking groups had their appeal sharply reduced and could not easily play a central revolutionary role. Thus the left organizations that were effectively revolutionary tended to be anti-Soviet and against the post-Maoist leadership of the People's Republic of China.

The coercive force constructed by the shah was a multiorganizational force centered on the large, well-trained, and reasonably competent organization known by its acronym SAVAK. The shah, like other totalitarian leaders, had to work out a means for maintaining personal control over the coercive apparatus. He did so by establishing independent organizations with overlapping functions, the leaders of each of which reported directly to him. But real effectiveness was a function less of the competence of the security forces than of their public image. In this regard SAVAK in particular achieved near optimal success. It came to be regarded as omniscient, omnipresent, and omnipotent. As such it destroyed a sense of revolutionary efficacy and reduced options so significantly that only the most dedicated persisted in antiregime activities. It follows that preservation of the image was essential if coercive control were to be effective.

A second vital element of Iranian coercive control was also rooted in imagery. The ease with which Musaddiq, the most popular figure Iran had known up to his time, could be overthrown simply reinforced a century-and-a-half-old view of the omnipotence of external force. Thus the shah, as the chosen instrument of Anglo-American policy, could expect if the chips were down that the same MI-6–CIA combination would keep him in power. Those Iranians who might be persuaded that SAVAK was not an insuperable obstacle to revolutionary success were still likely to conclude that ultimately the shah's external protectors would never allow him to fall from power. This image too was essential for coercion in Iran. Together these two forces were sufficient to convince the vast majority of Iranians of the regime's invulnerability.

Along with his ability to coerce, the shah had, thanks to the gift of oil, the ability to purchase support for his regime. But Iran had a large and growing population, around 40 million, and an economy that was increasingly complex. In an earlier period when most of the population was passively acquiescent and the economy relatively simple, a billion-dollar oil income could satisfy most aspirations. By the late 1970s, however, $20 billion in annual oil income could satisfy aspirations only differentially. The population could be broken down into three categories based on their degree of satisfaction with distribution of rewards: enthusiasts, accommodators, acquiescers.

Under the rubric of enthusiasts are placed first the officers of the security forces. High salaries, training abroad, and a whole array of perquisites were sufficient to preserve the loyalty of individuals many of whom already owed their positions of prestige in the community to the regime.[25] As events were to demonstrate, even with the defection in the revolution of much of the noncommissioned personnel, the officer corps remained essentially loyal to the regime.

Second is the large parvenu element in Iran. Many of them prospered beyond their wildest dreams under the shah and established his most numerically significant base of support. Indeed the shah's regime can appropriately be described as the dictatorship of the parvenu. He did not, however, make the effort to institutionalize this support in a way that could have helped his regime survive, and when the crisis came, much of this element fled the country.

Third, land reform under the shah as administered created a kulak class of peasants who were very appreciative of their newfound prosperity. This class would be difficult to mobilize in any activist way for regime support, however, and was able in fact to contribute little to the defense of the regime.[26]

25. Graham, *Iran*.

26. For a fine study of land reform in Iran, see Eric J. Hooglund, *Land and Revolution in Iran, 1960–1980* (Austin: University of Texas Press, 1982).

Accommodators included most significantly a large group of professional people and technocrats who almost certainly would have preferred the continuance of a Musaddiq-type regime. But the promise of a large salary plus the loss of any real hope of altering the system produced accommodation. Life for this group could be described as pleasant, and it could play some decisional role as long as it understood well the parameters of the range of options available to it. The sons and daughters of the secular and religious liberal nationalists of the Musaddiq era were largely located here. They did not know, and therefore exercised no influence over, those lower- and lower-middle-class youths now seeking participation in the system. The dichotomy was developing.

Also in this category were sons and daughters of the old conservative elite, often profiting very much from the regime but also very conscious of their families' loss of influence: skilled workers, unhappy with the lack of free trade unions but happy with their good salaries; bazaar merchants doing well economically but distressed at their loss of influence; clerics who were the recipients of often generous government subsidies for their activities but who were resentful of the low level of religious influence in governmental policy.

In the category of the acquiescers were the lower middle class, small merchants and white-collar workers, unskilled laborers, the dispossessed in the urban areas, and those peasants who had not profited much from land reform.[27] From 1963 through 1974 average real income for most of these people increased annually. They could therefore look forward to improvements in their standard of living year by year. But they were also aware of the large and widening income gap separating them from more favored elements of society. The rapid growth in predisposition for participation occurred largely among people in this category.

A major failing of the shah's control system was a concomitant of his unwillingness to share high-level decision making. He failed in every dimension to provide the institutions that could give Iranians a sense of participation in the process. Even at the ministerial and general officer level the assumption was accepted that the shah would make the basic decisions and his officials would execute them. This style in effect eliminated the second-level decision maker. What bureaucratic participation was allowed was at the level of interpreting basic policy directives—a level at which the shah lacked the time, interest, or expertise to participate.

Beginning in the late 1950s and ending with the Rastakhiz party of

27. See Farhad Kazemi, *Poverty and Revolution in Iran* (New York: New York University Press, 1980).

the 1970s, the shah did bow in the direction of party politics. But he was never willing to grant the parties he created any real decisional independence. They were viewed by the attentive public as political artifacts unable to develop an independent personality. It goes without saying that the newly participant had no institutionalized means for giving expression to their wishes.[28]

A major key to an understanding of the history of the Iranian Revolution is that the survival of the royal regime was remarkably dependent on the actions of one individual, the shah. Having failed in his efforts to achieve legitimacy, nationalist or religious, and having proved unable to provide any means for the awakening mass to participate in the political process, the shah lacked any possibility of attracting positive mass political support. He controlled Iran by purchase and coercion and he dared not share power with any other individual or group.

The strengths and vulnerabilities of the shah's control system are clear enough. The shah's stability rested heavily on his ability to satisfy a good deal more than minimal material demands of his people and to convince them that, given the efficiency of his coercive instruments, they could not possibly overthrow the regime. Were he to suffer, as he did, problems in the economy, the logic of the system would argue for an increase in coercive activity to suppress any manifestations of dissatisfaction. The regime was to fall ultimately because of the shah's failure to follow this procedure. It was here that he was to make his fatal mistake.

The shah's economic problems developed ironically as a consequence of the great oil price rise bonanza of 1973–74. His efforts to spend the added revenue on an accelerated economic development program led to an overheated economy and fairly serious inflationary pressures. From 1963 to 1974 Iran's inflation rate had been low. Now it reached the 35 percent level and higher, and this led to distress primarily within the element of society that was beginning to insist on more participation. Many in this element, suffering a real income decline, became receptive to revolutionary appeals. Clerical leaders associated with Khomeini and the Freedom Front sensed this receptivity and began giving sermons that were implicitly critical of the regime. The question was would they be permitted continuing access to their dissatisfied congregations or would they be reprimanded or punished? SAVAK was nowhere nearly as competent as its image suggested, but it was surely equal to the task of identifying

28. Amitai Etzioni, *A Comparative Analysis of Complex Organizations* (New York: Free Press, 1961). This book has a control scheme which, as adapted, is the conceptual basis of this analysis.

and intimidating these outspoken clerics. The regime had demonstrated frequently enough in the past its willingness to harass, incarcerate, torture, and even execute popular clerics. Yet now at a dangerous moment it held back. Why?

The explanation appears to lie in the personality and worldview of the shah. The shah had a history of indecision under stress. He was indecisive at the time of Musaddiq's overthrow and in the critical years of 1960–63. But he had appeared assertive, even arrogantly so, after 1963, and this earlier pattern had been forgotten. The shah's worldview is spelled out in his book *Answer to History*.[29] He, it appears, was always uncertain of American support and always fearful that the same CIA that had helped him into absolute power would help overthrow him. He saw American Democratic presidents in particular as dangerous. In 1977, with Iran's economy in crisis, a newly elected Democrat, Jimmy Carter, was making the observance of human rights a central tenet of his foreign policy. The shah knew very well that in a crisis period he had to be seen by his people as being so favored by the American government that it would not permit his being overthrown. He concluded therefore that he must please Jimmy Carter on human rights grounds even if in doing so he risked giving momentum to a developing revolutionary movement.

Carter's human rights program clearly did encourage the opposition, which began, gingerly at first and more confidently later, to test the waters of a changed situation. They held meetings, wrote condemnatory letters, printed pamphlets, and made strong demands for a return to the rule of law. On occasion they were incarcerated or brutalized but only sporadically so, and they thus concluded the risk was worth taking.[30] There was no lack of acts of official terror in this critical period. Indeed the casualties among demonstrators amounted to many thousands killed, including large numbers of children. But there was little system or obvious purpose to attacks on unarmed civilian crowds. They occurred at the same time that political prisoners were being released, and they rarely targeted influential opposition figures. The overall impression left was one of both weakness and sporadic brutality.

What was occurring in Iran was the erosion of two images vital to

29. Muhammad Reza Pahlavi, *Answer to History* (New York: Stein & Day, 1979). Even though the shah was mortally ill when the book was prepared, it captures very well his worldview, including some major implicit contradictions.

30. See Richard W. Cottam, "Arms Sales and Human Rights: The Case of Iran," in Peter G. Browne and Douglas MacLean, eds., *Human Rights and U.S. Foreign Policy* (Lexington, Mass.: Heath, 1979), 281–302.

the shah's retention of power. The failure of the security forces to suppress clerics and core revolutionary elements as they became increasingly bold had its impact on the image of the security forces. Perhaps they were not in fact all-knowing, ubiquitous, and all powerful! Then also the continuing emphasis placed on human rights by Carter and the shah's deferential attitude made people wonder if the United States really would save the shah were he to come under heavy attack. The shah's vulnerability might not be fatal, they felt, but it was sufficiently serious to warrant taking higher-level risks.

The rhythm of the revolution in those early days was clear. The revolutionary leadership at the highest level and its most articulate spokesmen were direct descendants of the Musaddiq movement. They were liberal rather than radical and included both secularists and individuals who favored a greater role for Islam. But the emerging mass support was coming from the acquiescent element—much of it newly participant, identifying intensely with the Islamic community, enormously attracted to Khomeini, and willing to follow prorevolution and pro-Khomeini clerics. They were inspired by increasingly revolutionary sermons at their mosques and became willing to follow the organizing directives of the mosque bureaucracy. There was close cooperation between the liberal leadership and men such as Ayatullah Muhammad Bihishti who were developing a mosque-based organization capable of raising the necessary funds and of putting together disciplined public demonstrations. But there was a major bifurcation developing, and some of the individuals at the top, such as Karim Sanjabi and Mihdi Bazargan, were very much aware of it.

The revolutionary high command was liberal and reformist. It was dominated by individuals who wished to restore the rule of law, basic freedoms, and liberal democratic institutions in Iran. The community of primary identification was the Iranian national community, although for some, such as Bazargan, the national and religious communities coincided. These leaders, however, spoke for very few of their people. Their natural constituency was among those Iranians described here as accommodationists, and in the early days of revolutionary activity this element saw little prospect for major change and continued to accommodate. The activist youth was revolutionary, not reformist. It no longer looked to Musaddiqist elder statesmen for leadership. The educated youth looked instead to secular Marxists or to men such as Ali Shariati who advanced an image of an Islam concerned with social justice. The less well educated looked to Khomeini.

The charismatic potential of Khomeini was easily apparent in the late spring of 1963. Khomeini presented an image of unquestionable sincerity, integrity of purpose, and uncompromising courage. He stood in marked contrast to much of the clergy who cared little for social justice. Khomeini spoke the language of the common people and appeared at once humble and yet willing and able to guide the umma, the Muslim community, toward a society in accord with his holistic view of Islam. He, with apparent deep sincerity, could present his picture in attractive symbolic terms. His self-proclaimed task was to show both the oppressed peoples and the oppressors that power relationships had changed forever and that the oppressed could throw off the yoke of oppression. For those vast numbers of Iranians who were now prepared to become politically participant, the attraction was enormous for this man who could give brilliant expression to their aspirations and who could be totally trusted. By 1978 Khomeini's great and growing charismatic attraction had become the central fact of the revolution. The revolutionary leadership at this stage was, and understood it was, completely dependent for its mass support on its alliance with Khomeini.

An event of particular importance occurred in February 1978 in the city of Tabriz. Religious leader–organized demonstrations there got out of the control of the internal security forces, and the government had to call in the army. Following this, the shah dismissed a number of SAVAK officials. This event more than any other served to damage the image of SAVAK and the coercive instrument generally. Now the vulnerability of the regime was beginning to appear to be fatal. But still the revolutionary rhythm continued as described. The rank-and-file participants looked to the clerics and to the charismatic figure of Khomeini. Cassettes of the latter's speeches were available at almost every mosque in the country.

By late summer and fall of 1978 the revolutionary momentum had developed further and was now incorporating the accommodators. Strikes were called by oil workers and government employees in support of the revolution, and demands were made for dramatic pay increases. It was these activities far more than the street demonstrations that were paralyzing the government. But in the streets the show was in the hands of the mullas. The liberal leadership at the top advanced a number of transition schemes which, had they been accepted and successful, might have brought some control to the revolutionary process. There was in fact a clear awareness at that level of the demagogic potential the situation was offering and hence of the possibility of the kind of authoritarian populism that was in fact to occur. But a transition scheme required the cooperation of the shah, Khomeini, the revolutionary leadership, and the American government and even with that would pose orchestration problems of great magnitude. Given these requirements no plan could be put into effect. The transitional government headed by Shahpur Bakhtiar, who was appointed by the shah, was not sanctioned by either Khomeini or the revolutionary leadership and hence had no chance for success.

After Khomeini's return to Iran, he held all the cards. Overwhelmingly the Iranian mass looked to him and not to the Musaddiqist reformists for leadership. Any possibility of avoiding polarization rested with Khomeini personally and his affection for and trust in Bazargan. But Khomeini tended to support radical, pro-clerical leaders, and in a period of several months polarization occurred.[31]

The point was made earlier that authoritarian populism occurs when a radical elite associated with a charismatic figure is able to bypass the established political and social elite and gain access to a large mass public and, with this mass support, overturn the established structure. This is precisely the pattern that was followed in the Iranian Revolution. The purpose of this chapter was to show why the established elite structure was vulnerable to this process. The case made was that this vulnerability was in large part a product of the interaction of various Iranian elite elements with the forces of external intervention. Iran moved in less than a hundred years from a society in which political participation was limited to a tiny traditional elite to the era of mass politics. The question answered by the Iranian Revolution was that of who would be successful in mobilizing this huge, newly participant mass. A comparison of Iran with other authoritarian populist regimes, however, suggests that the Iranian case fits the model in another important respect. The radical clerical elite that succeeded in mobilizing mass support is narrow and dependent for control

31. The accounts of the Iranian Revolution are by now numerous. Those giving important personal insights include John D. Stempel, *Inside the Iranian Revolution* (Bloomington: Indiana University Press, 1981); William H. Sullivan, *Mission to Iran* (New York: W. W. Norton, 1981); Mohamed Haikal, *The Return of the Ayatollah* (London: André Deutsch, 1981); Cyrus Vance, *Hard Choices: Four Critical Years in Managing America's Foreign Policy* (New York: Simon & Schuster, 1983); Jimmy Carter, *Keeping Faith: Memoirs of a President* (New York: Bantam, 1982); Zbigniew Brzezinski, *Power and Principle: Memoirs of the National Security Advisor 1977–1981* (New York: Farrar, Straus, Giroux, 1983); Gary Sick, *All Fall Down, America's Tragic Encounter with Iran* (New York: Random House, 1985). Of the myriad of books on the Iranian Revolution by academic authors, one by Jerrold D. Green, *Revolution in Iran: The Politics of Countermobilization* (New York: Praeger, 1982), is particularly important in the context of this article. It details a skillfully developed description of the process of mass mobilization.

on the appeal of the charismatic leader. It will have difficulty surviving his passing.

Are developments in Iran a portent of things to come in other parts of the Third World? The answer to that question is that there are indeed commonalities in the Iranian experience and those of much of the Third World. Virtually the entire Third World has been subject to interference by European powers and/or the United States. And wherever this has occurred the kind of elite formulas that had such an appeal in Iran for the external power have been similarly appealing. Where the external influence persists, leaders comparable to the shah or Zahidi are likely to be found, and they are subject to the same kind of vulnerability that the shah faced.

Also throughout the Third World the change process is pushing societies into the era of mass politics, and the rhythm of identity alteration seen in Iran is also apparent elsewhere. Identification with a national or ethnic community occurs early in the process. But, as in Iran, if the secular national elite is unable to establish permanent control, newly participant elements in lower and lower middle classes tend to identify more with a religious community. These patterns are particularly notable in the Arab world. Even in Arab states where the imperial influence is not strong, the inability of the national elites to deal effectively with the Israeli challenge has resulted in their being discredited and in an identity shift away from the secular national community to the religious community.

But there were unique qualities in the Iranian experience as well. The shah's paralysis in a crisis situation was a major precipitating factor for the revolution. Had he stood firm and then made a major effort to integrate the newly participant element in the political process, both the polarization and the populism that appeared in Iran conceivably could have been avoided. There was, in other words, no inevitability in the rhythm of Iranian developments. Moreover, Khomeini is sui generis. There will probably never again be another like him, and since, thanks to the magnitude of his charismatic appeal, he has given definition to the situation in Iran, he provides a unique quality that cannot be replicated.

In addition, Iran is in the eye of the storm of the Soviet-American dispute. It is of exceptional geopolitical importance and cannot avoid being the object of great-power preoccupation. Other less strategically vital Third World states can expect far less attention from the great competitors. Thus they will be freer to construct their own elite and institutional responses to rapid change.

A question of much contemporary concern is that of the universality of the attraction of the Iranian Revolution. Khomeini and members of his regime see the appeal of the revolution residing in its adherence to an Islamic ideology. But as noted above the regime has had great difficulty in providing programmatic translation of that ideology. Here again the Iranian Revolution appears to conform to an established pattern of authoritarian populism in that there is more illusion than reality in its claim to having an ideology. What appears to be an ideology is instead a set of attractive and integrated symbols.

Far more broadly appealing is Iran's negative goal—to rid the Third World of oppressor power domination including and especially the local agents of that domination. Khomeini is calling for a return to dignity in dealing with the great powers. He is calling as well for a recognition of the fact that as the world is changing so are relative power ratings and that the distance that separates the two superpowers from other important states is a declining one. Indeed he is saying that even today the states of the Third World—his oppressed world—are fully capable of containing the great imperial powers. It is not difficult to see the broad appeal of this message.

FRED HALLIDAY

Chapter Three # Iranian Foreign Policy since 1979: Internationalism and Nationalism in the Islamic Revolution

INTRODUCTION: IRANIAN EXCEPTIONALISM AND BEYOND

Imam Husayn was not to be killed again. Thus, he defeated Yazid in Iran last year. Imam Husayn, who is now leading a battle against a greater Yazid, will also triumph, God willing. The revolutionary Imam Husayn in Iran, who is fighting imperialism, is not alone now. In addition to some 35,000,000 Iranians who bravely and devotedly rally around him, there are billions of Muslims and non-Muslims everywhere in Syria, Libya, Algeria, Lebanon, Palestine, Pakistan, Africa, the Omani liberation front, Eritrea, the Chilean resistance, the Chadian liberation movement, the Canary Islands' liberation movement, the Futami liberation movement, Spain, Korea and many other places as well as the entire Islamic world, and the oppressed all over the world, who all support Iran, the revolution and Imam Husayn, represented in leader Imam Ayatollah Khomeini.[1]

The Iranian Revolution of 1978–79 was distinguished by at least four

This essay was a paper presented to the BISA Annual Conference in Durham, England, in December 1984.

1. BBC, *Survey of World Broadcasts,* Part IV (A), The Middle East (hereafter *SWB*), November 24, 1979, ME/6280/A/8. Yazid was the Umayyad monarch who slew the Shi'i leader Husain in 680 at the Battle of Karbala.

major characteristics from other revolutions of modern times. Three of these pertained to the internal dynamics of the upheaval. First, whereas the majority of these had been rural-based, relying on the mobilization of peasants against the state, the Iranian Revolution was urban-based, effected by a coalition of social and political groups centered in the major cities. Second, whereas recent revolutions have tended to involve the use of arms by the revolutionaries against their opponents, those who took power in Iran relied almost exclusively on political instruments, the mass demonstration march and the political general strike, to undermine the Pahlavi state. Only in the very last hours before Khomeini came to power did the revolutionaries take organized military action. Third, and most evident, was the prominent role of a religious belief, Islam, in the ideology of the revolution, which proclaimed the revolutionary goal as being the return to a seventh-century, divinely sanctioned ideal, and among the personnel of the revolutionary leadership and organizers, most of whom were clergymen who saw the revolution as a means of themselves obtaining power.[2]

There was, however, a fourth significant and distinguishing feature of the Iranian Revolution that separates it from other recent upheavals. Most of the latter had involved a strong and overt international catalyst: a foreign occupation or colonial presence to stimulate the revolutionary movement; a major foreign setback or defeat to undermine the prerevolutionary state; substantial assistance by interested outside parties in support of the revolutionaries; international assistance, military and political, to the challenged regime.[3] In the Iranian case these international factors did not apply. Iran was not under foreign occupation or rule; the shah's external policies during the 1970s had not led him into defeat abroad, but had, in the majority of cases, been quite successful and economic;[4] no significant foreign aid was provided to the Iranian opposition and Ayatullah Khomeini; and, despite some professions of support, none of the

---

2. I have gone into these features of the Iranian Revolution in greater detail in "The Iranian Revolution: Religious Populism and Uneven Development," *Journal of International Affairs* 26, no. 2 (Fall-Winter 1982–83). For an earlier survey of postrevolutionary foreign policy, see my "The Iranian Revolution in International Affairs," *Millennium* 9, no. 2 (Autumn 1980).

3. For an important analysis of the international socioeconomic and political components in revolution, see Theda Skocpol, *States and Social Revolutions* (Cambridge: Cambridge University Press, 1979), 19–24.

4. On the shah's foreign policy, see S. Chubin and S. Zabih, *The Foreign Relations of Iran* (Berkeley and London: University of California Press, 1974), and Fred Halliday, *Iran: Dictatorship and Development* (Harmondsworth: Penguin, 1978), Chap. 9.

shah's allies was able to come to his aid.[5] The Iranian Revolution was therefore atypical not only in its internal evolution but also in its apparent detachment from the broader international context within which Iran found itself and which played such an important role in most other revolutions.

This apparent Iranian exceptionalism does not, however, resist closer examination. The internal factors that led to the fall of the shah bear considerable comparison to the crises and movements that have emerged in many other Third World countries, where urban-based populist coalitions have developed. The "insulation" from international factors is also deceptive: for although in the immediate prerevolutionary period these external political catalysts of revolution were not so evident, the longer run causes of the Iranian Revolution certainly do include those exogenous factors that contributed to other revolutions. At the level of politics, the long history of foreign involvement in Iran, of overt occupation as in World Wars I and II, and of covert influence of the government, to which were added the imagined machinations so central to Persian political culture, produced a situation in which resentment at foreign rule was easily mobilized and maintained. In the socioeconomic sphere the expanded incorporation of Iran into the international capitalist system after World War II, and particularly after the launching of the shah's White Revolution in the early 1960s, led to a substantial transformation of Iranian society that itself shaped the tensions that underlay the revolution. The latter was in a direct sense a product of the widespread but uneven changes in Iranian society over the previous two decades and hence of the impact on Iran of its incorporations into the world economy. To these political and socioeconomic factors were added the cultural tensions produced by the impact of Western mores, goods, and communications on Iran, tensions easily played up either by those with a religious opposition to such imported and secular patterns of behavior or by those, such as the merchants of the bazaar, who saw in opposition to Western values one means of defending their own social and economic position. The revolutionary mullas were not, therefore, encouraged to avoid the temptation felt by

5. The reasons for the lack of direct Western support for the shah in the last months of his regime are explored in the memoirs of the American and British ambassadors to Iran at the time: see William Sullivan, *Mission to Iran* (New York: W. W. Norton, 1981), and Anthony Parsons, *The Pride and the Fall* (London: J. Cape, 1984). For the argument that more could have been done to save the shah, see Zbigniew Brzezinski, *Power and Principle: Memoirs of the National Security Advisor 1977–1981* (New York: Farrar, Straus, Giroux, 1983). The latter viewpoint, common in the hawkish strand of U.S. foreign policy, rests upon much fanciful second-guessing.

virtually all political leaders, to blame their country's ills on foreign influence.

The foreign policy orientations of the revolution were, to a considerable degree, a product of this pattern of international influence upon Iran in the pre-1979 period and the use made of it in the revolution itself. First and most evident of the foreign orientation was a hostility to the United States and to the strategic alliance it had developed with Iran since the 1940s. One of the first acts of the new government was to withdraw Iran from CENTO, the successor to the Baghdad Pact in which Pakistan and Turkey were also members, and which the United States had created and sustained. Second, there was the revolution's hostility to Israel and its support for the Palestinians. Israel had cooperated with the shah, and was involved in an important if unpublicized military, economic, and political collaboration with Iran. The strictly political reasons for breaking relations with Israel were compounded by the bigoted religious hostility to Jews which Khomeini's prerevolutionary writings had made clear. Solidarity with the Palestinians was a religious *and* political duty.[6]

Third, the Islamic revolutionaries were anticommunist and critical of the Soviet Union. This too had a historical component—opposition to the role of the Soviet Union in Iran in the twentieth century. But it also pertained to a more particularly Islamic consideration, namely hostility to the control and alleged persecution of Muslims inside the Soviet Union in areas with long-standing cultural and political ties to Iran.[7] Although Iran initially criticized the United States more than the Soviet Union, the combined hostility to both countries which the Islamic revolutionaries evinced was summarized in what became the leitmotif of Khomeini's foreign policy: *nah sharq, nah gharb,* neither East nor West.[8]

These general guidelines were supplemented by other themes in the new state's policies that pertained directly to foreign policy but arose from the domestic context of the revolution. First, the Islamic revolutionaries propounded a universalist ideology of revolutionary Islam. Although most revolutions have propounded such universal goals, the Islamic revolutionaries had their own particular Iranian reasons for doing so. They had to establish themselves in a country where other political traditions and

6. *SWB,* October 2, 1979, ME/6234/A/7, where Khomeini states, "It is imperative that every Muslim equips himself against Israel."

7. For example, *SWB,* May 21, 1979, ME/6121/A/2, July 15, 1980, ME/6471/A/6, October 7, 1983, ME/7458/A3.

8. Aryeh Yodfat, *The Soviet Union and Revolutionary Iran* (London: Croom Helm, 1984).

movements, secular and/or nationalist, had long existed. The opposition of the latter to the shah had been as evident, if not as ultimately successful, as that of Khomeini and his followers. The communists had been powerful in the middle 1940s, and it was the secular nationalism of Muhammad Musaddiq, premier from 1951 to 1953, that had won most support during the crisis over oil nationalization.[9] In order to weaken the legitimacy that such anterior traditions possessed, it was necessary for Khomeini and his associates to promote a distinctive ideology. This new ideology denied the significance of these earlier oppositions and their leaders, and substituted for the secular and nationalist ideas of earlier decades a new ideology, that of Islamic revolution. The legitimacy and authority of the Islamic Republic therefore required a depreciation of these other trends. Following the break with the National Front after the revolution, the name of the legislature was changed from National Assembly to Islamic Assembly in order to remove the word "National" (*milli*) from view.

The consequence of this policy of denying nationalist legitimacy and antecedents was that the Iranian Revolution has produced a legitimating ideology that is almost without historical antecedents, without the dates and heroes and anniversaries of other revolutions, with the signal exception of the events of the seventh century, notably the martyrdom of Husain at Karbala, from which Shi'ism derives its legitimacy. The heroes are Arabs and the new vocabulary of the revolution is derived from Arabic, in stark contrast with the practice of most nationalist movements that seek to purge their language of "foreign" words.[10] In this way, Khomeini has produced an ideology that appears to reject nationalism: it is not so much Iran that is struggling for freedom but the oppressed Muslims of the world.

Second, in the campaign to rid Iran of Western influence, the Islamic revolutionaries have sought to extirpate many of the cultural and economic features that they regard as products of this influence. For all their invocations of the past, they have not, as a whole, indulged in the kind of antitechnological romanticism found in some other Third World movements, such as that of Gandhi. There has been no promotion of cottage looms or romanticized peasant communities. But the religious and polit-

9. The best historical account is given in Richard Cottam, *Nationalism in Iran* (Pittsburgh: University of Pittsburgh Press, 1964). As this study makes clear, religious nationalism was a minority trend in twentieth-century Iran, but chapter 10, on "Religio-Nationalism and Pan-Islam" does document the precursors of Khomeini's international views.

10. Thus the words used for *oppressors* and *oppressed* (*mustakbarin* and *mustaz'afin*) are Qur'anic terms based on Arabic roots for *great* and *weak,* respectively. Khomeini's importation of Arabic words into Persian has, it is believed, caused considerable resentment in the country.

ical orientation of the revolution has been directed against what are portrayed as the values of consumerist, secular society, and in favor of a new economic model that is distinguished by two special features: self-reliance and austerity. The theme of self-reliance has been influenced by earlier Iranian nationalist views of an oil-less economy as well as by the autarky and "delinking" propounded in the 1960s and 1970s by Third World theorists of dependency, and self-reliance refers particularly to oil.[11] Iran produced over 6 million barrels of oil a day in the last years of the shah. The Iranian Revolution has brought this down to under 3 million barrels per day, a policy that reduces Iran's dependence on foreign income and prolongs the period in which the oil can be produced. The theme of austerity is one close to Khomeini's heart: the asceticism he espouses has become a generalized model for Iran, one that is, he argues, morally desirable in itself and one that enables Iran to survive more easily the economic pressures that conflicts with the outside world place upon it. During the hostage crisis with the United States, when Iran was threatened with an economic blockade that would have greatly reduced its food supplies, the Ayatullah was fond of reminding his listeners that the Prophet Muhammad ate only one date a day.[12]

This hostility to consumerism and luxury does, however, introduce a countervailing element in official ideology, since it brings in many of the themes normally associated with cultural nationalism. Albeit framed in an Islamic form, the kinds of denunciation Khomeini has made of Western values are very similar to those that nationalists around the world have made of foreign influence over the recent decades. The ideal of cultural purity and self-sufficiency, complementing that in the economic sphere, is a common enough element in nationalism as a whole. If its origins are multiple, so too are its functions: for if it serves to reduce or end what are indeed forms of foreign influence, values, and social activity, it also provides a legitimation for suppressing what are in reality internal conflicts, divisions within Iranian society and culture itself. Khomeini's claim to be expressing a "genuine," unadulterated, Iranian culture necessitates

11. For an example of Iranian dependency analysis, see Abol Hassan Bani Sadr and Paul Vieille, *Petrole et Violence* (Paris: Editions Anthropos, 1974).

12. Thus Khomeini: "We are a nation used to hunger—for thirty-five years or fifty years. We are used to these difficulties. We shall go on fasting, having one meal a day. If they resort to an economic blockade . . . it is a half-baked idea that will not materialize. . . . We shall eat meat once a week—after all, it is not a very good thing to eat meat. There they should not try to frighten us. If we are to choose between our honour and stomach, we prefer to keep our honour and go hungry" (*SWB*, November 12, 1979, ME/6269/A/7). For his denunciation of "Western" values, see *SWB*, September 11, 1979, ME/6216/A/U-5.

denial of the many other themes in Iranian history that are divergent from his. Cultural hegemony and authority, like that of politics, requires elimination or disqualification of the rivals—not just the corruption of the West but the poetry of Hafiz and the voices of women singers.

This adaptation to nationalism and the implicit use of its appeal become even more evident in the third central area of Khomeini's policy, namely in relation to the ethnic minorities in Iran. About half of Iran's population are Persians, and the rest is composed of Azerbaijani Turks, Kurds, Arabs, Baluchis, Turkomans, and smaller minorities. Although the main opposition to the shah was in the Persian cities, the revolution was also welcomed by the Kurds, Arabs, and Azerbaijanis, and the first two groups at least took advantage of the freedom following the shah's fall to advance their own claims for ethnic rights and regional autonomy. However, it then transpired that recognition of the ethnic diversity of Iran, and of the political problems following from this, was not something that the revolutionary government envisaged. Within months of the shah's fall, fighting between many of these minorities and the forces of the central government had broken out.[13] At the ideological level, the regime responded in two ways. On the one hand, it argued that since all Iranians were Muslims it was impermissible to accept the divisions into different ethnic groups. On the other hand, it aroused support for its policies in the Persian regions by resorting to implicitly nationalist propaganda, denouncing the Kurds and Arabs as enemies of the nation, and evoking long-standing chauvinistic themes to justify its policies. More practically, while it contributed to the worsening of relations between Persians and non-Persians by this hybrid Islamic-nationalist ideology, the regime also set out to convert those in the minority nationalities who were not Shi'is (that is, Sunnis). The result was that while Persian nationalism developed under the guise of Islamic universalism, Islam itself, in its Shi'i interpretation, came to be used as a factor that compounded the nationalist divisions within the country.

The particular origins and character of the Iranian Revolution, therefore, produced a foreign policy that was marked by two fundamental tensions or ambiguities. First, the Islamic Republic was committed to a universal goal, Islamic revolution, that it sought to preach to other countries. Yet the revolution had taken place within a very specific national context and in the absence of any general international crisis. Second, the

13. See my interview with Abdul-Rahman Qassemlu, Secretary-General of the Kurdish Democratic party of Iran, in *MERIP Reports,* no. 98 (July-August 1981), for an account of early relations between the Kurds and the Khomeini government.

ideology of the revolution contained apparently incompatible elements of internationalist or universalist ideas, and national and particular ones: Islamic revolution, an upheaval of the true believers without frontiers on the one side, Persian nationalism mixed with Shi'i fervor on the other. Yet it is precisely here, at the point of its most apparent uniqueness, that the Iranian Revolution appears to be more recognizable and typical. These two fundamental tensions were ones that have been seen in other revolutions; the French, Russian, and Chinese revolutions had all taken place in very particular national contexts and had sought, without success, to extend their influence elsewhere. These revolutions had also propounded ideologies that were both universal and nationalistic. The tensions that have marked Iranian foreign policy since the fall of the shah, for all their exceptionalism, consequently illustrate the general dilemmas that appear to be common to revolutions, as events simultaneously occurring within the national and international contexts.

THE PHASES OF IRANIAN FOREIGN POLICY

The evolution of Iran's foreign policy, and the manner in which these underlying tensions have been managed, becomes evident from considering the different phases through which Iran's foreign policy has progressed since 1979. In broad terms, four phases can be detected.[14]

The first, lasting from Khomeini's accession to power in February 1979 until the seizure of the hostages in November 1979, was characterized by the consolidation of the regime internally and a relatively cautious international policy. The Islamic regime canceled some of the major commitments of the shah's period: it broke diplomatic relations with Israel and South Africa, along with some other states recognized the PLO, left CENTO, and withdrew the remaining Iranian forces from Oman. A number of less overt Iranian military and financial commitments also ended, including the provision of signals-intelligence listening posts to the United States on the Soviet border. But Iran maintained diplomatic relations with the United States, avoided major conflicts with the Soviet Union, and continued to trade with the rest of the world. The most dramatic evidence of a shift in policy came in regard to Iraq, and in June 1979 there occurred the first of the major outbursts of mutual polemic and denunciation be-

14. For general surveys of post-1979 developments, see Sepehr Zabih, *Iran since the Revolution* (Baltimore, Md.: Johns Hopkins University Press, 1982), and Ramy Nima, *The Wrath of Allah* (London, 1984).

tween Iran and Iraq that were to lead to the 1980 war.[15] Nevertheless, although a number of Arab states appeared nervous about the consequences of the Iranian Revolution, no major political upheavals within their countries actually took place.

The second phase lasted from November 1979 to September 1980. This was marked by a sharpening of conflicts within and outside Iran: internally, the radical "Imam's Line" grouping that challenged the Bazargan government and forced its fall in November 1979 by the hostage affair was able to gain the upper hand and, with Khomeini's support, pursue a more militant foreign policy. While the hostage affair and the campaign against the "liberals" around Bazargan were designed to encourage a process of internal radicalization, the seizure of the U.S. embassy also became a symbol of revolutionary Iran's defiance of the established patterns of diplomacy and of the United States, seen as the historic oppressor of Iran. The supremacy of the more radical faction also coincided with increased criticism of the Soviet Union, following that country's intervention in Afghanistan in December 1979.

The combination of these two events, coming within the space of two months, therefore produced a situation in which Iran's initially cautious and restrained relations with both the major powers were followed by considerable deterioration. As if this was not sufficient, Iranian foreign policy also witnessed radicalization on a third front, namely in relations with Iraq. As the process of mutual recrimination and covert aid to each other's opponents increased during 1980, the Iraqi government decided that the best form of self-preservation was attack. As a result, in September 1980, it launched its war against Iran. The second phase of Iranian foreign policy therefore ended with Iran's international position at its weakest point—the unresolved crisis with the United States on one side, cooler relations with the Soviet Union on the other, and a direct assault by its western neighbor Iraq, leading to the occupation of parts of the oil-producing Khuzistan province.

The third period of post-1979 Iranian foreign policy, lasting from September 1980 until February 1983, involved a cautious but sustained drawing away from this abysmal position. First, after several failed attempts, the hostage crisis was resolved in January 1981. The U.S. diplomats were released, and a mutually agreed, if protracted, arbitration process for settling the economic disputes between the two countries in The Hague was established. Diplomatic relations were not reestablished

15. For an early and overt call to the Iraqi population to rise up, see *SWB*, June 18, 1979, ME/6144/A/5.

between Iran and the United States and hostility between the two states remained high, but the threat of a direct U.S. assault upon Iran had lessened. The ending of the hostage crisis also yielded a second benefit for Iran, namely, the removal of a major obstacle to improved relations with other developed capitalist countries, Japan and Western Europe. Trade with these improved considerably, and as the Iranian economy picked up after 1980, contacts between Tehran and the world business community expanded again. Third, after initially suffering heavy losses of men and territory in the war with Iraq, Iran began gradually to gain the upper hand; by July 1982 virtually all Iraqi troops had been driven out of the country and Iran, for the first time, gained control of some Iraqi territory. At the same time Iran was able to block all the mediation attempts made by outside parties and to repeat its insistence on major Iraqi concessions. Fourth, Iran was able in this period to develop relations of cooperation, if not friendship, with a number of regional states that had their own reasons for wanting improved relations. Syria and Libya provided some diplomatic and military support, in part because of their opposition to Iraq. Pakistan and Turkey, Iran's former partners in CENTO, developed major new trading links with Iran. They also developed co-operation in security matters, where issues of common interest, such as in Turkey's case the Kurds, were concerned.[16] While falling short of any formal alliances, these ties certainly provided Iran with support and access to the outside world that was of considerable benefit.

During this third period relations with the Soviet Union remained relatively constant—cool and occasionally polemical, but stable. The Russians must have been reassured by the continuingly poor state of U.S.-Iranian relations, and by the campaign against the "liberals" inside Iran, since the latter were cast as pro-American. The Russians must have welcomed Iran's ability to defend itself and push the Iraqis back. Iran also played little more than a rhetorical role vis-à-vis Afghanistan. What led to the fourth period was a marked deterioration in Soviet-Iranian relations, a tendency in train since 1982, but that broke into the open in 1983. The Russians had supported Iran in the war with Iraq as long as Iraqi soldiers remained on Iranian territory. This support was mainly diplomatic, but it also meant that the Soviet Union did not meet Iraqi requests for large arms supplies. Once the Iranians had crossed into Iraq, in July 1982, this policy changed, and criticism of Iran began to increase.

In February 1983 overt Soviet-Iranian conflict developed with the

16. Reports of a later Iran-Turkey mutual security agreement directed against the Kurds in *SWB*, November 30, 1984, ME/7814/i.

arrest of the leadership and members of the pro-Soviet Tudeh party in Iran, and the launching of an anti-Soviet and anticommunist campaign in the Iranian media. In May 1983 half of the Soviet embassy staff was expelled, and in December ten Tudeh members, accused of infiltration of the armed forces, were executed on charges of being Soviet spies. Although the Soviet media themselves were somewhat restrained in their criticism of Iran, the Soviet-based National Voice of Iran was more outspoken, denouncing the "fascist" character of the regime and, after some equivocation, singling Ayatullah Khomeini out for specific condemnation. If the Iran-Iraq War, and the persecution of the Tudeh, were the two main reasons for this deterioration in Moscow-Tehran relations, the third was Afghanistan. How far Iranian policy toward Afghanistan was itself a cause of this deterioration and how far it was a result of the deterioration in the two other spheres is impossible to say; but it appears that by late 1983 Iran was both stepping up its criticism of Soviet actions there and providing more aid to the guerrillas inside Afghanistan operating under Iranian control.[17]

This worsening of Soviet-Iranian relations was accompanied by a measure of improvement in Iran's relations with the West. Relations with the United States remained at a low level. The Reagan administration gave substantial backing to Iraq and continued to regard Iran as a threat to stability in the Middle East. This was both because of Iran's role in the Gulf, which was seen as threatening by the states of the Arabian Peninsula, and because of the role of Iran's followers in Lebanon, where they were believed to be behind the militant Shi'is who blew up the U.S. embassy and killed hundreds of members of the U.S. peacekeeping force there.[18] Relations with France, a state initially sympathetic to the Iranian Revolution, also deteriorated in this period, because of France's granting of asylum to opponents of the Khomeini regime. But relations with other major industrialized countries did improve. The Japanese foreign minister visited Tehran in 1983, as did the West German in 1984, and trade between the non-American OECD states and Iran continued to rise. While Iran preserved and developed its regional alliances, established in phase three, it also developed relations with China, and Peking's foreign minister paid a visit to Tehran in November 1984.

On the other hand, this fourth phase of Iran's foreign policy was

17. *Le Monde,* October 17, 1984. Iranian aid goes to three Shi'i groups operating among the Tajiks and Hazaras. (See the Edwards chapter in this volume.)

18. Despite official attempts to limit U.S. exports to Iran, considerable quantities of food and arms continued to be bought by Iran (*Time,* July 25, 1983).

marked by contradictory developments on the most vital international front of all, namely, the war with Iraq. On land, the major Iranian offensives launched after July 1982 won little ground and were very costly in lives. The Iraqis, in dire military and economic straits in early 1983, were gradually able to strengthen their defenses and build up their economy and, consequently, morale. A stalemate therefore set in from early 1984 onward. In the Gulf itself, the Iraqis began in 1983 to use their superior air power to attack Iran-bound oil tankers and so precipitated a major international crisis in which the United States threatened to intervene if Iran sought to close the Gulf to all shipping. Although this game of challenge and response continued during the early part of 1984, it at no time led to a decisive escalation—either a permanent throttling of Iran's oil exports or a determined Iranian attempt to close the Gulf. Iran was certainly affected by the tightening of the Iraqi blockade from March 1984 onward, but Iraq too was restrained from or unable to launch an all-out attack on Iran's exports. The relative worsening of Iran's position, on land and at sea, was therefore considerable, but did not lead to any overall reversal in the war or to a hastened conclusion.

A tentative balance sheet of the first five years of Iran's foreign policy would identify a number of major successes and failures in the record. On the positive side, the regime was able to sever many of the links, economic as well as military and political, that had been maintained by the old regime and establish a new, and widespread, set of diplomatic contacts. Second, it was able, despite the upheaval of the revolution and the crises with the United States and Iraq, to maintain the flow of imports vital for its military and economic goals and for the very survival of the regime. Third, it succeeded in warding off the major military and security threats that were directed at it from outside—the Iraqi attack most obviously, and the pressures from the United States and the Soviet Union as well. Fourth, it aroused in many countries of the Middle East and the Islamic world more generally a widespread interest and sympathy that were to outlast the initial enthusiasms of the revolutionary period. This sympathy and admiration were not something that could be cashed immediately for diplomatic benefit, but they constituted one of the major results of the Iranian Revolution, as well as one of the assets that Iran sought to exploit in pursuit of its foreign policy goals.

Iran's foreign policy was also marked by certain evident and substantial failures. First, despite the rhetoric about delinking and austerity, Iran's economy and political system remained perilously reliant on external inputs. The most obvious of these were food and arms, both of which were necessarily paid for by oil. Albeit the level of imports and exports was lower than in the days of the shah, Iran continued to use oil exports to feed its people, as well as to sustain its large military machine. Second, Iran failed to win any widespread international support for its position in the Iran-Iraq War. This was all the more notable, because Iraq was clearly the aggressor in the 1980 outbreak. Yet the U.N. did not condemn Iraq, and Iran found itself almost isolated in the international arena. Later, when Iran's position improved, it found little support for the conditions it was laying down for a cease-fire. Iranian indignation at what Tehran called "the imposed war" did not convert into diplomatic advantage.

Third, the Iranian Revolution did not internationalize itself. Despite the proclamation of universal Islamic goals, and much political and material support to radical groups elsewhere, no group sympathetic to Iran came to power in other Islamic societies. Most important, the attempt to export revolution to Iraq, a factor contributing to the outbreak of war and a policy continued subsequently, did not succeed. For a combination of reasons that can be only generally assessed, the Iraqi population did not rise up in support of the Iranian Revolution. Iran was left fighting a war between states, not a war in support of a revolutionary movement in a neighboring state. Elsewhere Iran's direct involvement in insurrectionary activities was also limited in impact: the well-planned and clandestine attempt at an armed insurrection in Bahrain was uncovered in December 1981;[19] the bomb explosions in Kuwait in December 1983, carried out by Iranian-trained members of the Iraqi Shi'i group al-Da'wah, were not followed by any greater upheavals in that state.[20] Support for Islamic opposition groups in such states as Morocco, Egypt, and Jordan remained at the level of the declaratory. The Iranian government rejoiced in undiplomatic tones at the deaths of Egypt's President Sadat in October 1981 and Saudi King Khalid in June 1982, but the Islamic groups active in the opposition movements of these states were not able to come to power.

ISLAMIC INTERNATIONALISM

To register this impasse, vis-à-vis Iraq in particular and the Islamic world more generally, can, however, tell us little about the future. The Russian and Chinese revolutions, as well as the Cuban, faced similar impasses in the years after their triumphs. It seemed then that increasingly normal

19. *SWB*, December 21, 1981, ME/6911/A/4–5.
20. *International Herald Tribune*, February 22, 1984.

state-to-state relations and state-versus-state wars would be the normal procedure for conducting their international relations. Yet over a longer period the example and influence of these revolutions did spread to neighboring states, albeit never in the form and through the means initially expected—to Eastern Europe and China after 1944, to Southeast Asia in 1975, and to Central America in 1979, respectively. In this longer run perspective, it may therefore be worth registering in more detail the particular manner in which the Iranian Revolution has sought to internationalize itself since 1979 and in particular to examine two aspects of this policy: the ideology and organization of Islamic revolutionary internationalism. It is indeed rather too early to assess how far the latter's impact has been spent.

Ideology

Since the establishment of the Islamic Republic, Iranian leaders and spokesmen have time and again stressed their view that Iran is the leader of a revolutionary movement encompassing all Muslims. A particularly clear exposition of this view was made by Khomeini soon after the beginning of the hostage crisis when he said:

> We hope that all Muslim nations may join in this struggle between infidels and Islam. This is not a struggle between ourselves and America; it is between Islam and the infidels. . . . I call on all Muslim nationals, all Muslims, all Muslim armies, all Islamic security forces and all Muslim countries' presidents to cooperate with our nation; the Muslims must rise in this struggle between infidels and Islam.[21]

A couple of months later he returned to the same theme on the occasion of Mobilization Week in Iran:

> I hope that the general Islamic mobilization will become a model for all the meek and the Muslim nations on the globe, and that the 15th century of the Hegira will be a century of the smashing of big idols and the substituting of Islam and monotheism for polytheism and atheism, justice and equality for injustice and iniquity, and of devoted men for cultureless cannibals.
> O meek of the world, rise and rescue yourselves from the talons of nefarious oppressors. O zealous Muslims in various countries in the world, wake up from your sleep of neglect and liberate Islam and the Islamic countries from the clutches of the colonialists and those subservient to them.[22]

21. *SWB*, November 24, 1979, ME/6280/A/7.
22. *SWB*, February 22, 1980, ME/6352/A/5.

These general appeals to the Muslim community as a whole, said in Iranian broadcasts to number one billion people, were accompanied by explicit and repeated calls for the export (*sudur*) of the revolution. Thus, on the second anniversary of the Iranian Revolution, the committee in charge of official celebrations stressed "the importance and advances of exporting and explaining the Islamic revolution" and sent delegations charged with this mission to thirty countries.[23] In November 1984 Rafsanjani, speaker of the Islamic Consultative Assembly, declared:

> The thing that none could conceal or have the intention of hiding is the export of Islamic revolution. The Islamic revolution does not confine its true and noble nature to geographical borders and deems the conveying of the message of revolution, which is the self-same message of Islam, as its own duty.[24]

In similar vein Tehran radio took to referring to Ayatullah Khomeini by the title "leader of the oppressed of the world"[25] and in the opening announcement to its Arabic transmissions presented itself in stark internationalist colors:

> "This is the voice of right, the voice of the oppressed, this is the voice of the Islamic Republic of Iran. Muslims everywhere, we transmit our programmes to you from Tehran, the bastion of the Islamic revolution, so that they will be a light for all oppressed people everywhere. We pledge to remain loyal to our Islamic mission, the mission of right, justice, and freedom."[26]

This universalist note in Iranian ideology was primarily directed at targets outside Iran, denying as it did the relevance of established frontiers and principles of sovereignty or noninterference. But it had, as already noted, a significant internal function, in denying the relevance of the ethnic divisions within Iran itself. Thus Khomeini, speaking just after the first clashes in Kurdistan, used Islamic universalism to this effect: "As far as Islam is concerned there is no question of Kurds, Turks, Fars, Baluchi, Arab or Lor and Turcomen. Islam embraces everyone and the Islamic Republic observes the rights of all groups under Islamic justice. . . . Everybody shall enjoy the protection of Islam."[27] It was these remarks that served to justify the later subjection of the Kurdish areas by the Islamic Guards.

23. *SWB*, February 6, 1981, ME/6642/i.
24. *SWB*, November 2, 1984, ME/7790/A/4.
25. *SWB*, July 27, 1982, ME/7088/A/1.
26. *SWB*, June 21, 1984, ME/7675/A/2.
27. *SWB*, September 4, 1979, ME/6210/A/8.

Organization

Since 1979, the Iranian government has announced numerous measures of support for Muslim groups struggling abroad against oppressive
governments. While Tehran radio and Iranian embassies have conducted
propaganda, relations with Islamic groups abroad have been handled by
the International Department of the Revolutionary Guards. A number of
conferences have been held in Tehran to which representatives of these
groups have been sent. Thus a meeting of liberation movements in January
1980 was reportedly addressed by representatives from Iraq, the Arabian
Peninsula, Oman, the Canary Islands, Lebanon, Morocco, and Moro (in
the southern Philippines).[28] Another such conference, held in June 1982,
called for the establishment of a united Islamic Front, composed of the
oppressed masses and Islamic liberation movements, and proposed the
formation of an ideological-political movement to propagate the ideology
of the Islamic revolution.[29]

Certain groups have been given special prominence in the public
statements and media of the Iranian regime. Prime among these have
been those from Iraq, who have received substantial facilities in Iran,
military training, and access to the media. Time and again and well prior
to the outbreak of war in September 1980 Khomeini and his associates
have endorsed these groups by themselves calling for revolution in Iraq
and the establishment of an Islamic government there.[30] The only other
groups given such explicit public support have been the Islamic Revolutionary Organization in the Arabian Peninsula (that is, in Saudi Arabia),
and the Islamic Front for the Liberation of Bahrain.[31] But the list of
countries whose representatives have been aided by Iran or have expressed support for the Islamic Republic has been a much longer one,
and there can be assumed to be a range of unpublicized clandestine contacts by groups seeking support from Iran for their particular activities.
The rebel Shi'is in Lebanon, aided via Syria, and Iran's supporters in
Afghanistan have certainly received substantial, if less overt, backing.

28. *SWB*, January 9, 1980, ME/6314/A/9. In the immediate aftermath of the revolution,
the Islamic government received, on several occasions, representatives of the People's Front
for the Liberation of Oman, the Marxist guerrilla group that had fought the shah's forces
in Dhofar from 1973 to 1975. But the PFLO's position was later taken by a hitherto unknown
Omani Islamic Front.

29. *SWB,* June 17, 1982, ME/7054/A/16.

30. *SWB,* June 19, 1979, ME/6145/A/7.

31. For the Saudi group, see *SWB,* March 17, 1980, ME/6372/A/1; for the Bahraini
Front, see *SWB*, April 14, 1980, ME/6394/A/4.

The three countries to which Iran is still committed to exporting revolution in deeds are Iraq, Lebanon, and Afghanistan.

The implementation of the universalist goals of the Iranian Revolution has not, however, been confined to assistance to Islamic groups elsewhere or the direct use of the Iranian armed forces to promote goals, as is the case with Iraq. Another dimension of internationalist organization and practice has been the use of the Iranian state itself to propagate the message of the revolution. Here three particular channels are worth mentioning.

One was the hostage crisis itself. Although occasioned by a U.S.-Iranian conflict and by a radicalization within Iranian domestic politics, it was used by the Islamic revolutionaries to propagate the message of the revolution as a whole, and during the crisis the Students Following the Imam's Line, the hostage takers, broadcast appeals to the peoples of the Muslim world, and the Arabian Peninsula in particular, to rise up. Symbolically, the hostage crisis was presented as a challenge to the United States and to the diplomatic practices it had, it was said, misused in the past; thus Iran did not deny the relevance of international conventions on diplomatic immunity, so much as argue that where diplomats used embassy protection to carry out espionage activities this should be lifted. Hence the U.S. mission was referred to not as an embassy but as a *jasus-khanih,* or spy-house. Practically, the period of the hostage affair was one that Tehran used to rally international support and build a network of contacts with Muslim groups around the world. The inability of the United States to take effective military action against Iran served only to strengthen Iran's image. In the words of one official commentary after the hostages were released:

> We hope that the rubbing of the snout of American imperialism in the dust of Iran and the regaining of our rightful and legitimate rights will be a lesson to all other deprived and captive nations that, if they accept Islam and if they accept God as greater than all, then all the powers and superpowers and tanks, cannons and planes are worth nothing, because "the hand of God is above all hands."[32]

A second channel of influence has been Iranian embassies abroad. It was reckoned that by the end of 1982 around 450 of the original 600-odd members of the Iranian diplomatic service had departed or been dismissed.[33] But their place was taken by a new generation of Islamic revo-

32. *SWB,* January 16, 1981, ME/6624/A/7.
33. Author's interview with Parviz Khazai, former Iranian consul in Norway, Oslo, November 1982.

lutionaries, some with experience abroad as students, others without, who turned Iran's embassies into centers for support and solidarity activities with their revolution. Part of this involved a domestic concern, namely, the surveillance of Iranian citizens, students, and opposition groups abroad. Each embassy had its security section and its *Hizbullahis,* vigilantes who were used to intimidate local Iranian communities. They set up associations (*anjuman*) of Islamic students. But these embassies also engaged in widespread propaganda activities in support of the revolution, and on several occasions Khomeini stressed the importance of this work, as well as the need to enforce "Islamic behavior" on women employees. On the other hand, Iranian embassies have confined their activities in the main to such diplomatic and political activities. The export of revolution has been primarily a publicity exercise. Embassies have not, in the Western world, become involved in direct attacks on political opponents, and the Iranians have seen the need and benefit of practical relations with established governments. Khomeini often spoke of the duties of diplomats. Just as in his day the Prophet had sent delegations to the countries of the world, so should the Iranian Revolution: in this way, he said, it would be possible to exert influence upon them. In late 1984 Khomeini spelled out this realism to his listeners by saying that Iran should establish diplomatic relations with all governments in the world, with the exception of the United States, Israel, and South Africa.[34]

A third channel of Iranian influence has been the specifically Muslim one of the hajj, the annual pilgrimage to Mecca. This has been accompanied by much official promotion in Iran. Iranian pilgrims in Mecca have used the occasion to distribute literature about ther revolution and pictures of Ayatullah Khomeini, and they have been involved in clashes with the Saudi police. This reflects the fact that, year after year, Khomeini and his followers have repeated that hajj is not just a religious occasion: rather, as the ayatullah put it, "the aim of Islam in making the pilgrimage a duty for Muslims was the awakening of Muslims, and their service of the interests of peoples and the world's oppressed."[35] On the eve of the 1982 hajj Khomeini, in appointing Khu'iniha as pilgrimage supervisor, developed this theme once again:

> The hajj period approaches. It is a great obligation of a worshipping, political and social character, which enjoys particular aspects among great acts of worship and about which the most Blessed, most Exalted

34. *SWB,* October 30, 1984, ME/7787/A/6.
35. *SWB,* September 9, 1981, ME/6823/A/1.

God has called upon the world's Muslims in special circumstances, to become informed of the social and political developments taking place in Muslim lands and while performing this great duty to discuss with each other any problem that they may have and to overcome such problems as far as possible. However, the political dimension has, unfortunately, been neglected by many Muslims. . . . you will, in religious sermons and centres, invite Muslims to unite in word and direction, so that you will inform them of what is taking place in dear Lebanon, in crusading Iran and in oppressed Afghanistan at the hands of oppressors and world-devourers and so that you will acquaint the esteemed Iranian hajj pilgrims with their great duties in confronting aggressors and international plunderers.[36]

CONCLUSION: THE RESURGENCE OF THE NATIONAL

If this internationalist orientation has remained strong throughout the Iranian Revolution, and if its longer run consequences cannot as yet be assessed, it can nonetheless be noted that it has been accompanied by a resurgence of nationalist themes in the ideology and practice of the revolution. First, as discussed, the very assertion of a pan-Muslim unity by the Tehran authorities has served within Iran as a means of denying the legitimacy of the claims of non-Persian ethnic groups fighting for various forms of regional autonomy. The "protection" offered to them by Islam has been in practice chauvinistic, all too reminiscent of that provided by the shahs. Second, the need for Iran to focus its foreign policy on the war with Iraq has led to a greater emphasis within Iran upon nationalistic values and themes. Khomeini did talk, prior to September 1980, of "the nation of Iran," but since the outbreak of war official propaganda has increased its stress upon this national element in appealing for support against the Iraqis, in a manner reminiscent of Stalin's shift to patriotic and away from internationalist themes after the German invasion of 1941. The word *mihan* (fatherland), so often invoked by the shah, has found its way back into official statements. Third, the new Iran has not abandoned all those nationalist themes that lay at the heart of the shah's foreign policy. Thus in May 1981 the then prime minister Raja'i instructed all government officials to use the term *Persian Gulf,* a denotation long resisted by the Arab states of that region.[37] Fourth, the very Islamic character of Khomeini's rhetoric has in part been perceived in restrictive nationalist terms; insofar as he has exalted the heroes and values of Shi'i

36. *SWB,* August 7, 1982, ME/7098/A/5.
37. *SWB,* May 9, 1981, ME/6719/A/7.

Islam and insofar as he is, as ayatullah and imam, seen as a Shi'i leader, Khomeini has widened the gap between the predominantly Shi'i population of Iran and the Sunni majorities elsewhere. The very discourse he has chosen to make his appeal more universal has itself confined his appeal and exacerbated sectarian feeling throughout the Muslim world.

The national character of the Iranian Revolution resides, however, in another, more fundamental dimension, one that returns to the comparison between the Iranian and other upheavals. For the very particularity of the conditions under which the revolution occurred has entailed that the revolution has not been automatically repeated elsewhere. Those groups outside Iran—in Iraq, Afghanistan, Bahrain, Lebanon, and elsewhere—that have been inspired by or directly assisted from Tehran have not, as yet, been able to come to power. In pursuing its goal of exporting revolution to Iraq, the Islamic Republic has had to resort to the classical instrument of influencing another state, namely, war, and this has become a self-defeating operation as far as the export of revolution is concerned in that it has apparently augmented the support of the Iraqi population for its government. At the same time, as Khomeini's speech of November 1984 made clear, the Iranian government has come to accept the need for diplomatic and economic relations with the majority of the world's governments in order to pursue its own state goals. It was even reported during 1984 that Vilayati, the foreign minister, had removed more radical elements associated with the guards from embassies, and told Iran's representatives to confine their activities to propaganda.

Necessary and recurrent as internationalist goals and actions appear to be in the policy of revolutionary states, the latter are also compelled, by the limits on their influence and the requirements of state survival, to offset this internationalism with an accommodation, of unforeseeable extent, to their own nationalisms and to the national sentiments, particularities, and states of the outside world. Iran's foreign policy, curious and in many ways idiosyncratic as it has been, nonetheless illustrates the dilemma that all revolutionary states have faced.

NAHID YEGANEH AND NIKKI R. KEDDIE

Chapter Four # Sexuality and Shi'i Social Protest in Iran

I

INTRODUCTION

BY NAHID YEGANEH

Twelver Imami Shi'ism has been the official religion in Iran since 1501. Students of its role and place within Iranian society have often described Shi'ism as a religion of protest. Various elements specific to Shi'ism, such as the theory of *imamat* (succession of the twelve Shi'i imams) and the practice of *ijtihad* (exertion of opinion on social and religious matters by religious leaders), have been taken as indicating an inherent oppositional tendency of Shi'ism (as opposed to other branches of Islam) to worldly governments.[1]

This view, however, has recently been challenged. It has been pointed out that at various stages of its development, Shi'ism has represented quietism and/or cooperation with central governments, as well as oppo-

The authors thank Sami Zubaida, Juan Cole, and Ali Zarbafi for reading and commenting on this essay.

1. As an example, see Hamid Algar, "The Oppositional Role of the Ulama in Twentieth Century Iran," in Nikki R. Keddie, ed., *Scholars, Saints and Sufis* (Berkeley and Los Angeles: University of California Press, 1972).

sition and protest. Social and political contexts have been emphasized as important in determining the stand of Shi'ism toward governments.[2]

The aim of this chapter is to extend the above challenge to encompass Shi'i protest on sexuality. Is Shi'ism inherently oppositional on questions of sexuality? To be oppositional, Shi'ism needs to contain its own specific concept of sexuality. It is important to ask, then, whether it is possible to talk about a *Shi'i concept of sexuality* as such.

It will be argued here that, as with politics, sociopolitical context is important in determining the place of sexuality in Shi'i social protest. Shi'ism is neither a mere reflection of Iranian social relations nor its sole determinant. Shi'ism, rather, is intricately interwoven with Iranian social relations. Its specific role and effect, however, must be seen within particular contexts. While Shi'ism has historically attained a specific concept of sexuality, yet often it is the dominant social relations that specify the Shi'i concept of sexuality. The relationship between the Shi'i and non-Shi'i concepts of sexuality can be determined only within a particular context.

We will discuss these questions in the context of the history of Shi'ism in Iran as well as Iran in the 1970s. Part I will assess the attempts within the literature to attribute an essential concept of female sexuality to Islam in general and to Shi'ism in particular. Part II will discuss the historical aspect of Shi'i social protest on the question of women, particularly in comparison with Sunnism, the mainstream branch of Islam. Part III will concentrate on the context of Iran in the 1970s and discuss a variety of contemporary Shi'i social protests on the question of sexuality, particularly in comparison with concepts of sexuality in secular writings.

THE GENERAL THEORY OF SEXUALITY IN ISLAM

The presence of a homogeneous concept of sexuality in Islam has been stressed by Fatima Mernissi and, with regard to Shi'ism, by Farah Azari.[3] Since views like theirs are widely accepted, they merit consideration.

The practices of veiling, seclusion, and polygamy in Muslim societies,

---

2. Sami Zubaida and Abbas Vali, "Religion and the Intelligentsia in the 1979 Iranian Revolution" (unpublished paper, 1979), 3; Nikki Keddie, "Religion, Society, and Revolution in Modern Iran," in Michael E. Bonine and Nikki Keddie, *Continuity and Change in Modern Iran* (Albany: State University of New York Press, 1981), 20.

3. Fatima Mernissi, *Beyond the Veil: Male-Female Dynamics in a Modern Muslim Society* (Cambridge, Mass.: Schenkman, 1975); Farah Azari, ed., *Women of Iran: The Conflict with Fundamentalist Islam* (London: Ithaca Press, 1983).

Mernissi argues, are due to the Muslim concept of female sexuality.[4] Mernissi takes the views of Freud and al-Ghazali as representative of their cultures and compares them. She then presents an interesting and well-informed analysis of the dynamics of the male-female relationship in modern Moroccan society.

Regarding the assumptions behind Mernissi's theory, problems arise from assigning a single conception of female sexuality to a complex of relations within a society, especially one as extended temporally and spatially as either Muslim or Western society. Mernissi's dichotomies of active female sexuality in Muslim society and passive female sexuality in Western society do not necessarily hold when dealing with different concrete situations. Also, taking a single thinker to represent each of two huge and changing cultures is a procedure of doubtful validity.

In practice, cultures are much more varied and complex than Mernissi's methodology allows. They contain contradictory elements and inconsistent conceptions. There are a variety of women's positions within every society, the determinants of which are related to various differences, such as ethnicity and class.

Mernissi herself acknowledges the presence of both passive and active conceptions of female sexuality among Muslims. Her choice of al-Ghazali, then, as the representative of a "Muslim" conception of female sexuality seems arbitrary. What is wrong is the assumption that women's present condition is the expression of an unchanging view of a passive or active female sexuality. Women's oppression is not seen as occurring within immediate practices and institutions but as functioning outside them. In the case of societies where the essential concept of female sexuality is called Islamic, the result is a confused conceptualization of the relationship between Islam and the prevailing social relations.

It remains unclear why al-Ghazali's "identity between male and female sexuality" should in some passages be praised as compared to Freud's differentiation of male and female sexuality, while at the same time, according to Mernissi, the former leads to female seclusion and the latter to lack of coercion and surveillance of women. Nor is it clear why al-Ghazali's concept is "Islamic." His belief in female ejaculation, which she stresses, was also widespread in Europe and is still part of common non-Muslim folk beliefs.[5] These criticisms, however, do not apply to the

4. Mernissi, *Beyond the Veil*, p. 6.

5. Mernissi's objections to Freud's theory of female sexuality are in many ways similar to those presented by the influential radical feminist movement in Western Europe and North America. I would like to draw the reader's attention to a different reading of Freud as presented in Juliet Mitchell, *Psychoanalysis and Feminism* (Harmondsworth: Penguin, 1974), and Juliet Mitchell and Jacqueline Rose, *Feminine Sexuality* (London: Macmillan Press, 1982).

second part of Mernissi's book, which deals with concrete Moroccan situations.

Following Mernissi's approach, Farah Azari has tried to demonstrate the social mechanism through which the suppression of female sexuality is maintained within Iranian society. In "Sexuality and Women's Oppression in Iran" (1983), Azari looks at various present-day practices and institutions within Iranian society, such as the ritual of mourning for the martyrdom of the third Shi'i Imam Husain in Karbala, the institution of the family, *hijab* (modesty/Islamic dress), prostitution, and virginity. She uses the psychoanalytical insights of Wilhelm Reich to show the ways in which social institutions in Iran operate to oppress women sexually and socially. Azari presents interesting and fresh points and opens up a new space for exploration in relation to women's position in Iran. Her efforts, however, are hampered by her application of a mixture of the two general theories of Mernissi and Reich to the case of Iran. Having relied so heavily on these general theories, Azari's analysis necessarily shares their inadequacies in accounting for the specificity of practices and institutions.

Following Wilhelm Reich's attempts to wed psychoanalysis to Marxism, Azari takes Shi'i practices, such as rituals of mourning, as a space through which "release from the 'inner tension' is sought not just in individual terms, but also in a religious ritual organized on a mass basis."[6]

Such practices, then, are spaces for the expression of a fixed and presocial biological "inner tension." There is no difference between the nature of the institutions and practices across various societies: they all produce the same effect. Indeed, in such an analysis, one can replace "Germany" with "Iran," and "Nazism" with "Shi'ism" without affecting the outcome of the analysis.

The specificity of various institutions and practices in constructing sexuality and sexual differences is hampered in Azari's work by adopting Mernissi's essentialized conception of what constitutes the social in a Muslim society. Azari finds the "sexual norms and attitudes of Iranian society" rooted in Shi'ism:

> With Ali's teachings forming the most important sources of Shi'ite ideology (after the Koran, of course), it is easy to see why in Iran— a predominantly Shi'ite society—Ali's attitudes to women and sexuality were established socially. These attitudes are reflected in the social institutions that affect male-female relationships, such as matrimonial affairs and in the sexual affairs of most men here.[7]

6. Azari, *Women of Iran*, 142.
7. Ibid., 104.

Institutions and practices in contemporary Iran are seen as passive recipients of a point of origin of women's oppression, 'Ali's sayings. The present is seen as a mere reflection of the distant past, and history is denied any relevance to the present, since it is seen not as a process but as a reified point of origin.

In contemporary Iran, popular religious practices, such as the rituals of mourning, *rauzih* ceremonies (religious recitals) and *sufrih* (religious feasts), Friday prayers, progovernment demonstrations, and chanting of slogans provide their own definitions of sexuality and express certain patterns of male-female relationships at the expense of others. Formal religion, too, depending on the context and its role and place within society, reproduces certain concepts and represses others. So do various other social and political institutions. These practices and institutions give rise to a variety of conceptions of male-female relationships that are heterogeneous and often contradictory. As long as they are seen as mere expressions of an essential "unconscious" or "Shi'ism," one cannot take into account the complexity and variety of discourses in one's analysis. One has to suppress many attributes of various societies in order to make them fit into a single general theory.

The problems involved in attributing a single universal concept of sexuality to Islam, or the West, indicate the need to look into the differentiations and varieties of concepts of sexuality within various cultures and the need for studying such concepts contextually.

II
VARIATIONS IN PAST IDEOLOGY AND PRACTICE
BY NIKKI R. KEDDIE

To an outsider, or even an insider acculturated to new ways, the whole of a foreign culture (or foreign-seeming domestic culture) often appears similar. The visual aspects of this are well known, as in the frequent observation that to white Westerners all Chinese or all blacks may look similar, whereas differences among one's own ethnic group are easily noticed. So too, sweeping generalizations about traditional Islam, Hinduism, or whatever are based not wholly on bad faith but also on the tendency to lump together a set of unfamiliar beliefs and practices that indeed have many elements in common, but whose inner differences often pass unnoticed. Having criticized views that tend to see both Islamic and Western approaches to women and sexuality as internally identical over long periods of time and great distances, we should note concretely some of the evidence of differences in Muslim, and more specifically Shi'i, views and practices regarding women that precede the theories of the 1970s on which the final section of this essay concentrates.

Even within the Qur'an there are some passages suggesting near equality for women and others speaking of women's subordination to men. Men are told that, unless they fear they cannot treat them equally, they may marry up to four wives; but later in the same sura men are told that no matter how hard they try they will not be able to treat their wives equally—exactly the same Arabic verb for "equal treatment" is used both times. This sura, and also others, has been the source of quarrels between liberal modernists and conservatives, in this case over whether the Qur'an intended to encourage, permit, discourage, or disallow polygamy. Traditionally the propolygamy view was dominant, but not exclusive, whereas in the last century antipolygamy views have grown, not because of textual changes, but because of social ones.[8]

Questions of veiling and seclusion are others in which there has been a far wider variation in theory and practice even in the area of early Muslim conquest than most people realize. Contrary to widely held opinion, veiling is nowhere enjoined in the Qur'an, which has just two passages that discuss women's dress. One calls on Muslim women to draw their cloaks (*jalabiyah*) tightly around them when they go abroad so that they may be recognized and not annoyed; the other tells believing women to cover their bosoms and hide their ornaments (*zinah*).[9] The latter was later often interpreted, usually on the basis of supposed traditions from the Prophet, to mean covering all but the hands, feet, and perhaps the face, though some interpreters said this too should be covered. This interpretation, which became widespread, is improbable; if the Qur'an had wanted this much covered, why would it have referred specifically to the bosom, which would automatically have been included in later formulas? Also, the widespread interpretation of zinah to cover hair, neck, forearms, and so on is linguistically farfetched.

Nonetheless, strict veiling and seclusion became the ideal, although

8. For a convenient translation of verses of the Qur'an relevant to women, see Elizabeth Warnock Fernea and Basima Qattan Bezirgan, eds., *Middle Eastern Muslim Women Speak* (Austin: University of Texas Press, 1977), 7–26. The verses I discuss I have read in the Arabic original. The traditional and modern literature giving varying interpretations of the meaning of many of these verses is vast.

9. Fernea and Bezirgan, pp. 20, 25; Auran, xxiv: 31; xxxiii: 59. Frequently these and other verses are translated so as to imply the meaning preferred by the translator; hence some English speakers, for example, may get the impression from translations as well as from interpretations that veiling is enjoined by the Qur'an.

they could in fact be practiced only by a small minority of Muslim women—those who did not have to work in the fields or elsewhere in public—and they were a sign of class status. More important, they were a sign of male control over a wife whose fidelity was guarded even more by household seclusion than by veiling. Veiling and seclusion also made it difficult for many women really to control their property or to be entrepreneurs.

Veiling did not originate with Muslim Arabs, but in the pre-Islamic Near East, many centuries before Muhammad. We have an early Palmyran bas-relief of veiled women and know the practice existed among elite Sassanian and Byzantine women.[10] Veiling and seclusion in various forms and at various times was also practiced in European Mediterranean cultures, Hindu India, and elsewhere. It has been more tenacious in many Islamic countries than elsewhere partly because of its presumed sanction by the Qur'an, believed to be the word of God, and partly as a reaction against the culture of Western imperialism. Largely because the Western impact began earlier in the Middle East than elsewhere, and because of Europe's proximity geographically and associations with the state of Israel, it has brought a stronger cultural counterreaction in Muslim countries than elsewhere in the Third World.

Veiling, however, was never a universal phenomenon in Islam, among either Sunnis or Shi'is. Nomadic and peasant women have evidently rarely veiled unless they were forced to, or they or their husbands wished to emulate the traditional bourgeoisie of the towns. We know that many dynasties of nomadic origin spread the custom of nonveiling among part of the elite and even beyond. This was true of Turko-Mongol rulers who ruled Iran for many centuries.[11] The miniatures of this period showing women in diaphanous head coverings similar to those worn by many modern nomads are surely depicting dress realistically, and we know that Italian travelers spoke of being shocked at the dress of Iranian women in early Safavid times![12]

As to the position of women, there are also significant differences in theory, and far more in practice, regarding their traditional rights to prop-

10. Nikki Keddie and Lois Beck, Introduction to *Women in the Muslim World* (Cambridge, Mass.: Harvard University Press, 1978), 25; and, especially on Sassanian veiling and seclusion, Guity Nashat, "Women in Pre-Revolutionary Iran: A Historical Overview," in Guity Nashat, ed., *Women and Revolution in Iran* (Boulder, Colo.: Westview Press, 1982), 5–35.

11. Ibid.

12. Nikki R. Keddie, *Roots of Revolution* (New Haven: Yale University Press, 1981), 14, and the original sources cited therein.

erty and inheritance. The Qur'an lists legal heirs and says that daughters inherit half as much as sons, which Muslims rightly note was more than women inherited and held in most traditions. Without entering the controversy over the position of Arab women before Islam—which seems to have been better in some tribes and in some respects and worse in others than after Muhammad—one may agree with Coulson and others who have shown that, very soon after the Qur'an, representatives of the patriarchal tribes quickly whittled away at women's Qur'anic rights, including property rights. Thus, the Sunni schools of law added to the Qur'anic heirs a series of agnates, or relatives on the male side, to those who had rights to inherit, whereas relatives on the female side had no such rights. The Shi'is, however, developed a significantly different inheritance law, based in part on their desire to legitimize succession in the female line (Muhammad had no adult sons, and the Shi'i imams descended from his daughter, Fatima) and in part on Shi'i belief that Muhammad and the Qur'an had intended to end the old tribal system of inheritance in favor of a more equitable one. The Shi'is, therefore, gave rights to female-line relatives to inherit and did not recognize the prior rights of distant male relatives; so, for example, in Sunni law, a single surviving daughter was limited to a maximum of half of the inheritance, no matter how distant the next eligible male-line relative was, but in Shi'i law the same daughter got the whole Qur'anic inheritance.[13]

Another Sunni-Shi'i difference was less favorable to women. This was *mut'ah* (temporary marriage, or more literally, marriage for pleasure), a pre-Islamic custom, never renounced in the Qur'an, by which a man paid a sum of money for sexual rights to a girl or woman for a specified period of time. It differed from prostitution mainly in that it and its offspring were legitimate. Among the Sunnis it was forbidden by Caliph Umar, who was not recognized by the Shi'is, and the Shi'is have insisted on mut'ah's legitimacy under Muhammad and since. Like many institutions mut'ah developed a variety of uses according to context, from filling up the harems of the powerful to allowing two people who might have no sexual relations to mix freely in a common home. In the twentieth century, however, many Shi'is saw it as an abuse, especially as poor families might "sell" or "rent" their daughters at ages as young as nine.

In the Islamic Republic, however, it has again come into its own with some new justifying arguments. It is now said that since teenagers have sexual urges but are not ready for permanent marriage, mut'ah is a way

13. Noel J. Coulson, *Conflicts and Tensions in Islamic Jurisprudence* (Chicago: University of Chicago Press, 1969), 31–33.

for them to fulfill these urges or, more often, to have a kind of trial marriage before taking the big step of permanent marriage. Some Shi'i writers note that since boys and girls cannot get to know each other in view of sexual segregation, it is recommended that they undertake temporary marriages, while at the same time vowing not to have sexual relations, as a means of getting acquainted.[14] Here we have a mixture of an age-old institution with a "modern" usage designed precisely to overcome some of the barriers imposed by the "traditionalist" Islam that these writers on temporary marriage support.

Variation according to time, place, and class in Muslim institutions has existed in veiling and seclusion, as has been shown primarily by certain anthropologists and sociologists. It also existed regarding women's holding and controlling of property, whatever the law might say. Very early there were legal attempts to get around the requirement of female inheritance, and, as noted by Schacht, this was one of the main motives behind the early creation of the family *waqf,* an endowment in favor of descendants that kept property from being divided and allowed the endower (it might be said, against the intent of the Qur'an), to name his own heirs instead of having to respect the Qur'anic heirs.[15] Claude Cahen argues persuasively on the basis of early sources that these family waqfs developed first among Arabs and preceded the pious waqfs that receive more attention. Further, he writes regarding waqf:

> We are certain that from the best known early times until today the institution was in fact used to undermine as far as possible the rulings of Muslim succession law in favor of daughters. . . . the great majority of planned endowments excluded, if not the daughters of the founder, at least their descendants, reserving the benefits for the descendants of sons. . . . There seems to be no doubt that the waqf was utilized right away to reinforce the patriarchal family, beyond, or contrary to, Qur'anic law.[16]

14. Shahla Haeri is continuing the most complete study of mut'ah. See especially her "The Institution of Mut'a Marriage in Iran: A Formal and Historical Perspective," in Nashat, ed., *Women and Revolution in Iran,* 231–51.

15. Joseph Schacht, in relation to waqf, enumerates its roots, among which "a fourth, which expanded enormously, particularly in Iraq, in the first half of the third/ninth century, and which was, perhaps, most decisive in shaping the final doctrine of Islamic law concerning *waqf,* arose from the desire of the Muslim middle classes to exclude daughters and, even more so, the descendants of daughters from the benefits of the Qur'anic law of succession; in other words, to strengthen the old Arab patriarchal family system" (J. Schacht, "Law and Justice," in P. M. Holt, Ann K. S. Lambton, and Bernard Lewis, eds., *Cambridge History of Islam* [Cambridge: Cambridge University Press, 1970], 2:561).

16. C. Cahen, "Reflexions sur le Waqf ancien," *Studia Islamica* 14 (1961): 37–56; the quotation is on pp. 54–55.

In this matter, despite their relatively profemale position on Qur'anic inheritance, the Shi'is have not been shown to have behaved differently from the Sunnis, although further research may indicate a difference. A minority of waqfs gave women larger inheritances than they would otherwise have had, and some women were waqf trustees, again indicating significant variations.

Other forms of absolute or relative deprivation of females of Qur'anically due inheritance have been noted, especially by anthropologists and especially among tribal and rural groups, and it is reasonable to suppose that further research in legal documents and elsewhere will underline that this is not solely a modern phenomenon. Naturally, some women did inherit as they were supposed to, and, especially in times of prosperity or of relatively greater freedom for women, some might even use their money and property entrepreneurially or for planning their own pious donations.[17] Also, even poorer women who might not inherit might find other means to exercise significant control or influence over the use of family income. Thus, although there has been great similarity in mainstream legal views, there has always been much variation over time, place, and class in the actual property rights and control exercised by women.

When one turns away from the main legal schools to other Islamic groups and movements, one finds even greater variation in both theory and practice regarding the position of women. Movements labeled heterodox by the main legal schools, which were mostly proto-Shi'i or Shi'i rebellious movements, frequently preached and practiced a more egalitarian treatment of women. Scholars have shown that the charge of "communism of women" often lodged against such frequently rebellious movements was almost surely based on their opposition to the concentration of women in the harems of the rich and powerful, which left some ordinary men without wives and lowered the overall position of women. Some Shi'i movements held special reverence for Muhammad's daughter, Fatima, putting her at the same level, or occasionally higher, than her descendants, the imams. Eyewitness reports tell us of the higher role of women among the Shi'i Fatimids and especially the radical Shi'i Qarmatians, both of whom came to be rulers.[18] They were associated with Isma'ili, or Sevener Shi'ism, which at least through the thirteenth century

17. See Ian C. Dengler, "Turkish Women in the Ottoman Empire: The Classical Age," and Ulku U. Bates, "Women as Patrons of Architecture in Turkey," in Beck and Keddie, *Women in the Muslim World,* 220–24 and 245–60.

18. The best brief discussion of this is in a manuscript in progress by Laila Ahmed on the history of Middle Eastern Muslim women.

was the most radical of the three major branches of Shi'ism in both sexual and nonsexual matters.

Although Twelver Shi'ism does not have the same radical record on women (or, until modern times, on other questions), it does show some significant differences from mainstream Sunnism. For example, there have been "heresies" within Twelver Shi'ism, especially among Turks, Iranians, and Kurds, that have promoted a higher position for women. One of these is the Ahl-i Haqq, often called Ali Ilahis, concentrated among Iranian Kurds, who allow women a freer and higher position in ritual and daily life than do their orthodox Shi'i neighbors. More dramatic is the Babi movement that began in Iran in the 1840s, and most of whose adherents converted to the new Baha'i revelation in the 1860s. In both Babism and Baha'ism women were given a higher position and polygamy was limited or discouraged. The early Babi woman poet and preacher Qurrat al-'Ain apparently preached unveiled.[19]

Among both Sunnis and Shi'is, many mystic or Sufi teachers and writings also promoted greater equality for women, and some prominent teachers and poets were women. It must be added that, although these "heterodox" movements were convinced that *they* represented true Islam and the spirit of the Qur'an, the association of greater women's equality with what the legists considered heterodoxy probably hurt the cause of greater gender equality among the legists.

There is also a social class question to be noted. Whereas since the nineteenth century it has been, on the whole, the upper classes and those with better posts in the modern economy who have adopted Western ways, including greater equality for women, in earlier times the heterodox movements that often favored greater equality arose more from nonelite urban tradespeople, peasants, and nomads. (When nomads with more egalitarian gender relations, whether heterodox or not, took over a dynasty, some of them became part of the elite, but might still retain many of their egalitarian customs regarding women, as in Iran.) In recent times it has often been the popular classes, rather than the elite, who have clung to gender inequalities. The reasons for this change need study, but one of them surely is that "modernizing" the position of women brought far more advantages for those benefiting from the modern economy and world system than it did for the popular classes, who might be hurt by it. Running

19. Discussion of the Babis and Baha'is, including their position on women, is found in numerous works; see Mangol Bayat, *Mysticism and Dissent: Socioreligious Thought in Qajar Iran* (Syracuse: Syracuse University Press, 1982), chap. 4; and Keddie, *Roots of Revolution*, 49–52.

a modern economy requires mothers well enough educated to facilitate their children's education and at least some women specifically educated for such jobs as nurses, teachers, secretaries, and so on. Also, mixing with international society is far easier if women are not secluded. Peasant, nomadic, and working women, however, were not generally perceived as deriving any tangible benefit from education, and greater equality for them might end the one sphere in which popular-class men could exercise dominance; elite men had other spheres for this. In earlier times, by contrast, extreme female seclusion and the arbitrary placing of significant numbers of women into large harems, along with the widespread use of slave girls in court for entertainment and sex, were all elitist privileges that at times aroused the anger of the popular classes, especially when they knew that the strict sexual rules that seclusion was supposed to protect were not in fact followed by most of the elite.

If mainstream Twelver Shi'ism, which has its own juristic orthodoxy based on its own school of law, did not enter heavily into revolts including a profemale element, it did have some features that might be considered favorable to women. The relative favoring of women in its inheritance law has been noted. In addition to Twelver Shi'ism, at least in its main centers, Iran and Iraq, and possibly elsewhere, orthodox women religious leaders have held a position closer to that of male religious leaders than in most Sunni countries. These leaders, among Shi'is called mullas like their male counterparts, preside over frequent women's religious ceremonies. In Iran, these are especially women's rauzihs, where stories of the imams, and especially the martyred Imam Husain, are recounted, and women's sufrihs, ceremonial meals involving vows at which women mullas read from the Qur'an and explicate it.

In addition, some Iranian women have, in the centuries Iran has been Shi'i, received enough higher religious education and certification of education to be capable of ijtihad, or independent judgment on legal and other questions. There is disagreement among authorities as to whether these women are properly to be called *mujtahids,* as many say that being male is a prerequisite to being a mujtahid and to giving rulings binding on a group of followers. In any case, such women have often given their opinions orally or in writing, and have had an important influence.[20]

20. This discussion is based largely on my own interviews and observations, including women's religious ceremonies led by women mullas, in Iran. The first writer to draw attention to women mullas in Shi'i Iraq was Elizabeth Warnock Fernea, *Guests of the Sheik* (New York: Doubleday, 1965), and with Robert A. Fernea, "Variations in Religious Observance among Islamic Women," in Keddie, ed., *Scholars, Saints and Sufis.* Disagreement over mujtahid status comes from several oral and written sources.

Playing a different role were those Iranian women who, from the early nineteenth century on, wrote treatises advising women how to get around their husbands, carry on flirtations, and otherwise subvert strict "Islamic" rules. There seem to have been groups of women, probably mostly elite, who consciously followed such advice, while many in all classes no doubt did similar things without having to read about them. This was not a specifically Shi'i phenomenon. Also not exclusive to Shi'ism was the great influence in Iran as elsewhere of many royal family women on government policy, which scholars have begun to reevaluate as a more positive phenomenon than had been thought.[21]

Iranian women also entered heavily into many riots, revolts, and revolutions, whose aims were not specifically profeminist. In bread riots, frequent in the nineteenth century, women were often the leading element, partly because popular-class women shoppers experienced directly the price of bread and partly, it seems, because men preferred to have *chadur*-clad anonymous and theoretically inviolate women do the dangerous work. Women participated in the 1891–92 tobacco movement, and especially in the constitutional revolution of 1905–11, where there were a few women's societies and newspapers and more than one dramatic demonstration by women.[22] Women's rights became an important issue in the twentieth century, but was promoted mostly by the educated and modernized elite and even Muhammad Reza Shah's government, neither of which popular-class women could relate to.

The heavy and multiclass women's participation in the revolution of 1978–79 involved a minority of modernized women, whose agenda included some feminist demands, and a great majority of popular-class women. The latter, like their male relatives, were more likely to identify the wealthier classes, even if anti-shah, with being favorable to Western economic and cultural domination than they were to join their elite sisters in such things as abandoning chadurs. The Iranian revolutionary ulama were successful both before and after the revolution in emphasizing discontent with Western ways. Such ways were associated with Western domination, with attacks on the bazaar economy, on the nomads, and on many peasants in the name of modernization, and with cultural changes such as Western dress and sexual mores. Even more than in most Muslim countries, an idealized Islam became an increasingly popular alternative for those who associated their ills and those of their country with the West

21. See especially Guity Nashat, "Women in Pre-Revolutionary Iran."
22. See especially Mangol Bayat-Philipp, "Women and Revolution in Iran, 1905–1911," in Beck and Keddie, *Women in the Muslim World*, 295–308.

and Westernization. In this process, at least in its current fundamentalist stage, women seem almost bound to lose out, as Pahlavi-period reforms in family law, seclusion, and so on are seen by fundamentalists as being against the Qur'an—even if what is really involved is the especially patriarchal interpretation of the Qur'an that evolved in later centuries. Among important Iranian groups only the Mujahidin-i Khalq attempted a reinterpretation of the spirit of Islam and the Qur'an in twentieth-century terms that included substantial equality for women as well as a form of socialism.

The popularity of the Mujahidin, despite brutal repression, is the most recent example we will give of the variability of Islamic theory and practice according to time, place, social class, and other factors. There is no doubt that the much-needed documented studies of the history of women, for which there are good sources in legal, waqf, and other documents, biographical dictionaries, art, poetry, folklore, and material culture, will reveal and explain far more variations and complexities in the history of Muslim women than have been suggested above. This history, in addition to the existence of current Islamically oriented organizations and thinkers who take a variety of positions on women, should show that if Islam, like most religions, has until now mostly reinforced patriarchy, other developments are possible within it, despite cultural difficulties.

As to the question of whether Shi'ism contains elements that might particularly encourage social protest among women, this too appears to be a matter of context. The tradition of the martyrdom of Husain and his followers, who included brave women, has been used in both Iranian twentieth-century revolutions to justify revolt against tyranny. And yet, as Mary Hegland has shown, in nonrevolutionary periods the role of Husain as intercessor for the individual believer is stressed, not his role as a rebel against unjust tyranny.[23] Shi'ism contains elements that in some periods are interpreted as denying the legitimacy of any temporal government, but this has not always been presented as a cause for revolt. On the contrary, some religious thinkers have stressed solidarity between ulama and government. As a matter of fact rather than theory, it may be noted that Shi'i Iran has had an extraordinary number of rebellions and revolutions since the mid-nineteenth century. To a degree, though not exclusively, this was because of the growing ideological and material split between the government and frequently dissenting ulama. The ideological

23. Mary Hegland, "Two Images of Husain: Accommodation and Revolution in an Iranian Village," in Nikki R. Keddie, ed., *Religion and Politics in Iran* (New Haven: Yale University Press, 1983), 218–35.

part of this estrangement stressed the illegitimacy of temporal rulers, and some preachers even, during both twentieth-century revolutions, compared the shahs to the tyrant Yazid who ordered Husain's death. There were thus elements in Shi'ism that were developed in a rebellious direction, although in earlier centuries many of the same basic doctrines had been interpreted in favor of clerical-state cooperation. Some ulama continued to be so, although political neutrality was preached by many non-royalist clerics. It was only with Khomeini that the argument that Islam is intrinsically antimonarchical became popular.

There seems little in Shi'ism, as compared to Sunnism, that would lead women in particular to protest, and so Shi'ism is probably not a major cause of women's participation in revolts. But the very development of many crises and rebellions in Iran that involved great numbers of people in antigovernment actions did encourage women's political action. As long as this action was not directed toward feminist goals, it was on the whole encouraged by revolutionary ulama. The constitutional revolution of 1905–11 was accompanied by modernist measures, including the beginnings of feminist literature and women's organizations and newspapers, whereas the 1978–79 revolution has resulted in antifeminist measures. In neither case was an "essence of Shi'ism" important but rather a changed socioeconomic and cultural context.

III
SEXUALITY IN CONTEMPORARY SHI'I TEXTS
BY NAHID YEGANEH

The period between the late 1960s and early 1980s was a fertile time for the production of various Shi'i texts on the position of women. Basically, the 1970s were a period within which a degree of plurality of social thought existed alongside the shah's strong and dictatorial central government. Although the state set limits on the expression of thought, censorship focused mostly on party political opposition and to a lesser extent on social opposition. While a severe crackdown on Marxist-Leninist and other guerrilla movements was going on, Marxist academic thought was finding some expression through publications, university lectures, and public debates. In the realm of Islam, too, although the Fida'iyan-i Islam (a small Iranian analog of the Muslim Brothers) had been suppressed and the anti-shah political movement led by Ayatullah Khomeini in 1963 was crushed, various Shi'i texts were taking up the issue of the position of women in Islam. The clergy's position in this period was that of a diverse social category, simultaneously in dialogue with and in opposition to the Pahlavi state.

The question of change was a social issue and the question of women a subject for public debate. Various trends of thought expressed ideas on sexuality and different aspects of women's position. The official state ideology, and its associated women's organization, Shi'i texts of various kinds, Marxist pamphlets, fiction and poetry, all reflected conceptions of female sexuality in explicit or implicit terms. Looking at some of this literature one finds that although the prescribed legal and social position of women in each text is often very different from the others, they all share many of the same ideas about female sexuality. Moreover, one often finds it difficult to differentiate, within this literature, which conception of sexuality is Shi'i and which secular.

The complex of social relations ensured that, whether in Shi'i or non-Shi'i texts, certain definitions of sexuality were reproduced widely while others could find only minimum expression.

One of the views that had little space for expression was the idea of sexual equality between men and women. Some Marxist writings, the poetry of the outstanding woman poet Furugh Farrukhzad, and the lifestyle of a small section of Iranian intellectuals and artists, who risked social stigma, implied sexual freedom for women. Another socially disfavored view, at the opposite end of the scale, was advocacy of polygamy and mut'ah (temporary pleasure marriage). The most accepted view of sexuality favored legitimate monogamous marriage. This view was represented across a whole series of ideologies, including state ideology and its associated feminism, Shi'ism, nationalism, and Marxism. In many ways, there was nothing specifically Shi'i about Iranian social thought of the time. Indeed, various views, from those presented in Shi'i texts to the idea of sexual liberation of women, found their parallels in Western social thought and fed intellectually on it. Iranian social relations defined what views on sexuality were to be taken as Shi'i and what as secular.

The shah's secular conception of female sexuality expressed the following doubt about women's emancipation:

> Just what constitutes the emancipation of a woman? To hear some so-called feminists talk, you would think it means freedom not to marry, freedom not to have children, freedom not to devote themselves to their children's welfare. . . . The women of Persia can enjoy all those freedoms if they want to—there is nothing in either law or binding custom which prevents it—but our enlightened women reject

them all. They know that women possess certain unique endowments, and that with those go unique responsibilities.[24]

As we will see, the shah left it to the Shi'i theorists to formulate what women's "unique endowments" and their corresponding "unique responsibilities" were.

The Pahlavi regime, however, was associated with the idea of women's emancipation and legal reforms in the position of women. Such associations encouraged oppositional groups, both Shi'i and Marxist, to reject feminism as a bourgeois preoccupation.

Marxist-Leninist pamphlets (mainly distributed outside Iran) occasionally specified their conception of women's relationship to the institution of family. One pamphlet argued:

> It has recently become fashionable amongst the educated and progressive women to complain about women's housework and childrearing duties. . . . Those who are concerned with their own individual liberation are no more than bourgeois and daydreaming intellectuals. . . . Any one demanding women to give up domestic responsibilities, or perform them partially and share them with men should know that this will not lead to mobilisation of the masses. The masses know very well that under present conditions housework, and reproduction and rearing of children are a necessity to ensure the continuance of the struggle of the masses.[25]

In the realm of fiction, too, certain concepts of sexuality found widespread expression. During the 1970s it became popular in fiction and poetry to object to the conception of women's emancipation advocated by the official state ideology. Furugh Farrukhzad objected to the hypocrisy involved in the official conception of female emancipation, and some other writers complained about the disturbance of old ways and the uprooting of women's traditional role.

During this decade, quite a range of Shi'i texts were available on the question of women. To cover the range reasonably, we can look at texts by Ayatullah Khomeini, Ayatullah Mutahhari, Ali Shariati, the organization of Mujahidin-i Khalq, and Zahra Rahnavard.

Ayatullah Khomeini's main text discussing women was a *Tauzih al-Masa'il* (book of religious instructions). Tauzih al-Masa'ils were the place within which various major Shi'i *marja'-i taqlids* (sources of imitation) provided instructions on bodily, religious, and social functions for their

---

24. Muhammad Reza Shah, *Mission for My Country* (London: Hutchinson, 1960), 235.
25. International Confederation of Iranian Students, *Roshana-i*, no. 3 (n.d.): 6.

followers. Sexual functions usually constituted an important section of these books, and other sections also referred to sex-related taboos and pollutions. In these texts, instructions on sexual intercourse had a degree of frankness and detail that went well beyond the soft-porn fiction that was becoming increasingly popular (though denounced by the clergy). In this, Tauzih al-Masa'ils enjoyed the kind of status accorded to medical books on these matters. Yet, in a sexually repressed social atmosphere, they also functioned as pornography. Ayatullah Khomeini's text was quite similar to other Tauzih al-Masa'ils.[26] In his text, the definition of male and female sexuality and the institutions built around them is one that favors a maximum rate of reproduction. Incest is defined narrowly,[27] marriage age is the lowest possible,[28] and polygamy and temporary marriages are allowed.[29] Sex and reproduction are separated to a considerable extent in male but not female sexuality. Male sexuality is active; female sexuality is passive. Women, as was true since early Islamic times, have the religious duty to submit to their husband's sexual wishes. Sexual intercourse is equated with penetration. Marriages can be dissolved and inheritance annulled if penetration does not take place.[30] Pregnant women are treated with favor in Khomeini's text and a whole series of regulations are built around breast-feeding.[31] All this creates the broadest conditions for legitimate reproduction. Khomeini's opposition to women's enfranchisement and to the new family protection laws introduced by the shah in the 1960s and 1970s expressed a fear of damage to the reproductive capacity of the "Muslim community."

Yet, this does not necessarily dictate a corresponding political position for Khomeini under all circumstances. Khomeini's conceptions of sexuality, like anybody else's, mean different things in different contexts. The "Muslim community" he tried so hard to preserve and multiply in his Tauzih al-Masa'il was asked to offer its youth for martyrdom for the Islamic Republic.[32] In the same context, women's enfranchisement, which

---

26. Ruhullah al-Musavi al-Khomeini, *Risalih-i Tauzih al-Masa'il* (Qum, n.d.); Adele K. and Amir H. Ferdows, "Women in Shi'i Fiqh: Images through the Hadith," in Nashat, ed., *Women and Revolution*, 56, say Khomeini's rulings on women are almost identical to those of the late Safavid theologian Muhammad Baqir Majlisi (whose own works draw on earlier Shi'i treatises).

27. Khomeini, *Risalih,* Instructions: 238–2411.

28. Ibid., 2410, 2379.

29. Ibid., 2412–2432.

30. Ibid., 2775, 2381.

31. Ibid., 2464–2497.

32. Ibid., 312–14.

Khomeini had previously found "disturbing to the peace of mind of the religious leaders,"[33] after the revolution brought him peace of mind.

Ayatullah Mutahhari was a reformist Shi'i clergyman and professor of theology at Tehran University. After February 1979, he became a member of the Revolutionary Council and was assassinated by a fundamentalist group in May of that year. His major text on women's position is a collection of his articles published in a women's magazine (*Zan-i Ruz*, Today's Woman) as a debate with Westernized Iranian women.

Ayatullah Mutahhari's text concerns biological differences between men and women.[34] For him biology includes both physical and psychological attributes, and sexuality is strictly biological. Reproductive sexuality is the only "natural" form, nonproductive sexuality being against nature. The family, the only legitimate site for sexual intercourse, is therefore in the realm of "nature."[35] This view of the physical and psychological attributes of humans creates a fertile ground for Mutahhari's production of stereotypes of "femininity" and "masculinity": man is rational, woman is emotional; nature has invested in man the need to love and seek, and in woman the need to be loved and sought; man is strong, woman weak; man seeks beauty in woman, while woman wants strength in man; man is a slave to passion, woman is a prisoner of love and affection; man is zealous, woman is jealous.[36] Sexual intercourse is defined as a moment of total unity and possession. The only "natural" form of marriage for Mutahhari is monogamy, with polygamy and temporary marriage reserved for times of crisis when men and women must sacrifice for the sake of society. Men and women are both monogamous by nature. Men's tendency to seek variety in sex has social reasons and can be changed.[37] Sexual instinct is active, strong, and deep in both men and women. The difference between them lies in women's greater ability to bring her sex drive under control.[38]

Mutahhari is aware of modern debates and tries to choose allies

33. Khomeini's telegram to the shah in October 1962; quoted in Haleh Afshar, "Khomeini's Teachings and Their Implications for Iranian Women," in Azar Tabari and Nahid Yeganeh, eds., *In the Shadow of Islam: Women's Movement in Iran* (London: Zed Press, 1982). See also pp. 98–103 of this book for Khomeini's changing position toward women's status during and after the revolution of 1979 in Iran.

34. Murtaza Mutahhari, *Nizam-i Huquq-i Zan dar Islam* (The System of Women's Rights in Islam) (Qum, 1979).

35. Ibid., chap. 6.

36. Ibid., 172–75.

37. Ibid., 332, 389, 391.

38. Murtaza Mutahhari, *Mas'alih-i Hijab* (The Question of Modesty) (Tehran: Arjuman-i Islami-i Pizishkan, 1969), 69, 71, 96–106.

within them. He allocates a chapter to the question "is the idea of biological differences between men and women a medieval one?"[39] His answer is negative, and the Western intellectuals he mentions regarding this
position range from French biologists to English philosophers and Alfred
Hitchcock.[40] Yet Mutahhari wants to think independently of these trends
in the West that, in his words, despite the outcries of Western natural
scientists and philosophers, argue for sexual liberation. These include
Freud, the women's movement, the Declaration of Human Rights, prostitution, pornography, alcohol, drugs, and so on. These are all seen as
"inherently" Western, and if we see them in Iranian society, it is because
of the power of the West to export them and Iranians' intellectual dependency which leads Iranians to accept them. The effect of these Western
trends for Mutahhari is to dilute the boundaries of the family and social
spheres. In Mutahhari's writings, once sexuality is defined in biological
terms and situated in the realm of nature, other human activities gain a
nonsexual character. All sexual functions are to take place within the
sphere of the family. The sphere of the social is for thinking and working,
and sexual difference does not belong here.[41] This separation is to be
achieved through Islamic devices such as modest dress and behavior in
public.

Mutahhari's concept of nature was a cultural construction that went
well with the then-dominant image of woman as part-time mother and
part-time worker. The social atmosphere of the time encouraged a partial
release of women from home to take up social and political responsibilities.

Ali Shariati was a lay Shi'i reformer who opposed the shah in much
more radical terms than Mutahhari and was imprisoned for it. Shariati
studied at the University of Paris. In the 1970s his ideas gained enormous
support among Iranian youth and formed the cornerstone of a new Shi'i
opposition to the West and its manifestations within Iranian society. He
died in 1977 in exile. Shariati produced a number of texts on the Shi'i
model of revolutionary women, within which he rejected the tauzih al-
masa'il approach toward women.

In one text Shariati praised Mutahhari's model of the natural family:

> Although Islam is strongly against "prejudices" against women, it
> does not support "equality" for them. Islam tries to find the "natural
> place" of men and women within society. . . . Nature has created

39. Mutahhari, *Nizam*, 167.
40. Mutahhari, *Hijab*, 51–57.
41. Mutahhari, *Nizam*, 150–53

man and woman as complementary beings in life and society. This is why unlike Western civilisation, Islam offers men and women their "natural rights" and not "similar rights." This is the most profound word to be said on the matter and its depth and value should be clear to those conscious readers who would dare to think and see without Europe's permission.[42]

But Shariati's alliance with Mutahhari on women's "natural position" and "natural rights" ends here. Shariati must have had a different definition of nature to conceptualize his ideal woman as an asexual one. Shariati's text revolves around a criticism of a conception of woman as a sex object. In his attempt to deobjectify woman, Shariati desexualizes her. There is no place for sexual instinct in his discourse. Woman is an object of desire, but the desire should be for her love, not her body. The main fault with the capitalist system is that it has replaced love with sex. In the hands of capitalism, woman, who was the main source of inspiration throughout history, has become a sexual image aiding the transformation of the values of a traditional spiritual society into an absurd consumer society.[43]

For Shariati sex is not only opposed to love but also opposed to work, intellect, leisure, political struggle, and spiritual inspiration. Freud's "sexual liberation" is a Western conspiracy against all innovative activities by Muslims.[44] Shariati's ideal woman, Fatima, is simple and pure. She has a heart full of love for Islam. She challenges social and political injustice and respects just authority.[45] She reproduces and provides service to her family. But she has no sexual desire and is not sexually desired by any man, including her husband, 'Ali. Fatima's shyness and chasteness is counted by Shariati as among her virtues.[46]

Her father, the Prophet, however, is allowed to desire women and be desired by them. Shariati goes out of his way to describe the Prophet's love for one of his wives, Aisha, and her emotions toward him[47] and his romance with Zainab (the wife of the Prophet's adopted son).[48] The nature of the Prophet's desire, however, is portrayed to be beyond the com-

42. Ali Shariati, *Zan dar Chishm va Dil-i Muhammad* (Women in the Eye and Heart of Muhammad) (1979), 5.

43. Ali Shariati, *Fatima Is Fatima,* trans. Laleh Bakhtiar (Tehran: Shariati Foundation, 1980), 100–05.

44. Ali Shariati, *Intizar-i Asr-i Hazir az Zan-i Musalman* (The Expectation of Present Era from Muslim Woman) (n.p., n. d.), 27.

45. Ibid., 20, 32.

46. Shariati, *Zan,* 6.

47. Ibid., 8.

48. Ibid., 13.

prehension of ordinary mortals. His love is not the sexual, biological, and impure desire portrayed by the Christian clergy and Western Orientalists.[49] His love and desire are divine. It is a silent, patient, humble, and painful love that inspires him to do good and brings him close to God. For Shariati, it cannot be otherwise. Love is a "reality" like anger, hatred, and fear. Therefore, Muhammad (as a prophet) is bound to feel love, and feel it in a pure and divine sense.[50] This is the ideal type of love toward which Muslims should aspire.

For Shariati, "pure desire" should replace "sexual passion" in the minds of the new generation of Muslims. This conception of sexuality in his view matches the new militant role of Shi'i women. A woman who is militant and responsible for her society is a source of inspiration for the Muslim man. She is an object of man's desire, but does not have an independent desire of her own for men. Shariati, then, attempts to purify and cleanse Khomeini's and Mutahhari's biological essentialist conception of sexuality, by replacing "sex instinct" with "love instinct." This is in accord with a popular interest in romance and pure love among the young generation of the early 1970s. Mutahhari's regulation of sexuality released women's labor power by making the sphere of the social nonsexual, and Shariati's political ideology gave the nonsexual militant woman an important role to play on the political scene. Both of these were part of general trends within Iranian society. The role of woman as mother/worker/politician was propagated by the formal state ideology as well.

Shariati's conception of women is mainly a result of the problematic of his discourse. The discourses of Khomeini, Mutahhari, and Shariati are not concerned with the same problem. The distinctive and traditional function of Tauzih al-Masa'il within Iranian religious culture determines its problematic. The relationship between marja'-i taqlid and followers within the context of the prevailing definition of authority made Tauzih al-Masa'ils religious guidebooks that gave instructions on sex and reproduction without a need for rationalizing them.

Mutahhari was not a marja'-i taqlid and his book was not a Tauzih al-Masa'il. As a reformer who saw Islam as an ideology opposed to Western infiltration of Iranian society, Mutahhari tried to construct a rationalized Shi'i system of the male-female relationship, centered on an ideal Shi'i family.

Shariati's discourse centered on concerns different from those of either Khomeini or Mutahhari. He was neither in a position to issue

49. Ibid., 13–15.
50. Ibid., 16.

religious instructions on sex and reproduction, nor was he interested in rationalizing and regulating these matters. His mission was to create an ideal model for Muslim women to follow, and his concern was primarily political. He tried to provide the ideological basis for creating a new generation of Iranian women who, by relying on their "Shi'i" tradition, would resist and fight "cultural imperialism." Shariati allowed nothing to stand in the way of the militant Shi'i woman: neither her role as mother nor her legal position. His ideal woman, Fatima, was a wife and mother and was subject to all the Qur'anic injunctions on the position of women. Shariati's Shi'i woman could not exist without Marxist theories of dependency, existentialism, the Algerian resistance to French rule, Arab Islamic reformism, Iran's subordination to the superpowers, and a concrete anti-imperialist movement in Iran.[51] A combination of such elements, with which Shariati was acquainted, formed the condition of existence for Shariati's concept of sexuality.

As is true of Khomeini, Mutahhari, and Shariati, the discourse of Mujahidin-i Khalq on women can also not be reduced to a historical concept of sexuality. The context within which Mujahidin's series of articles appeared in their paper was that of revolutionary fervor and freedom of expression. The Iranian Revolution of 1979 had just succeeded, and various ideologies were struggling for a place within the future social and political order.

The Mujahidin-i Khalq organization was an anti-imperialist group that engaged in armed struggle against the shah's regime. By 1979, most of its members were killed by security forces, executed, or in prison. The imprisoned members of the Mujahidin were released during the revolution and led the organization into a popular Shi'i movement. The Mujahidin supported the leadership of Ayatullah Khomeini during the revolution, but were alienated from power by the postrevolutionary Islamic state. Today the Mujahidin constitute the major Shi'i force in armed struggle with the regime of Ayatullah Khomeini.

The Mujahidin's text on women's position presented a challenge to a tendency among some members of the 1979 assembly of Islamic experts to give "priority to the element of sexuality before that of humanity"; for making "absolute the motherhood role of women to such extent that it confines them to the house and deprives them of any social and political activities"; and for regarding "women as delicate and in need of sup-

---

51. On Shariati and Khomeini, see Sami Zubaida, "The Ideological Conditions for Khomeini's Doctrine of Government," *Economy and Society* 11, no. 2 (May 1982): 138–72.

port."[52] For the Mujahidin, the attempt by this tendency to portray "the social reality of discrimination between men and women" as "a natural and necessary phenomenon, and even try, by means of various justifications to present it as scientific or even divine law"[53] had to be challenged. This was mainly because it encouraged many Muslim women to accept their second-class position as the natural order of things.[54] The Mujahidin's alternative was a *tauhidi* (nonantagonistic) society that was "against any class, racial, national and sexual discrimination" and could not, therefore, "accept the discrimination between women and men as a holy matter and approve it."[55]

The Mujahidin replaced the appeal to nature with an appeal to reality, which was their primary reference point in exploring the position of women. Iranian social reality for the Mujahidin was the discriminatory class and sexual structure of that society. This reality was rooted in history and could only be changed in the future. Any attempt to change the position of women here and now faced disapproval from the Mujahidin. The liberation of women, they argued, means a "total destruction of the historically determined relations within the society that oppresses women," and not "just minor changes and superficial reforms."[56] This view, placed in the context of anti-imperialist sentiments preceding the revolution, determined the Mujahidin's position on the question of women's rights. Addressing women's demonstrations in March 1979 against the intention of Ayatullah Khomeini to make the hijab compulsory for women, the Mujahidin invited women to abandon their protest "because the heavy burden of the imperialist culture cannot be eliminated all at once and other than through a long term and gradual process."[57]

However, the Mujahidin's realism and ideology of nonantagonism contained a conception of equality of rights for men and women in all spheres, including the family, excluding the hijab. They rejected the argument of "equal but not similar." The exact translation of their conception of equality into legal rights, however, would depend on the political context—as is true of any ideology. The Mujahidin's position on the male-female relationship was no different from the general Marxist-Leninist

52. The Organization of Mujahidin-i Khalq of Iran, *Zan dar Masir-i Rahai* (Woman in the Path of Liberation) (Tehran, 1981). All my references to this text are to its English translation in Tabari and Yeganeh, *In the Shadow of Islam*, 115.

53. Ibid., 113.

54. Ibid.

55. Ibid.

56. Ibid., 114.

57. Ibid., 127.

trend of the time. Neither included sexual liberation as part of women's liberation. Sex outside marriage was considered a "bourgeois perversion" for both sexes. Yet, the social atmosphere ensured that female members received tougher treatment than male members if they committed the sin. Sex and reproduction were firmly placed within the family, and in this sphere, mutual and two-sided relationships, including sharing of domestic responsibilities, were encouraged.[58]

What separated the Mujahidin from purely Marxist-Leninist groups was the woman's hijab. This was the link they insisted on preserving with popular religion within Iranian society, which also ensured the ideological identity and uniformity of their followers. What constituted the Mujahidin's Shi'iness was the hijab; they kept the institution without believing in all that went with it in Mutahhari's system. Hijab is defined in their educational text as "the boundary of dressing for men and women" set by "the culture of revolutionary Islam." But why has this culture asked women but not men to cover their hair? There is no justification apart from a reference to "tradition" and the personal choice of "Iranian militant Muslim women."[59]

One can find much that is "moral" in the Mujahidin's views on women, but little that is "Shi'i" as such. In that sense, the Mujahidin's religiosity is to be found in the expression rather than the content of their ideology. This can be said about the texts on women written by other Shi'is, nationalists, Marxists, feminists, royalists, and so on at the time. The immediate indigenous and international relations set the terms for various discourses and debates on the male-female relationship in Iranian society.

The revolutionary and postrevolutionary context provided a fertile ground for the birth of another Shi'i protest on women's position. Tens of thousands of Iranian women took part in the revolution of 1979, and many Iranian women turned to Shi'ism for their liberation. During the revolution, a heterogeneous body of Shi'i women's movements began to take shape, and soon after the revolution various Shi'i women's groups began to educate the masses of women about their Islamic rights and attempted to mobilize them. The Shi'i women's movement was not an oppositional movement. An ideologically significant section of it, however, soon came face to face with the practices and policies of the postrevolutionary Islamic state. The works of a few individual women assumed par-

58. Ibid., 113.
59. Ibid., 121.

ticular significance for the direction of this movement. One of the major ideologues of the Shi'i women's movement was Zahra Rahnavard.[60]

Zahra Rahnavard studied in the United States and was an active supporter of the Islamic revolution. After the revolution she became editor of the women's magazine, *Ittila'at-i Banuvan* (Women's Information) and changed its name to *Rah-i Zainab* (Zainab's Way). In the summer of 1980, the magazine was stopped by the board of directors of the *Ittila'at* newspaper on the grounds of economizing. In November 1981, Rahnavard's husband Mir-Husain Musavi became the prime minister of Iran. Some members of the Islamic Parliament objected to his premiership because of Rahnavard's feminist ideas. This, no doubt, further contributed to her silence since the closing of her magazine.

Rahnavard's major text is an expression of a Shi'i feminist protest.[61] She begins the book by pointing to a change of mind on her part about the importance of the question of women:

> To be honest, earlier on when the question of women was raised, both in Iran and abroad, I used to think it was a passing and momentary matter. I used to believe that the materialists talk about it in order to make women weary of Islam, and the ruling system made it an issue in order to implement its conspiracies against women. But with further contemplation, I perceived the one-dimensional nature of my thought. I realised that the woman question is a historical one and it is a social and political necessity to find a solution for it.[62]

No doubt the availability of writings on Shi'i woman, her oppression and her rights, made an important contribution to the transformation of Rahnavard's (and many other women's) thought regarding the question of women.

Rahnavard adopts Shariati's protest against the Western infiltration of Iranian society. She complains about the imperialist conspiracy to rob Iran of its economic resources and cultural heritage by winning the hearts of women (through makeup and fashion), and turning men's attention away from poverty and oppression by preoccupying them with sex. Following Shariati's protest against the exploitation of Iranian women through superstitious Shi'ism and corrupt Western culture, Rahnavard

60. For a more detailed discussion of Shi'i women's movement and its role within the postrevolutionary society, see Tabari and Yeganeh, *In the Shadow of Islam*, 26–74. For exposition of the works of other ideologues of the Shi'i women's movement, see pp. 171–200 in the same book.

61. Zahra Rahnavard, *Tulu'i Zan-i Musalman* (The Dawn of Muslim Woman) (Nashr-i Mahbubih: n.p., n.d.). The book became available in Iran after the revolution of 1979.

62. Ibid., 6.

condemns both women's imprisonment in the house and her liberation as a sex object.[63]

Having established the fact of women's oppression in Iran and having discussed the reasons behind it, Rahnavard turns to Mutahhari to explain women's Islamic rights. Following Mutahhari, she argues that in the Qur'an the question of *value* is treated as separate from the question of *right*. Therefore, the existence of division of labor in the economy, which is based on the physical and psychological differences between men and women, should not give rise to social superiority of one sex. She believes it is "natural, very beautiful, both fair and reasonable" for men to offer financial support to women.[64]

It would be wrong, however, to see Rahnavard's text as a mere repetition of Shariati and Mutahhari. Rahnavard was involved in a concrete feminist politics within a concrete political situation. As an ideologue of a Shi'i women's movement, she relied on the ideological tenets provided by male theorists and presented her own special articulation of what women's Islamic rights consist of. Rahnavard defined the objective of a Shi'i women's movement as equality of opportunity for men and women to develop their talents and capacities. She argued for participation of women in every sphere and field. Yet she emphasized women's participation in politics as the most significant step in liberating them.[65] For Rahnavard, Western feminism has gone wrong in assuming men to be the main enemy, and communism has failed to liberate women because of its emphasis on the importance of women's participation in production. Both, she argues, have resulted in recklessness, chaos, and prostitution, and only the systems have benefited from it, women themselves being left helpless and unhappy.[66]

In her search to find a system that would make women "happy," Rahnavard discovers "the true Islam": "Muslim woman is a perfect woman, a multidimensional being."[67] The true Islam, she argues, allows woman to realize both her motherhood instinct and her need to participate in the liberation of her country. Communism violates the latter by leaving the care of the infant to the nursery, and capitalism violates the former by turning woman into a sex object. Islam, by advocating monogamous family with the man as the breadwinner, makes this possible. In the mo-

63. Ibid., 10–12.
64. Ibid., 81. See also pp. 77–82 and pp. 100–03.
65. Ibid., 22–23, 103–18.
66. Ibid., 32–37.
67. Ibid., 91.

nogamous family, woman has the opportunity to free herself from productive activities in order to give birth and look after her infant. Her need
for physical and psychological support is also fulfilled within the monogamous family. With the attainment of political consciousness, and with
progress of technology to allow her to control and limit her housework
duties, Muslim woman, Rahnavard argues, can be on her way to liberate
her country and herself.[68]

Rahnavard's Shi'i feminism presented yet another conception of
women's emancipation to be added to those of the prerevolutionary official
women's movement and the poetry of Furugh Farrukhzad. All three conceptions were protests against Ayatullah Khomeini's taken-for-granted
conception of women's place in Iranian society. Mutahhari, Shariati, and
the Mujahidin, too, rejected lawful and unlawful pleasure and polyga-
mous sexuality, although in different degrees and for different reasons.
Mutahhari emphasized "fulfillment of sexual needs of the partners" in the
setting of the "ideal family." Shariati prescribed pure love and romance
between the partners. The Mujahidin added to the variety of Shi'i conceptions of women's position by protesting against the "dissimilarity of
rights" among men and women.

CONCLUSION

It has been argued in this essay that the attribution of a universal concept
of sexuality to Islam is untenable. The study of Shi'i history in Iran and
the contemporary Shi'i movements demonstrate that sociopolitical context
is important in determining the form and content of Shi'i social protest
on sexuality.

We saw that, historically, Shi'i ideology on women's position has
varied contextually and that Shi'i protest at one time and place became
the status quo in another time and place. The history of Shi'ism in Iran
does not suggest intrinsic elements in Shi'ism to activate social protest on
women's position regardless of contextual factors.

In contemporary Iran, too, there is no substantial evidence of intrinsic
Shi'i concepts of female sexuality. Social and political relations in this
period were important in specifying what concepts of sexuality were
counted as Shi'i and what constituted a Shi'i protest on sexuality. In this
period, the available Shi'i concepts of sexuality were drawn into the context of immediate social and political issues, and there emerged new for-

68. Ibid., 99.

mulations of relevance to present conditions. The Shi'i texts of the 1970s presented a variety of views. Each of these texts had different functions and was written for different purposes. Although certain concepts of female sexuality were often reproduced, nevertheless, these discourses were far from repetitions of an essential Shi'i concept of sexuality. Immediate indigenous and international relations were major factors in setting the terms for various Shi'i discourses and debates on male-female relationships in Iran of the 1970s.

HELENA COBBAN

Chapter Five # The Growth of Shi'i Power in Lebanon and Its Implications for the Future

A new factor has emerged into the Lebanese body politic. This is the newly articulated community interest of the country's Shi'i Muslims, who today constitute the largest of the seventeen religious sects officially recognized in Lebanon.[1]

In late 1983, the importance of the Lebanese Shi'is impressed itself on Americans in a shocking way, when a terrorist presumed to be a Shi'i extremist drove a truck-bomb into the U.S. Marines' compound near Beirut airport, killing 241 Marines.[2]

Then, in February 1984, Nabih Berri, leader of the broad-based Shi'i militia group Amal, caused the collapse of the Lebanese army in West

The author would like to thank As'ad Abu-Khalil, doctoral candidate at Georgetown University, for the help he has given her in connection with this essay. She remains responsible, of course, for all mistakes and judgments herein.

1. In my analysis of Lebanese affairs, I use the word *sect* to describe the Shi'is, as well as other religious groups in Lebanon, in two of the senses defined in *Webster's Ninth New Collegiate Dictionary*: "a religious denomination, . . . a group adhering to a distinctive doctrine or to a leader."

2. After the truck-bombing, an anonymous man called some news media to "claim" it in the name of a group called the Islamic Jihad. This claim may not in itself have been genuine, or may have been part of a black propaganda exercise by parties interested in discrediting Muslim organizations. Nevertheless, mounting evidence in this and other truck-bombing incidents began to point to the responsibility of Shi'i extremists.

137

Beirut, by hinting that the Shi'i soldiers in the army should resign. Around 60 percent of the army's rank-and-file were members of the Shi'i sect. As if they had only been waiting for Berri's call, nearly all did resign. Those tumultuous two days completely redrew the shape of Lebanese politics.

The bombing of the Marines' compound had prompted the first serious discussions in the United States about how to get the Marines out of Lebanon. The collapse of the Lebanese army in West Beirut then prompted the United States to announce that the Marines would be pulled out soon thereafter. On both occasions, the "Shi'i factor" had made itself strongly felt.

THE HISTORY OF SHI'ISM IN LEBANON

The irruption of the Shi'i factor into the Lebanese system caught many traditional analysts of Lebanese politics unawares. Most previous writing about the country had concentrated on the role of the two sects that had dominated its politics since 1943—the Maronite Christians and the Sunni Muslims. Little attention was paid to developments inside the rapidly growing Shi'i community.

However, the Shi'is' presence in Lebanon is by no means a recent phenomenon: it dates back to the first days of the disagreements that split the world Muslim community into Shi'i and Sunni camps in the seventh century. (Most Lebanese Shi'is became associated with the Twelver subgroup of the sect.) In the eleventh century, each of three local Shi'i dynasties enjoyed a brief moment of glory in Lebanon under the overall protection of the Sevener Shi'i Fatimid dynasty, which, from its base in Egypt, dominated much of the eastern Mediterranean at the time. In that century, too, the Shi'i communities in Lebanon and Syria were rent by another schism, out of which emerged the closed and esoteric Druze sect.

From the twelfth century onward, however, the Shi'is of Lebanon were reduced to the status of dissenters, at first from the Christianity of the Crusader kingdoms and then, for long centuries, from a surrounding orthodoxy dominated by the Sunnis.

The Shi'i population eventually became concentrated in two areas of present-day Lebanon. The first of these was Jabal 'Amil (Mount 'Amil), which is the part of the Mount Lebanon range that lies in South Lebanon, between the Shouf and northern Galilee. The second area was in the northern reaches of the Bekaa, around the towns of Baalbek and Hirmil. Each of these two major groups of Shi'is followed a distinctive path of development.

Jabal 'Amil was nearly always able to support a steady form of rain-fed agriculture. Its society was settled and became dominated by a handful of large landlords, who exercised strong feudal power over their cultivators. The power of these landowning families was balanced only slightly by that of the local Shi'i learned men, or ulama. The ulama played an important role in the life of the Jabal through the centuries. They retained and transmitted the people's beliefs, and they kept this small group of Shi'is in touch with the much larger Shi'i communities in southern Iraq and elsewhere. The ulama network of Jabal 'Amil produced many religious teachers whose fame spread throughout the Shi'i world. Indeed, when Iran's new Safavid ruler decided in the early sixteenth century that Shi'ism should be the official religion of his new state there, he imported scores of ulama from Jabal 'Amil to teach the new belief to his formerly Sunni subjects.

The northern Bekaa was very different from Jabal 'Amil. There, settled agriculture was seldom feasible. The driest part of Lebanon, this region could support only a seminomadic society. The Shi'is from there were clanspeople, living under the same kind of honor code that regulated the life of seminomads throughout the great deserts of the Syrian interior.

The two groups of Lebanese Shi'is took little part in the events that led to the establishment of a new, intersectarian political system in the central parts of Mount Lebanon from 1585 on. The Ottoman Empire, which ruled the whole region in that period, did so in the name of Sunni Muslim orthodoxy. The Ottomans were willing to recognize a degree of separateness for the Maronite Christians and Druze who dominated the population of central Mount Lebanon. But they were reluctant to do the same for the Shi'is and treated them as normal Muslim citizens.

During the latter years of Ottoman rule, the Shi'is constituted only about 5 percent of the population of the intersectarian regime that was emerging in central Mount Lebanon. Then, in 1920, the French incorporated Jabal 'Amil and the Bekaa along with Mount Lebanon and the Sunni-dominated coastal cities to its west into the new state of Greater Lebanon. The proportion of Shi'is in this new entity now reached around 17 percent.

The French continued to control Greater Lebanon under a mandate from the League of Nations until 1943. The Maronite Christians, who had been the strongest group in the previous regime in Mount Lebanon, remained the strongest local group in Greater Lebanon. The major threat to the new French-backed regime emanated from the Sunnis of the coast, who agitated to resume their previous links with the Syrian interior. The

Shi'is were not generally thought to constitute as strong a threat as the Sunnis.

The French and their Maronite friends were easily able to co-opt the handful of landowning families from Jabal 'Amil and the key clan leaders from the Bekaa. They gave them honorary positions in the state administration, good salaries, and access to Beirut's commercial riches. In return, these community leaders dealt with any opposition movement that might arise inside their own villages and clans. They were generally able to deliver on their part of the bargain because they still retained near-total control over their community's internal affairs.

During World War II, French power in the eastern Mediterranean eroded seriously and then was replaced by that of the British. In 1943, under the auspices of the British, Sunni and Maronite merchant leaders from Beirut reached an unwritten agreement called the National Pact, which was to become the political basis for the country's independence.

The pact divided the most important positions in the Lebanese administration among the country's major religious groups. First and second places in the system were allotted to the Maronites and Sunnis, respectively. The Maronites were given the presidency and the powerful post of army commander. The Sunnis were given the premiership, which in theory could make or break any individual president's regime. The Shi'is came in a poor third. They were given only the speakership of the Parliament, a largely symbolic job offering only occasional opportunities to affect the course of power.

When the last Allied troops left Lebanon in 1945, the country declared its independence as a parliamentary republic. The coming of independence did not make much difference inside the Shi'i communities, however. The large landowners continued to dominate the life of Jabal 'Amil, and the clan leaders, the life of the northern Bekaa.

NEW FORCES

Within thirteen years, change was to come to these outlying regions of the new republic. In 1958, Lebanon was swept up in a brief civil war, caused in part by the gross inequalities that had grown up between the wealthy trading center of Beirut and the depressed rural hinterland.

The crisis of 1958 was resolved when Fuad Shihab succeeded to the presidency. Shihab was a Maronite, a member of the extraordinary multi-confessional family that throughout two centuries had dominated the emergence of an intersectarian entity in Mount Lebanon. Prior to 1958,

Shihab had been the commander of the national army. In this capacity, he had traveled to more of the country's outlying villages than most Beirut-based politicians ever knew existed. He had seen the poverty in the villages and realized that the inequalities within the country had to be eased if a stable regime was to evolve.

In the presidency, Shihab sought to build a nationwide economic infrastructure. He brought in French experts with plans to bring roads, schools, and basic social facilities to all parts of the country. He hoped that later he might build on these first steps by bringing modern agriculture and industrial development to all the outlying regions. Shihab was able to implement nearly all of the first part of this scheme. The school-building program he launched increased the number of students in the Bekaa and South Lebanon (including Jabal 'Amil) from 62,000 in 1959 to more than 225,000 in 1973.[3] All but a half dozen of the furthermost villages were tied into the national road network.

In 1964, Shihab was succeeded by Charles Helou, who tried to follow through on Shihab's economic development schemes. But the continued opposition of the merchant class slowed down his momentum. Then the deep regional upset caused by the 1967 Middle East war brought all development planning nearly to a halt. Shihab and his friends were thus only partially successful in realizing their overall economic plan for the country. But they were much more successful in spurring the social development of its rural areas.

Previously, the most enterprising Shi'i youths had often found their ambition checked by the conservatism of their communities' traditional leaders. Many of the best of these youth had ended up emigrating, to West Africa and elsewhere, so that they could get ahead.

After Shihab had finished his work, however, a Shi'i youth could go to a government school, pursue his or her studies at the new national university in Beirut, and return to his village to work as a teacher or lawyer. The whole process would cost the youth's family very little. And the local landowner or clan leader was powerless to stop the process of social change thus set in motion.

But not all the newly mobilized Shi'is returned to their villages. The migration of Shi'i families to the suburbs of Beirut became a flood from the late 1950s onward. By the early 1980s fully one-third of Lebanon's whole Shi'i population was found there. The large-scale Shi'i migration

3. Salim Nasr, "La Transition des chiites vers Beyrouth: Mutations sociales et mobilisation communautaire à la veille de 1975," in *Mouvements communautaires et espaces urbains au Machreq* (Beirut: CERMOC, 1984).

to Beirut accelerated the process of social change within the sect. In addition, in the city, Shi'is from Jabal 'Amil and the Bekaa mingled for the first time; and they went through many of the same traumatic experiences there together. Urbanization thus helped weave the interests of what were now three distinct areas of Shi'i settlement into something like a single national Shi'i constituency.

The Shi'is' true integration into the Lebanese system, as spurred by the Shihabists, set the stage for the rise of new radical movements which threw out a strong challenge to the sect's traditional leadership, as well as to the Maronite ascendancy. (There were many parallels here with what had happened inside Maronite society 150 years earlier. In that period, a radical movement had grown up among Maronite peasants that had challenged both the existing landowning aristocracy inside their own sect and the Druzes' continuing predominance in the political system.)

The first form the new Shi'i radicalism took was leftist in tone. In the late 1960s, a broad leftist movement was emerging in Lebanon under the leadership of the idiosyncratic socialist leader Kamal Jumblatt—who was also hereditary heir to the leadership of the socially conservative Druze sect! In 1969, Jumblatt formed a coalition called the Lebanese National Movement (LNM), which grouped progressives from many ideological groups. In the LNM, there were socialists and communists, Arab nationalists, and various other leftists and secularists. Although the leaders of many of these groups came from the Christian communities, a large proportion of their foot soldiers were Shi'is.

The civil war that erupted in Lebanon in 1975 and 1976 represented Jumblatt's armed challenge to the Maronite ascendancy in Lebanon and the Maronite militias' armed defense of it. In the course of 1976, the Maronites were saved from military defeat by the Syrians.

The Shi'i community suffered heavily in 1975–76. Shi'is fought and died in disproportionately large numbers during Jumblatt's bid for power. So strong was the tide of Shi'i radicalism in those months that old-style Shi'i leaders such as Kamil al-As'ad and Kazim al-Khalil had to seek protection in the Maronite-held enclave throughout the war. Perhaps as many as half of the thirty thousand to forty thousand killed in the 1975–76 war were Shi'is. In the middle of the fighting, too, the Maronite militias evicted all non-Christians from the areas they controlled to the east and north of Beirut. In late 1975, the militias moved into the Shi'i quarter of Harat al-Ghawarina in East Beirut and evicted all its residents. In January 1976, they stormed the two miserable and predominantly Shi'i shanty-towns of Maslakh and Qarantina, evicting the surviving residents at gunpoint before they razed the zinc-sheet shanties to the ground.

In August 1976, the militias captured the vast and longer established Shi'i suburb of Nabaa. Its 100,000 inhabitants were similarly forced to flee, and the homes they left behind were looted. The other smaller pockets of Shi'i settlement in and around East Beirut which the militias (in their own term) "cleansed" of Shi'i presence in 1975–76 included Sabtiyeh, Za'triyeh, Batshay, and Kfarshima.

After 1976, when Jumblatt's movement was beaten back, it started to fall apart. The movement's particular mix of radical ideals—which revolved principally around nonsectarianism and pan-Arabism—fell out of fashion. The old-style Shi'i leaders tried feebly to stage a comeback in their own community. However, the causes of Shi'i radicalism still persisted, as acute as ever. And a majority of Shi'is still blamed most of their problems on the Maronite extremists behind whose guns the traditionalists continued to shelter. The breakup of Jumblatt's movement was thus followed not by the return of the conservative Shi'i ancien régime but by the growth of another form of radicalism, the Shi'i sect-consciousness of the Amal movement.

AMAL AND THE SHI'I RENAISSANCE

Amal was the brainchild of Musa al-Sadr, who was born in 1928 in the Iranian Shi'i theological center of Qom. His family had branches in Iran, Iraq, and Lebanon. Young Musa was only following a strong family tradition when he opted for a Shi'i religious education in his hometown.

In 1960, al-Sadr had succeeded to the leadership of the Shi'i community in Tyre on the recommendation of his predecessor there. From the beginning, the new young leader tried to take the group of Shi'i ulama beyond the juridical role they had traditionally played in the Lebanese Shi'i community into the leadership of a broad-based campaign against social injustice. In advocating this, he quickly aroused the ire of the established feudal families of neighboring Jabal 'Amil, who considered he was trying to loosen their total domination of community representation.

In addition to his campaign for social justice, al-Sadr also concentrated his activities on combating the central government's failure adequately to protect South Lebanon (including Jabal 'Amil) from Israeli attacks. Throughout the early 1970s he mounted a militant but nonviolent campaign around these issues, trying to weld his supporters into a modern-style mass organization as he did so. Most of his supporters were Shi'is, but from the beginning al-Sadr recognized the need to make inter-sect alliances. From 1960 onward, he worked with a radical Catholic archbishop, Grégoire Haddad, in a broad-based movement to improve the social conditions of the poor of all faiths.

In spring 1975, the armed movement al-Sadr called for came into formal existence as an outgrowth of the Movement of the Deprived. It bore the title Afwaj al-Muqawamah al-Lubnaniyah (Battalions of the Lebanese Resistance), but quickly became known by its acronym, AMAL, which means "hope." Over the years that followed, Amal developed into much more than simply a military movement. It built around itself its own broad-based political and social infrastructure. At the same time, it moved from being a movement representing all the underprivileged of Lebanon of whatever sect, narrowing its focus to the interests of the sect that had spawned it.

Musa al-Sadr himself had no institutional position within Amal. Instead, he was described simply as the organization's *murshid ruhi* (spiritual guide). This same description, exactly, was later used to describe Ayatullah Khomeini's relationship to the revolutionary Iranian state.

During the 1975–76 civil war, al-Sadr and his movement notably abstained from joining the attack on the Lebanese status quo that was led by Kamal Jumblatt. Instead, al-Sadr seemed to be generally in line with the Syrians' efforts to restore the internal balance in Lebanon—at a time when the pro-Jumblattis who were bitterly opposed to Syria still seemed strong in many Shi'i areas. By the end of 1976, much of the original fire seemed to have gone out of al-Sadr's movement, and for a while it even seemed possible that it might become just another of the many small movements that have swirled around the broader historical currents in modern Lebanon.

But Amal was uniquely placed to spearhead the Lebanese Shi'is' gathering renaissance. For it was able to utilize the full energies of the new classes of Shi'i businesspeople and professionals in a community-building effort that was free of the potentially divisive influence of imported leftist ideology. Amal had no need to import any ideologies, for the ulama tradition in which it was rooted already contained many important strands of social radicalism. These were emphasized by al-Sadr's movement at the expense of other, more conservative ideas also encompassed by ulama traditions. The teachings of the Prophet Muhammad's companion, Abu Dharr al-Ghifari, one of the Shi'i movement's earliest social radicals, became especially popular in the Lebanese Shi'i community.

It was on the basis of Amal's new, specifically Shi'i appeal that, from the late 1970s on, Shi'i doctors would move out of their successful practices in Beirut to do volunteer work in Amal's rural clinics. The owners of Shi'i banks in Beirut—a group that had not even existed there before 1977—secured loans for Amal's rehabilitation and development projects. And many of Amal's expenses were met by the Shi'i emigrants of an earlier generation. The emigrants had their own long grudges against their sect's old-style leaders, and many of them had prospered in West Africa and the Arabian (Persian) Gulf.

PAINFUL DAYS

By the early 1980s, the Lebanese Shi'i community was experiencing a whole social, political, and economic renaissance. Taken in conjunction with the sect's raw numbers, this renaissance brought the Shi'is near the point where they could challenge the Maronite ascendancy in the country. Before this challenge could be articulated, however, the Shi'is had to live through further painful days in Jabal 'Amil and in the suburbs of West Beirut.

Ever since the late 1960s, the rolling slopes of Jabal 'Amil had been a battleground between the Palestinian guerrillas who trained there for missions against Israel and the Israelis who were bent on stopping them at the source. The Shi'i villagers of the area generally supported the Palestinians' demand to be allowed to return to their former homeland. But they had been largely incidental to the harsh Israeli-Palestinian dispute. Nevertheless, they bore a heavy proportion of its casualties.

Then, in 1976, the Israelis launched a new policy toward their neighbors across the Lebanese border. The harsh retaliations of previous years were replaced briefly with a "good fence" policy, which offered services designed to "win friends and influence people." Within months, this policy had succeeded to the extent that a half-dozen of the Christian villages near the border now boasted their own Israeli-supplied militias.

When the civil war fighting around Beirut subsided at the end of 1976, the new Christian militias in the South went into action. They were commanded by the rebel Lebanese army major Saad Haddad. Throughout 1977, the Israelis helped Haddad to keep up the pressure against neighboring Shi'i villages, trying to force the villagers to end the support they still maintained for the PLO. Haddad's men shelled villages, kidnapped villagers, extorted large ransoms from them, and generally tried to terrorize the whole border area. Still, many villagers continued to aid the PLO.

Finally, in March 1978, the Israelis launched their biggest punitive raid to date. As Israeli planes swooped and bombed from overhead, some twenty-five thousand Israeli ground forces pushed in across the border to march steadily toward the Litani River. Civilian casualties from that invasion were estimated at around two thousand dead. In one hundred southern villages, a total of twenty-five hundred houses were destroyed completely, and twice that number were partially damaged.[4] The vast majority of those who suffered these losses were Shi'is.

During the 1978 invasion, hundreds of thousands of southern villagers streamed northward toward Beirut. As late as 1983, one demographic researcher was reporting that a total of 141,000 Shi'is who had originally left their Jabal 'Amil homes during that exodus were still living as refugees in and around West Beirut five years later.[5] This was despite the Lebanese government's policy of delivering relief aid only in the refugees' home villages.

The vast migration of 1978 once again radicalized those affected. But the losses of March 1978 were so huge that they started to have something of the effect intended by the Israelis. Over the years that followed, the Shi'is started cutting back on their support for the PLO. In some cases, they even started collaborating with Haddad.

The gap between the Shi'is and the PLO grew ever wider. In August 1978, Musa al-Sadr's disappearance in Libya caused the tide of Shi'i opinion to swing against the pan-Arab leftism represented by Libya's gadfly leader, Mu'ammar al-Qadhafi. The PLO leaders in Beirut were forced to choose between the Shi'is and those Lebanese who remained with the left; and finally, they chose the latter. Then, after the Iran-Iraq War started in September 1980, PLO leader Yasser Arafat refused to give the Iranians the outright backing they asked for. That further aggravated the tension between the Shi'is and the PLO. From early 1980 onward, the rivalry between the two sides erupted into frequent armed clashes in West Beirut and South Lebanon. Many, many Shi'is in these areas were fed up both with the left and with the PLO.

In June 1982, the Israelis invaded Lebanon again. As their units leapfrogged up toward Beirut, they found that many southern Shi'is seemed to welcome their arrival. The feeling was widespread among the southerners that their region had suffered for fourteen years now from the Israeli-PLO confrontation. They welcomed any development, however cataclysmic, if it promised to bring that conflict to an end.

4. Walid Khalidi, *Conflict and Violence in Lebanon: Confrontation in the Middle East* (Cambridge, Mass.: Harvard Center for International Affairs, 1979), 128.

5. Salim Nasr, "Conflit libanais et restructuration de l'espace urbain de Beyrouth," in J. Mettral, ed., *Politique urbaines au machreq et au maghreb* (Lyon, France: Presses Universitaires de Lyon, 1984[?]).

This feeling was not echoed, however, among the Shi'is of the vast suburb slums that ringed the southern fringes of Beirut. It was true that over the preceding months tension had built up in the suburbs between Amal on the one hand and the PLO and leftists on the other. Nevertheless, the slum dwellers still continued to consider that the major threat to the lives they were trying to eke out there came not from the PLO or the leftists but from the Maronite militias just across the Green Line in East Beirut. And as the Israelis advanced, it was clear that they were doing so in close coordination with these militias.

The Shi'is of the Beirut area thus joined with the PLO and the leftists in resisting any further Israeli advance. The Israelis found themselves blocked at the entrances to West Beirut; then they cut off water and other vital supplies to that part of the city. Its Shi'i residents suffered from this brutal siege as much as anybody else.

The political effects of the Israeli invasion—at the Lebanese level—did not take long to appear. In late August 1982, the parliamentary speaker (and old-style Shi'i feudal leader) Kamil al-As'ad convened a special session of the House to elect the country's next president. The sole candidate was Bashir Gemayel, youthful supreme commander of the Maronite militias. Under As'ad's urging, the session was successfully convened—in an army barracks that lay well within the area controlled by Israel. Bashir Gemayel was duly elected president of Lebanon.

U.S. officials who had supported Bashir Gemayel's candidacy considered that, once in office, he would cease the narrow pursuit of Maronite interests he had practiced up till then and seek the kind of inter-sect compromises that would make him truly president of all the Lebanese.[6] Whether he would indeed have done so must remain an unanswered question. For with nine days still to go before his inauguration, Bashir Gemayel was killed in a massive bomb blast in his headquarters in East Beirut.

The next day, the Israeli army moved into West Beirut in violation of the U.S.-brokered agreement under which the PLO had earlier left the city. Behind the shield provided by the Israelis, Gemayel's grief-crazed militiamen were brought into two Palestinian refugee camps, where for two days they committed a slaughter that later shocked the world. Some of the reporters who saw the results of that massacre estimated that upwards of one-fourth of the victims had been Lebanese citizens—members of families so poor that the only shelter they could find had been inside the refugee camps. Most of those near-pauper Lebanese had been Shi'is.

Revelation of the refugee camp killings prompted the United States

6. Sentiments expressed to me by Philip Habib in Atlanta, Georgia, November 1983.

and three other Western nations to send back the units of the Multinational Force (MNF) that had been withdrawn from Beirut only days before. It also sent a sharp *frisson* of fear throughout all the Muslims of Lebanon. In that atmosphere, many Muslims welcomed the election of Bashir's elder brother Amin Gemayel, which took place the following week. Amin had a reputation for being much more sensitive to their interests than Bashir had been. The Muslims hoped that, if they threw themselves completely on Amin's mercies, he would protect them from the extremism of the Maronite militias. This was not what President Amin Gemayel chose to do, however. Instead, he transformed the presidency into a virtual extension of his family's pro-Maronite Phalangist party, seeking to use the whole state apparatus—including the army—to further the Phalangists' aims.

Even before he formed his first government, Gemayel had ordered the remnants of the Lebanese army into action against the people of West Beirut. Army roadblocks fanned out throughout West Beirut, sweeping many young Muslims off to crowded detention centers for questioning. Several hundred of those thus detained—against whom no charges had ever been preferred—simply "disappeared" while in custody. A high proportion of the "disappeared" were Shi'is.

Other army roadblocks meanwhile set about demolishing slum housing, which had been built in contravention of planning regulations in the Shi'i suburb of Ouzai. In mid-October 1982, five thousand Ouzai residents staged a demonstration against the demolitions. They complained that no analogous measures were being taken against gross violations of the law in Christian East Beirut.

AFTER ISRAEL'S 1982 INVASION

In the months following the 1982 invasion, Lebanon's three major Shi'i communities found themselves living under very different conditions. The Shi'is of the Beirut suburbs were chafing under the measures Gemayel was taking to "pacify" and disarm them. The Shi'is of the Bekaa were living under continued Syrian occupation. And the Shi'is of Jabal 'Amil were still living under the Israelis.

The welcome many southern Shi'is had accorded the Israelis when they first arrived did not last long. The tide of opinion in Jabal 'Amil rapidly swung against the new occupiers. The Israelis found that guerrilla attacks against their troops increased as their stay wore on. And their assailants were generally not members of the cowed Palestinian refugee community, but rather local Shi'is. Moreover, the more vigorous the Israelis were in trying to punish the Shi'is, the stauncher became the Shi'is' opposition. The trend of opinion among the Lebanese of the South was summed up by the mayor of Sidon, who said of the Israelis: "They invaded us to hunt Palestinians and have stayed to occupy our land."[7]

Riding the wave of increased anti-Israeli feelings among southern Shi'is was Amal. Amal's national leadership had never altered the movement's official view of Israel, which Musa al-Sadr had described in the seventies as "the very embodiment of evil." So from Beirut and from the Syrian-occupied Bekaa, Amal now did what it could to strengthen Shi'i resistance to the Israelis in Jabal 'Amil. The Syrians, whose lines almost abutted the Israelis' in the southern Bekaa, were only too happy to help in this endeavor.

The Syrians were also happy to support the movement that was growing inside Beirut itself in opposition to the pro-Maronite partisanship of Gemayel's rule. Ever since Gemayel had come into office, the Lebanese army had taken draconian measures against West Beirutis who were suspected of involvement with the leftist or Muslim militias. But Gemayel's army had been unable to prevent the re-formation of these militias, especially in the densely packed southern suburbs.

In July 1983, the re-forming Amal units in Beirut engaged in their first open confrontation with the army. This clash took place in an area peopled by Shi'i refugees near the Green Line, which divided the city. The army command was trying to clear refugee families out of a local school. But the families refused to budge, arguing that they had literally no other place to go. The army then tried to clear them out by force. But Amal militiamen opened fire, and the clash that resulted lasted throughout the next two days. During that clash, a number of the individual soldiers who were ordered to take part reportedly deserted to Amal. This was significant, for although the highest levels of the army command were now dominated by pro-Phalangist Maronites, the rank and file had been boosted by a general conscription in the Greater Beirut region. Sixty percent of the products of this conscription were Shi'is.

At the end of August, the army again confronted Amal in West Beirut—this time in much larger battles. The army's next major chore, however, was not in Beirut but in the mountainous Shouf region to the southeast. The Israelis, for their own reasons, were preparing to leave the

---

7. Augustus R. Norton, "Making Enemies in South Lebanon: Harakat Amal, the IDF, and South Lebanon," *Middle East Insight* (Washington, D.C.) 3, no. 3 (January-February 1984): 19.

Shouf, and Gemayel wanted to prevent it falling into the hands of the Druze militia. In early September 1983, before Gemayel could reach any agreement with the Druze, the Israelis did pull out of the Shouf. As they left, full-scale battles erupted there, in which the Druze rapidly gained ground at the expense of the army and the Phalangists.

The Shouf fighting soon overflowed into the capital. On September 23, Amal units started attacking the army's positions throughout most of West Beirut. The army, assailed from the front and the rear, was on the point of collapse. But that same day the Americans moved up the refurbished battleship *New Jersey* to join the considerable flotilla off the Lebanese coast. All the parties, including the Syrians, now agreed to a cease-fire, which was supposed to lead to political talks aimed at national reconciliation. But Gemayel delayed on convening the talks, and his American backers did not seem to be hurrying him.

Meanwhile, the pressures were mounting on those in the Amal leadership who had agreed to the cease-fire. After Musa al-Sadr had disappeared, back in 1978, the leadership of Amal had passed ("until al-Sadr should return") to a lawyer from a prominent Bekaa family, called Husain al-Husaini. Then, in 1980, al-Husaini was replaced in new elections by Nabih Berri, a much younger lawyer from a second-echelon family in the Jabal 'Amil village of Tibnin. Berri, whose major credentials were his years in a mainstream organizing cadre of Amal, had long been subject to some criticism from more conservative sectors of the community. These critics included, of course, the old-style feudal leaders who had always been opposed to Amal's activities; but they also came to include al-Husaini and the religious scholar Shaikh Muhammad Mahdi Shams al-Din, who had taken over al-Sadr's former position at the head of the HSIC.

After the 1982 Israeli invasion, however, the Lebanese Shi'i community was subject to a new wave of radicalization, which came to produce another threat—far more serious than that posed by the conservatives—to Berri's position. In the summer of 1982, a member of Amal's Command Council, a schoolteacher from the Bekaa called Husain Musawi, split away from the movement to form his own group, which he called Islamic Amal. Musawi's supporters were limited in number, but he gained additional importance in his home region from the presence there of some hundreds of Iranian Revolutionary Guards, who generally appeared to back him.

Not long after Musawi's schism, another group emerged in the West Beirut suburbs, which brought the radical threat to Berri nearer his Beirut base of operations. This was the Hizbullah group, headed by the charismatic religious scholar Shaikh Muhammad Husain Fadl Allah. This group, like Musawi's, had strongly criticized Berri's agreement to the September 1983 cease-fire.

Then on October 23, a terrorist drove a truck laden with explosives into the U.S. Marines' main compound near Beirut airport, killing 241 Marines; another 57 French soldiers died in a simultaneous explosion in a French MNF barracks. A shadowy front organization calling itself Islamic Jihad claimed responsibility for those bombings. The existence of any formal group of this name seemed unlikely, however, and it was generally believed in Lebanon that the suicide bomber and his accomplices had been linked to either Musawi's or Fadl Allah's group.

After the bombing, the Americans quickly nudged Gemayel into convening the promised political talks. But at the same time, they insisted that he could not discuss the abrogation of the Israeli-Lebanese agreement of the previous May, which they had brokered. Abrogation was a major demand of all the opposition parties, and so the talks, briefly convened in Geneva in October, almost immediately stalled.

At the beginning of February 1984, a new clash erupted between Amal and the Lebanese army in Beirut. This time, the army started firing its tank guns directly into some of the heavily peopled Shi'i neighborhoods along the Green Line. On February 4, Amal leader Nabih Berri asked the Muslim troops in the army not to take part in the shelling of civilian areas. Berri was still *not* calling on the Muslim troops in the army to desert. However, in the tension of the hours that followed his appeal, a majority of Shi'i soldiers did just that. Their flight from the army was so massive that by the morning of February 6, the army's authority had collapsed completely throughout West Beirut.

Amin Gemayel was faced with the imminent collapse of his regime, and the Americans, with the possibility of their Marines being caught in the midst of a major new Lebanese maelstrom. Within hours, the U.S. president had announced his intention to withdraw the Marines, and Amin Gemayel, in an abrupt about-face, went to Damascus to ask the Syrians to help save his regime. The Syrians helped negotiate the formation of a new Lebanese government. Presidential power still rested with Amin Gemayel, a Maronite, and the premier still came from the Sunni community. But one of the new government's most powerful members was the Amal leader, Nabih Berri, who was being asked to help Gemayel govern the country.

With the question of Shi'i political representation in Beirut thus at least partially resolved, the community's attention turned to the South.

(Berri himself underscored this development by insisting that his ministerial portfolio include responsibility for southern affairs.) From April 1984 on, Shi'i resistance to the Israeli presence in South Lebanon mounted dramatically, increasing the Israelis' casualties there.

The Israelis had been hoping to rely on their local allies in Haddad's militia, now renamed the South Lebanon Army (SLA), to continue to police the area after their occupation. But the SLA was never able to shed its image as a Maronite-dominated body, so the majority of the southern Shi'is continued to oppose it. The rise in the casualty toll throughout 1984 forced the Israelis to withdraw from most of South Lebanon even without leaving the SLA to cover their withdrawal. By June 1985, the Israelis had pulled out of all but the narrow border strip they and their allies had controlled since 1978.

The liberation of most of South Lebanon greatly increased Shi'i power throughout the country. In West Beirut, Amal turned on its erstwhile allies in the Lebanese Sunni community and in the Palestinian refugee camps, trying to suppress any independent forces these groups might hope to maintain.

In June 1985, Amal leader Berri achieved brief international prominence during the negotiations to free American hostages hijacked by Shi'i hardliners. The following month, he participated in Syrian-sponsored talks, which resulted in new proposals for constitutional reforms. But whether these proposals would get any further than the now defunct reform plan the Syrians had presented nine years previously remained to be seen.

CONCLUSIONS

Despite the high hopes expressed by secularists in the early 1970s, sectarian divisions in Lebanon have strengthened over recent years. In the mid-1980s, the country now looks as if it is in the midst of a historic shift in the balance among its sects. The preeminence within Lebanon's unique intersectarian system may be passing from the Maronites to the Shi'is. The Shi'i community is not simply the largest single religious group presently in the country. It is also one of the most vigorous, having experienced a considerable internal renaissance since it was brought into the system in 1920.

The Maronite community, by contrast, has been losing much of its relative strength over recent decades. It has lost the numerical predominance it once enjoyed and even longer claimed. (Indeed, one result of the actions of the Maronite militias over recent years has been sharply to increase the rate of Maronite emigration.) Meanwhile, the Maronites have also lost much of the relative advantage they previously retained over other Lebanese communities in terms of social and economic development. For the other groups, including the Shi'is, are no longer very far behind the Maronites in these respects.

Few human groups, however, ever give up power gracefully to their successors. The history of Lebanon itself well illustrates this, for around 150 years ago, the country saw an earlier shift, very similar to the present one. In it, the prime place within the inter-sect system passed from the Druzes to the Maronites. That earlier process took about thirty-six years to be completed, from the first disruptions of 1825 down to the institution of the Maronite-dominated *mutasarrifiyah* in 1861. There is no particular reason to think that the present shift from the Maronites to the Shi'is could be completed in a shorter time—and it really started only in 1975.

But it is to be hoped that at some stage, the Maronite community can come to terms with the changing realities of power in Lebanon. They cannot reverse long-term demographic trends nor turn the socioeconomic clock backward. And after the various debacles of 1975 to 1984, they surely can no longer hope that any outside power will be able to solve their problems for them.

Where might Shi'i preeminence within Lebanon be expected to lead the country? It is, of course, far too early to tell yet; but some key pointers about the Shi'is' interests have already emerged. The first is the stress most Shi'i politicians put on Lebanese national unity. The Shi'i community in Lebanon is far less compact than either the Druze or the Maronites. There are three distinct areas of Shi'i settlement, and Shi'i politicians fully realize that, if their sect's numbers are to be used to full advantage, these areas cannot be split from one another.

The Jabal 'Amilis have shown they do not want to be ruled forever by Israel. The independent-minded Shi'i clanspeople of the Bekaa would meanwhile certainly not be happy under a highly centralized regime such as that in Damascus.

Politicians within other, more geographically compact sects, have at times considered the possibility of decentralization as a solution to Lebanon's problems. But Shi'i politicians have consistently opted to strengthen the role of the Lebanese central government. In their continuing advocacy of this type of policy, the present generation of Shi'i leaders in Amal is only echoing a concern felt by earlier generations of their sect's leaders.

Do the Shi'is seek an Iranian-style Islamic takeover of the whole Lebanese system? The answer, with reference to the present leadership of Amal, must surely be—on the basis both of pronouncements and of actions—that they do not. In November 1983, for example, Nabih Berri was telling an American journalist that he wanted "a new Lebanon where every Lebanese has the same rights and the same obligations—no difference between Christian and Muslim."[8] And after Amal had swept to power in West Beirut in February 1984, Berri made a point of reopening some of the bars that had been closed by Shi'i militants.

The renaissance that the Lebanese Shi'i community has experienced in recent years, however, gained a great part of its momentum from sources that were specifically radical, cultural, and religious in content. The radicalization of the Shi'i community stemmed from the fact that the urbanization process it underwent from the early 1960s on was very rapid. It was also, from 1968 onward, accompanied by forced uprootings and evictions on a truly massive scale. The cultural and religious aspects of the Shi'i renaissance stemmed, in part, from a rejection of the Western-style social values that were imported wholesale into Lebanon during the later decades of Maronite domination. By the early 1980s, the *dernière mode parisienne* of the Maronite teenager was met not with emulation by her Shi'i counterpart but by the latter's return to the traditional Islamic clothing.

All these aspects of the Lebanese Shi'is' renaissance were stimulated by the victory of political Shi'ism in Iran. This is not to say that the Lebanese Shi'is follow blindly wherever the Iranians lead them. Indeed, the few hundred Iranian Revolutionary Guards who stayed in Baalbek from 1982 onward often felt the weight of their local cobelievers' hostility. But the Shi'i ulama of Jabal 'Amil have always maintained close links with their counterparts in Iran. So developments in Iran will continue to have some resonance inside the Lebanese Shi'i community.

According to some Shi'i sources, there has been a continuing debate inside the ruling revolutionary circles in Iran over whether the establishment of an Islamic republic in Lebanon is or is not an attainable objective. That debate has been echoed inside the Lebanese Shi'i community, where advocates of an Islamic republic gained supporters during the turmoil of 1982–85. But they were still, in the middle of 1985, a minority in the community.

The presence of these hard-liners, however few, forms a constant

8. Lally Weymouth, "What the Shias Want in Bloody Lebanon," *Los Angeles Times,* November 13, 1983, pt. 4, p. 2.

source of potential pressure on Nabih Berri and his colleagues in the leadership of Amal, and it increases the urgency with which they seek a just political settlement in Lebanon. For in a situation of continuing civil disorder, Shi'i families can be expected to come under further pressures of forced uprootings, bereavements, or other troubles, which would increase the radicalization of the community.

Developments far away on the Iranians' battlefront with Iraq can also be expected to have continuing repercussions inside Lebanon. A clear Iranian victory over Iraq would almost certainly raise Shi'i political expectations in Lebanon as well.

By mid-1985, the Shi'is stood on the threshold of a new era of power, and also of responsibility, within Lebanon's intersectarian system. There was still no guarantee that the problems of political transition in the country were over. But from the beginning of 1984 onward, the Shi'is had demonstrated that they had enough power to play the strongest role inside the system and also that, in Amal, they had a leadership that knew how to use that power. Throughout Amal's decade in existence, its leaders had shown themselves to be deft players in the game of inter-sect alliances inside Lebanon. They also showed that they knew how to use alliances with non-Lebanese parties, when necessary, without totally abandoning their movement's independence.

With the Shi'i community's rise toward preeminence, however, the risks at stake for the Amal leadership have also risen dramatically. For until that leadership can realize a good proportion of the community's general political objectives, it will continue to come under pressure from the very forces that fueled its meteoric rise.

AUGUSTUS RICHARD NORTON

Chapter Six   Shi'ism and Social Protest
in Lebanon

Few of the standard works on politics in Lebanon have made more than
a passing reference to the country's Shi'i community. Indeed, for many
authors, the Shi'is were no more than a curious artifact of the early succession
struggles in Islam. Impoverished, underdeveloped socially, and
underrepresented politically, Lebanon's Shi'is hardly seemed to merit serious
attention. A mid-nineteenth-century traveler, David Urquhart, described
the Shi'is as a listless, subservient people reveling in squalor, a
description that many found apt even a century later.

> They are all in rags, except some of the Sheiks, and are all mendicants.
> They will come and stand round the cooking which goes on in
> the open air, and if one is asked to go and get some eggs, he will
> shrug his shoulders, and when told he will be paid for his trouble, he
> answers, "there is none." If another is asked to sell a sheep or a fowl,
> he answers, "it is not mine." The filth is revolting. It would seem as
> if they took a particular pride in exhibiting their rebellion against the
> law, originally proclaimed from Horeb and afterwards from Mecca,
> both in regard to their persons and the cleanliness of their villages.[1]

The views expressed in this chapter are those of the author and do not express the
position of any institution or branch of the U.S. government.

1. David Urquhart, *The Lebanon: (Mount Souria) A History and Diary,* 2 vols. (London:
Thomas Cautley Newby, 1860), 233.

156

Even as recently as the late 1950s and early 1960s, the Shi'is seemed most notable for their invisibility and irrelevance in Lebanese politics. Yet in the space of a quarter of a century these same people have made a remarkable political transformation. For so long only a minor factor in Lebanese politics, the Shi'is are now playing a major role in shaping the future of this strife-torn state. In this chapter we consider the recent political history of this long-ignored community, in particular emphasizing the key role played by a distinctively Shi'i movement (Amal) in mobilizing a long quiescent and politically mute community.

BACKGROUND

When Lebanon won its independence from France in 1943, the Shi'is were recognized—on the basis of a 1932 census—as the third largest communal group in the fledgling republic. The National Pact (al-Mithaq al-Watani) of 1943, essentially an unwritten compact between the two largest and politically dominant sects at the time—the Maronite Christians and the Sunni Muslims—accorded the Shi'i community the third most important political office in the land, the speaker of the Chamber of Deputies. However, this allocation of office was less a recognition of the community's size than an acknowledgment of the power of the traditional political bosses (or *zu'ama'*) who dominated their respective slices of the community. For the most part, the community—or more aptly, fragments of it—languished under the domination of a relatively small number of zu'ama', whose political power stemmed from land wealth and the political ineffectualness of their clientele.

Urban and town-based merchant families such as the Usayrans of Sidon, the al-Khalils of Tyre, and the al-Zayns of Nabatiya gained their influence in the late nineteenth century when they acquired landed property or became tax agents (*multazims*) on behalf of the Ottoman rulers of the Levant. Other families, especially the al-As'ads of al-Tayibi or the Hamadas of Baalbek, represented historically powerful clans or tribes (*'asha'ir*) who buttressed their traditional role by also becoming multazims. After independence these political bosses dominated communal politics, winning parliamentary seats and cabinet ministries again and again. As Albert Hourani aptly noted more than forty years ago, the first need of the Shi'is was a reformed social organization and improved economic conditions, an observation well justified by their subservience to the zu'ama'.[2]

---

2. Albert H. Hourani, *Syria and Lebanon: A Political Essay* (London: Oxford University Press, 1946), 135.

The zu'ama' dispensed favors much in the style of Chicago ward bosses, but perhaps with more asperity. Fouad Ajami recalls a vignette from his childhood in South Lebanon, in which a peasant slaughtered one of his own sheep for Ahmad Bey (literally Lord Ahmad; Ahmad al-As'ad, father of Kamil, the long-time speaker of Parliament), and returned to his village extolling the generosity of the bey who had given him a small hunk of the meat.[3] Survival in such a system meant being a *zilm* (follower of a *za'im*), voting the prescribed electoral slate, defending the za'im's interests and property, and affecting the proper respect for the patron. Even when they moved from their villages to the Beirut slums, the peasants' links with their respective za'ims remained strong. These links were reinforced by Lebanon's electoral laws, which make it nearly impossible to change from one electoral constituency to another, thus spawning the phenomenon of the election bus dispatched by a za'im to retrieve his followers and their votes at election time. Moreover, those Shi'is who relocated to the environs of Beirut found that the Sunni political bosses of the capital were usually unwilling to integrate them into their patronage networks.[4] Since the Shi'i zu'ama' had neither the political reach nor the incentive to assist their clients in breaking their political ties, the migrant had little choice but to maintain fealty to his za'im. So for most Shi'is significant political and social ties were limited not just to their region but to their village.

Although accurate socioeconomic data are not readily available, it is clear that by any reasonable measure the Shi'is fared poorly whether their status might be measured relative to other Lebanese sects or in absolute terms. They earned less, had a lower standard of literacy, lived in the poorest regions (the Jabal 'Amil region of South Lebanon, the northern Bekaa Valley, and the Beirut suburbs), toiled more often than not as unskilled wage earners or farmers, and paid most dearly in blood for the enduring violence that has plagued Lebanon for more than a decade. Well into the 1960s, the Shi'is were underrepresented in bureaucratic appointments and the officer corps, as well as in business and commerce. For instance, in 1962 only two of seventy senior civil service positions were held by Shi'is. Even in 1984, only one in twelve Lebanese embassies were headed by Shi'i diplomats.[5]

3. From a private interview, January 1984.

4. For a very useful analysis, see Michael Johnson, "Popular Movements and Primordial Loyalties in Beirut," in Talal Asad and Roger Owen, eds., *Sociology of "Developing Societies": The Middle East* (New York: Monthly Review Press, 1983), 178–94.

5. For a fuller discussion and analysis of the socioeconomic status of the Shi'is, see Augustus R. Norton, "Harakat Amal," in Myron Aronoff, ed., *Religion and Politics,* vol. 3, *Political Anthropology* (New Brunswick, N.J.: Transaction Books, 1984), 105–31.

Although there has not been a census since 1932, most authoritative estimates agree that the Shi'i community today constitutes the largest single sect in Lebanon.[6] This population growth reflects the larger mean size of the Shi'i family, as well as the Shi'is' propensity to return to Lebanon after working abroad (typically in West Africa or the Gulf) rather than emigrating permanently. Of the three million Lebanese living in Lebanon, between 30 and 35 percent are probably Shi'is. The potential impact of changing demographics is well illustrated by a simple consideration of the allocation of parliamentary seats to the Shi'is and the Maronites. The present ninety-nine-seat parliament (elected in 1972) includes nineteen Shi'i seats and thirty Maronite seats. Yet if the seats were allocated according to the realities of changed demographics, the Shi'is might gain as many as ten seats while the Maronites would lose an equal number. Moreover, if parliamentary representation were to be split evenly between the Muslims and the Christians—a reform that has been on the agenda since 1976—the Shi'is would have a claim on the lion's share of the Muslim seats, much to the detriment of the previously dominant Sunnis, who now comprise only about 20 percent of Lebanon's population, and the Druze, who account for less than 10 percent. But numbers are no more a guarantee of political success than impoverishment, although both factors help to clarify the demands, if not the newfound assertiveness, of the Shi'is.

FINDING A POLITICAL VOICE

Although they still lagged far behind their countrymen by all the standard measures of socioeconomic status, the Shi'is were not insulated from the processes of modernization that affected Lebanon as a whole. The bonds of their social isolation began to be broken by the instrusions of the media, agricultural mechanization, and improved transportation. Their schools were still inferior in quality to those of their non-Shi'i cohorts, yet education, especially at the primary level, became far more readily accessible. In short, the Shi'i community was, by the 1960s, caught in the throes of socioeconomic change, change that would undermine the traditional po-

6. Useful population estimates and demographic analyses may be found in Joseph Chamie, "The Lebanese Civil War: An Investigation into the Causes," *World Affairs* 139 (Winter 1976–77): 171–88; Idem, *Religion and Fertility: Arab Christian-Muslim Differentials* (Cambridge: Cambridge University Press, 1981); and Riad B. Labbarah, "Background to the Lebanese Conflict," *International Journal of Comparative Sociology* 20, nos. 1–2 (1979): 101–21.

litical system and make ever larger numbers of Shi'is available for political action.[7]

Not unexpectedly, the effects of such change were first felt at the leadership level. As Michael Hudson noted in his seminal 1968 book, *The Precarious Republic,* one of the most interesting developments of the post– World War II period was the gradual modernization of the Shi'i political leadership.[8] The Shi'is were beginning a political awakening, which, while largely unnoticed, would play an important role in shaping the destiny of Lebanon in the 1970s and 1980s. Nonetheless, there was nothing deterministic about the direction that the awakening would follow. Given the absence of a movement or party with communitywide appeal, it is hardly surprising that the newly politicized Shi'is lent their numbers to a wide variety of political organizations. Long under the heavy thumbs of the zu'ama', who controlled land, wealth, and access to the political system, the Shi'is were appealed to by party slogans pledging equality, improvement in social and health services, and better conditions of employment and housing. Thus, quite a large number of Shi'is joined the Lebanese Communist party and other antiestablishment organizations, such as the Organization of Communist Action (Munazzamat al-'Amal al-Shuyu'i).

Many Shi'is, impressed by the similarities between their plight and that of the Palestinian refugees, joined various *fida'i* organizations, as well as parties that were closely affiliated with the Palestinian resistance. Thus, sizable numbers of Shi'is joined the Arab Liberation Front and the Popular Front for the Liberation of Palestine, as well as the Arab Nationalist Movement and the branches of the Baath party. But it should be noted that not all members were motivated by political principles; many joined simply to win a salary. No single party was overwhelmingly successful in the recruitment of Shi'i members, and in point of fact, it is the relatively broad ideological spectrum covered by the organizations that seems noteworthy in retrospect.

The secular antiestablishment parties did not have the field to themselves. Juxtaposed to the secular parties and the fida'i groups was a distinctively Shi'i movement led by a Shi'i cleric, Sayyid Musa al-Sadr (who came to be known to his followers as Imam Musa). This movement, known today as Amal, was only in its incipient stage in the early 1960s, yet it has, in large measure, come to dominate Shi'i politics in present-

7. See Augustus R. Norton, "Lebanon's Old Politics Must Yield to the New," *New York Times,* January 3, 1984.

8. Michael C. Hudson, *The Precarious Republic: Political Modernization in Lebanon* (New York: Random House, 1968), 31–32.

day Lebanon. Through a combination of good fortune and astute leadership it has submerged many of its competitors. While the founder of
Amal has not been heard from since he disappeared during a 1978 visit
to Libya, al-Sadr's formative influence is irrefutable. For that reason it is
important to consider the career of this "giant" (as he is often characterized by his followers).

Imam Musa and the Mobilization of the Shi'is

Musa al-Sadr was born in Qom, Iran, in 1928, the son of an important
religious leader, Ayatullah Sadr al-Din Sadr. He attended secondary and
primary school in Qom and college in Tehran. He did not intend to study
religion, but instead hoped to follow a secular career. It was only upon
the urging of his father, who believed that Reza Shah was destroying Iran's
religious institutions, that he discarded his secular ambitions and pursued
an education in Islamic jurisprudence (*fiqh*). Initially he studied in a Qom
madrasah (religious school), and while still in Qom he edited a magazine,
Makatib-i Islami (Islamic Schools), which is still published in Iran. One
year after his father's death in 1953 he moved to Najaf, Iraq, where he
studied fiqh under the Marja' al-Kabir Muhsin al-Hakim.

He first visited Lebanon, which he claimed as his ancestral home, in
1957. During this visit he made a very strong and positive impression on
his coreligionists in Lebanon. Following the death of the Shi'i religious
leader of the southern coastal city of Tyre, al-Sayyid 'Abd al-Husain
Sharaf al-Din, he was invited by the Shi'i community of South Lebanon
to replace Sharaf al-Din. In 1960, he moved to Tyre, with the active
support of his teacher and mentor, Muhsin al-Hakim. One of his first
significant acts was the establishment of a vocational institute in the southern town of Burj al-Shimali, which was constructed at a cost of half a
million Lebanese pounds (about $165,000) with monies provided by Shi'i
benefactors, the Ministry of Education, and bank loans. The institute
would become an important symbol of his leadership; it is still in operation
providing vocational training for about five hundred orphans.

A physically imposing man of intelligence, courage, personal charm,
and enormous energy—one of his former assistants claims that he frequently worked twenty hours a day—al-Sadr attracted a wide array of
supporters, ranging from Shi'i merchants making their fortunes in West
Africa to petty bourgeois youth. Imam Musa set out to establish himself
as the paramount leader of the Shi'i community, and his timing could not
have been more auspicious. He did not single-handedly launch the com-

munity's political consciousness, but he capitalized on the budding politicization of the Shi'i community, invigorating and rationalizing it.[9] At the time of his arrival there were a number of signs of incipient political organization, including a remarkable expansion in family associations, small political discussion groups, and other social organizations that often carried political import.[10]

Imam Musa helped to fill a yawning leadership vacuum that resulted from the increasing inability of the traditional political bosses to meet the cascading needs of their clients. From the 1960s on, the Shi'is had experienced rapid social change and economic disruption, and the old village-based clientelist system was proving to be ever more an anachronism.[11] Unlike the zu'ama', Musa al-Sadr was able to stand above a fragmented and victimized community and see it as a whole. For a man of Iran, Lebanon is a country of modest size indeed. While the Lebanese might speak of "distant" Lebanese towns as if they were foreign countries, al-Sadr was unimpressed by the minuscule distances that separated the South from the Bekaa Valley and Beirut. Despite the sometimes palpable sociological differences between the slum dweller of Beirut, the peasant of the South, and the clansmen of the Bekaa, he succeeded in giving many Shi'is an inclusive communal identity.[12] Furthermore, he reminded his followers their deprivation was not to be fatalistically accepted, for so long as they could speak out through their religion they could overcome their condition. As he once observed, "Whenever the poor involve themselves in a social revolution it is a confirmation that injustice is not predestined."[13]

He arrived in Lebanon as a Persian, but he was soon accepted—legally and emotively—as a Lebanese. (President Shihab bestowed Lebanese citizenship on him in 1963.) In fact, Karim Pakradouni notes that upon arrival he "murdered the Arabic language," but by 1975, although he still retained a Persian accent, he spoke the Arabic language with an

9. The incipient political organization was verified by a senior associate of Musa al-Sadr in a private interview, February 1984.

10. A useful discussion of family associations and their role in the political and socio-economic development of Lebanese communal groups may be found in Samir Khalaf, "Adaptive Modernization: The Case for Lebanon," in C. A. Cooper and S. S. Alexander, eds., *Economic Development and Population Growth in the Middle East* (New York: American Elsevier Press, 1972), 567–98.

11. For a detailed discussion, see Augustus R. Norton, "Harakat Amal and the Political Mobilization of the Shi'a of Lebanon" (Ph.D. diss., University of Chicago, 1984), chap. 2.

12. This observation is borrowed from Fouad Ajami, who made it in a private interview, April 1984.

13. Quoted in *al-Sadr!?* (Beirut: Dar al-Khalud, 1979), 27.

elegance that matched his personal grooming and demeanor.[14] He well understood the affective potential of religion and its symbols, which he exploited effectively. He shrewdly recognized that his power lay in part in his role as a custodian of symbols. But above all else he was a pragmatist, as the record of his political alliances shows. It is both a tribute to his political skill and a commentary on his tactics that one well-informed Lebanese should have commented that nobody knew where the Imam stood. At one point, for instance, he backed al-Fatah against al-Sai'qah (the guerrilla organization created by his Syrian ally), leading one Syrian official to note: "We suddenly realized that our friend and ally, Imam Musa, was a check that bounced."[15]

His followers today often characterize him as a vociferous critic of the shah, but it was only after the October war of 1973 that his relations with the shah deteriorated seriously. From the fall of 1973 he became a vehement critic of the shah, accusing him of suppressing religion in Iran, denouncing him for his pro-Israel stance, and describing him as an "imperialist stooge." However, for more than a decade he had maintained close, even cordial ties with the Pahlavi regime, and during his visits to Tehran in the 1960s and early 1970s he was warmly received. Shahpur Bakhtiyar goes so far as to claim that al-Sadr was originally dispatched to Lebanon by the shah in furtherance of a scheme to create a pan-Shi'i union encompassing Iran, Iraq, and Lebanon.[16] There is no convincing evidence to support this assertion, but there seems little doubt that the shah did provide significant funding to support Imam Musa's efforts in Lebanon (some believe that the source of their falling-out was monetary rather than moral or political). Whatever the source or sources of the failing relationship, it is patent that Imam Musa was not averse to hedging his bets. Thus, as his relations with Iran deteriorated after 1973, he improved his relations with Iraq from which he may have received significant funding in early 1974.

Like the Maronites, the Shi'is are a minority in a predominantly Sunni Arab world, and for both sects Lebanon is a refuge in which sectarian identity and security can be preserved. It is not surprising that many Maronites saw a natural ally in Imam Musa.[17] Imam Musa was a reformer,

14. Karim Pakradouni, *La Paix manquée* (Beirut: Editions FMA, 1983), 105–07, quotation at 106.

15. Quoted in Raphael Calis, "The Shiite Pimpernel," *Middle East*, November 1978, 52–54, quotation at 54.

16. Shahpur Bakhtiar, excerpts from his book, *Ma Fidelité*, *al-Watan al-Arabi*, October 8–14, 1982, 54–56.

17. For example, Juan Cole recalls that in 1974, while he worked in Beirut, many Beirutis were speaking in admiring terms about al-Sadr's recent address to the congregation of a Maronite church (private communication, September 1984).

not a revolutionary. He sought the betterment of the Shi'is in a Lebanese context. He often noted, "For us Lebanon is one definitive homeland." Despite his appreciation of the dramatic demographic shifts that had made the Shi'i community the largest single one in Lebanon, he declined to call for a new census. Indeed, Musa al-Sadr recognized the insecurity of the Maronites, and he acknowledged their need to maintain their monopoly hold on the presidency. Yet he was critical of the Maronites for their arrogant stance toward the Muslims, and particularly the Shi'is. He argued that the Maronite-dominated government had neglected the south since independence and had made the Shi'is a disinherited subproletariat in Lebanon.

Imam Musa was anticommunist, one suspects, not only on principled grounds but on the grounds that various communist organizations were among his prime competitors for Shi'i recruits. While the two branches of the Baath party (pro-Iraqi and pro-Syrian) were making significant inroads among the Shi'is of the South and the Beirut suburbs, he appropriated their pan-Arab slogans. Although the movement he founded, Harakat al-Mahrumin (or the Movement of the Deprived), was aligned with the Lebanese National Movement (LNM) in the early stages of the Lebanese civil war, he found its Druze leader, Kamal Jumblatt, irresponsible and exploitative of the Shi'is. As he put it to Pakradouni, the LNM was willing "to combat the Christians to the last Shi'i." He imputed to Jumblatt the prolongation of the war: "Without him the war in Lebanon would have been terminated in two months. Because of him, it has been prolonged two years and only God knows how long the encore will last."[18] Thus, it was hardly inconsistent with his political stance that he should have deserted the LNM in May 1976, when Syria intervened in Lebanon on the side of the Maronite militias and against the LNM and its fida'i allies. He was a friend and confidant of Syrian president Hafez al-As'ad, yet he mistrusted Syrian motives in Lebanon. It was, in Imam Musa's view, only the indigestibility of Lebanon that protected it from being cut up by Syria. Nonetheless, the Syrians were an essential card in his very serious game with the Palestinian resistance.

He claimed to support the Palestine resistance movement, but his relations with the PLO were tense and uneasy at best. During the 1973 clashes between the fida'iyun and the Lebanese army, Imam Musa reproached the Sunni Muslims for their chorus of support for the guerrillas. On the one hand he chastised the government for failing to defend the

18. Quoted in Pakradouni, *La Paix manquée,* 106.

South from Israeli aggression, but on the other he criticized the PLO for shelling Israel from the South and hence provoking Israeli retaliation. He consistently expressed sympathy for Palestinian aspirations, but he was unwilling to countenance actions that exposed Lebanese citizens, and especially Shi'i citizens of the South, to additional suffering. Given the chronic weakness of the Lebanese army and its relative inferiority in arms and numbers to the Israel Defense Forces (IDF), it was natural that Musa al-Sadr would demand restraint from the PLO.[19]

After the 1970 PLO defeat in Jordan, the bulk of the PLO fighters relocated to South Lebanon where they proceeded to supplant the legitimate authorities. Imam Musa prophetically warned the PLO that it was not in its interests to establish a state within a state in Lebanon. It was the organization's failure to heed this warning that helped spawn the alienation of their "natural allies"—the Shi'is—who actively resisted the fida'iyun in their midst only a few years later. "The PLO is a factor of anarchy in the South. The Shi'is are conquering their inferiority complex with respect to the Palestinian organizations. We have had enough!"[20] In private he challenged the revolutionary bona fides of the Palestinians. He argued that they lacked a sense of martyrdom and that above all else the PLO was a military machine that terrorized the Arab world, extorting money and support, and the sympathy of world opinion. For their part, some PLO officials believed that Musa al-Sadr was a creation of the Deux-ième Bureau (the Army Second—or intelligence—Bureau).[21]

But his unremitting opponent was Kamil al-As'ad, the powerful za'im from the South, who quite accurately viewed the Imam as a serious threat to his political power base. In 1967 the Chamber of Deputies (or Parliament) passed a law establishing a Supreme Shi'i Council, which would for the first time provide a representative body for the Shi'is independent of the Sunni Muslims. The council actually came into existence in 1969, with Imam Musa as its chairman for a six-year term—a stunning confirmation of his status as the leading Shi'i cleric in the country and certainly one of the most important political figures in the Shi'i community. The council quickly made itself heard with demands in the military, social, economic, and political realms, including improved measures for

19. For representative comments by Musa al-Sadr about the fida'i presence in Lebanon, see *al-Musawwar,* May 27, 1977, 22–24; *al-Hawadith,* December 24, 1976, 15–17; and *al-Dustur,* June 26–July 2, 1978, 9–11.

20. Quoted in Pakradouni, *La Paix manquée,* 106.

21. Based on private interviews by the author with al-Fatah officials in South Lebanon, 1980–81.

the defense of the South, the provision of development funds, construction and improvement of schools and hospitals, and an increase in the number of Shi'is appointed to senior government positions.

One year after the formation of the Supreme Shi'i Council, Imam Musa organized a general strike "to dramatize to the government the plight of the population of southern Lebanon vis-à-vis the Israeli military threat."[22] Shortly thereafter, the government created the Council of the South (Majlis al-Janub) which was capitalized at thirty million Lebanese pounds and was chartered to support the development of the region. Unfortunately, the Majlis al-Janub quickly became more famous for being a locus of corruption than for being the origin of beneficial projects.[23] The creation of the council was a victory for al-Sadr, but it was the formidable Kamil al-As'ad who dominated its operation. As one observer reported, "Certain people insist that to be helped by the Council of the South, one must hang Kamil al-As'ad's picture in the house."[24]

With the influx of thousands of fida'iyun in 1970 and 1971, following the bloody conflict in Jordan, the existing social and economic problems of the Shi'is were compounded by a rapidly deteriorating security environment in the South. Although the army made a few attempts to control the Palestinian militants, it soon became clear that the political and social divisions among the Lebanese precluded any decisive measures to bring them under control. Thus the Cairo Agreement of 1969, which was to limit the guerrillas' activities in and from Lebanon, served instead to license the establishment of a rump state. Although the Supreme Shi'i Council seemed a useful vehicle for the promotion of the community's interests (as mediated by Musa al-Sadr, of course), the council was ineffectual in a milieu that was quickly becoming dominated by militias and extralegal parties. Hence in March 1974, at a well-attended rally in the Bekaa Valley city of Baalbek, Imam Musa declared the launching of a popular mass movement, the Harakat al-Mahrumin (the Movement of the

22. David R. and Audrey C. Smock, *The Politics of Pluralism: A Comparative Study of Lebanon and Ghana* (New York: Elsevier Scientific Publishing Co., 1975), 141.

23. Many Lebanese refer to the council as the Majlis al-Juyub (the Council of the Pockets) in recognition of the council's reputation for bribery and illegal diversions of funds. The council became an important target of Amal activism in 1980, when it occupied council offices in Sidon to dramatize its demands that the council be more honestly and efficiently operated. Since 1982, under the chairmanship of Husain Kanaan, an early associate of al-Sadr, the council has apparently been operated with much greater integrity.

24. Quoted in Thom Sicking and Shereen Khairallah, "The Shi'a Awakening in Lebanon: A Search for Radical Change in a Traditional Way," in *Vision and Revision in Arab Society, 1974,* CEMAM Reports, 1974, vol. 2 (Beirut: Dar el-Mashreq Publishers, 1975), 97–130, quotation at 110.

Deprived). With his movement he vowed to struggle relentlessly until the social grievances of the deprived—in practice, the Shi'is—were satisfactorily addressed by the government. As Kamal Salibi, a prominent Lebanese historian, notes: "He even warned that he would soon have his followers attack and occupy the palaces and mansions of the powerful if the grievances of the poor and oppressed were left unheeded."[25]

Just one year later, al-Sadr's efforts were overtaken by the onset of civil war in Lebanon. By July 1975 it became known that a militia adjunct to Harakat al-Mahrumin had been formed.[26] The militia, Afwaj al-Muqawamah al-Lubnaniyah (the Lebanese Resistance Detachments), better known by the acronym AMAL (which also means "hope"), was initially trained by al-Fatah (the largest organization in the PLO) and it played a minor role in the fighting of 1975 and 1976. As we have already noted, Musa al-Sadr's movement was affiliated with the LNM and its fida'i allies during the first year of the civil war, but it broke with its erstwhile allies when the Syrians intervened in June 1976 to prevent the defeat of the Maronite-dominated Lebanese Front.

Four months before the Syrian intervention President Sulaiman Franjiya accepted a "Constitutional Document" that Imam Musa indicated was a satisfactory basis for implementing political reform. The document—which called for an increase in the proportion of parliamentary seats allocated to the Muslims, as well as some restrictions on the prerogatives of the Maronite president—seemed to offer a basis for restoring civil peace to Lebanon. When it was combined with the prospect of bringing the PLO under control through the Syrian intervention, there appeared to be a prospect for a new beginning. Unfortunately, the opportunity to stop the carnage was more apparent than real. Although the pace of fighting had decreased by the end of 1976, the violence continued.

The growing influence of Musa al-Sadr prior to the civil war was certainly a bellwether of the increased politicization of the Shi'is; however, it bears repetition that Imam Musa led only a fraction of his politically affiliated coreligionists. It was the multiconfessional parties and militias that attracted the majority of Shi'i recruits, and many more Shi'is carried arms under the colors of these organizations than under Amal's. And

25. Kamal S. Salibi, *Crossroads to Civil War: Lebanon 1958–1976* (Delmar, N.Y.: Caravan Books, 1976), 78.

26. Ibid., 119. While most accounts indicate that Amal was founded in 1975, an examination of obituaries in *Saut al-Mahrumin* (a magazine published by the Harakat al-Mahrumin) indicates that the militia existed in 1974, and perhaps earlier. This research will be reported in the author's "A Tentative Sociology of Shi'i Martyrs in the Lebanese Civil War" (in progress).

even in war the Shi'is suffered disproportionately; by a large measure they incurred more casualties than any other sect in Lebanon. Perhaps the single most important success achieved by al-Sadr was the reduction of the authority and the influence of the traditional Shi'i elites, the zu'ama', but it was the civil war, and the associated growth of extralegal organizations, that conclusively rendered these personalities increasingly irrelevant in the Lebanese political system.

Whatever he may have been, despite his occasionally vehement histrionics, Imam Musa was hardly a man of war. (He seems to have played only a most indirect role in directing the military actions of the Amal militia.) His weapons were words, and as a result his political efforts were short-circuited by the war. He seemed to be eclipsed by the violence that engulfed Lebanon. Ironically, it was his disappearance in 1978 that helped retrieve the promise of his earlier efforts.

The Revitalization of Amal

Three events transpired in the ten-month period from March 1978 to January 1979 that accelerated the mobilization of the Shi'i community and contributed to the consolidation of Shi'i political influence in a revitalized Amal (the name Harakat al-Mahrumin having fallen into disuse).[27] In March 1978, Israel launched its first major invasion of Lebanon, Operation Litani; in August 1978, the Imam Musa al-Sadr disappeared during a still enigmatic visit to Libya; and in January 1979, the Islamic revolution in Iran toppled the shah. It was the occurrence of these three events that resuscitated Amal and rendered it an organization that would come to play an unprecedented—if possibly passing—role in Lebanese politics.

The 1978 invasion by Israel, which claimed about one thousand (mostly Shi'i) lives and destroyed a significant number of homes throughout South Lebanon, not only demonstrated the heavy human costs that the Israelis would exact from the residents of the South as a result of the armed fida'i presence; it also signaled the onset of an accelerated Israeli campaign aimed at alienating the Lebanese Shi'is from the Palestinians

---

27. I have analyzed the critical events of 1978–79 in much greater detail elsewhere. An early consideration was presented at the Middle East Institute of Columbia University in December 1981. A full development may be found in "Harakat Amal," a paper delivered at the annual meeting of the American Political Science Association, Denver, Colo., September 2–5, 1982. A revised version of "Harakat Amal" is reprinted in Aronoff, ed., *Religion and Politics*.

in their midst. After Operation Litani, the IDF moved far beyond all but the slimmest pretense of retaliation. Instead, Israel sought to keep the PLO (and its supporters) constantly on the defensive with a relentless series of air attacks, raids, kidnappings, and house bombings. Helped by the callous, arrogant, and shortsighted behavior of the fida'iyun, the Israeli campaign was a tremendous success. In large part spurred by the desire to protect their families, homes, and villages, many Shi'is either joined Amal or actively supported it. By 1980 and 1981 important clashes were taking place between Amal on the one side, and the fida'iyun and their allies on the other. Al-Fatah officials struggled unsuccessfully—and sometimes disingenuously—to arrange a rapprochement between Amal and its most visceral foes (such as the Iraqi-sponsored Arab Liberation Front and the Libyan-funded Arab Socialist Union), but the imperatives of the Shi'is and the fida'iyun were almost diametrically opposed. By the spring of 1982, after particularly heavy fighting between the Palestinians and Amal, many Shi'is were expecting a Shi'i-fida'i war to erupt at any moment.[28]

The second development was the disappearance of the leader of the Amal movement, the Imam Musa al-Sadr. After arriving in Libya on August 25, 1978, Imam Musa disappeared under circumstances that remain mysterious. While Libya's ruler, Mu'ammar al-Qadhafi, claims that al-Sadr left Libya on an Alitalia flight bound for Rome, only his luggage and an impostor arrived. Most Amal leaders believe that al-Qadhafi is responsible for the disappearance of their leader. Such suspicions have not evaporated, as a chain of anti-Libyan skyjackings, kidnappings, and sundry other attacks on Libyan officials and facilities attest.[29]

While Imam Musa was extraordinarily important when he was alive and active in Lebanon, he became even more important after his enigmatic disappearance. His persona has been elevated to that of a national martyr for many Shi'is. Had Imam Musa passed quietly from the scene, it is likely that Shi'i politics would have been even more fractious than they had been prior to his arrival in Lebanon. In short, many Shi'is have found in their vanished leader a compelling and culturally authentic symbol for an expression of their discontent with the cruel malady they have had to suffer. In private interviews, several movement leaders have conceded the

28. Based on the author's observations during a thirteen-month stay in South Lebanon, 1980–81.

29. Documents made available by a former Libyan ambassador who defected to Jordan reportedly indicate that al-Sadr was liquidated in Libya. See *al-Watan al-Arabi*, September 30–October 6, 1983, 38. Although many Amal leaders publicly profess that Imam Musa is still alive, when speaking privately they concede that he is probably dead.

irony that their leader is probably more valuable to them in his current "hidden" status than he would be in the flesh.[30]

Immediately following the fall of the shah in January 1979, the success of the Islamic revolution spawned enormous excitement among the Shi'is of Lebanon—and not without good reason. The events in Iran demonstrated dramatically what a well-organized and mobilized Shi'i community might accomplish. The traditionally close ties between the two religious communities helped ensure that the events in Iran would reverberate in Lebanon. Furthermore, the links between the Shi'is of Iran and Lebanon transcended the symbolic level. Many Lebanese shaikhs received their clerical training in Qom, and the links between Iran and Jabal 'Amil have a long history.[31] Several Amal officials were to play an active role in the unfolding events in Iran, most notably Iranian-born Mustafa Chamran who served as chairman of Iran's Supreme Defense Council until his death in 1981 (many believe he was the victim of foul play).

However, it must be remembered that the typical Lebanese Shi'i— much like his Muslim cohorts throughout the Middle East—has a bifurcated view of the Islamic revolution. On the one hand, there is the notion that it is an exemplar for what a pious, mobilized Shi'i community can accomplish. Yet, on the other hand, many of the same Shi'is roundly and freely condemn the excesses of the revolution (summary executions, torture, and so on), as well as the anachronistic visions of many of the principals. Furthermore, even in the unlikely event that a preponderance of Lebanese Shi'is sought to create an Islamic republic, the feasibility of such an endeavor is not high, given that as many as 65 to 70 percent of the Lebanese are non-Shi'is. The important point, reservations aside, is that the Islamic revolution has served as an important spur to the political mobilization of the Shi'i community, and the effective and affective agent of that mobilization has been Amal.

30. Juan Cole's comments well capture the popular reaction to the imam's disappearance: "I was in Beirut most of 1978 and until mid-1979, and I was interested to note the widespread popular conviction that al-Sadr was still alive, but in hiding. One rumor had it that he had gone underground to sneak into Iran and help the revolution against the shah. In any case, people were constantly expecting him to appear (zuhur) in almost messianic terms. In fact, one often heard rumors in Beirut that the imam *had* appeared in some part of the city. He almost rivaled the statue of the Virgin at Jounieh for miraculous charisma in the war-torn land. In any case, the popular conviction of his imminent appearance no doubt lent hope to many Shi'is in the uncertain autumn of 1978" (Private communication, September 1984).

31. For example, see Tarif Khalidi, "Shaykh Ahmad 'Arif Al-Zayn and Al-'Irfan," in Marwan R. Buheiry, ed., *Intellectual Life in the Arab East, 1890–1939* (Beirut: Center for Arab and Middle East Studies, 1981), 110–24.

Facing the Post-June Challenges

In the months preceding the Israeli invasion of June 1982, the Amal movement was rapidly gaining adherents throughout the Shi'i community. The movement's support for the unity of Lebanon, its demand for the abolition in sectarianism in Lebanese politics, and most important, its increasingly effective opposition to the widely detested fida'i presence helped fortify its popularity. However, much as the onset of civil war in 1975–76 arrested the mobilization of the Shi'is by Imam Musa, the Israeli invasion threatened to obviate its raison d'être—security. With the PLO presence largely excised, the critical question to be faced was whether a membership fed in large part by the attraction of collective defense would be lost.

As anyone who visited Lebanon in the months following the invasion can attest, this was a period of great euphoria. The Lebanese had been waiting for the "last battle," and now, finally, the last shot had been fired. Even after the massacres in the Sabra and Shatila camps, there was a remarkable ebullience afoot. The United States had finally decided to solve the Lebanese crisis, the "external forces" (the Israelis and the Syrians, as well as the PLO) would soon withdraw, and Lebanon had a president, Amin Gemayel, whose hands were relatively bloodless and who seemed to be a proponent of intersectarian reconciliation. Unfortunately, even before the end of 1982 it became apparent that Lebanon's prospects were cloudy indeed. U.S. diplomacy was moving at a desultory if self-satisfied pace. Fighting between Druze and Maronite militias flamed in the Shouf region, south of Beirut. Lebanon's new president, far less popular in his own Maronite community than his assassinated brother Bashir, proved more concerned with buttressing his following among his coreligionists than among the populace as a whole. In addition, President Amin Gemayel was far more inclined to deal with traditional rather than emergent leaders from the Shi'i community. And Israel, flushed with the hubris of victory, began to hunker down for a long stay in Lebanon.

Fissures, some latent and others new, began to open within the Shi'i community. Kamil al-As'ad, za'im par excellence, and speaker of the National Assembly,[32] emerged as President Gemayel's preferred Shi'i interlocutor. Traditional leaders, who seemed to have been rendered increasingly irrelevant by a decade of conflict and several decades of profound socioeconomic change, appeared anew to reclaim political fief-

32. In 1979 the Chamber of Deputies was renamed the National Assembly.

doms, though typically with little success. In the South the Israelis fever-ishly set about creating alternative militia structures to replace Amal, which they had unsuccessfully attempted to co-opt during the summer of 1982. Within Amal there were a number of defections. The movement had never been a tightly integrated organization. There were regional splits that roughly corresponded with relative proximity to Israel. In ad-dition, Amal had subsumed an admixture of political perspectives and ideological perspectives, and more than a few members rejected the rel-ative moderation of the movement. One member of the movement's twenty-five-member Command Council, Husain Musawi, accused Amal of collaboration with Israel and of deserting its Islamic principles (accu-sations that were not baseless, but that were—in the main—false). In mid-1982 Musawi formed the Islamic Amal, apparently with significant Iranian support. He is widely believed to have played a role in the de-struction of the U.S. embassy in April 1983, as well as the truck-bombing of the French and U.S. contingents of the Multinational Force in October 1983.

In the Bekaa Valley bordering Syria, a number of Shi'i clerics revi-talized the Hizbullah (Party of God), which had been founded in the wake of Ayatullah Khomeini's victory in Iran. Shaikhs Subhi Tufaili, 'Abbas Musawi, Ibrahim Amin, and Hasan Nasr Allah set about to lead an Is-lamic revolution in Lebanon. The shaikhs were reinforced by a contingent of Pasdaran (Revolutionary Guards), manned by as many as one thousand men and dispatched in the summer of 1982 by Iran for the ostensible purpose of fighting the invading IDF. (There is no evidence to suggest that the Pasdaran ever engaged the IDF in combat.) Hizbullah has also won a significant and expanding following in the Shi'i suburbs of Beirut. Sizable numbers of disaffected Amal members have lent support to the party, a fact that reflects their impatience with Amal's leadership, as well as the continuing polarization that has marked the postinvasion period.

Although it is not clear whether he plays an official role in Hizbullah, Shaikh Muhammad Husain Fadl Allah's lucid sermons and writings and public statements have proved to be an important recruitment impetus for the party. In contrast to Amal, which has eschewed the establishment of an Islamic state in Lebanon, Fadl Allah and Hizbullah call not only for dialogue and mutual understanding among sects but for the eventual cre-ation of a state ruled by Islam. Shaikh Fadl Allah cleverly argues that the Muslim, unlike his Christian counterpart, is required by the tenets of his faith to live in an Islamic state. "When a Muslim lives in a state that does not adopt Islam, his life remains confused because of the dualism [of authority] that he is living under. . . . The Christian, by contrast, does not have this problem when living in an Islamic society."[33]

Hizbullah's political program, as enunciated in February 1985, is marked by a pungent anti-American tone, a reflection of the widely held belief that the United States has been behind Israel's aggression in Lebanon. In addition, the program is critical of Amal's comparative moderation and particularly the participation of Amal officials in the activities of what is viewed as an illegitimate government under the presidency of Amin Gemayel.[34] As Hizbullah has gained strength in the environs of Beirut, and to a lesser extent in the South, the Amal leadership has been persistently pressed to adopt ever more extreme positions in order to conserve its following. By 1984, armed clashes between Amal and Hizbullah militiamen were occurring with some regularity. Although Berri and his deputies strove to minimize the differences between the two organizations, their profound disagreement over the establishment of Islamic rule guaranteed their irreconcilability.

In the South, the initial impotence of Amal under Israeli occupation fostered a fissuring of the Shi'i community. The ulama of Jabal 'Amil, who had accepted Amal authority—albeit often begrudgingly—in the period between the 1978 and 1982 invasions, were now adopting a far more militant and independent role. Personages like Shaikh Raghib Harb of Jibshit (assassinated in February 1984), Shaikh Said Ali Mahdi Ibrahim of Adloun, and the militant Islamic Students' Organization of Nabatiya were taking an ever more assertive stance against the Israeli presence and, in doing so, were diminishing the prestige and the influence of Amal. In point of fact, the very imperatives of resistance activities—secrecy and small resistance cells—militated against a large, well-ordered, and responsible organization. One senior U.N. official remarked in early 1984, "The most important legacy of the Israeli occupation might well be a fragmented Shi'i community under the grip of the clergy."[35] By mid-1984, however, the Amal leadership in the South began playing a central role in directing resistance activities against the Israelis (who have proven most adept in alienating even the most moderate Shi'i leaders). As a result, the movement seems to have reversed the erosion of its authority in the South, and its control now seems much surer in the South than in Beirut.

33. Quoted in an interview in *Monday Morning*, October 15–21, 1984, 40–45.
34. *Nass al-risalah al-maftuha allati wajjahaha hizb allah ila al-mustaz'afin fi lubnan wa al-'alam* (Text of the Open Message which the Party of Allah Sends to the Oppressed in Lebanon and the World) (N.p. [Beirut]: February 16, 1985).
35. Private communication, January 1984.

Another serious challenge to Amal's primacy in the leadership of the Shi'is did not come from the Israelis, local religious leaders, Hizbullah, or Iranian militiamen but from the influential Shi'i cleric, Mufti Muhammad Mahdi Shams al-Din. Before his disappearance Imam Musa al-Sadr literally dominated Shi'i politics; he chaired the Supreme Shi'i council and led the popular movement. After his disappearance, however, the two leadership positions have been split along clerical-lay lines. Husain al-Husaini, and now Nabih Berri have led Amal, while Mufti Shams al-Din has served as deputy chairman (Imam Musa is still considered the chairman) of the Supreme Shi'i Council. Al-Husaini, a member of the National Assembly, aligned with Shams al-Din in the contest to determine who would speak for the Shi'i community. Al-Husaini's victory over Kamil al-As'ad in the October 1984 election for assembly speaker has helped to make the Shams al-Din–al-Husaini dyad increasingly formidable. The mufti has attempted to place himself above the fray, calling for the disarmament of all militias and coordinating his role with leading clerical officials and politicians from the Druze and Sunni communities. Israel's inept and oppressive occupation of South Lebanon afforded Shams al-Din ample opportunity to exploit the mantle of legitimacy the Supreme Shi'i Council provides. In October 1983, after an Israeli military convoy desecrated the Ashura commemoration in Nabatiya, Shams al-Din issued a *fatwa* (an authoritative interpretation of religious responsibility), calling on all Muslims to conduct "comprehensive civil opposition" to the Israeli occupation. The Ashura incident with the resultant fatwa made even quiet collaboration with Israel impossible.[36] Subsequently, in March 1985, Shams al-Din declared a "defensive jihad" (or *al-jihad al-difa'i*), thus making it a religious obligation to fight against Israel as long as it occupied any part of Lebanon.[37]

Upon inspection, it is clear that the competition between the mufti and Berri has less to do with the substance of platforms than with the allure of power. Indeed, with minor modification the positions espoused by the two sides are interchangeable. They both support the integrity of a free Arab Lebanon, the preservation of Lebanon as a parliamentary republic, the commitment to a free economic system, the redress of social

36. See Augustus R. Norton, *External Intervention and the Politics of Lebanon* (Washington, D.C.: Washington Institute for Values in Public Policy, 1984), 12–13, for more details on the Nabatiya incident.

37. Shams al-Din's call for a defensive jihad was reported on Lebanese radio, Beirut Domestic Service, March 4, 1985, trans. in Foreign Broadcast Information Service, *Daily Report, Middle East & Africa*, March 5, 1985, 62.

inequality, the rejection of the partition of the country, the abolition of sectarianism as a desideratum of politics and administration, and the end of the Israeli occupation.

In an important sense Berri—a lawyer trained in Beirut and Paris—represents the newly emergent Shi'is, first-generation participants in politics. Berri, like many of his financial supporters, is the scion of a relatively obscure family from the southern town of Tibnin. Indeed, it is fitting that he was not even born in Lebanon but in West Africa (in Freetown, Sierra Leone), where many of the newly politicized Shi'is have sought and, in some cases, earned their fortunes. By no means anti-American or anti-Western, Berri lived in the United States in the early 1960s and for a brief period in the 1970s, acquiring a deep sense of affection for the country. His former wife and six children still live in Dearborn, Michigan, where he visits yearly in order to maintain his U.S. immigration documents. (Some of his colleagues refer to him as "the American," and they do not do so wholly in jest.)

In contrast, Mufti Shams al-Din is no stranger to authority. His family is well known in Shi'i religious circles for the many clerics it has produced. His support stems in large measure from the Shi'i establishment, the men who have grown accustomed to power and are discomfited by the loud voices of the previously quiescent. But like Berri, Shams al-Din has also been able to draw on the generous support of Shi'i merchants who have profited by migrating to Africa. In the fall of 1982, the mufti was able to collect the equivalent of $15 million in a short tour of Shi'i communities in West Africa, and in February 1984, Berri collected impressive sums as donations from wealthy Shi'is in the Beirut area. Although funding for Shi'i political activities has not been lavish, it is important that stereotypes about the Shi'is' impoverishment not be allowed to mask the considerable wealth that a fair number of them have accumulated. (Contrary to erroneous reports in the press, the Lebanese Shi'is hardly need to depend on outside funding to pursue their political interests.) Both Berri and Shams al-Din control important political assets: on the one hand, manpower, armed might, and street popularity, and on the other, the symbols of religious legitimacy and esteem. It remains to be seen whether the two sides will reconcile their ambitions.

FUTURE PROSPECTS

On May 7, 1984, after a tumultuous period that saw the retreat of the Multinational Force, the abrogation of the May 1983 agreement with Israel, the seizure of West Beirut by Amal and Druze militiamen, and the subsequent enfeeblement of the Lebanese army, Berri accepted a role in the cabinet of Rashid Karami. Among his portfolios is the newly created post of minister of state for the affairs of the South and reconstruction, a fitting post for the leader of a movement so closely identified with South Lebanon and its travails. Some, including Berri's competitors, believe that he has put his head in a noose. But noose or not, Berri had no choice but to attempt to strengthen his increasingly tenuous grip on his constituency.

Berri's delicate situation was well illustrated during the TWA hijacking incident of June and July 1985. Although Amal was not involved in planning or carrying out the hijacking, Berri quickly found himself in a situation wherein his more extreme competitors in Hizbullah (who may themselves have co-opted the hijackers) were stealing his limelight and undercutting his authority among the Shi'is. Accordingly, Berri acted by taking custody of the hostages, much as he had acted in February 1984 when his move into West Beirut was in part calibrated to arrest the erosion of his following. But the very limitations of his action serve to illustrate his dilemma and the dynamics of the political environment in which he operates. We are dealing with political movements, not well-defined political parties in the Western sense. Followers are more easily swayed, cajoled, or enlisted than directed. Suasion is the technique of a man in Nabih Berri's situation. He can do no more than the political mood of his constituency permits, and if he forgets this norm he risks finding himself without a following. In the case of the ill-fated TWA flight, Berri could secure the hostages, but their release had to await the intervention of a far more secure actor, Syria. At best, Berri managed to keep the lid on the pot. He denied his competitors a clear-cut victory, but they succeeded in demonstrating his lack of clear-cut authority. In short, Berri gained a temporary stalemate, but the internecine competition continues.

The looming test of Amal's vitality (and Berri's survivability) will be in South Lebanon, during and following the Israeli withdrawal announced in January 1985. Israel's watershed decision to leave the deepening morass is in no small part the direct result of the deadly effectiveness of Shi'i resistance activities. Amal has come to play a significant role in attacking the Israeli occupiers and their Lebanese collaborators, but other forces played significant parts as well. The National Resistance Front, largely manned by leftists, began its attacks while Amal was still sitting on its hands in 1982 and during most of 1983. Local religious leaders, emboldened by the unpopular occupation, have made their contributions as well. Now that the Shi'i genie has, as Yitzhak Rabin noted in a December 1984 discussion with me, been let out of the bottle by the Israeli occupation, the major question is whether Amal will be able to contain it within the bounds of moderation. U.N. forces, and whatever elements the Lebanese army may be able to deploy to the South, will be hamstrung unless Amal can consolidate its control in the South. Radical Shi'i forces have proliferated in an environment where law and order has been seen as a complement to the continuing occupation. Thus, time itself is a crucial variable. In my judgment, the balance of power—however delicate—is still held by Amal. But, if the Israeli withdrawal was significantly delayed, the balance could have changed. Indeed, it was the belated recognition of just this dynamic that led Israeli policymakers to treat the withdrawal with a keen sense of urgency. It is clear that no single political organization will enjoy a monopoly on the allegiance of the sect's members, but if Amal emerges supreme in the South it will hold a strong card. The South is not only the geographic center for the sect but its spiritual heartland as well, and those Shi'i politicians who hold sway there will have an extraordinary role to play in shaping Shi'i politics throughout what remains of Lebanon.

Moreover, only time will tell how far-reaching the effects of Israel's expulsion from Lebanon will prove to be. Within Lebanon, there are widespread apprehensions about the ascendant Shi'i community. For many non-Shi'i Lebanese the Shi'is appear as a behemoth threatening to dominate Lebanon culturally, socially, and politically. Thus, all manner of novel realignments among Lebanon's other sects are possible. Many suspect that the Druze-Shi'i marriage of convenience will be the first casualty. The Druze, although geopolitically intact in the Shouf, lack the numerical strength of the Shi'is, and they have opted to create a statelet rather than pursue the reunification of the state. In this way the Druze and the Maronite Christians both seem to be seeking regional autonomy instead of intercommunal reconciliation. The wounds of more than a decade of civil war, with its resultant bloodshed, hatred, and suspicion, will not heal quickly. Although many mourn the demise of Lebanon, it is obvious that Lebanon will be a state-in-fragments for many years to come. Some have predicted that the Shi'is will dominate the state, but there is, in fact, little of the state left to dominate.

External powers will continue to exert considerable influence over events within Lebanon. Israel, despite its failures in Lebanon, maintains ties with the Druze and the Maronites, and Iran is continuing to shop for suitable Lebanese clients. Amal's relatively moderate political program and its nonclerical leadership have not played well in Tehran for several years, and Iran is likely to continue to lend at least rhetorical support to Amal's adversaries. The enigma, at this point, is Syria, which has shown itself to be wary of "Khomeinists" but, on the other hand, has been leery of Amal's past attempts (especially in 1982) to strike an independent path. If past performance is any guide, Syria may be counted on to support a variety of Shi'i contenders, including the Amal leadership, Mufti Shams al-Din, and Speaker Husain al-Husaini, to ensure an equilibrium of dependent and pliant "allies." The Syrian ploy will be a difficult one though, and the possibility of an anti-Syrian backlash should not be underestimated. Although Lebanon may well be an ailing—even terminally ill—patient, Lebanese nationalism is more alive among the Shi'is than most people realize.

Whatever the play of events within Lebanon, it is indisputable that the expulsion of Israel from Lebanon will reverberate through the Middle East for a long time to come. Well-informed Israeli officials are already reporting that the example provided by the South Lebanese Shi'is has begun to echo on the West Bank, where imitative attacks on the Israeli military have already begun. Israel, marked by defeat in Lebanon, will no doubt feel the results of its venture for years to come, as its adversaries assimilate the lesson that it is not invincible. Thus, the Shi'i Arabs of Lebanon, often dismissed or ignored by other Arabs in the past, have made a significant contribution to Arab nationalist struggles.

The Shi'is have a clear stake in the territorial integrity and independence of Lebanon, and they may—after a time—provide the glue for putting Lebanon back together (in whatever form), but even the most optimistic Shi'i politicians see a long and hard road awaiting them. No matter what course events follow, it is clear that the mobilization of the Shi'is will be an enduring fact. They are no longer mendicants.

HANNA BATATU

Chapter Seven   Shi'i Organizations in
Iraq: Al-Da'wah
al-Islamiyah and
al-Mujahidin

In the 1970s and early 1980s Shi'i revivalist elements were very active in
Iraq's underground, but they now count only a few isolated and scattered
cells. In recent years their activity has been more evident outside their
home country, in particular among the Iraqi refugees and prisoners of war
in Iran. Some of their organizations—the Soldiers of the Imam, for example—are obscure, diminutive, and of little effect. The most significant
are al-Da'wah al-Islamiyah (the Islamic Call) and al-Mujahidin (the Muslim Warriors).

Strongly affected by Iran's popular upheaval, the Mujahidin emerged
in Baghdad in 1979. The Da'wah is an older movement: it had its beginnings in the late 1950s or early 1960s in the holy city of Najaf.

In terms of material resources and membership the Da'wah surpasses
the Mujahidin who have been, however, distinguished by their energy,
zeal, and bold actions. Moreover, the Mujahidin are free from the taint
of connection with the late shah of Iran which the Da'wah still bears.

Men of religion form the crucial core of the leadership in the Da'wah.
They include, among others, Muhammad Mahdi al-Asafi, the official
spokesman of the party, Sayyid Kazim al-Ha'iri, Mahdi Ali Akbar Shariati, 'Ali Muhammad al-Kurani, Mahdi al-Khalisi, and Hamid Muhajir.
Al-Asafi, al-Ha'iri, and Shariati are of Iranian origin. The others are

179

Arabs: Muhajir and al-Khalisi hail from Iraq and al-Kurani from Lebanon. There are also some laymen among the top leaders of the Da'wah, such as Murtada al-'Askari, who is Iranian by birth and citizenship but had long resided in Iraq.

Religiously oriented graduates of modern schools and colleges play a greater role among the Mujahidin than the trainees in traditional religious learning. Most of the Mujahidin are also fighting men, which follows naturally from their belief in the primacy of armed struggle. There is little specific information on their leading cadre. Their foremost guide, however, is Sayyid 'Abd-ul-'Aziz al-Hakim, the youngest of the surviving sons of the late chief Shi'i *marji'* (authority) Muhsin al-Hakim. Although the Hakim family is surnamed al-Tabataba'i, a name for descendants of the Prophet common in Iran, it has had—like numerous other families of Iranian descent—its roots in Iraq for many generations and has intermarried with Iraqis. Its members assert that, being *sayyids* (descendants of the Prophet), they are therefore Arabs. They also insist that they stem from the Arab Shi'i region of Jabal 'Amil in southern Lebanon. At any rate, the mother of 'Abd-ul-'Aziz al-Hakim is from the Arab Lebanese family of al-Bazzi.

The Mujahidin differ at present from the Da'wah in one other important respect: they yield unequivocally to the Islamic overlordship of Ruhullah Khomeini, whereas, according to reliable reports, strong opposition to his supremacy has lately developed among some of the leaders of the Da'wah, who are said to favor the prospect of an independent Iraqi Islamic regime.

The two organizations have at least one thing in common. They both draw their inspiration from the thought of the late Sayyid Muhammad Baqir al-Sadr, the most learned of Iraq's ayatullahs.

Muhammad Baqir al-Sadr, who was born at Najaf, probably in the early 1930s, into an Arab family of Lebanese origin famous for its learning throughout the Shi'i world, is best known for his *Falsafatuna* (Our Philosophy, 1959), *Iqtisaduna* (Our Economy, 1960), and *al-Bank al-Laribawi fi al-Islam* (The Nonusurious Bank in Islam, 1973). But he was a prolific writer and ranged far and wide. Here only his view on the Islamic polity and his guidelines for a Muslim economy can be treated, and only in the briefest manner.

His fundamental points of departure and the chief clues to his entire work are the traditional Muslim propositions that God is the source of all power, the only legislator, and the sole owner of all the earth's resources.

In support of these propositions he adduces appropriate Qur'anic verses and these words of 'Ali ibn Abi Talib: "The worshippers are the worshippers of God and property is the property of God."

From the principle of God's exclusive supremacy and the related idea that man owes homage to God alone, Muhammad Baqir al-Sadr infers that "the human being is free and that no other human being or class or human group has dominion over him." Similarly, the principle of God's sole ownership of the riches of nature involves, in his view, the prohibition of "every form of exploitation . . . of man by man." Moreover, since whatever resources of the earth man holds he holds as a trust from God, he has to use them according to God's orders.

At bottom the call for a return to Islam is a call for a return to God's dispensation and necessitates a "social revolution" against "injustice" and "exploitation," but it is a revolution that has a "universal" rather than a "class" character and one in which the virtuous rich and the virtuous poor stand shoulder to shoulder.[1]

The concrete objective of the social revolution is the realization of the Islamic polity that would derive its force from the foregoing principles and would apply the values of Islam in every sphere of life. The prototype of the Islamic polity is the present Islamic Republic of Iran. Its supreme representative and the commander-in-chief of its armed forces would be the highest marji', that is, the most authoritative Shi'i mujtahid. The mujtahid is a legist capable of giving a *fatwa*, or binding opinion. His rise to the position of highest marji' is in practice the result of long years of study. In an Islamic polity it would also depend upon universal or general recognition by the learned men of the community, or nomination by a Council of One Hundred chosen from the best of the ulama and Muslim thinkers and comprising no fewer than ten mujtahids, or, ultimately, in the instance of a lack of consensus, election by the whole community through a general popular referendum. With the help of the Council of One Hundred, the highest marji', who is in effect general deputy for the absent imam, would have overall supervision of the state, approve candidates for the office of chief of the executive branch of the government, and pronounce on the "constitutionality of laws" passed (on matters on

---

1. Muhammad Baqir al-Sadr, *Lamhah Tamhidiyah 'an Mashru' Dustur al-Jumhuriyat al-Islamiyah* (A Preliminary Glance at the Draft of the Constitution of the Islamic Republic) (Beirut: At-Ta'aruf Publishing House, 1979), 17–18, and *Surah 'an Iqtisad al-Mujtama' al-Islami* (An Image of the Economy of the Muslim Society) (Beirut: At-Ta'aruf Publishing House, 1979), 7–18.

which the *shari'ah* is silent) by a popularly elected assembly of *ahl al-hall wa al-'aqd* (those who bind and loose).[2]

In the economic sphere the Muslim polity would closely relate incomes to effort and need, prohibit any gain arising out of usury or the hoarding of money, reestablish money in its natural role as a means of exchange, transform banks from being instruments for the growth of capital into tools for enriching the community, continually bring prices of labor and commodities near to their genuine exchange values by combating monopoly in every area of economic life, equalize or narrow differences in standards of living by providing a reasonable minimum of material comfort for all and preventing waste, extravagance, and the concentration of capital by the few, devote one-fifth of the country's oil income to social security and the construction of houses for the citizenry, and provide free education and free health services for all.[3]

There is perhaps little that is original in al-Sadr's economic or philosophic works, but his style was lucid and, for his followers, compelling. Moreover, his writings, rather than requiring the abdication of reason, stressed its value. His admirers, who are quite numerous, describe him in superlatives. From their standpoint he was the best representative of Islamic thought or, as one of them put it, "its symbol and its summit." Even in other respects he is compared favorably with Ruhullah Khomeini. Unlike the latter, who is emotional and impulsive, al-Sadr was said to have been calm, deliberate, and sound in his judgments. One thing is beyond doubt in any event: after his execution on April 8, 1980, by the Baath regime, Iraq's Shi'i movements declined in intellectual significance.

The conditions that in the 1970s and early 1980s disposed Shi'is of humble background favorably toward the Da'wah or the Mujahidin were quite different than the conditions that actuated their leaders and organizers.

In Greater Baghdad the two parties drew much of their support from al-Thaurah,[4] a township which accounts for more than a quarter of the

2. Muhammad Baqir al-Sadr, *Lamhah Tamhidiyah*, 19–22.

3. Muhammad Baqir al-Sadr, *Surah 'an Iqtisad al-Mujtama' al-Islami*, 36–37, and *Khutut Tafsiliyah 'an Iqtisad al-Mujtama' al-Islami* (Detailed Lines on the Economy of the Islamic Society), 2d ed. (Beirut: At-Ta'aruf Publishing House, 1979), 36–73. For a detailed discussion of "the Islamic economy in its principal features" and "the responsibility of the state in the Muslim economy," consult his *Iqtisaduna* (Our Economy), 11th ed. (Beirut: At-Ta'aruf, 1979), 293–307, 696–728.

4. Other secondary sources of support were the districts of al-Salam and al-Gray'at in which live, for the most part, laborers of rural origins and the district of Karradah al-Sharqiyah, which is inhabited by teachers, tradesmen, and lower ranking state employees.

entire population of the capital and in which were to be found Baghdad's worst slums. In militant Shi'i literature, al-Thaurah was identified as "the stronghold of heroes."[5]

The inhabitants of al-Thaurah were clearly disgruntled with their living conditions. At first glance this seems to be at odds with pertinent statistics. Thus, the minimum daily wage for unskilled laborers—a class to which most of the people of al-Thaurah belonged—rose from 450–550 fils[6] in 1973 to 1,100 fils in 1977, that is, by 200 to 244 percent, and to 1,300 fils in 1980, that is, by 236 to 289 percent. Moreover, a pick-and-shovel workman could earn in 1980 as high as 2 or 3 dinars a day.[7] At the same time, thanks to control or subsidies by the state, prices increased from 1973 to 1978, according to official figures, by only 53.4 percent for foodstuffs, 54.7 percent for housing, 55.9 percent for clothes, and 108.1 percent for shoes.[8]

However, it is difficult to say how careful or conscientious the government was in its statistical calculations. Its figures on changes in housing costs, for instance, do not appear to reflect the actual state of affairs. Because of the sharp increase in the population of metropolitan Baghdad (from 1.5 million in 1965 to 3.2 million in 1981) and the related galling housing shortage, the monthly rent for what Iraqi laborers disparagingly call "a garage," that is, a modest dwelling of one bedroom, one sitting room, and the barest of necessities, was in 1981 from 50 to 60 dinars, compared with 10 or 15 dinars a decade before. Similarly, the price of a kilogram of Iraqi mutton rose from about 900 fils in 1970 to 2.5 dinars in 1981 (the flesh of a native sheep slaughtered by Muslims is preferred to imported meat, which sold at only 750 fils a kilogram). Furthermore, if the price of various products was relatively low by decree, their actual supply was erratic owing to inefficiencies in the state distribution services. Even the nominal earnings of the unskilled classes, at least in the sector of construction, tended to decrease because of the copious flow of Egyptian labor into Iraq: the number of Egyptians engaged in services, con-

5. The Party of al-Da'wah al-Islamiyah, *Bayan al-Tafahum al-Sadir min Hizb al-Da'wah al-Islamiyah ila al-Ummah fi al-'Iraq* (The Manifesto for Mutual Understanding Issued by the Party of al-Da'wah al-Islamiyah to the Nation in Iraq) (N.p., 1980), 8.

6. One dinar or 1000 fils exchanged for U.S. $3.37 in 1975, $2.90 in 1980 before the Iraq-Iran War, and for $2.20 thereafter.

7. For the 1980 figures I am indebted to Fakhri Karim and 'Abd al-Razzaq al-Safi, members of the Politbureau of the Iraqi Communist party, in conversation, January 10, 1981. For the 1973 and 1977 figures, see Hanna Batatu, *The Old Social Classes and the Revolutionary Movements of Iraq* (Princeton: Princeton University Press, 1978), 1095–96.

8. Iraq, Ministry of Planning, *Annual Abstract of Statistics, 1978*, p. 158.

struction, and agriculture in and around Baghdad alone was roughly estimated by a U.N. official in 1980 at no fewer than 700,000.[9]

The Iraq-Iran War was also beginning to have a negative impact on the daily life of the laboring people. It is true that there was in the early 1980s an import boom, that trade in the cities was still buoyant, and that the government went out of its way to shield consumers from the effects of the war. But the shortage of oil and electricity slowed down industrial activity. Over and above this, the escalating cost of the long drawn-out conflict and the need to finance the replacement or the repair of badly damaged oil and other economic installations eventually pinchéd the government's ability to spend for social welfare.

Finally, the people of al-Thaurah had an additional reason to be aggrieved: the government had not been providing their district with such services as sewers and asphalted streets because of its belief that the town lay over a rich oil field.

In brief, it is clear that the living conditions of the Shi'is of al-Thaurah had much to do with their susceptibility to the influence of the Da'wah and the Mujahidin. By way of further evidence, one could underline that it is from this same township or its old component districts that the Communist party derived much of its strength in the 1940s, 1950s, and 1960s. In fact, the deep wound inflicted upon the Communists in 1963, the course of compromise with the Baath regime that their leadership steered from 1973 to 1978, and the departure into exile in 1979 of no fewer than three thousand of the Communist party's hardened members left the disadvantaged of the capital with no organized means of protest and produced a void in the underground which the Da'wah and Mujahidin hastened to fill.

But what role did the Shi'ism of the sympathizers of the Da'wah and the Mujahidin play in their affection for these militant movements? Of course it would be foolish even to attempt to infer what was in their hearts, and the analysis must confine itself to the objective and observable phenomena of Shi'ism. In this connection, it is necessary to bear in mind that the inhabitants of al-Thaurah are all of recent rural origins and hail from districts in which, as is evident from the accompanying table (due allowance being made for possible statistical deficiencies), religion was very feebly organized. Thus in the overwhelmingly Shi'i rural districts of the provinces of Basra, Karbala, Diwaniyah, Hillah, 'Amarah, Muntafiq, and Kut, where more than 49 percent of the total rural population of Iraq lived, there were in 1947 only thirty-nine religious institutions or, to put

9. Conversation with an official of the U.N. Economic Commission for Western Asia, January 23, 1981.

Population and Religious Institutions in Urban and Rural Shi'i Districts
in 1947

Old (and New) Name of Province	Population[a] (in thousands)		Number of Religious Institutions[b]	
	Urban	Rural	Urban	Rural
I. Mixed Shi'i-Sunni Arab provinces				
Baghdad	522	266	1,303	16
Basra	136	220	188	6
II. Overwhelmingly Arab Shi'i provinces				
Karbala	95	33	725	10
Diwaniyah (Qadisiyah)	80	297	82	2
Hillah (Babylon)	72	189	308	20
'Amarah (Maysan)	61	246	98	—
Muntafiq (Thi-Qar)	54	287	71	1
Kut (Wasit)	48	175	36	—
III. Other provinces	536	1,247	2,017	714
IV. Total for Iraq	1,604	2,960	4,828	769

[a]The population figures do not, of course, include nomadic tribesmen, which in 1947 were roughly estimated at 170,000.

[b]The religious institutions are not differentiated in our source, but they presumably comprise, among other things, *husainiyahs* (places where Shi'is gather, especially in the Muslim month of Muharram, to commemorate and lament the martyrdom of Husain), *takiyahs* (dervish places of retreat and prayer mostly in the Kurdish provinces), *maqams* (tomb-mosques), *madrasahs* (religious schools), *masjids* (mosques), *jami's* (mosques where the Friday prayers are held), and Christian and Jewish institutions.

Source: Government of Iraq, Ministry of Social Affairs, Directorate General of Census, *Census of Iraq, 1947* (Baghdad, 1954). The figures were computed from all the tables numbered 2 and 3 relating to the various districts of Iraq in Volumes 1, 2, and 3.

it differently, there was on the average only one religious institution for every 37,000 persons. In rural 'Amarah and Kut, from which come a great number of the people of al-Thaurah Township and in which lived upwards of 421,000 inhabitants, there was not a single religious institution. In the census for 1947 from which these figures are drawn the term *religious institution* is not defined but obviously refers to such things as mosques, religious schools, and *husainiyahs*, or places where Shi'is normally gather to accept condolences upon the death of a relative and, more particularly, to lament the martyrdom of Husain in the Muslim month of Muharram.

What accounts for the paucity of religious institutions in the Shi'i countryside?[10] Part of the explanation lies in its extreme poverty, but the

10. It should be pointed out that religious institutions were also scarce in the Arab Sunni rural areas. The Kurdish Sunni rural belt, however, swarmed with *takiyahs* or *khanaqahs* (dervish places of retreat and prayer).

phenomenon is also related to the fact that for very long and well into the first decades of this century vast segments of the countryside were the home of semimobile tribal groups. Moreover, until recent years the Tigris and Euphrates seasonally overflowed their banks and flooded large areas from Kut to the outskirts of Basra. About a quarter of the provinces of 'Amarah and Basra and 10 percent or so of the Muntafiq consisted of permanent or seasonal marshland. Inside the marshes no buildings could be found other than reed huts which stood above the level of the water on *chabashas*, or artificial mounds of bulrushes.

Does the scarcity of rural religious institutions argue a lack of religious vigor on the part of rural Shi'is? Of course, there is here no intrinsic correlation of cause and effect. Moreover, at least in the past, in certain villages resident tribal sayyids used their *mudif*, or guest house, as a sort of mosque or husainiyah. To other villages itinerant preachers—the *mu'mins*—came from neighboring towns. However, although some of these preachers were trainees of religious schools and bona fide representatives of Shi'i religious leaders, others specialized in superstition or even quackery and lived off the peasant tribesmen. Certain of the sayyids were also of this latter type.

At the same time it is necessary to remember that many of the rural Shi'is were of relatively recent bedouin origin and the bedouin have not been known for the vigor of their religion. Ibn Khaldun remarked in 1377 that although, in view of their primitive and "untainted" nature, they were the quickest people to accept the "right way," no religious quality could be firmly established in them.[11] More recently, in 1826, Ibn Sanad, a Sunni man of religion and a historian of the Mamluks of Baghdad, in a specific reference to tribesmen in southern Iraq who had turned not long before toward Shi'ism, complained with obvious partiality, but not without some degree of truth, that "nomadic Arabs are gullible people and have no notion of the religion or of its tenets."[12] In 1907, Chiha, a long-time resident of Baghdad and a man well versed in tribal affairs, asserted that in his days most of the bedouin neglected their prayers and the other precepts of Islam and often if asked in what their faith consisted would simply answer that they were the followers of the religion of their

11. *Muqaddimat al-'Allamah Ibn-Khaldun* (The Introduction of the Savant Ibn-Khaldun) (Cairo: Press of Mustafa Muhammad, n.d.), pt. 2, chap. 27, p. 151, and pt. 3, chap. 52, p. 329.

12. Ibn-Sanad al-Basri al-Wa'ili (1766–1834), *Matali' al-Su'ud Bitayyibi Akhbar al-Wali Da'ud* (Fortune's Preludes to the Happy Annals of the Governor Daud), as abridged in 1873 by Amin b. Hasan al-Halwani al-Madani (Cairo, 1951), 169.

shaikh. They would not scruple, he added, at swearing falsely on the Qur'an but would hesitate to do so on their "chance and destiny" for fear of being miserable all their life.[13]

One other relevant factor, which needs to be stressed, is that not a few of the tribes to which the rural Shi'is belong were relatively recently converted to Shi'ism. For example, the important tribes of Rabi'ah, Zubayd, and Bani Tamim turned to Shi'ism only within the last 180 years or so.[14] Ibrahim Fasih al-Haidari, a Sunni man of learning who brought this fact to light in 1869, blamed their conversion on "the lack of ulama among them" and the temptations of the "devils of the disavowers."[15] But Shi'ism's antigovernmental motif, its preoccupation with oppression, its grief-laden tales, and its miracle play representing Husain's passion accorded with the instincts and sufferings of tribesmen-turned-peasants and must have eased the tasks of the traveling Shi'i mu'mins.

It is also significant that the agricultural, sheep-tending, or marsh-dwelling tribesmen are not strict in their Shi'ism or well versed in their faith. It is true that on the whole they conform to certain traditional rites and participate in great religious events. For example, most of them—but not the Shi'is of the marshes—will not eat the meat of an animal slaughtered by Muslims as yet uncircumcised. Many will also not miss participating in the lamentation for the martyred Husain or visiting in their lifetime the sacred places at Najaf and Karbala if they can afford it, and the followers of the Usuli sect—as contradistinguished from the Akhbaris[16]—nurse the hope their bodies will be taken after death for burial in Wadi al-Salam (the Valley of Peace) between the resting places of the Commander of the Faithful 'Ali ibn Abi Talib and Husain, "the Lord of Martyrs."

On the other hand, except for those who live on the Euphrates in the neighborhood of the Shi'i holy cities, the tribesmen are by and large

13. Habib K. Chiha, *La province de Bagdad. Son passé, son présent, son avenir* (Cairo, 1908), 313–14.

14. Ibrahim Fasih b. Sibghatullah al-Haidari, *'Unwan al-Majd fi Bayan Ahwal Baghdad, Basrah, wa Najd* (The Sign of Glory or the Elucidation of the Conditions of Baghdad, Basra, and Najd) (Baghdad: Dar al-Manshurat al-Basri, 1962), 110–12, and 'Ali al-Wardi, *Dirasah fi Tabi'at al-Mujtama' al-'Iraqi* (A Study on the Nature of Iraqi Society) (Baghdad: Al-'Ani Press, 1965), 225.

15. Al-Haidari, *'Unwan al-Majd,* 111–12.

16. The basic difference between the two sects is that, unlike the Akhbaris, the Usulis favor the method of ijtihad, that is, the development of Islamic law through binding independent opinions of recognized Shi'i legists (mujtahids) (Great Britain, *Personalities, Iraq (Exclusive of Baghdad and Kadhimain)* [Baghdad, 1920], 51–52). The Usulis hence follow mujtahids; the Akhbaris do not.

lax about their prayers or in keeping the fast.[17] They are also much prone to perjury, having for so long been harassed by usurers and tax collectors and by the importunities of arbitrary shaikhs.[18]

Moreover, at some unknown point in the past, they developed a heterodox cult around 'Abbas, Husain's half-brother, who stood out for his bravery and tenacity in the historic battle of Karbala in A.D. 680. They would indeed swear falsely by God, the Prophet, his cousin 'Ali, and his grandson Husain, who are all, in their view, compassionate and forgiving, but not by 'Abbas, who was stern and quick to anger when roused. A violation of an oath by him, they believe, is bound to be visited by a swift and apposite punishment.[19]

More than that, down to the 1958 revolution and even afterward, they continued on the whole to be governed more by their ancient tribal customs than by the shari'ah, or Islamic law as developed and interpreted by the twelve Shi'i imams and the great Shi'i marji's.

When peasant tribesmen moved to Baghdad (and Basra) from the countryside in the 1930s and succeeding decades in great waves, sometimes emptying whole villages, and hundreds of thousands became fixed in what eventually came to be known as al-Thaurah Township, little concern was at first shown, except by the Communists, for their ideological development. Shi'i men of religion were not conspicuous in their districts until after the mid-1960s and the rise of the Da'wah movement, when the migrants became the object of sustained attention.

It was not a reviving Islam or an ascendant Shi'ism that prompted elements within the circle of ulama (*hauzah al-'ilmiyah*) at Najaf to organize ranks in the late 1950s or early 1960s and set on foot the Da'wah party.

On the contrary, they were moved by a growing sense that the old faith was receding, that skepticism and even disdain for traditional rites were rife among the educated Shi'is, that the belief of even the urban Shi'i masses was not as firm and their conformity to ancient usages not as strict or as reverent as in times past, and that the ulama were losing ground and declining in prestige and material influence.

17. This is particularly true of the people of the marshes. Consult Wilfred Thesiger, *The Marsh Arabs* (Harmondsworth: Penguin, 1967), 105, and "The Ma'dan or Marsh-dwellers of Southern Iraq," *Journal of the Royal Central Asian Society* 41, pt. 1 (January 1954): 20.

18. 'Ali al-Wardi, *Dirasah fi Tabi'at al-Mujtama' al-'Iraqi*, 240.

19. Ibid., 240–42.

There were many signs of the weakening of the religious sense of the people. For one thing, the students of religion had been palpably decreasing. In 1918, no fewer than 6,000 students attended the theological madrasahs, or schools of Najaf.[20] By 1957 the number of students had declined to 1,954, of whom only 326 were Iraqis.[21] Because of the lack of any time limit on the learning process, which went on for very many years and could be continued for life, the ages of the students ranged from twenty to sixty, and the turnover of graduates was not large. Moreover, some Iraqis enrolled in the madrasahs only in name in order to secure exemption from military service, a privilege accorded to all students of religion.

For another thing, the monopoly of the Shi'i ulama over the molding of the worldview of their followers, which they enjoyed down to the 1920s, had been broken by reason of the entry of Shi'is into modern schools and the penetration of European influences. As early as 1929 they found themselves defied in their own citadel when the government took the decision to open a girls' school at Najaf itself. The governor of the place dismissed their vehement protests against this step as dictated by "selfish motives." "With the advance of education and knowledge," observed another high official, "the influence the ulama at present exercise over the more ignorant people is bound to be weakened with a consequent falling off in their income."[22]

Indeed, their material position depended on the strength of the old pieties, inasmuch as they could expect little financial backing from the government and did not have control over rich endowments (*auqaf*)[23] as did their Sunni counterparts. "The Shi'i *'ulama'*," wrote King Faisal I confidentially in 1933, "have no connection with the government and are at present estranged from it, particularly inasmuch as they see the Sunni *'ulama'* in possession of funds and properties of which they are deprived, and envy, notably among the religious classes, is something well-known."[24]

Formerly, however, the distinguished Shi'i ulama received large contributions from their coreligionists in the form of *zakat, khums, radd*

20. Great Britain, "Annual Administration Report, Shamiyyah Division, 1918," *Reports of Administration for 1918 of Divisions and Districts of the Occupied Territories in Mesopotamia,* vol. 1 (Baghdad, 1919), 87.

21. Of the other students, 896 were from Iran, 665 from the Indian subcontinent, 47 from Syria and Lebanon, and 20 from Bahrain, Hasa, and Qatif (Fadil Jamali, "The Theological Colleges of Najaf," *Muslim World* [Hartford] 50, no. 1 [January 1960]: 15).

22. Iraqi Public Security *File No. 2198* entitled "Girls' School in Najaf."

23. Properties or funds entailed to pious or charitable purposes.

24. The text of Faisal's memorandum is in 'Abd al-Razzaq al-Hasani, *Tarikh al-Wizarat al-'Iraqiyah* (The History of the Iraqi Cabinets), vol. 3 (Sidon: al-Irfan Press, 1953), 286–93. The quoted statement is on p. 291.

mazalim, and *saum wa salat.* The *zakat* was the tithe for the poor. The *khums,* or a fifth part of one's income, formed the perquisite of the claimants of descent from the Prophet. *Radd mazalim* was the special forgiveness purchased from the ulama for earning state salaries derived from taxes, which to a strict Shi'i were forbidden. *Saum wa salat* were fees for the observing of prayers and fastings on behalf of certain persons for periods varying in accordance with the amount paid. In 1918 these contributions were so ample that the chief Shi'i marji' at Najaf, Sayyid Muhammad Kazim al-Tabataba'i al-Yazdi, alone distributed upwards of 100,000 pounds sterling in charity.[25] But in 1953 the Najafi Imam Ayatullah Muhammad al-Husain Kashif al-Ghita complained:

> In bygone days the people and the chiefs of tribes were virtuous and open-handed. They showed deference to the *'ulama'* and came to their aid. The religious schools lived on their gifts and charities. . . . But since the change in conditions, the shrinking of benevolence, and the corruption of the wealthy . . . the religious schools have fallen on bad days. . . . The Ministry of Education sends us every year only a small grant-in-aid . . . and the contribution of the *Awqaf* Department is even less substantial.[26]

A visitor to Najaf in the 1960s could not help noticing the straits to which many of the Shi'i legists and students of religion were reduced.[27]

The deep penetration of communism in the 1940s and 1950s into Najaf itself also alarmed the conservative instincts of many of the ulama. Ayatullah Kashif al-Ghita noted in 1953 with a sense of peril not untinged by wonder how "wide nests" comprising "spirited and ardent young men" throve in its name in the holiest of Shi'i cities, even though it was "without logic or proof and unassisted by funds or patronage or dignity of rank."[28] Even more disconcerting must have been the conversion to communism of descendants of ulama and provincial town sayyids.[29]

The pronounced Sunnism of the regime of 'Abd al-Salam 'Arif (1963–66) and the secularly oriented policies of the Baath government that came to power in 1968 were other important factors in galvanizing the Shi'i ulama into action.

25. Great Britain, *Reports of Administration for 1918,* 106.
26. *Muhawarat al-Imam al-Muslih Kashif al-Ghita al-Shaikh Muhammad al-Husain ma'a al-Safirain al-Baritani wa al-Amiriki fi Baghdad* (The Conversation of the Reforming Imam Kashif al-Ghita . . . with the British and American Ambassadors to Baghdad) (Najaf: al-Haidariyah Press, 1954), 15–16.
27. 'Ali al-Wardi, *Dirasah fi Tabi'at al-Mujtama' al-'Iraqi,* 231.
28. *Muhawarat al-Imam al-Muslih Kashif al-Ghita,* 5.
29. See Hanna Batatu, *The Old Social Classes,* 752, 1000.

The origins of the Da'wah are still somewhat unclear. The relevant sources do not agree on the facts or their precise sequence. They are also at variance concerning the relationship between the party and Sayyid Muhammad Baqir al-Sadr. Recently a correspondent of *Le Monde diplomatique* maintained, apparently on the basis of conversations with leading members of the party in Iran, that the Da'wah was founded in 1957–58 by "a certain number of Shi'i *'ulama'* [who had] regrouped around Muhammad Baqir al-Sadr."[30]

This version of the origins of the Da'wah differs somewhat from the account given to the Iraqi political police by captured members of the party. According to this account, a group called Jam'iyat 'Ulama' al-Din (the Association of Ulama) in Najaf came into being after the 1958 revolution but was renamed Hizb al-Da'wah al-Islamiyah in 1960 by Muhammad Baqir al-Sadr. Muhammad Mahdi al-'Asafi, Murtada al-'Askari, 'Ali Muhammad al-Kurani, and Mahdi Ali Akbar Shariati, who with other persons[31] still lead the Da'wah in Iran, were mentioned as other founding members of the party.[32]

A third source—*al-Muqatilun,* an organ of the Da'wah—depicted al-Sadr as the founder between 1958 and 1960 at Najaf of Jama'at al-'Ulama' (the Community of Ulama), but interestingly enough, in the biographical sketch that it drew of al-Sadr it did not link him at any point with the Da'wah party.[33]

More in harmony with the groundwork of fact is the account provided by Muhammad Baqir al-Hakim, a son of the late chief marji' Muhsin al-Hakim. Writing in 1981, he explicitly denied that al-Sadr was a founder or member of Jama'at al-'Ulama'; al-Sadr, who had been born in 1932[34] or 1935,[35] was still too young and had not attained the necessary rank in juristic learning to join the society. Moreover, in 1960 some members of Jama'at al-'Ulama' attacked al-Sadr personally and deplored the intellectual influence he exerted over the younger ulama who had charge of the society's journal *al-Adwa' al-Islamiyah*. It is significant that in the same

30. Chris Kutschera, "Nouveaux espoirs pour l'opposition chiite irakienne," *Le Monde diplomatique,* April 1984, p. 15.

31. See p. 179.

32. This account was conveyed to this writer in May 1984 at Baghdad by an influential member of the Baath party.

33. *Al-Muqatilun,* no. 20 (April 1984): 1, 5.

34. *Al-Jihad,* no. 14 (April 1981): 13.

35. Statement of the Supreme Islamic Shi'i Council in Lebanon, April 23, 1980, *Al-Safir* (Beirut), April 24, 1980.

article Muhammad Baqir al-Hakim connects neither al-Sadr nor Jama'at al-'Ulama' to the Da'wah party.[36]

Al-Sadr does not appear to have had any organizational links with the Da'wah. This, at least, finds support in a statement made to this writer in 1981 by a founding member of the Lebanese Shi'i Movement of the Deprived and of its offspring Amal:

> In 1974 I visited Iraq to verify reports of the execution by the Iraqi government of five ulama on a charge of affiliation with the Da'wah party. The persons involved turned out not to be ulama but three laymen and two turbaned students of religion. I saw Sayyid Muhammad Baqir al-Sadr at that time. He protested against the manner in which the judicial proceedings were conducted but expressed his disapproval of the Da'wah. His opposition to this party derived from its links with the shah of Iran. The accusation of leading the Da'wah leveled later against Sayyid al-Sadr by the Iraqi government and which formed the ground for his execution is absolutely without foundation. Sayyid al-Sadr was neither the leader nor an affiliate of the Da'wah party.

Be that as it may, it is reasonable to conclude that the Da'wah was founded at Najaf either in 1960 or sometime in the early 1960s. It is also certain that the next few years were for the party a period of clandestine preparation, and this explains why for the better part of that decade few Iraqis, even in Najaf, were aware of its existence.

The 1964 exile from Iran of Ruhullah Khomeini, who went first to Turkey and then to Najaf, marked an event in the life of the Shi'i ulama. The power he exercised, and continues to exercise, over others lies in his stern and unswerving idealism. He was one of the few of Iran's religious dignitaries who did not kiss the hand of the shah or fawn at his feet. "I am a Husaini not a Hasani," he often reminds his followers, referring to the claim that Husain held fast to his principles and won martyrdom, whereas Hasan compromised with the Umayyads only to die by poison at their instigation. Consistently, Khomeini had no hand in the progress of the Da'wah party, which, as already mentioned, is known to have had in the earliest phase of its history links, probably of an indirect nature, with the shah, whose objective from 1968 to 1975 was the overthrow of the Baath regime.

At the outset the Da'wah penetrated among the men of religion in Najaf, Karbala, and Kazimain and tended to attract in particular elements from their lower and younger ranks. In this connection it should be

36. *Al-Jihad,* no. 14 (April 1981): 22–26.

pointed out that the Shi'i ulama are of different grades. Lowest in influ-
ence are the *mutadayyins,* or pious men, who are addressed as *Thiqat al-
Islam* (the Trust of Islam) and are qualified to receive charity and settle
minor shari'ah cases. Of more significance are the lesser mujtahids, or
Hujjat al-Islam wa al-Muslimin (the Proof of Islam and of Muslims) and
the greater mujtahids, or *Hujjat al-Islam wa al-Muslimin, Ayatullah fi al-
'Alamin* (the Proof of Islam and of Muslims, the Sign of God in the
World). Both the lesser and the greater mujtahids are capable of giving
a fatwa, but the fatwas of the latter are given more consideration in view
of their greater influence and the larger number of their followers. The
most important mujtahids are the marji's who are addressed as Ayatullah
al-'Uzma (the Great Sign of God). As a rule, their fatwas stand for their
lay followers unless revoked by the highest marji', which is unusual. It
should be added that after the death in 1970 of the chief marji', Muhsin
al-Hakim, there were only three marji's in Iraq, all at Najaf: his successor
Abu'l-Qasim al-Khu'i, Ruhullah Khomeini, and Muhammad Baqir al-
Sadr. Only al-Sadr was Arab; the others are of Iranian extraction. None
became associated with the Da'wah party.

It is also worth emphasizing that the Shi'i men of religion in Iraq are
not as numerous per capita as they are in Iran. A recent French book
affirmed that in 1979 there were in Iran 180,000 mullas.[37] An informed
Shi'i source gave a more conservative estimate of 120,000. This, if true,
would mean that there was in that year one mulla for every 308 Iranians,
assuming a total population of 37 million. There are no up-to-date statistics on the size of the religious class in Iraq, but in 1947, when the population was about 4.5 million (at present it is 14 million), the number of
persons employed in the religious services of all denominations did not
exceed 7,763,[38] and this figure included persons who were not men of
religion, such as servants in mosques or churches. As could be expected,
more than one-sixth of the total were concentrated in the Shi'i holy cities:
601 at Karbala, 474 at Najaf, and 232 at Kazimain.[39]

It is in the mosques of these cities that the Da'wah began spreading
its ideas. It also gave considerable attention to the vast crowds that take
part there annually in the ceremonial processions commemorating the

37. Paul Balta and Claudine Rulleau, *L'Iran insurgé* (Paris, 1979), 152. This figure is
almost surely overstated.
38. Government of Iraq, Ministry of Social Affairs, Directorate General of Census,
Census of Iraq, 1947 (Baghdad, 1954). The figure was computed from all the tables numbered 7 relating to the various districts of Iraq in vols. 1, 2, and 3.
39. Ibid., pp. 48, 195, 205.

martyrdom of Husain on 20 Safar, and hoped to attach the people's feelings to its ideological conclusions.

In its efforts the Da'wah was greatly assisted by the drought that struck the Najaf-Karbala region and other Shi'i areas in the middle 1970s in the wake of the reduction of the flow of the Euphrates River because of Syria's newly built dam at Tabqah. The drought ruined fruit orchards and the rice crop, affecting hundreds of thousands of peasants.

The Da'wah's first test of strength with the government came in 1974 when the Husaini processions broke up into angry political protests. But this was as nothing compared to the fury that greeted the forces of the police in 1977 when they attempted to interfere with the processions halfway between Najaf and Karbala. Outraged, the crowds stormed a police station at nearby al-Haidariyah chanting rhythmically: *"Saddam, shil idak! Sha'b al-'Iraq ma yiridak!"* (Saddam, remove your hand! The people of Iraq do not want you!).

The Iranian Revolution of 1978–79 radicalized the Da'wah and prompted the appearance of the Mujahidin. This signaled before long a shift in the method of struggle, the two movements now resorting to sporadic guerrilla attacks on the posts of the police, the Baath party, and the People's Army.

The Iranian Revolution also turned the gaze of the Shi'is increasingly toward Sayyid Muhammad Baqir al-Sadr, who, it will be remembered, was Iraq's most distinguished and most enlightened Shi'i legist and inspired much devotion among the common people. Moreover, without any encouragement from him, more and more Shi'is began to look up to him for political leadership and Iran's Arabic radio broadcasts repeatedly referred to him as "the Khomeini of Iraq." In the eyes of the government he loomed as a rival pole of attraction and a symbol of approaching danger.

How did the regime react to militant Shi'i activities?

Theoretically, Saddam Husain laid down a number of guidelines for his followers. In the first place, he insisted that the attitude of the Baathists toward religion and with regard to "religious or sectarian fanaticism" should be "free from ambiguity or evasiveness" because "we have no wish to win over the majority within determinate temporal limits or for transient causes or merely to get past a temporary trying situation." "Our party," he added, "is not neutral between belief and unbelief; it is on the side of belief always, but it is not a religious party and should not be so."

He also pointed out that "certain oppositional forces" sought "under the cover of religious observances" to provoke the apparatuses of the regime into interfering in matters of faith in an "undisciplined and insensible" manner in the hope of isolating the Baath from its masses and throwing it into "the situation of the interpenetrating trenches . . . where it becomes difficult to distinguish between friend and foe." The political line of those forces was based upon the supposition that "we would make a tactical mistake whose consequences they would generalize with negative effects on our strategy."

It was necessary, therefore, for the government and party to avoid at all costs "the politicizing of religion" and to permit every sect to observe its rites according to its wishes. For the regime to meddle in affairs of faith was bound not only to divide the people into believers and unbelievers but to split the believers themselves in the light of their varying views and their different religious and sectarian affiliations. "Is this not tantamount to entering a foredoomed policy by its most perilous channels?"

At the same time, Saddam Husain left the Shi'i movements under no misapprehension that "the use of religion as a cover for politics" or the veering of religious observances toward a course of "incompatibility or collision" with Baathi policies would incur "stern punishment" and bring the perpetrators under "the iron fist of the revolution."[40]

In practice Saddam Husain pursued two tactics, one of *tarhib* (intimidation) and the other, *targhib* (incitement to cupidity). As Iraqis would say, he terrorized with one hand and offered rewards with the other. In 1974 he executed five members of the Da'wah party; in 1977 he sent eight other Shi'is to their death; in June of 1979 he ordered the arrest of the popular and widely respected Sayyid Muhammad Baqir al-Sadr, and when the people of al-Thaurah took to the streets in protest he suppressed them with violence. His crackdown on the Shi'i opposition precipitated a split in the ruling Revolutionary Command Council, which was to lead in the following August to the physical elimination of twenty-two of his Baathi critics or rivals.[41] In the first quarter of 1980, in the wake of stepped-up grenade attacks in and around Baghdad, he expelled 15,368 Iranian nationals who descended from families that had been living in Iraq for many

40. Saddam Husain, "Nazrah fi al-Din wa al-Turath" (A Glance at Religion and the Historical Heritage), a talk given on August 11, 1977; in Saddam Husain, *Al-Turath al-'Arabi wa al-Mu'asarah* (The Arab Heritage and Contemporary Life) (Baghdad: al-Hurriyah Printing House, 1978), 5–17.

41. The Party of al-Da'wah al-Islamiyah, *Bayan al-Tafahum,* 7–9; *International Herald Tribune* (Paris), February 25, 1977; *al-Hawadith* (Beirut), April 1, 1977; and *New York Times,* August 8, 1979.

generations.[42] In the fall of that year, after the outbreak of the Iraq-Iran War, which was intimately related to Shi'i unrest, he pressed harder on the Da'wah party. According to its own perhaps exaggerated account, from 1974 to the end of 1980 "no fewer than five hundred of the best men of Iraq" were put to death, including the Shi'i marji' Sayyid Muhammad Baqir al-Sadr, eight other ulama and Dr. 'Ala' al-Shahristani, one-time director of the Iraqi Atomic Energy Authority.[43]

Side by side with this, Saddam Husain showed greater deference to the Shi'i ulama and went out of his way to win them over to his regime. In 1979 alone, he spent as much as 24.4 million dinars on shrines, mosques, husainiyahs, pilgrims, and other affairs of religion, dispensing funds impartially to both Shi'i and Sunni establishments.[44] He also declared the birthday of 'Ali ibn Abi Talib a national holiday and took pains to pay frequent visits to the holy places and to tour the Shi'i country, promising new services and further reforms. At Najaf he undertook in a speech to crowds gathered near the Alid sanctuary "to fight injustice with the swords of the Imams" and called for "a revival of heavenly values."[45] In another speech, referring to his family's claim of descent from the Prophet, he asserted, "We have the right to say to-day—and we will not be fabricating history—that we are the grandsons of Imam Husain."[46]

But he did not succeed in getting into the good graces of the highest authoritative Shi'i legist, the chief marji' Ayatullah al-'Uzma Abu'l-Qasim al-Khu'i, who remained wrapped up in religion and unshaken in his determination not to approve or oppose the government. Nor was he able to conciliate the only other Shi'i marji' in Iraq, Sayyid Muhammad Baqir al-Sadr, who is said to have firmly adhered right up to his execution to the view that relationships with the regime were *haram,* that is, religiously forbidden, on account of its palpably "un-Islamic" character.

However, Saddam Husain won over a number of Shi'i religious dignitaries such as the imam Shaikh 'Ali Kashif al-Ghita and Shaikh 'Ali al-Saghir, both of Najaf.[47] But from the standpoint of militant Shi'is these dignitaries belong to the category of *'ulama' al-hafiz,* or service ulama. *Al-hafiz* is a distortion of the English word *office* and is an appellation of

42. *Al-Safir* (Beirut), April 15, 1980.

43. The Party of al-Da'wah al-Islamiyah, *Bayan al-Tafahum,* 7–8.

44. *Al-Jumhuriyah* (Baghdad), January 10, 1980.

45. *Al-Hawadith* (Beirut), January 4, 1980.

46. Baghdad Radio, Arabic Service, August 8, 1979, *Foreign Broadcast Information Service,* August 9, 1979, p. E4.

47. For the support to the regime expressed by Imam 'Ali Kashif al-Ghita and others, see *Baghdad Observer,* October 7, 1980, and *al-Jumhuriyah* (Baghdad), October 10, 1980.

disesteem attached originally to ulama who collaborated with the English and is now pinned to ulama who place their learning at the disposal of regimes unsanctioned by Islam.

It remains to underline that Saddam Husain does not discriminate against Shi'is and thinks in Arab rather than sectarian terms. This is not without its appeal to many in Baghdad or the southern part of the country who are Arabs first and Shi'is after. It is true that few Shi'is hold crucial threads in his regime, but this is less a result of sectarian influences than of the fact that, by dint of the relative thinness of his domestic base and the repressive character of his government, he has been driven to lean more and more heavily on his kinsmen, or members of his own clan, or old companions from his underground days. More than that, in the last five years or so he has spared no efforts to recruit Shi'is into the Baath party and to associate them with his regime. But many of the Shi'is he attracts appear to be impelled more by interest than conviction and tend to be careerists rather than devotees.

What are the present conditions and future prospects of Iraq's Shi'i movements?

It should be reemphasized that in recent years their oppositional activity has been most perceptible outside Iraq. The most salient fact in this connection was the coming together in 1982 at Tehran of the Da'wah, the Mujahidin, and other less significant groups under an umbrella organization, the Supreme Council of the Islamic Revolution in Iraq. In a brochure issued by its publicity unit, the new council was said to represent "all the Muslims in Iraq, the Sunnis as well as the Shi'is" and to view the Islamic Republic of Iran as "the foundation (and the prime mover) of the World Islamic Revolution."[48]

In Iran the Da'wah, the Mujahidin, and the council's other component organizations have their anchorage in the thick of the Iraqi refugees but appear to have made gains also among the Iraqi prisoners of war whom they have been indefatigably wooing. Moreover, they have a foothold in what they call the "liberated part of Iraq," that is, the Kurdish district of Hajj 'Umran. In this area, which is controlled by their allies Mas'ud and Idris al-Barzani, they claim to have no fewer than a thousand fighters who, however, do not appear to be highly trained or heavily armed or as ardently motivated as Khomeini's Revolutionary Guard.

The Da'wah party, in particular, has also won converts in Bahrain

---

48. The Publicity Unit of the High Majlis of the Islamic Revolution in Iraq, *The High Majlis (Supreme Council) of the Islamic Revolution in Iraq* (Teheran?, 1983), pp. 21–25, 46.

(as is evident from the arrest there of fifty-two of its followers on December 16, 1981), in Kuwait (where eighteen of its members were involved in the bombings of December 12, 1983), and among the tens of thousands of Iraqi refugees who live in camps in Syria near the border with Iraq or in the Sitt Zaynab quarter of Damascus. Significantly enough, these refugees, who were alleged to be of Iranian descent, had originally been expelled to Iran but, feeling lost in their new environment, "returned to the Arab culture by way of Syria."[49]

In Iraq itself, however, Shi'i oppositional organizations have shrunk sharply. At present they are capable only of mounting disruptive acts— like the bombing assaults against the Ministry of Planning on August 1, 1982, and the offices of the Iraqi Airways on April 8, 1983—that are suicidal in character and of limited effect. The hand of the government is discernible in much of their decline. Its agents have been stern in their vigilance and relentless in their repression.

The Shi'i religious class as a whole has been tangibly weakened by the exile of the ulama of Iranian origin and the ulama suspected of Iranian sympathies and by the execution in May of 1983 of six and the arrest of many other members of the al-Hakim family. The treatment meted out to the Hakims is obviously tied to their prominence in the Shi'i anti-Baathi opposition in Iran. Only a skeleton network of men of religion is said to have survived. Academic theological activity has noticeably declined. Even the chief marji' Ayatullah al-'Uzma Abu'l-Qasim al-Khu'i reportedly offers courses only at his home and for a limited number of students.

Al-Thaurah district of Greater Baghdad is no longer a stronghold of the Shi'i underground as it was in the 1970s. Since 1980 the government has spent much money on this district, providing it with drinking water, sewers, paved streets, and other essential services, and has renamed it Saddam's Town.

But factors other than the role of the government have contributed to the ebb in the fortunes of the Shi'i clandestine organizations. One has been their inability to span a bridge even for temporary purposes with the other elements of the Iraqi opposition, except for the Kurdish National Union, led by Mas'ud and Idris al-Barzani. The chasm between their worldview and that of such secular oppositional forces as the Communists and Jalal al-Talabani's Kurdish Democratic Union is too wide to permit authentic or enduring cooperation among them.

Another negative factor has been the division that characterized the

49. *Al-Ghad ad-Dimuqrati* (Organ of the Iraqi Democratic Rally, Damascus) no. 9, Year 2, May 1984, p. 3.

Shi'i groups prior to 1982 and has fragmented them again in recent months. In the pre-1982 period the Da'wah did not have only the Mujahidin for Shi'i rivals. It had to contend also with Munazzamat al-'Amal al-Islami (the Organization for Islamic Action), a group of lower importance which had its original base in Karbala and is presently led by Muhammad Taqi al-Mudarrisi, a nephew of Shaikh Muhammad al-Shirazi. Even though the various groups, spurred by the Tehran regime, closed ranks in 1982, the Da'wah has—since the spring of 1984, if not earlier—been in practice distancing itself from the other organizations and is apparently no longer represented in the Supreme Council of the Islamic revolution. In a meeting held by the council last May to commemorate the execution of the six members of the Hakim family, the representative of the Da'wah was denied the floor and could not read his party's statement.

The Da'wah has not only opted for an independent Iraqi Islamic regime, thus tacitly rejecting the overlordship of Khomeini; but some of its leaders, such as Murtada al-'Askari, have openly questioned the appropriateness for Iraq of the principle of *wilayat al-faqih* (the sovereignty or guardianship of the jurist) to which Khomeini firmly adheres.

The close embrace of the Shi'i movements by Iran has been a problem not only for the Da'wah but for many dedicated Iraqi Shi'is. "In their heart of hearts," as one of them told this writer in 1981, "Iraq's Shi'is like things to grow from their own soil." This is why they took so much pride in Muhammad Baqir al-Sadr, who, they felt, was one of their own[50] and the only Arab among the eight marji's of the Shi'i world.[51] Moreover, at least in the past it was possible to sense in Najaf itself an undercurrent of tension between Iranian and Arab ulama not dissimilar to that which prevailed between the Greek and Arab clergy within the Orthodox church in Syria and Palestine. Some of the Iranian men of religion tended to look down on their Iraqi counterparts and entertained the notion that Iranians were, on the whole, more devoted to their faith than the Arabs and that had the religious message not descended upon an Arab prophet, no Arab would have ever embraced Islam. At any rate, Iraq's Shi'is are clearly more comfortable with their own kind and prefer that real leadership should be in the hands of Shi'is who are Iraqi.

50. It should be noted, however, that he came from a family that migrated to Iraq from southern Lebanon in the latter part of the eighteenth or early in the nineteenth century.

51. The other seven marji's in 1980 were Abu'l-Qasim al-Khu'i of Najaf, Ruhullah Khomeini, Kazim Shariat Madari, and Gulpaygani of Qom, and 'Abdullah al-Shirazi, al-Najafi al-Mar'ashi and Hasan al-Qummi of Mashhad, who were all Iranians, although Shariat Madari was of Azerbaijani Turkish origin.

Besides, one of the side effects of the Iraq-Iran War has been a sharpening of the feeling of distinction between Arab and Iranian among at least a part of Iraq's Shi'is, particularly among those who have all along held that their Arab or Iraqi identity is more important than their Shi'i or Islamic affiliation. Others could not help noticing that the status of the Arab Shi'i minority in Iran has not improved under the new religious dispensation. There is also a strong opinion to the effect that Shi'i causes in Iraq should not be identified with Iran's military effort.

In fact, the most telling thing about the Iraq-Iran War is that the Shi'i soldiers, who form the bulk of the rank and file of Iraq's army, have so far not shown any inclination to sacrifice their country to their religion, which suggests that national bonds may be stronger and sectarian ties weaker than is often imagined.

However, Shi'i themes and symbols remain powerful, and the Shi'i opposition is poised to benefit if the regime of Saddam Husain falters politically or suffers a serious military defeat, which according to all present indications appears unlikely. The fortunes of the Shi'i opposition also obviously depend to no inconsiderable degree on the fortunes of Iran's theocracy.

DAVID BUSBY EDWARDS

Chapter Eight # The Evolution of Shi'i Political Dissent in Afghanistan

During the 1970s research on Afghanistan expanded widely, particularly
in the fields of history and anthropology, but one area that was generally
ignored was the study of Islam and its place in Afghan society and politics.
Thus, if one were to judge the relative importance of Islam and Buddhism
in Afghan history and society on the basis of the number of journal articles
published on each subject, Buddhism would undoubtedly win even though
it had effectively died out in Afghanistan by the seventh century. Today
hindsight tells us what few scholars apparently realized in the seventies:
that, far from being inconsequential, Islam could reassert itself as a vital
social force still capable of providing a framework for political mobilization in a time of grave crisis.

Seven years after the first uprising against the communist government, analyses of the Afghan resistance movement are still hampered by
the absence of previous research on Islam in Afghanistan. Existing
sources provide little help in deciphering the confusing political situation
that prevails today in the Pakistani cities of Peshawar and Quetta, where
the major Sunni and Shi'i parties, respectively, are located, not to mention
the situation in Afghanistan where each region is a story unto itself. This
essay provides a preliminary and admittedly incomplete sketch of the
evolution of Islamic political protest in Afghanistan from the late nine-

teenth century to the present. The focus here is on Shi'i Islam, but it should be noted that sectarian boundaries between Sunni and Shi'i have varied in importance during the period under consideration, and sometimes have faded from sight completely as Islamic political activists sought new ideas and forms to embody their faith. At other times, sectarian divisions have reemerged to frustrate attempts to develop a unified approach to the problem of redefining Islam as a political ideology. I will indicate here the major events in the history of Islamic and, specifically, Shi'i political development in Afghanistan during the last ninety years and will set forth some of the patterns of conflict and change that can be discerned in the course of this history. Of principal concern is the division between rural and urban segments of the Shi'i population and the different roles Islam has played in galvanizing political dissent in these two contexts.

QIZILBASH AND HAZARA: SHI'ISM AND ETHNIC DIVERSITY IN AFGHANISTAN

The Imami Shi'i population of Afghanistan consists of three principal ethnic groups: the Mongol Hazaras who inhabit the central Hazarajat region; Farsiwan who are located primarily near the Iranian border but who have also settled in towns and villages in eastern Afghanistan; and the urban Qizilbash most of whom live in Kabul, Herat, and Qandahar. In addition to these groups, there also exist smaller communities of Shi'is, such as the Shi'i Turkomans of Surkh-i Parsal (Parwan Province), Kabul-based Kashmiris, and scattered lineage groups of Shi'i sayyids who claim descent from the Prophet through the Alid line. Although census figures for Afghanistan are notoriously inexact, it can be estimated that Shi'i comprise approximately 10 to 15 percent of the total population.[1]

With the exception of the Turkomans and some groups of Farsiwan and Qizilbash living in Pashtun areas, all these ethnic groups speak Persian dialects; but aside from this and their adherence to Imami Shi'ism,

1. See Louis Dupree, *Afghanistan* (Princeton: Princeton University Press, 1973), 58–64; W. Smith et al., *Afghanistan—A Country Study* (Washington, D.C.: American University, 1980), 70–79; Editors, *L'Islam en Afghanistan* in *Les Nouvelles d'Afghanistan,* supp. to nos. 12–13, March 1983 (AFRANE, Paris). All succeeding quotations and other information not otherwise cited derives from interviews conducted with Afghans in Pakistan between 1982 and 1984 during the course of gathering background material on the origins of the Afghan jihad and refugee migration. This research was made possible through a Fulbright-Hays predoctoral fellowship and a grant from the National Science Foundation whose support is gratefully acknowledged.

they have little else in common with regard to their sociocultural traditions and economic conditions. This is particularly true of the Hazara and Qizilbash communities, which are of primary concern here because of their involvement in the evolution of Shi'i political protest in Afghanistan. The originally tribal Qizilbash, for example, who first settled in Herat and Qandahar in the Safavid period, were closely associated with the Sadduzai dynasty, which was founded by Ahmad Shah Durrani in the late eighteenth century and continued to serve in positions of influence as royal bodyguards and clerks in the court until the end of the nineteenth century.[2]

In contrast to the urbanized Qizilbash, the tribally organized Hazaras, the largest Shi'i community in Afghanistan, are one of the poorest groups, inhabiting a mountainous region that is characterized by long, cold winters and a paucity of arable land. Unlike the Qizilbash, whose practice of Shi'ism allowed them to prosper as dependent outsiders among contending royal factions, the Hazaras "had raided and plundered the neighboring subjects [of the Afghan confederacy] for about three hundred years past, and none of the kings had had the power to make them absolutely peaceful."[3] As famous for their internal feuds as for their raids the Hazaras were able to keep both the government and the Pashtun nomads who coveted their pastures at bay until the late nineteenth century. The Hazaras have differed historically from the Qizilbash in their fierce independence and unwillingness to compromise their autonomy to any outside power.

Qizilbash and Hazara also differ in their traditional understanding and practice of Islam. Given their social position and high literacy, the Qizilbash produced a number of scholars (ulama) capable of writing learned tracts on religious subjects. They also had contacts with Persian mujtahids, whom they visited during pilgrimages to Karbala and Mashhad, and appear generally to have been connected to the Shi'i world outside Afghanistan.[4] At the same time, their minority position required

2. Hasan Kakar, *Government and Society in Afghanistan: The Reign of Amir 'Abd al-Rahman Khan* (Austin: University of Texas, 1979), 91–94. Kakar, one of Afghanistan's finest scholars and the source of most of the information contained here on the reign of 'Abd al-Rahman Khan, has been in prison in Kabul for the last several years for having established a human rights monitoring group in Afghanistan.

3. Mir Munshi, S.M.K., *The Life of Abdur Rahman, Amir of Afghanistan* (London: John Murray, 1900), 1:279. See also R. Canfield, *Faction and Conversion in a Plural Society: Religious Alignments in the Hindu Kush* (Ann Arbor: Museum of Anthropology, 1973), 95–97.

4. Kakar, *Government*, 148.

that they sometimes practice dissimulation (*taqiyah*) and that they keep to themselves within their own walled enclaves of Chindawal and Murad Khani in Kabul. Although the Shi'i community in Kabul maintained *takyah khanahs* where they performed the mourning ceremonies of Muharram and listened to the sermons (*khwandan*) of their religious leaders, theirs seems to have been an undemonstrative faith subordinated to the pragmatic realities of their status in the society and court.[5]

The traditional practice of Islam among the Hazaras seems to have been different. According to Kakar, they "neither had mosques nor observed the *muharram* ceremonies in their *takyah khanahs*."[6] Hazara informants dispute the idea that they had no mosques but admit that because of the impoverished conditions prevailing in the Hazarajat most villages had to combine the activities of the takyah khanah and mosque in one building. Regardless of which description is most accurate, it appears certain that their practice of Islam was one that had little connection to scriptural traditions, if only because literacy was a rare accomplishment, even for the local imams who led the communal prayers. One result of this was the development of an insular tradition focused on the person of 'Ali who was (and still is) seen by many as an autochthonous progenitor. While it was recognized that 'Ali was a historical figure who lived in a relatively recent era, this fact was not thought to be incompatible with the belief that with his great sword *dhu'l-fiqar* he created the lakes at Band-i Amir, cleaved mountains, and left giant footprints visible in the geological formations of the region. Like the Qizilbash, Hazaras also journeyed to the shrine cities of Mashhad and Karbala in great numbers each year and paid visits to the mujtahids of those cities. However, lacking an established and broadly based literate tradition of the kind that existed among the Qizilbash, they were dissociated from the more profound currents of Shi'i thought and were more likely to seek the blessing than the advice of the mujtahids. We can characterize the Hazara brand of Shi'ism as an insular, self-contained faith that emphasized veneration of shrines and uncritical reverence for sayyids as bearers of *karamat* (miracles) while downplaying formal theology and the purely historical significance of shrines and sacred descent in Shi'ism.[7]

5. Writing during the reign of Amir Amanullah, Sirdar Ikbal Ali Shah noted that "the spectacular demonstration of mourning during the Muharrum is a practice which many of their own [Qizilbash] Shiah reformers do not favour" (*Afghanistan of the Afghans* [London: Diamond Press, 1928], 213).

6. Kakar, *Government,* 148.

7. Several exceptions to this general statement, all historical works, should be noted: Faiz Muhammad Hazara, *Saraj ul-Tawarikh*; Muhammad Afzal ibn Watandad, *Mukhtasar ul-Manqul Fi ul-Tarikh Mughul*; and Mir 'Ali Asghar Sho'a, *Dairat ul-Ma'rif Afghanistan.*

Although the Qizilbash and Hazara represent very different societies and traditions, their histories became intertwined with the outbreak of the so-called Hazara War (1891–93). This conflict was one of a number that broke out in various parts of what was to become the nation of Afghanistan during the reign of 'Abd al-Rahman, but the Hazara campaigns differed from, and in many ways were more virulent than, the battles waged against other groups in that they were formulated specifically in sectarian terms. Thus, the amir secured a fatwa (a document of religious sanction) from the chief religious authorities in Kabul declaring the Hazaras and all other Shi'is to be infidels. Proclamations to this effect were distributed widely throughout the country, and stipendiary mullas were dispatched to accompany the tribal levies and further incite them with the prospect of *ghaza* (holy conquest) and *ghanimat* (booty).[8]

'Abd al-Rahman's reasons for premising his campaigns on sectarian grounds appear to have been essentially pragmatic since a declaration of jihad not only legitimized military action but also helped to attract tribal levies who were promised their share of the booty according to Islamic precedents. However, in exploiting this line, 'Abd al-Rahman created a number of additional problems for himself as well. For one, he escalated a relatively isolated tribal conflict into a much larger religious war. Since the early 1880s, a number of campaigns had been waged against Hazara tribes, but, because of the normal divisions that existed between Hazaras, these conflicts had remained localized with some Hazara tribes even assisting the government.[9] This situation changed dramatically, however, once the conflict was transformed into a religious war, and by the fall of 1892, virtually all the normally fractious Hazara tribes joined in defense of their homeland and religion. Like 'Abd al-Rahman, the Hazara also sought religious legitimacy and received "the *fitwa* of the *mujtahids* of Meshad who declared '. . . a religious war against Afghan Sunnis to be lawful and worthy of the martyr's reward.' "[10] Further, when in 1892 'Abd

8. See Hasan Kakar, *Afghanistan: A Study in Internal Political Development, 1880–1896* (Lahore, 1971), 165, and Ashraf Ghani, "Islam and State-Building in a Tribal Society," *Modern Asian Studies* 12, no. 2 (1978): 269–84. Amir 'Abd al-Rahman premised other military campaigns as well on religious grounds. Thus, Sardar Muhammad Ishaq was condemned for rebelling against the legitimate Sunni ruler, and the 1895 invasion of Kafiristan, an area of northeastern Afghanistan that retained its own religious belief system, was justified as a jihad to convert the kafirs. In the latter instance, 'Abd al-Rahman succeeded beyond what might have been expected considering that the area was not only converted to Islam but also became known in recent decades as a bastion of Panj Piri mullas espousing a conservative theology similar to Wahhabism.

9. Kakar, *Afghanistan*, 165.

10. Ibid., 177.

al-Rahman launched his final invasion of the Hazarajat, his forces faced not the usual collection of quarrelsome Hazara tribes but a tribal coalition united behind a sayyid named Timur Shah.[11]

The Qizilbash found themselves implicated in this conflict, for the Amir suspected that both they and the mujtahids of Mashhad were responsible for Hazara intransigence toward their Sunni rulers. Lacking specific proof to back up his suspicions, 'Abd al-Rahman launched a campaign of persecution against the Qizilbash on the pretext that Shi'is generally were guilty of blasphemy in their devotion toward 'Ali and neglect of the other companions of the Prophet.[12] Beyond this, the Amir also outlawed the traditional Muharram ceremonies and allowed Shi'is to operate only three takyah khanahs in Kabul. Later, after an apparent assassination attempt by a mentally unbalanced Qizilbash boy, even more restrictions were applied, including the abandonment of Shi'i faith, conversion of all takyah khanahs to mosques, and the appointment of Sunni mullas to ensure mosque attendance by Qizilbash and other Shi'is living in Kabul.

According to Kakar, there was little resistance to these measures, and in 1896, leading members of both the Qizilbash and Hazara communities in Kabul "informed the amir that they had become Sunnis."[13] Such declarations were very likely examples of dissimulation as allowed by the doctrine of taqiyah, but, from the evidence available, it does seem that the Kabul Shi'is of the late nineteenth-century period were far from militant in their attitude toward Sunni persecution. Acquiescence, however, did not help them regain their former positions of power, and most Qizilbash were eventually forced to turn to shopkeeping and other professions to earn their livelihoods.

Among the Shi'is of the Hazarajat, the ultimate defeat of the Imami coalition under Timur Shah brought about a number of fundamental social and political changes. One such change was that the effective power of both sayyids and tribal leaders was much reduced. Many of the more important leaders were either relocated by the government to other regions or forced into exile, mostly to Quetta and Mashhad where large Hazara communities were established after the final defeat in 1893. Many

11. Ibid., 170.

12. Kakar, *Government,* 159. Kakar writes that a hundred thousand members of both the Qizilbash and Hazara communities traveled to Mashhad annually. Although the figure would appear to be significantly exaggerated, it does illustrate that large numbers from both communities traveled to Iran and certainly had contacts among themselves while there.

13. Ibid., 159.

of the leaders who stayed had land confiscated and redistributed to Pashtun agriculturalists, sixteen thousand of whom were relocated in Uruzgan, and to nomads who "were awarded indisputable grazing rights in central Afghanistan."[14]

Beyond these assaults, the imposition of an extrinsic administrative system tied to the national government in Kabul undermined the importance and coherence of both tribal and religious structures. Thus, for example, the introduction of a central system of land ownership and taxation "contributed to the formation of private property on the level of lineage segments or even families," thereby eliminating one of the bases of tribal solidarity.[15] Through their involvement in judicial cases and other matters requiring decision making, government officials also usurped many of the responsibilities and prerogatives of the tribal and religious leaders who had formerly handled such matters themselves. The overall effect of these changes was to limit the role of traditional leaders, and in the place of the larger religious coalitions of the past, "smaller *pir-murid* [sufi leader-follower] networks based on more closed and many-stranded relations succeeded the former system."[16]

This diminution in the role of traditional leaders was only one of many fundamental changes brought about by the invasions of the late nineteenth century and the absorption of the Hazarajat into the Afghan state. As noted, political coalitions in the Hazarajat appear to have continued as they had before, albeit on a reduced scale, but after the final defeat of the Hazara confederacy in 1893, large numbers of Hazaras began to be incorporated into the mainstream of Afghan society. Many of these Hazaras were forcibly relocated, and still others were sold into slavery, a practice that was not finally outlawed until the reign of Amir Amanullah Khan (1919–29). Other Hazaras, however, began to leave the Hazarajat because of economic strains, for with the confiscation of lands that occurred under 'Abd al-Rahman, the already inadequate land base became even more tenuous, leading considerable numbers of Hazaras to migrate to Kabul and other cities. Here, they took over many of the least desirable jobs that other groups refused, most of which involved such forms of low-paying day labor as carrying backbreaking loads around the city.[17]

14. Canfield, *Faction and Conversion,* 103. See also Kakar, *Afghanistan,* 174.

15. L. Kopecky, "The Imami Sayyed of the Hazarajat: The Maintenance of Their Elite Position," *Folk* 24 (1982): 104.

16. Ibid., 104.

17. See C. Jung, "Some Observations on the Patterns and Processes of Rural-Urban Migrations to Kabul," Occasional Paper no. 2, Afghanistan Council of the Asia Society, n.d. (1971?).

YAGHI AND GHAZI: FROM RURAL BANDITRY
TO URBAN POLITICAL PROTEST

With the increasing consolidation of the Afghan state after the ascension of Zahir Shah to the throne in 1933, the focus of Shi'i political protest began to move from the country to the city. This does not mean that the Hazarajat was entirely pacified, but the forms of protest changed, becoming once again more localized and sporadic as well as less overtly religious in formulation. Thus, most of the remembered incidents of "political protest" from 1933 until the present period involved what are called *yaghi,* "bandits." Characteristically, these were men who, after getting into some kind of trouble with the government, fled to the mountains and then took up arms against government despotism (*istibdad*) and the abuses of Pashtun nomads who were protected by local government officials.

In this regard, Hazara informants accused nomads of killing innocent people, taking farmers' harvests to feed their animals, and plundering houses. Whether such actions were generalized or not, it is clear that nomads were given favorable treatment by the Pashtun administration and that, with this support, they managed not only to obtain access to pastures but also to gain outright control of much of the agricultural land in the Hazarajat. This was accomplished through a traditional nomadic enterprise—moneylending—which Pashtun tribes engaged in as far afield as Burma and Bengal and which, in the Hazarajat, accelerated the process of disenfranchisement begun under 'Abd al-Rahman. By the late sixties, this process had proceeded so far that it was estimated that in some areas 20 percent of the land was owned by nomads and that 60 to 80 percent of all Hazaras suffered under some degree of indebtedness.[18]

With no channel of redress through the government, the yaghi became folk heroes in the Hazarajat. Stories are still told of one such individual named Yusuf Beg, who managed to avoid capture in the region of Shahristan (Uruzgan Province) for nineteen years. He was finally apprehended by Abdullah Khan Wardak, the *hakim* (subgovernor) of Deh Zangi, and was taken before Prime Minister Hashim Khan in Kabul and eventually executed.

A more serious (and storied) event occurred in the late 1940s when Ibrahim Gausawar, known as Bach-i Gausawar, instigated a revolt, again

---

18. Ibid., 10. See also K. Ferdinand, "Nomad Expansion and Commerce in Central Afghanistan," *Folk* 4 (1962), and J. A. Robinson, *Notes on the Nomad Tribes of Eastern Afghanistan* (1934; reprint, Quetta, 1978). Ferdinand notes that government officials in Deh Zangi commented to him in 1954 that a more modest 5 percent of land in the region was in the hands of nomads (p. 133).

in Shahristan. This uprising was explained by one Hazara informant as follows:

> After this rebel [Yusuf Beg], the tyranny of the government increased, and they wanted to collect *rughan* [clarified butter] from the people. But all the people fled. They still continued to collect *rughan* by force and would bind people in iron chains and make them stand in their bare feet on thorns until they gave them the *rughan*. Then Bach-i Gausawar rebelled and completely destroyed the *hukumat* [government center] of Shahristan. For one winter, he was the *padshah* [king] in that district.[19]

Bach-i Gausawar's rebellion was brought to an end the following spring when the government in Kabul sent a delegation of prominent Hazaras to Shahristan to offer amnesty in return for an end to the resistance. Subsequently, Bach-i Gausawar accompanied the delegation to Kabul where he was pardoned by Zahir Shah. But despite Bach-i Gausawar's notoriety, the situation remained as before: both government officials and Pashtun nomads continued their economic exploitation of the Hazarajat, and the Hazara people were legally and politically powerless to effect a remedy.[20]

In analyzing the activities of Yusuf Beg and Bach-i Gausawar, we are warranted in seeing them as representatives of the phenomenon that Hobsbawm has called "social banditry." In Hobsbawm's analysis, banditry represents a form of political protest characteristic of societies in transition, societies undergoing the first stages of incorporation within larger state systems. In this regard, Hobsbawm notes that "tribal or kinship societies are familiar with raiding, but lack the internal stratification which creates the bandit as a figure of social protest and rebellion. However, when such communities . . . develop their own systems of class differentiation, or when they are absorbed into larger economies resting on class conflict, they may supply a disproportionately large number of social bandits."[21]

Although complex social relations such as those between nomads and Hazaras do not fit neatly within the definition of "class conflict," it is

19. Interview with Hazara leaders, conducted in Peshawar, Pakistan, January 1984.

20. That this was not an isolated incident is evinced by the fact that at least two other bandits (Qurban from Shahristan and Khudai Dad from Deh Kundi, also in Uruzgan Province) took up arms following the surrender of Bach-i Gausawar and that the people of Garnaw also mounted a brief revolt against the government.

21. E. J. Hobsbawm, *Bandits* (New York: Pantheon, 1981), 18–19. See also Hobsbawm, *Primitive Rebels: Studies in Archaic Forms of Social Movements in the 19th and 20th Centuries* (New York: Norton, 1965).

nevertheless the case that, for the first time, Hazaras were being incorporated within a larger economic and social system and that this was occurring on terms other than their own. As a result, Hazaras were also beginning to acquire a sense of shared Hazara identity through their common experience of exploitation, and it was this and the absence of alternative channels of political redress that gave rise to social banditry during this period. Like the social bandits of Hobsbawm's study, Yusuf Beg and Bach-i Gausawar lacked an ideological basis for their protest other than their bald opposition to injustice. There was also no channel available to them to voice their protest to the government nor any organizational structure capable of galvanizing the people into a popular political force. As with others who became social bandits, their inchoate opposition to exploitation led in due course to their taking up arms against the oppressors, which, of course, led the government to characterize them as criminal bandits even as the people looked up to them as folk heroes.

It is significant in this regard that the principal bandit of the period should be called by the humble appellation *Bach-i Gausawar* (son of the cow-rider) rather than by a title such as *arbab,* which would indicate his holding an established position in society.[22] The symbolic connotation of the name would appear to link it to that of *Bach-i Saqau* (son of the water-carrier), the popular name of the Tajik bandit from the Koh-i Daman region of Kabul who unseated Amir Amanullah in 1929. In both cases, the name conveys the sense of modest origin. Because they do not contain the usual tribal or regional designation but rather are descriptive of the bearers' association with a lowly occupational class, the names point to a change in the frame of reference within which the individual assumes his identity.[23] It is perhaps in the nature of bandits that they portray themselves and are portrayed by others not as individuals from a particular tribe or place but as humble "sons of the people," both universal and anonymous. This seems to be the case here, and it is symbolic of a society that is leaving behind its insular past and beginning to see itself as part of a larger social universe in which class oppression is an inescapable reality.

22. According to Hazara informants, Gausawar was in fact an *arbab* (tribal leader) in Shahristan, although he was not known by this title.

23. In *'Ayyari az Khurasan: Amir Habibullah, Khadim-i Din-i Rasul Allah,* a work of lyric—and, for non-Pashtuns, revisionist—history by the noted Afghan poet Khalilullah Khalili, the claim is made that the title *Bach-i Saqau,* "son of a water-carrier," refers to the father's having transported water to the mujahidin entrenched on the Koh-i Asmai during the battle for Kabul during the Second Anglo-Afghan War. Whether this claim is accurate or not cannot be judged, although no one doubts that Bach-i Saqau was from a poor peasant family in the village of Kalakan in the Koh-i Daman region.

In considering this process of evolving political consciousness, it should be noted that our understanding of the significance of the bandit is in accord with the native understanding. Thus, the word *yaghi* conveys many of the characteristics that we have come to associate with social banditry. Besides its connotation of "bandit," the word also signifies "dissidence," and it is usually used with the locational suffix *-istan* to convey the idea of a "land of dissidence," in opposition to a land where the rule of the government holds sway.[24] The banditry of Yusuf Beg and the rebellion of Bach-i Gausawar can be seen in this light not only as a reaction against the oppressive actions of specific government officials and the incursions of nomads into their region but also as a response to the government's attempts to upset the traditional balance of tribe and state. To this extent then, the localized and episodic protests of Hazara bandits can be thought of as essentially reactionary in nature, rather than revolutionary, in that the objective of the protest was the reassertion of a previous status quo. At the same time, the very fact that such actions were taking place is indicative of the fundamental transformations that were taking place in Hazara society. These transformations were such as to produce outbreaks of social banditry even as they portend the annihilation of the conditions within which banditry might arise.

During this same period, the political activity of sayyids appears to have remained parochial and self-interested. Generally speaking, it did not involve larger national issues. Thus, for example, while the pir-murid networks of the mystical brotherhoods tended to be "highly politicized," the nature of their political concerns was apparently quite insular and unrelated to the larger dynamics of political and economic exploitation. This would seem to be the case at least with the pir-murid networks investigated in the late 1960s by Canfield, who reports that all the major public issues of concern to members of one such group were generated out of a dispute over the right of succession between two collateral lines of the pir's lineage.[25]

Whether this parochial detachment from larger political issues ac-

24. For a detailed explication of this dichotomy in relation to Pashtun tribes, see J. Anderson, "Khan and Khel: Dialectics of Pakhtun Tribalism," in R. Tapper, ed., *The Conflict of Tribe and State in Iran and Afghanistan* (London: Croom Helm, 1983), 119–49.

25. R. Canfield, "Islamic Coalitions in Bamiyan: A Problem in Translating Afghan Political Culture," in M. N. Shahrani and R. Canfield, eds., *Revolutions and Rebellions in Afghanistan: Anthropological Perspectives* (Berkeley: Institute of International Studies, 1984), 223. Although neither Canfield nor Kopecky (1982) discusses the specific characteristics of pir-murid networks in detail, the use of this term would indicate that they are spiritual groups comprising the spiritual guide (pir) and his disciples (murid) and that their principal activity centers on the performance of dhikr recitations. To my knowledge, no author has written on such matters as the tariqat affiliation of Afghan Shi'i groups.

curately reflects the concerns of all or most pir-murid groups is unknown, but in numerous interviews conducted with Hazaras in Pakistan between 1982 and 1984, none of the informants mentioned any significant political activities initiated by sayyids or by other religious figures in the Hazarajat prior to the outbreak of anticommunist resistance in 1978, and several informants stated that some religious leaders had actually worked in opposition to popular figures like Bach-i Gausawar.[26] This disconnection of Shi'i leaders from larger political concerns, if typical, would seem to be related to the general decline in the importance of both the traditional secular and religious leadership in the Hazarajat after the incorporation of the region into the Afghan state.

At the same time, however, the fact of incorporation also established the conditions for the expansion of Shi'i political activity outside the Hazarajat. Thus, the development of the central government during the mid-twentieth century led to a massive increase of the population of Kabul, much of which was directly attributable to the influx of Hazaras into the city. Although Sunnis were the chief beneficiaries of the expansion in government jobs and the economic development of the period, Hazaras were also attracted to Kabul where they congregated in traditional Shi'i enclaves like Chindawal, Kart-i Sakhi (Jamal Mina), and Qala-i Musa as well as in the squatter settlements that rose up on the slopes of the hills that ring the city.[27]

Opportunities offered to other groups, particularly to Pashtuns, were less readily available to Shi'is in general and the Hazaras in particular. Thus, for example, although Hazaras supplied a large percentage of conscripts for military service, the officer corps was dominated by Pashtuns and, to a lesser extent, by Tajiks, the second largest ethnic group in Afghanistan who, like the Pashtuns, are Sunnis of the Hanafi school. High

26. Afghan informants have indicated that, whereas the term *yaghi* has positive connotations when used in rural areas like the Hazarajat, it has negative connotations in Islam and indicates one who rebels against a legitimate ruler. This difference in interpretation might therefore be used to justify opposition by religious leaders to individuals like Bach-i Gausawar, but it also indicates a fundamental disjuncture between this leadership and the people at large as regards the state and what constitutes legitimate political protest.

27. In Jung's study made in the sixties of the rural-urban migration situation in Afghanistan, it was estimated that 29 percent (127,432) of Kabul's total population (435,203) had not been born in the city, and approximately half of the immigrants (63,466) had arrived within the preceding four years. It was further estimated that 31 percent of the immigrants came from the central provinces of Afghanistan, areas that are inhabited entirely or predominantly by Hazaras, and that 42 percent of the migrants were between fifteen and thirty-four years of age. In this group, there were twice as many males as females, two-thirds of the males were unmarried, and 70 percent were illiterate (Jung, *Observations*).

schools and the university also had disproportionately large numbers of Pashtuns, and whereas the government established several boarding schools for tribal Pashtuns, no such institutions existed for Hazaras. This is not to say that Hazaras and other Shi'i were entirely shut off from advancement during this period; for the first time, many did attend school and university, and even the officer corps gradually began to admit Shi'is to its ranks. However, these were recognized to be limited and inadequate concessions which only reinforced the sense of exploitation established in the rural context and added to the bitterness and resentment felt by the Shi'i population toward the Pashtun majority and the Afghan monarchy that represented their interests.

Although Hazaras living in Kabul felt the same anti-Pashtun resentment as those in the country, the resulting political activity in the two contexts was very different. As previously discussed, the uprisings that broke out in the Hazarajat over government abuses and nomad incursions never managed to become more than localized—and therefore easily suppressed—incidents involving individual tribes, and it does not appear that these uprisings had any religious component in terms of either ideological content or organization. In Kabul, however, members of the various Shi'i groups began to identify with one another as Shi'is and to perceive their common economic and social problems in Shi'i ideological terms, which is to say, as one more instance in the long history of Sunni persecution that began with the paradigmatic martyrdom of Imam Husain by the forces of Yazid on the plains of Karbala.[28]

The institutional foci for this emerging sectarian identity were the takyah khanahs, which became important gathering places for Shi'is of different ethnic backgrounds and which provided a location for communal expression and solidarity. This is illustrated in the following statement by one Hazara informant who noted, "In Kabul, at one time, a person could not say that he was a Hazara. People would belittle him. But, later, during the time of Zahir Khan, a number of sayyids and ulama got permission from the government to set up *minbars*. After that, the sectarian beliefs [*'aqayid-i mazhabi*] of the Hazaras in Kabul became free."

During the month of Muharram, thousands of Shi'is would fill the takyah khanahs of distinguished ulama like Agha Bulbul who were revered for their dramatic recitations of the events of Muharram which could fully render the emotion and anguish associated with the martyrdom of Husain. Considering that the king or one of his representatives generally

28. See M. Fischer, *Iran: From Religious Dispute to Revolution* (Cambridge, Mass.: Harvard University Press, 1980), 13–21.

made an appearance each year at the major takyah khanah of Chindawal on the eleventh day of Muharram, it does not appear that these ceremonies were overtly political in orientation. However, the inherent political content and symbolism of the Karbala story cannot be dissociated from the Muharram ceremonies, particularly among a population that, like the Shi'is of Kabul, had come in a short period of time to form an economic and social understratum within the urban milieu.

If Kakar is right in his statement that Muharram was little celebrated in the Hazarajat, then it can be further assumed that the elaborate ceremonies conducted in the takyah khanahs of Kabul's Shi'i quarters must have been especially novel and potent for many of the recently arrived immigrants who had previously had little exposure to the full richness of their cultural traditions or to the emotional resonance of the Karbala story. Thus, even though there might have been no explicitly political dimension to the takyah khanahs and to the Muharram ceremonies conducted therein, the establishment of these places of worship served as a necessary precondition for the gradual politicization of the Shi'i community.

SAYYID ISMA'IL BALKHI AND THE ADVENT OF ISLAMIC POLITICS IN AFGHANISTAN

The first step in the politicization process was taken by Sayyid Isma'il Balkhi, who has come to be thought of as the founder not only of Shi'i but also of Islamic political protest generally in Afghanistan. Balkhi was born in 1919 in Balkhab, an area of Juzjan Province on the northern edge of the Hazarajat. Besides being of sayyid descent, Balkhi was also an *'alim* who first studied religious subjects with his father and later completed his training in Iraq, as was common among the more learned of the Shi'i ulama. Many of the details of Balkhi's early career are obscure, and it is unclear what influences led to his taking what was at the time the unprecedented step of engaging in political activism along religious ideological lines. However, it is known that after his return to Afghanistan he settled for a time in Balkh where he gained sufficient prominence as a political speaker to be arrested and exiled to Kabul.

In 1949, Balkhi was involved in an attempted coup d'état against the government of Prime Minister Sardar Shah Mahmud Khan. Other leaders involved in the plot were Ibrahim (Bach-i) Gausawar, who had been pardoned by King Zahir Shah approximately two years earlier for his part in the Shahristan uprising, and Khwaja Muhammad Na'im, from a well-known *khwaja* family of Kabul. Na'im was a security commander in Kabul and, as such, had foreknowledge of the movements of the prime minister and other officials. The coup attempt was scheduled to occur while King Zahir Shah was away from the country; the occasion was an agricultural exhibition held in Kart-i Sakhi to commemorate the Afghan New Year (March 21) which was to be inaugurated by Shah Mahmud Khan.

The plan the conspirators had devised called for one group of those involved in the coup to capture or assassinate the prime minister on his way to Kart-i Sakhi, while a second group under Lt. Mir Ahmad Shah Rizwani would capture the palace. Thereafter, Bach-i Gausawar was supposed to capture the radio station and announce that the coup had taken place, that a new Islamic government would be formed with Balkhi serving as amir and Khwaja Muhammad Na'im as defense minister, and that Zahir Shah would remain abroad (as later happened after the coup d'état of Sardar Muhammad Da'ud). Shortly before the inaugural ceremony, however, a Sunni informer named Guljan Wardak disclosed the plan, and the three principal architects of the coup plot were arrested along with a number of other well-known Shi'i figures like Mir 'Ali Ahmad Gauhar, Mir 'Ali Ahmad Zia, and Abdul Latif Sarbaz.

In prison, both Balkhi and Gausawar continued their involvement in political activity, but along divergent lines. Each established covert organizations or, more accurately perhaps, the nuclei of what were to become organizations, under the names Payam-i Islami (the Message of Islam) (Balkhi) and Qiyam-i Islami (the Uprising of Islam) (Gausawar). Those who look on Balkhi as the founder of the Islamic movement in Afghanistan state that the reason for this split between Balkhi and Gausawar was that Gausawar capitulated to the government after his arrest and that this was why he was released sooner than Balkhi who remained in prison until 1964; unlike Gausawar, Balkhi is said to have kept his *iman* (faith). Whatever the truth of this assertion, the split between Balkhi and Gausawar signals a profound break with the past. Indeed, rarely does one find such transitions so clearly manifest, for lacking a coherent ideological foundation, the bandit Gausawar slipped out of the front rank of those Hazaras leading the political opposition to the government. Although he remained a respected figure, particularly for Hazara "nationalists" who rejected both Islam and communism as bases for their political objectives, it was Balkhi who provided the symbolic focus and inspiration for the more potent political movement that was then emerging in Kabul.

This was accomplished primarily through his poetry, which was widely circulated among both Shi'is and Sunnis, particularly students to whom Balkhi addressed much of the explicitly political rhetoric in his verse. The main themes that emerge in his poetry are the need for sacrifice and hardship, especially on the part of young people, and the eventual triumph over oppression that can be achieved only through the shedding of one's own blood. In expressing these themes, Balkhi became the first figure in the modern era of Afghan history to embody personally the Islamic conception of sacrifice by refusing to compromise his beliefs for his freedom. In this respect, Balkhi actualized the Karbala paradigm, bringing the lesson of the martyrdom of Husain into the Afghan political context of 1960. The full significance of this was not to be realized until somewhat later, but it remains the case that in establishing this precedent of personal sacrifice, Balkhi transformed political ideology and action in Afghanistan and provided a potent symbol in a society that was in the midst of fundamental structural changes.

ISLAMIC PROTEST DURING THE
CONSTITUTIONAL ERA: 1964–73

Balkhi's release from prison in 1964 coincided with the advent of the experiment in parliamentary democracy that was to continue more or less fitfully until the coup d'état of 1973. Although Balkhi was ill when released and was to remain infirm until his death in 1969, he helped establish a new political party named Paiman-i Islami (Islamic Alliance) headed by Mir 'Ali Ahmad Gauhar, a Shi'i spiritual leader from Ghorband who like Balkhi had been arrested for his part in the coup attempt of 1949 and had spent the following fourteen years in prison. During this same period, Qiyam-i Islami was also resurrected, though covertly as an underground party under the leadership of Gen. Mir Ahmad Shah Rizwani, who, as a lieutenant, had been involved in the 1949 coup attempt but had not been captured. This group was active primarily within the military and included both Shi'a and Sunni among its members.

Two other Islamic groups that were active during the late sixties and that also had both Shi'i and Sunni members were the university-based student organization, Jawanan-i Musulman (Muslim Youth), and a group led by a Sufi spiritual figure, Mawlana Faizani, which was called Madrasah-yi Qur'an (School of the Qur'an). Initially inspired by the private teachings of Prof. Ghulam Muhammad Niazi, a graduate of al-Azhar who had been exposed to the ideology of the Muslim Brotherhood while in Cairo, the Jawanan group took their mentor's teachings to heart to a degree that he himself was unwilling to do. Thus, while Niazi remained publicly uninvolved in political issues so that he could continue teaching at the university, his students became increasingly militant, in response particularly to the radical rhetoric of the communist students who had become actively engaged in organizing students on campus a few years earlier. Between these two camps, great bitterness developed, and each side sought out every opportunity for confrontation and violence.

In contrast to this group, Mawlana Faizani's Madrasah-yi Qur'an developed first as a Sufi order (of which Faizani was the pir) and only later took on an active political dimension. However, even after becoming involved in politics, Faizani continued to teach his followers that political progress could come only after personal spiritual advancement. In addition, Faizani was also concerned with another fundamental problem largely ignored by other Islamic groups, namely science. During the late sixties, the traditional ulama had found it increasingly difficult to explicate the advances of Western sciences within the established teachings of Islam. Most responded by closing their eyes to the problem, and when asked about such matters as the moon landings that began in 1969, a number of mullas argued that since the earth was surrounded by a crystal sphere, rockets would have crashed into it and therefore no trip to the moon could ever have occurred. This attitude toward science was an embarrassment to Muslim students and a source of ridicule for communists, who could point to such utterances to prove their contention that Islam was no longer relevant to the twentieth century. Faizani, however, tried to demonstrate both how scientific knowledge is presaged in the Qur'an and how the Qur'an contains a philosophy that is coherent in the light of scientific knowledge.

Another dimension of Faizani's appeal, which apparently developed somewhat later, was the implicitly messianic quality of his personality and message, for, to his followers, Faizani was more than a pir. To them, he was (and is) considered the representative of the mahdi himself who will appear on the Day of Judgment. This belief in Faizani's extraordinary spiritual status was apparently not manifest early and even later was not generally broadcast.[29] However, the fact that Faizani was a Sufi and that

29. Although he was himself a Sunni from Herat, Faizani claimed a number of Shi'i disciples, especially among the student generation, and it can be argued that one factor that helps account for Faizani's ability to transcend sectarian divisions was that he had no connection to any established sufi tariqat and claimed to have attained his own spiritual progress individually without the guidance of a pir. His path therefore remained basically uncategorizable, and this presumably helped break down traditional divisions, including that of Sunni and Shi'i. The belief that Faizani was the *khalifa-i mahdi akhir al-zaman* was expressed to me in separate interviews by several disciples of Faizani. That Faizani's disciples believe this about their pir is not widely known among Afghans, a fact that is probably not surprising

he sponsored an active *dhikr* (mystical chanting) circle in his home led some of the Muslim activists, particularly members of Jawanan-i Musulman, to condemn his followers as shaikhs who were leading people to the caves rather than toward political activism.

During this formative stage, however, such accusations were not made, and the different groups were not rigidly divided into separate parties. Initially, many of the students who were members of Jawanan-i Musulman also studied in the Islamic library that Faizani maintained near the Pul-i Khishti mosque in Kabul, and some even participated in the dhikr ceremonies conducted in his home. Also, many members of Faizani's group, as well as many student members of Paiman-i Islami and Qiyam-i Islami, worked with Jawanan-i Musulman and supported them in their victorious campaign in the university elections of 1969. What united these groups during this period was the belief that they shared a common cause—the advancement of Islam—and that the furtherance of that cause outweighed whatever divisions existed among them. In addition, it appears that the divisions reflected not so much ideological differences but rather the emergence of new interest groups and sodalities that were partly replacing or transforming traditional ethnic and tribal structures in Kabul society. For a brief period, it mattered more that one was a student or a military officer than that one was a Shi'i Hazara or Sunni Pashtun insofar as it was the former rather than the latter that tended to have greater weight in the determination of which of the Islamic political parties an individual joined.

However, as extremism and confrontational politics began to predominate and the parliamentary system to appear increasingly anemic, differences that had previously been subordinated became more apparent. One of the first fissures to open was between Shi'i and Sunni students within the Jawanan-i Musulman party. The overt reason for this split was the student group's association with Jama'at-i Islami Pakistan and their advocacy of a "foreign" ideology which many students—Shi'i in particular—considered dogmatic in nature and inappropriate to the Afghan context. As these problems began to come into the open in 1970, a number of students who were members of both the underground Qiyam-i Islami and

---

considering the antagonism that has been aroused every time a member of the Qadiyani sect has attempted to preach in Afghanistan (see Sirdar Ikbal 'Ali Shah, *Afghanistan of the Afghans,* 213–14, for an illustration of such a controversy). Although Faizani was arrested in 1973 for his part in the coup attempt described below, his original execution order was reportedly commuted to a life sentence, and his disciples believe that he remains alive today in a prison in Kabul.

Jawanan-i Musulman, including a Hazara named "Farid," Akhtar Muhammad Sulaimankhel, and Sayyid Isma'il Pasikh, who like Farid was
Shi'i, discontinued their association with the Jawanan. Other students who
had been members of both Paiman-i Islami and Jawanan-i Musulman also
left the latter group during this period.

Before turning to developments during the period of Da'ud's rule, it
should be noted that, in addition to the groups discussed above, many
other Shi'i students were involved in political activities. As occurred in
the Islamic camp, communist splinter groups (for example, Sitam-i Milli
and Shu'lah-i Jawid) were formed by non-Pashtuns who feared both Pashtun and Soviet hegemony. Other groups such as Jawanan-i Mughal (Mongol Youth) and Tanzim-i Nasl-i Nau-i Hazara (Organization of the New
Generation of Hazaras) that espoused no particular political ideology but
that were militantly committed to advancing the rights of minorities and
the independent cultural traditions of the "Mongol" (that is, Hazara)
peoples of Afghanistan were also active during this period. Although
these groups have not been discussed in this essay because they contained
no specifically Shi'i components, it should be kept in mind that Islamic
political protest was only one among many forms of dissent that emerged
in this era and that a complete understanding of political developments
requires comprehension of this continuum of ideological issues and organizational forms.

DA'UD AND THE SUPPRESSION OF ISLAMIC DISSENT: 1973–78

Following the successful coup d'état of Sardar Muhammad Da'ud in July
1973, Islamic political activists were suddenly thrown on the defensive,
since Da'ud relied on the support of leftist groups like the Parcham party,
many of whose members had been involved in conflicts with Islamic activists on campus and still had old grudges to settle. In this respect, members of Jawanan-i Musulman were most vulnerable, and many left Kabul
for exile in Pakistan soon after Da'ud came to power. Most members of
Paiman-i Islami, Qiyam-i Islami, and Madrasah-yi Qur'an, however, who
were less exposed since they had not been as involved in the confrontations on campus, were nevertheless distressed by the change in government. Thus, while Zahir Shah was certainly not beloved by the Islamic
groups, Muslim activists, like Afghans generally, tended to place the
blame for unpopular policies and actions on those around the king (his
uncles, Hashim Khan and Shah Mahmud Khan, prior to 1953; later, his
cousin, Muhammad Da'ud, and son-in-law, Sardar Wali) rather than on

the king himself. Reflecting this attitude, Faizani is reported to have turned down a proposal for a coup d'état against the king on the grounds that even if he was sometimes an unwise ruler, he was not unjust.

This position changed, however, after the 1973 coup, for Da'ud's opposition to Islamic groups was well known from his period as prime minister from 1953 to 1963. As a result, following Zahir Shah's overthrow, Madrasah-yi Qur'an formed an alliance with Qiyam-i Islami and Payam-i Islami under the name Madrasah-yi Tauhid (the School of Monotheism). Faizani was chosen as amir of the new alliance, and almost immediately he put in motion a plan designed to topple the Da'ud regime using the extensive network of military supporters that had been developed by the three individual parties. As occurred with Balkhi's coup in 1949, however, this coup was also discovered prior to its initiation, and Faizani, Engineer Habib al-Rahman (one of the few members of Jawanan-i Musulman who continued to support Faizani after the break in 1970), and a number of military officers were arrested and imprisoned.

In the summer of 1975, another unsuccessful plot—this one to be set off by a number of small-scale provincial insurrections—was put in motion by the exiled members of Jawanan-i Musulman. Although this plan managed to reach fruition, its result was even more disappointing since the members of the group had predicated their operation on their ability to elicit the support of the local populations in and around the government centers under attack. Instead, in those places where attacks actually occurred, it was frequently local people who captured the activist "schoolboys" and turned them over to the government. In no instance was an effective assault raised, and the government managed to capture the majority of those involved in the abortive attacks, thereby eliminating in one stroke all but a handful of the leaders of the Jawanan-i Musulman.[30] The next year, 1976, a third coup was planned and discovered prior to implementation. This plan, which was to have been carried out within the military, was organized by Gen. Mir Ahmad Shah Rizwani, and following detection of the proposed coup, he, Sayyid Isma'il Pasikh, Akhtar Mu-

---

30. The only important leader of the Jawanan-i Musulman directly involved in these abortive uprisings to survive was Ahmad Shah Mas'ud, the renowned commander of the Panjshir Valley. Ironically, considering his later stature, Mas'ud's attack on the government in Panjshir was stopped largely because of the opposition of local people who were unprepared for such an attack and unready to support it. The other principal figure involved in these uprisings was Engineer Gulbadin Hikmatyar who was one of the architects of the plan though he remained in Peshawar while the other leaders participated. That Hikmatyar inherited the mantle of leadership by remaining on the sidelines has long created suspicions and given ammunition to the controversial leader's enemies.

hammad Sulaimankhel, and a number of other members of Qiyam-i Islami joined the ranks of Islamic activists already in prison.

As a result of these abortive plots, the vast majority of the Islamic political leadership in Afghanistan was either in prison or had already been executed by the time of the communist coup of April 1978.[31] Those who remained were suspicious of one another and divided on ideological and pragmatic grounds as to the best way to recoup the damage that had been inflicted on the Islamic movement. One of the most significant of these divisions was that between Sunni and Shi'i activists. There remained an abiding distrust among members of the different groups, who suspected one another of the subversions that had led to the uncovering of their various plots.

The cooperation that had existed previously was thus replaced by almost complete separation, as the Sunni groups set up their base of operation in Peshawar in Pakistan's Northwest Frontier Province and the Shi'is established theirs in Quetta where a sizable community of exiled Hazaras had remained in exile since the reign of 'Abd al-Rahman. Even groups like Madrasah-yi Tauhid that had included both Sunni and Shi'i members were divided along sectarian lines with one group composed of Sunni Pashtuns remaining in Peshawar and a second group of Shi'i members led by Asadu'llah Nuktadan moving their center of operations to Iran after the overthrow of the shah. This latter group has been particularly active in publishing various materials under the name Islam Maktab-i Tauhid.

THE PERIOD OF POPULAR PROTEST: 1978–79

Given the state of disarray of the established parties, it is not surprising that after the Marxist People's Democratic party of Afghanistan (PDPA) overthrew President Da'ud's regime in April 1978 the first resistance to the communist government arose spontaneously from the people. It is also not surprising that the two areas where revolts first broke out were Nuristan and the Hazarajat, the last two regions of Afghanistan to submit to the central government under 'Abd al-Rahman. According to Hazara

31. Those Islamic leaders arrested prior to 1978 included Engineer Habib al-Rahman, Maulawi Habib al-Rahman, Engineer Saif al-din Nasratyar, Khawja Mahfuz, and Dr. Umar from the Jawanan-i Musulman; professors Ghulam Muhammad Niazi and Abdul Rasul Sayaf (head of the fundamentalist Ittihad-i Islami Mujahidin Afghanistan ["Seven Party"]) who were faculty members at Kabul University; Gen. Mir Ahmad Shah Rizwani, Akhtar Muhammad Sulaimankhel, and Sayyid Isma'il Pasikh from Qiyam-i Islami Afghanistan; and Mawlana Faizani.

informants, the first antigovernment violence broke out in the Hazarajat in the region of Pasawand in October 1978, less than a month after the Nuristan revolt began and only six months after the communist coup.

The Pasawand uprising failed, but it was succeeded the following spring by a series of local rebellions against the district administrative centers of Shahristan, Deh Kundi, La'l wa Sar Jangal, Nawar, Dara-i Suf, and Behsud. Although all informants state that the motivation behind these uprisings was ideological (to defeat the communists and advance Islam), other factors were involved as well, and most of these had to do with the pragmatics of power as exercised by the local leadership of the Communist party. These uprisings occurred before the inauguration of land redistribution or any of the other reform programs; they also occurred at a time when the regime in Kabul was still downplaying its ideological orientations and portraying itself as the champion of the rights of the ethnic minorities in Afghanistan.

Therefore, it seems that what inspired the first antigovernment reactions were the actions of local officials rather than those of the distant policymakers in Kabul. Since the local officials installed by the Khalq regime were frequently recent university graduates who had been away from the Hazarajat for some time, they tended to be out of touch with local problems and antagonistic to traditional power structures, which they viewed as feudal remnants waiting to be swept away by the historical forces they themselves represented. Without waiting for directions from Kabul, many of these local communist cadres immediately set out to undermine and discredit traditional leaders. To this end, the Khalqis not only arrested prominent local figures but also attempted to disarm those they suspected of opposing them. In the process, they searched homes and interfered in the domestic lives of the people, acts that are violations of honor (*namus*) and that are neither forgiven nor forgotten in Afghanistan. Violence inevitably broke out, and incidents of Khalqi injustices became the subject of rumor and sermon, spreading quickly throughout the Hazarajat and to other regions as well.

In this way, incidents of government abuse set off a string of small-scale and spontaneously organized uprisings that, because of their dispersed nature, overwhelmed the capacity of the government to respond in any effective way. By June 1979, virtually all the government forces in the Hazarajat were either pushed out or confined to a few well-fortified bases. Most of the rural areas were liberated, and the nucleus of a political organization was established in the town of Waras in Bamiyan Province.

This first organization of the Hazara resistance, which became known as Shura-yi Ittifaq-i Islam-i Afghanistan (United Islamic Council of Afghanistan), comprised mostly sayyids, tribal chiefs, and a number of nationally prominent Hazaras, including some former parliamentary representatives, all of whom began assembling in Waras from throughout the Hazarajat in June 1979. Of these component groups, the nonreligious elements initially dominated the council. However, within a short period of time, leadership of the Shura was taken over by the sayyid contingent, and one of their number, Ayatullah Bihishti, who had been educated in Iraq, was chosen as the president (*ra'is*) of the council.[32] Bihishti's deputy (Ayatullah Husain Nasiri) and chief military commander are also sayyids, the latter of these being Sayyid Muhammad Hasan Jagran, who was one of the leaders of the popular uprising in Ghazni and a former major (*jagran*) in the Afghan army.

Jagran's fronts are considered to be the best organized of any commanded by the Shura, and because of their location on the eastern fringe of the Hazarajat, they have engaged in more regular combat than other fronts and have played a more important role in maintaining outside contacts with non-Hazara fronts, including those of Ahmad Shah Mas'ud in Panjshir and Qari Taj Muhammad ("Qari Baba") in Ghazni. Other active Shura fronts have been those similarly located on the periphery of the Hazarajat, such as the front in Onnai, east of Bamiyan, and in Garau, on the northern fringe.[33]

Except for the activities of these fronts, the reputation of Shura-yi Ittifaq-i Islam-i Afghanistan has been shaky, as the organization has been open to charges of being a bastion of clerical interests unresponsive to the needs of Hazaras. Non-Hazaras also accuse the Shura of being inactive in their prosecution of the war. This arises from the fact that since the early stages of the resistance the Hazarajat has been relatively immune from attacks by the government, the last major operation having been the unsuccessful summer offensive of 1980.[34] Possible reasons for the govern-

32. Although both Bihishti and Muhsini are referred to as ayatullahs, it is not clear whether they signify the achievement of the same scholarly status as in Iran or Iraq. That both men are considered respected ulama is unquestionably the case, but within the Afghan resistance groups, there are a great number of "engineers" and "doctors" who completed only a year or two of university and presumably more than a few maulawis who were mullas before 1978.

33. See *Afghan Information Centre Bulletin,* no. 21 (December 1982): 8–9 (published monthly in Peshawar, Pakistan).

34. *Afghan Information Centre Bulletin,* no. 21 (December 1982): 8. It should be noted that while there may not have been a major offensive unleashed on the Hazarajat, there have been frequent cases of indiscriminate bombing of villages. See, for example, *Afghan Information Centre Bulletin,* no. 31 (October 1983): 2–3; and B. Almquist, "The Afghan War in 1983: Strengthened Resistance versus Soviet 'Nazi' Tactics," *Central Asian Survey* 3, no. 1 (1984): 23–45.

ment's ignoring the Hazarajat in its military operations include the fact that because of its rugged isolation and location away from international borders the region is of secondary strategic importance and would not justify the cost required to capture it. In addition, it is argued that the present prime minister, Sultan 'Ali Kishtmand, a Hazara who is thought to carry considerable power in the ruling Parcham party hierarchy, is perhaps protecting the region while also advancing the cause of minority rights in an effort to gain the eventual support of the Hazaras.

If gaining the adherence of the Hazaras is in fact a part of Parcham's policy, it has not been successful. At the same time, however, it could be argued that the policy of leaving the Hazaras to their own devices has not been without its benefits from the government's point of view. Ignoring the Hazarajat has allowed the government to concentrate its forces elsewhere while remaining secure in the knowledge that the traditional isolation of the Hazaras from other groups would prevent any large-scale mobilization of Hazara forces in support of non-Hazara territory.[35] In addition, over the six years of resistance, there has grown up considerable discontent among Hazaras over the theocratic rule of Shura, and the government has undoubtedly enjoyed this development. However, what they may have enjoyed somewhat less is the rise of pro-Iranian parties, which, since the success of the Islamic revolution, have come to play an increasingly dominant role in the politics of the Hazarajat.

FACTIONS IN THE SHI'I RESISTANCE: 1979–84

Before considering the impact of the Islamic revolution of Iran on the situation in the Hazarajat, it should be mentioned that during the first stage of popular resistance to the communist government, the Shura was not the only political organization that was active among Hazaras. Many of those aligned with the Shura, especially the younger members, also belonged to one of the many parties that emerged after the communist revolution, and at least one of these parties, Harakat-i Islami Afghanistan (Islamic Movement of Afghanistan) led by Ayatullah Shaikh Asaf Muhsini, managed to establish a number of independent combat fronts. Others

35. Although there has not been any large-scale mobilization of Hazaras to assist non-Hazaras (or vice versa), there have been a number of incidents of cooperation. The most famous such case was one from the first year of the jihad in which Pashtun elders from the province of Wardak (on the eastern border of the Hazarajat) went to Kabul to petition for weapons from the communist government to be used against the Hazaras. Seeking to exploit traditional animosities, the government turned over a large number of weapons to the Wardak elders who immediately turned them on the government upon their return from Kabul.

like the Ittihadiyah Mujahidin-i Islami Afghanistan (Union of Islamic Mujahidin of Afghanistan) of Abdul Husain Maqsudi have set up fewer fronts but have nevertheless come to play an important role in coordinating the flow of supplies into the Hazarajat from Pakistan.

Of all the affiliated parties, however, these two have been the exceptions. The majority have a negligible presence outside of the exile community in Quetta, Pakistan, and many have consisted of little more than a name, an office, and, in some cases, a newspaper.[36] Most of these Quetta parties have some reference to Islam in their name, although this reference often serves simply as protective camouflage for leftist or moderate nationalist groups. To remain viable these groups have had to demonstrate a more active concern for Islam than they may in fact possess, because without such protestations of true faith they have no chance of attracting supporters and a great deal of opportunity to find themselves—quite literally—removed from the scene.

During the initial period of the jihad, the existence of these parties was accepted as compatible with the authority of the Shura, which was viewed as an alliance (*ittifaq*) and therefore qualitatively different in structure and purpose from a party (*hizb*). This exalted status has gradually eroded, however, partly as a result of Shura's problems and partly because of the expanding influence of Iran in the region. In considering the impact of the Iranian Revolution on the situation in the Hazarajat, it should be noted that the initial reaction of the Hazaras to Ayatullah Khomeini's rise was extremely favorable. Pictures of Khomeini appeared throughout the region, and even though there have been strains in the relationship between Hazaras and Iranians in the past, Khomeini was viewed as someone who represented all Shi'is. This attitude was short-lived, however, for the assistance expected from Iran did not arrive, or at least not in the form anticipated.

Rather than backing the indigenous Shura or one of the Shi'i parties such as Harakat-i Islami Afghanistan, the Iranian government threw its support to Hizb-i Islami Afghanistan, the Sunni fundamentalist party of Engineer Gulbadin Hikmatyar who was one of the early members of the Jawanan group at Kabul University. From Iran's perspective, the Shura certainly must have appeared as hopelessly retrograde, but their initial rejection of Ayatullah Muhsini is more puzzling. A Shi'i religious scholar of some repute, Muhsini is from Qandahar, and although he was apparently not actively engaged in politics prior to the communist revolution,

36. See "B. M.," "The Present Situation in the Hazarajat," *Central Asian Survey* 1, no. 1 (July 1982): 87.

he had organized a cultural group known as Subh-i Danish (Dawn of Knowledge) whose members became early and vigorous opponents of the communist regime. Nevertheless, in August 1980, Iran banned Muhsini's Harakat-i Islami party from Iran and backed Hikmatyar, whose strident fundamentalism was more in line with Iran's ideological position even if he did not adhere to Shi'ism.[37]

In retrospect, this action appears to have been as much a holding action by the Iranian authorities as true endorsement. At the time, the Iranians were preoccupied with their own affairs, and there was no organized group among the Shi'is that could adequately serve as an appropriate representative of their position. The first such representative to appear was a party known as Sazman-i Nasir-i Islami-yi Afghanistan. Nasir is composed primarily of young, ideologically committed funda mentalists. Among these are a former deputy of Ayatullah Bihishti's named Sadiqi, who led an attempt to take over the Shura at an early stage in its development, and an individual known as Mazari, who is reported to have spent time in an Iranian prison with the current president of Iran, Hujjat al-Islam 'Ali Khamene'i.

Starting with little support and a limited base of operations on the northern periphery of the Hazarajat, Nasir gradually increased its influence in the region, in part through superior organization but largely because of the financial and logistical backing received from Iran. This was accomplished in the face of concerted opposition from the Hazara people in general and the Shura in particular, who were, and are, distrustful of the extremism of the group. Much like its Sunni ally and ideological stablemate, Hizb-i Islami, Nasir has also been frequently accused of attacking other parties, as in 1982 when five hundred mujahidin were reported to have been killed in a battle between Nasir and Muhsini's Harakat-i Islami.[38] Nasir has also been accused of other acts of intimidation as in the reported kidnapping and execution of a popular Shi'i Turkoman leader, Haji Nadir, who was affiliated with the Shura and opposed Nasir's activities in his area of Surkh-i Parsal.

Despite the opposition to them, Nasir managed to strike a decisive blow against the Shura in the summer of 1984, when it forced Ayatullah Bihishti to flee his headquarters in Waras. He is now said to be under the protection of Sayyid Jagran, who is perhaps the only Shura commander

37. See O. Roy, "Islam in the Afghan Resistance," *Religion in Communist Lands* 12, no. 1 (1984), and D. K. Duran, "Afghanistan's Struggle for National Liberation," *Journal of the University of Baluchistan* 1, no. 1 (1982?).

38. *Afghan Information Centre Bulletin*, no. 21 (December 1982): 14.

with sufficient strength and influence to hold his own in these factional conflicts. Ironically, however, as Nasir's power has grown, its main opposition has come not from the Shura, whose fortunes have been on the decline for some time, but from another Iranian product, Sipah-i Pasdaran. According to the French researcher, Jean-Jose Puig, who has made several trips into the Hazarajat, Sipah was initiated in 1982 because of Iranian dissatisfaction with Nasir. At that time, the Iranians sent a delegation to the Hazarajat to investigate Nasir's activities and to monitor how their financial aid and weaponry were being used. They were reported to be unhappy with what they saw and convinced of the necessity of personally coordinating operations through their own Sipah-i Pasdaran. An Afghan contingent of this organization has therefore been established, using mostly Afghan personnel but operating directly under the command of the Iranians.[39]

CONCLUSIONS

In considering the evolution of Shi'i political protest in Afghanistan over the last ninety years, certain distinctive patterns and stages can be discerned. During the latter part of the nineteenth century, Hazaras living in their ancestral homeland of the Hazarajat mounted a major defensive operation against the Afghan forces of Amir 'Abd al-Rahman. Normally divided tribes united in this instance as Shi'is under the leadership of a sayyid commander and in opposition to a Sunni state. The inability of this coalition to hold off the encroachment of the Afghan government marked the last time until 1979 that the people of the Hazarajat would come together on a sectarian basis for the achievement of common objectives. Subsequent political activity in the Hazarajat appears to have been fragmentary, sporadic, and secularly based. The closest approximations to political protest were the various incidents of banditry that sprang up during the reign of Zahir Shah and the short-lived rebellion of Bach-i Gausawar which failed to provoke a general uprising in the region despite popular resentment at abuses by government officials and nomads. During this same period, the political activities of Shi'i sayyids in the Hazarajat

39. J.-J. Puig, Interview, *Afghan Information Centre Bulletin*, no. 32–33 (November–December 1983): 27–28, and no. 42 (September 1984): 8. See also B. Almquist, "The Afghan War in 1983," 32. Another group that has recently begun operations in the Hazarajat and that takes a similar ideological position to that of Sipah is an organization called Mustaz'afin. This party publishes a newspaper in Iran under the same name and is said to be in close cooperation with Ahmad Shah Mas'ud, the Panjshir commander.

appear to have been parochial, self-interested, and generally unrelated to the larger political dynamics of the Hazarajat or the Afghan state.

The situation in Kabul, however, was very different as a religiously based political culture began gradually to emerge among the Shi'i population during the 1940s and 1950s. The first stage in this process was the establishment of takyah khanahs in the city, which provided a focus for communal activities and exposed many Shi'is for the first time to their religious traditions. In this sense, the takyah khanah served as the incubator in the formation of Shi'i political ideology in Afghanistan. Prior to this time, it appears that the ceremonies of Muharram did not have a central place in the lives of Afghan Shi'is, and consequently they would have been shut off from the central event and symbolic core of Shi'i belief and experience. The inauguration of takyah khanahs in Kabul therefore provided a forum for the dramatic remembrance of the sacrifice of Husain and, in so doing, laid the groundwork for the subsequent development of an ideology of Shi'i political activism. In the next stage, however, the Muharram story was taken out of the takyah khanah, becoming in the process more than just a pretext for individual catharsis and dramatic communion. With the development of political parties, the sacrifice of Husain became a living symbol. No longer simply a metaphor for human suffering in this world, it became an ideal of political action and commitment based on the expectation of personal sacrifice on the part of every Shi'i.

The figure responsible for this transformation was Sayyid Isma'il Balkhi. In evaluating Balkhi's role here, it should also be noted that he made his appeal for political action and personal sacrifice during a period of rapid social change. In this context, Balkhi galvanized Islam and gave it new vitality as an ideology capable of accommodating change within a traditional system of meaning. At the same time, political parties became an alternative basis for social identification, which reflected the emergence of new interest groups (government workers, students, military officers) and compensated for the declining importance of traditional kinship networks at least in the urban environment.

With the advent of the communists in 1978, the lead in opposing the new government came not from the urban parties but from the people themselves. Thus, from all available evidence, it seems clear that the uprisings that began within six months of the communist takeover were indigenous expressions of dissatisfaction with the new status quo and with the abuses of specific officials and were not inspired or organized by any outside agency. Reflecting this, the Shura, the political assembly that was set up to coordinate resistance activities in 1979, was controlled by traditional religious and secular leaders and probably had more in common with the Hazara coalition that opposed 'Abd al-Rahman than with any of the political parties that emerged in the 1960s.

These political parties initially had little role in the resistance because their leadership had been decimated in the failed coup attempts of the 1970s and because they lacked a popular base in the rural areas. Gradually, however, they have regrouped and asserted themselves not only as opponents to the regime but equally as would-be successors to the traditional and, by their lights, regressive and un-Islamic Shura. This development has become particularly apparent since the early 1980s and has been caused in large part by the increased involvement of Iran and its allied and surrogate parties in the Hazarajat.

These parties have succeeded in forging a bond to Iran and to the Islamic revival Iran represents, but so too have they alienated many Afghan Shi'is who view with pride the accomplishments of the Iranian Revolution but nevertheless resist subordination to Iranian control. From the perspective of Iran and her Afghan proxies, this may represent the last stirrings of a corrupt band of sayyids with vested interests in maintaining their authority over the illiterate Hazara peasantry.

To the majority of Hazaras, however, the radical ideology emanating from Iran represents a dangerous innovation that has little in common with their own understanding of Shi'ism and would put power in the hands of individuals with no popular backing or conception of what is traditional and valued in Hazara culture. Ultimately, the Iranian-backed parties may overwhelm the less disciplined and more poorly organized coalition that comprises the Shura; but in the meantime, this division in the ranks of the resistance severely hampers the ability of Hazaras to mount an effective and unified opposition to the government and therefore enhances the likelihood of an eventual communist victory, a victory that the vast majority of Afghan people continue to oppose.

JACOB GOLDBERG

Chapter Nine   The Shi'i Minority
in Saudi Arabia

Saudi Arabia's indigenous population is more homogeneous and cohesive, ethnically and religiously, than that of any other Arab state. The Shi'i community is the only major exception to this homogeneity and the most divisive element in the kingdom. Estimates of the number of Shi'is vary from 200,000 to 275,000,[1] 300,000,[2] 400,000,[3] and even 440,000.[4] In the absence, however, of a reliable census, it is impossible to ascertain the exact figure, though many indications would suggest that 350,000 is a realistic estimate. Given the overall indigenous population of approximately 6 million, this would mean that the Shi'is constitute no more than 6 percent of the Saudi populace.

Although figures may vary, the location of the Shi'is is quite precise and well-defined. The Shi'is are concentrated in only one region of the

1. David Holden and Richard Johns, *The House of Saud* (New York: Holt, Rinehart & Winston, 1981), 528.

2. William Quandt, *Saudi Arabia in the 1980's* (Washington, D.C.: Brookings Institution, 1981). Quandt gives two figures: on p. 39 it is 200,000; on p. 96 it is 200,000 to 300,000.

3. James Buchan, "Secular and Religious Opposition in Saudi Arabia," in Tim Niblock, ed., *State, Society and Economy in Saudi Arabia* (London: Croom Helm, 1982).

4. James A. Bill, "Islam, Politics, and Shi'ism in the Gulf," *Middle East Insight* 3 (1980): 6.

230

900,000 square miles of Saudi territory: the Eastern Province, also known as Hasa.[5] More than one-third of the inhabitants of that important province are Shi'is. Some 95 percent of the population of the city of Qatif and its surrounding communities and one-half of the people of the Hufuf district are Shi'is.[6] This places the Shi'i minority in one of the most strategically crucial areas of the kingdom, in view of three central factors: (1) its proximity to Iran, especially postrevolutionary Iran, the only Islamic country dominated and ruled by Shi'is; (2) its location along the Persian Gulf shores with all the strategic importance this entails; and (3) its being the region that contains all the oil fields and oil reserves of the kingdom. Some of the largest oil fields in the world, such as Ghawar and Qatif, are located in areas predominantly Shi'i in composition.

Since the beginning of modern Saudi history in 1745, with the alliance between the Sunni tribal leader Muhammad Ibn Sa'ud and the strict Sunni religious reformer Muhammad ibn 'Abd al-Wahhab, the Shi'is in Hasa came under Saudi rule during three distinct periods: 1792–1818, 1830–72 (with a brief interval in 1837–43), and 1913 to the present day. This chapter explores the position of the Shi'is in the Saudi kingdom religiously, politically, socially, and economically. It traces the evolution of their relations with the Saudi authorities and analyzes the differences in their position between the period prior to the revolution in Iran and the postrevolutionary period. It also examines the policies and attitudes of the various Saudi regimes toward the Shi'i minority and identifies the determinants and criteria with which the Saudi state has approached the Shi'i problem. Special emphasis will be laid on the Saudi need to reconcile the Wahhabi perception of Shi'ism, on the one hand, and the pragmatic constraints of day-to-day rule on the other.

The Wahhabi view of the Shi'is is a logical development of the cornerstone of Wahhabi ideology: the doctrine of *tauhid* (the Unity of God). Abhorrence of such Shi'i practices as saint worship, shrine and grave cults, and veneration for imams became a central tenet of Wahhabism. Viewed as shifting faith from the creator to the creature, these practices were perceived as obliterating the distinction between God and man and thus constituting *shirk* (polytheism) or "the association of anyone or thing with God." One of the early Wahhabi texts explicitly stipulates that "visiting places and the domes over tombs found in many countries is the greatest

5. This article does not deal with the problem of the Zaidis, also Shi'is, located in the province of 'Asir, the southwestern part of the kingdom, close to the Yemeni border.
6. Bill, "Islam," 6.

shirk which the polytheists perform."[7] In addition, these practices, including the celebration of festivals, were regarded as intercession between God and man because they verged on idol worship.

Given such a fundamentalist approach, the Wahhabis easily classified the Shi'is as falling into the category of shirk. Indeed, the Shi'is were viewed as the incarnation of infidelity, and the Shi'is as a community were referred to as polytheists (*mushrikun*). One of the basic tenets of the Wahhabi doctrine centered on the duty imposed by God on the believers (*mu'minun*) to manifest enmity to the polytheists. Furthermore, "when religion applies to something other than God, then fighting is obligatory."[8] Indeed, the Shi'is were perceived as unbelievers (*kuffar*), and were therefore liable to the severest sanctions including that of holy war (*jihad*).

The Wahhabi view of the Shi'is was first applied following the conquest of Hasa by the first Saudi state in the last decade of the eighteenth century. The Saudi-Wahhabi forces destroyed all the domed tombs and all other objects of Shi'i worship and pilgrimage. The Wahhabi conqueror, Saud the Great, imposed a Wahhabi infrastructure and launched a comprehensive campaign aimed at the indoctrination of the Shi'i population. Mosques and schools were established, and Wahhabi preachers and religious scholars (*ulama*) were dispatched to Hasa, half of whose population was thought to be Shi'i. The basic goal of this drive was to establish the practice of the doctrine of tauhid.[9] The Wahhabis' attitude toward the Shi'is was further manifested in April 1801 when a considerable Saudi force attacked the town of Karbala, sacred to the Shi'is and anathema to Wahhabism. In the course of the attack, some five thousand Shi'is were massacred, the domes of various tombs—including that of the Prophet's grandson, Husain—were demolished, and the whole city was plundered.[10] Wahhabi-Shi'i relations were also shaped by the assassination in 1803 of the Saudi ruler 'Abd al-'Aziz by a Shi'i, in revenge for the massacre of Karbala in which the latter's family perished.[11]

The Wahhabi rule over Hasa was, however, short-lived. In 1810 the Ottoman sultan ordered Muhammad 'Ali, the pasha of Egypt, to embark

7. Christine M. Helms, *The Cohesion of Saudi Arabia* (London: Croom Helm, 1981), 82, 99.

8. Ibid., 100.

9. John B. Philby, *Saudi Arabia* (London: Benn, 1955), 82, and George Rentz, "Wahhabism and Saudi Arabia," in Derek Hopwood, ed., *The Arabian Peninsula* (London: Allen & Unwin, 1972), 58–59.

10. Philby, *Saudi Arabia*, 93, and John Gordon Lorimer, *Gazetteer of the Persian Gulf, Oman and Central Arabia* (Calcutta, 1908–1915), 1:1060.

11. Philby, *Saudi Arabia*.

on a campaign aimed at "suppressing the Wahhabi rebellion in Arabia." By 1818 the Saudi state was destroyed, and Wahhabi rule over the Shi'is in Hasa came to an end. It was only in the 1830s that the founder of the second Saudi state, Turki, and his son, Faisal the Great, managed to restore Wahhabi control over Hasa. However, owing to the brevity of the first Saudi conquest of Hasa and the profound Shi'i antagonism toward the new Wahhabi doctrine, Wahhabism failed to establish roots among the Shi'is there. Turki and Faisal had, therefore, to reestablish schools and mosques, assign ulama and teachers to reeducate the Shi'is, and appoint prayer leaders (*imams*) and Sunni judges (*qadis*) in various towns of Hasa.[12]

The overall attitude of the second state toward the Shi'is was, admittedly, more tolerant than that of the first state. At one point, a Shi'i, Muhammad al-Farisi, was appointed to the post of judge of Hasa. But the change was not rooted in any shift from the concept that underlay the Saudis' approach toward the Shi'is, that is, the Wahhabi doctrine. It reflected, rather, the inherent overall weakness of the second state, its desire to consolidate its rule without antagonizing the population of Hasa, its limited—shakable at times—control over Hasa, and a distinct decline in the religious fervor and dynamism that had characterized the first state.

The attitude of the first two Saudi states toward their Shi'i subjects was, thus, based on the Wahhabi conceptual framework. This framework was strictly applied by the first state; it was much less intensely imposed by the second state, owing to its weakness.

With the conquest of Hasa by Ibn Saud in 1913, the third chapter in the Saudi-Shi'i relations began. Following the pattern of former conquests, the Saudi authorities reintroduced Wahhabism into Hasa and attempted to impose it on the population.[13] Two distinctly divergent approaches, however, evolved on the Saudi side as to the attitude to be adopted toward the Shi'is. In one camp were the exponents of the newly established organization of the Ikhwan. Created by Ibn Saud in 1912, it was based on bedouins of different tribes establishing joint colonies, obtaining strict Wahhabi education, and finally forming the nucleus of the Saudi army. This organization, which had no connection with the Egyptian al-Ikhwan al-Muslimun (the Muslim Brotherhood, established in 1928), was to give the Saudi state a larger degree of unity, cohesion, and permanence. The Ikhwan argued that the Wahhabi doctrine had to be im-

12. Ibid., pp. 162–63, and R. Bayly Winder, *Saudi Arabia in the Nineteenth Century* (London: Macmillan, 1965), 77.
13. Philby, *Saudi Arabia*, 269.

posed, forcibly if necessary, on the Shi'is and that the latter had to stop observing all their Shi'i customs and basically change their pattern of conduct. On the other hand, Ibn Saud and his cousin Ibn Jiluwi—whom he appointed the first governor of Hasa—sought to pursue a different policy. They essentially tried to draw a line between the Shi'is' conduct in public and their behavior in the privacy of their homes. The basic formula they attempted to apply was that the Shi'is could continue to observe their religious customs in their homes, provided they did not demonstrate their religious distinction in public.

In reality, the attitude toward the Shi'is in Hasa fluctuated between these two positions, reflecting an ongoing struggle—both political and ideological—between Ibn Saud and the Ikhwan. For almost a decade, until 1922, the Ikhwan had the upper hand in Hasa. The Shi'is were prevented from engaging in religious worship and from holding religious meetings. A number of them who continued to hold meetings in their husainiyah were killed.[14] Even smoking in the privacy of their own homes was prohibited. The Ikhwan took the law into their own hands and punished all transgressors. Thus, those who were caught observing Shi'i religious customs and women who were improperly dressed were killed by the Ikhwan.[15] After 1922, however, it seems that Ibn Saud managed to assume more control over the activities of the Ikhwan. This was reflected in Hasa, where the condition of the Shi'is was considerably alleviated. They were now permitted to engage in Shi'i worship, as well as to smoke, in the privacy of their homes, as long as their public conduct conformed with Wahhabi principles and tenets. In addition, their economic condition was significantly improved, and a general atmosphere of tranquility came to prevail in Hasa. Such changes were obviously regarded with disfavor by the Ikhwan, who consistently tried to impose their will on the Shi'is. The governor, Ibn Jiluwi, was therefore forced to restrain the Ikhwan and defend the Shi'is from their molestations.[16]

Underlying the differences between Ibn Saud's attitude toward the Shi'is and that of the Ikhwan was, however, a much more profound dis-

14. Lawrence Goldrup, "Saudi Arabia, 1902–1932: The Development of a Wahhabi Society" (Ph.D. diss., University of California at Los Angeles, 1972), 416. A husainiyah is a mourning center where the Shi'is congregate during the month of Muharram to commemorate the martyrdom of the Imam Husain.

15. Hafiz Wahba, *Jazirat al-'Arab fi al-Qarn al-'Ishrin* (Cairo: Cairo repr. Maktabat an-Nahdah al-Misriyyah, 1961), 310; and John Habib, *Ibn Saud's Warriors of Islam: The Ikhwan Movement of Najd* (Leiden: Brill, 1978), 38.

16. H. R. P. Dickson, *Kuwait and Its Neighbours* (London: Allen & Unwin, 1956), 155, 281.

agreement over the nature and orientation of the Saudi state. The Ikhwan represented the twentieth-century successors of traditional Wahhabis whose approval, or disapproval, of any phenomenon was based solely on its conformity with their doctrine. In a broader perspective, then, they sought to approach the Shi'i problem with the same guidelines employed by the two former Saudi states—Wahhabi considerations. Ibn Saud, however, represented a new type of Saudi-Wahhabi ruler, motivated more by dynastic-pragmatic aspirations than by religious-Wahhabi messianism. Such a shift resulted also in his attempt to formulate a new policy toward the Shi'is that was not totally in line with, let alone based upon, the Wahhabi doctrine.

The fundamental differences between the two streams, concealed and subterranean during the first quarter of the twentieth century, surfaced in late 1925 with such intensity that they threatened the very existence and unity of the Saudi state. At the heart of the confrontation was the Ikhwan's charge that Ibn Saud had deviated from the Wahhabi ideology in his foreign and domestic policies. In foreign affairs he refused to fulfill his duty of expansion in order to spread and impose the Wahhabi faith and to restore Muslims to the "correct path." Domestically, they accused him of introducing Western innovations (such as the telephone, telegraph, and cars), which should have been considered by Islam as *bid'ah* (unacceptable innovations). It is in this context that they also challenged Ibn Saud's policy toward the Shi'is.

In 1926 the Ikhwan called a conference in Artawiyah, in which they censured Ibn Saud and submitted a list of grievances and accusations against him. Figuring prominently in the list was the charge that he had abandoned the duty of jihad against the polytheists, that is, Shi'is, incumbent upon all believers, that is, Wahhabis. Article 7 in the list concerned "his failure to enforce the Unitarian [Wahhabi] doctrine on the Shi'is of Hasa and Iraq." The Ikhwan demanded that Ibn Saud should either force them to embrace Wahhabism or, if they failed to comply, kill them.[17]

In response to the Ikhwan's challenge, Ibn Saud convened a major conference in Riyadh in early January 1927, which many tribal leaders and religious scholars attended. Unwilling to further strain relations between himself and the Ikhwan, Ibn Saud felt that he had to placate them and was, therefore, ready to compromise. This was formulated in the form of a fatwa issued at the end of the conference, in which the following demands were made on the Shi'is: (1) that they accept Wahhabi Islam,

17. Helms, *The Cohesion*, 253; and Habib, *Ibn Saud's*, 122.

(2) that they make a profession of Faith, (3) that they abandon all forms of innovation in their faith and at private and public assemblies, (4) that they pray five times a day, (5) that they cease all prayer to the saintly members of the Prophet's house, (6) that the places erected for the practice of their rites be destroyed, (7) that they study the principles of Wahhabi Islam, and (8) that they attend classes in Wahhabi Islam. Those Shi'is who refused to comply with these demands would be exiled.[18]

The fatwa, however, has never been put to the test, let alone implemented. For relations between Ibn Saud and the Ikhwan deteriorated to the point where the latter openly challenged his authority and embarked on what became known as the Ikhwan rebellion. Because the Ikhwan were utterly defeated in 1929, Ibn Saud felt he was not bound any longer by the fatwa regarding the Shi'is—which he had accepted in the first place only for the sake of compromise—and he never enforced it. Thus, in the somewhat historical confrontation between the protagonists of traditional Wahhabism—the Ikhwan—and the founder of the twentieth-century Saudi state—Ibn Saud—the latter had the upper hand.

What were the ideological foundations of Ibn Saud's attitude and policies toward the Shi'is? There could have been no better testimony than Ibn Saud's own response as divulged to the Lebanese author, Amin al-Rihani:

> When the Saudi ruler was asked whether he considered it a religious duty to wage war against the mushrikin to the end of making them Unitarians, he gave the following reply: "No, no! take Hasa, for instance. We have there thirty thousand of the Shi'a, who live in peace and security. No one ever molests them. All we ask of them is not to be too demonstrative in public on their fête-days. Rest assured . . . we are not as some people imagine us." Then the question was rephrased and Ibn Saud was asked whether he considered it a political duty to fight the mushrikin till they become religious. His answer was: "Politics and religion are not the same. But the people of Najd desire nothing that is not sanctioned by religion. Therefore, if religion sanctions our desire, the political measures we adopt for its realization must be lawful. If politics fail, then war. And in war everything is permissible."[19]

Such a rationale attests to a fundamental shift from the traditional Wahhabi approach to religion and politics in general and toward the Shi'i

18. Habib, *Ibn Saud's*, 123–29; and Buchan, "Secular," 118.
19. Ameen Rihani, *Ibn Sa'oud of Arabia* (London: Constable, 1928), 234–35; and Helms, *The Cohesion*, 114–15.

problem in particular. The new attitude did not evolve from a Wahhabi starting point, nor was it defined in Wahhabi terms of reference, nor was it anchored in the Wahhabi concept of the Shi'is as mushrikun liable to jihad. Furthermore, there was no *religious* duty to fight the Shi'is and convert them to Wahhabism. This was not the goal. The objective was essentially a *political* one, namely, securing the allegiance and loyalty of the Shi'is to the Saudi state.

Indeed, the approach outlined by Ibn Saud has served, since 1930, as a guideline governing the Saudi regime's attitude toward the Shi'is. They could continue to observe all their religious customs, including those anathema to Wahhabism, as long as they confined it to the privacy of their own homes. In public, they had to restrain themselves and avoid too overt a demonstration of their religious distinction.

With Ibn Saud's victory over the Ikhwan, the Shi'is started to be integrated into Saudi society and economy. The discovery of oil in commercial quantities in the region of Hasa during the 1930s introduced a major turning point in this direction. A considerable number of Shi'is were employed by the Arab American Oil Company (ARAMCO), and during the 1970s it was estimated that over 25 percent of the workers in the oil fields were Shi'is. Aramco's experience has been that Shi'is show a greater willingness to undertake manual tasks, skilled or otherwise, than Sunnis of bedouin origin. The launching of the long-term development project of the industrial and port town of Jubail provided yet another field for the integration of the Shi'is; indeed, in 1976 a Shi'i was appointed head of the project.[20] In addition, many Shi'is from Hufuf were the goldsmiths and leather workers of the Hasa area, and the Shi'is of Qatif came to be known as the contractors and food suppliers.[21]

On the other hand, the overwhelming majority of the Shi'is working in the oil fields and the Jubail project merely performed manual labor, and very few succeeded in penetrating the managerial level. Furthermore, the Shi'is as a whole were excluded from all but the lowest ranks of the armed forces—both the army and the National Guard—and all but low-level clerical jobs in the ever-expanding government bureaucracy and civil service. By 1984, only one Shi'i had held ministerial rank. Some scholars, such as Bill, have asserted that "Saudi Shi'is are very prominent in every

20. Buchan, "Secular," 119.
21. Bill, "Islam," 7.

phase of the oil industry,"[22] but all evidence suggests that they are not prominent at all beyond the manual labor level. Furthermore, unlike the other Gulf states in which wealthy Shi'i families play a prominent role in the economic and financial systems of the states, the Saudi Shi'is are very marginal actors in the Saudi economy. They were distinctly less well-off with fewer opportunities to advance than Saudi Sunnis, and they felt they had profited very little from the services and construction boom generated by the oil industry in Hasa. The feeling was growing that Shi'i towns and villages in Hasa, such as Hufuf and Qatif, remained neglected and under-developed in contrast with such towns as Dammam, Jubail, and Khubar, which benefited from the oil boom and prospered. In addition, the Shi'is complained that because of insufficient budgetary expenditures and long-term investments, Shi'i areas suffered from lack of both an appropriate infrastructure and basic public services—schools, hospitals, clinics, paved roads, and so on. Some of their most serious grievances were in the fields of education and culture. Shi'i literature and history were not taught in local schools and universities, and teaching—one of the few occupations open to Saudi women—was barred to Shi'i women by the Saudi author-ities. Thus, a general sense of discrimination evolved among the Shi'is, who perceived themselves as second-class citizens, deprived of equal so-cial and economic opportunities.[23]

This state of affairs was epitomized by the fact that in the last five years of his reign, King Faisal never visited Hasa. The Shi'is felt not only that nothing was done to overcome discrimination against them but also that no effort was made to integrate them into society. As one Shi'i put it, "In Saudi eyes, there are the Sunnis; below them are the Christians, and below the Christians are the Jews. We are below the Jews."[24] Never-theless, the 1929–79 period was characterized by tranquility and peace in the Shi'i-populated areas of Hasa, the social and economic discontent remaining largely subterranean. Alienated from the religion and customs

22. Ibid. Bill makes several sweeping statements, such as "at the core of the economies of the Gulf states, Shi'i merchants and financiers dominate in the *suqs* and the traditional market place," or "each Gulf country has a wealthy cadre of Shi'i merchant families whose members maintain close ties with the ruling families and are critical forces in the economic and financial systems." These statements, as well as his sweeping conclusion that "the Shi'a populations of the Gulf have extraordinary resources" and that "the Gulf Shi'is are a central force driving the economies of the Gulf countries" are totally inapplicable in the case of Saudi Arabia.

23. Jacob Goldberg, "The Saudi Arabian Kingdom," *Middle East Contemporary Survey* 4 (1979–80): 688–90.

24. Interview, *New York Times* (hereafter *NYT*), January 3, 1980.

of the mainstream in Saudi Arabia, the Shi'is looked for guidance to the ayatullahs of Iran, across the Gulf from Hasa, and of Iraq, to the north.

But lacking support for their cause from any external force, the Shi'is of Hasa were intimidated by the power of the Saudi regime, and they conducted their affairs in a highly subdued and cautious manner. Indeed, there were very few incidents involving Shi'is from Hasa. One of these occurred in late 1966 when several hundred people in Hasa, most of them Shi'is, were arrested on the suspicion of having links to the Baath party.[25] It seems, however, that what figured prominently in this case were questions of security and subversion, not the sectarian affiliation of the suspects.

The revolution in Iran in early 1979 seems to have produced a new consciousness among the Shi'is in Hasa and served as a model for their future conduct. It clearly gave them the courage to challenge the Saudi regime and make demands such as they had never dared to do in the past. Throughout 1979, postrevolutionary Iran played an important role in fueling the situation in Hasa. Leaflets began circulating in the towns and villages, calling on the Shi'is not to cooperate with the royal family. The leaflets—echoing the propaganda carried over Radio Tehran's daily Arab-language program directed at the Arab Gulf states—were undoubtedly inspired by Iran. In addition, cassette recordings of Khomeini's religious speeches, with strong political overtones, circulated in Hasa during 1979. Some leading Iranian clerics, notably ayatullahs Khalkhali and Ruhani, had singled out Hasa and Bahrain as areas where "Shi'i brothers" were being persecuted and, hence, needed help.[26]

The first indication of unrest in Hasa came in the summer of 1979 when Shi'i leaders announced that they would publicly stage the Ashura ceremony. The holy day of Ashura, commemorating the martyrdom in battle of the third Shi'i imam, Husain, is the most solemn in the Shi'i calendar and the emotive peak of a major religious period observed by the Shi'is—the month of Muharram. On the basis of their distinction between public and private practices of Shi'i customs, the Saudi rulers had always banned the Ashura ceremony. Nevertheless, on November 28, 1979, the eve of Ashura, the Shi'is did hold the traditional mourning procession. This led to demonstrations by thousands of Shi'is in various parts of the region, which turned quickly into violent clashes with the security forces stationed in the area and to the burning of cars and the

25. Holden, *The House,* p. 280.
26. *The Financial Times* (London) (hereafter *FT*), March 12, 1980.

looting of shops. It was as if the decades-old frustration had at last found public expression.

The demonstrators were reported to have called on the Saudi government to stop supplying the United States with oil, and to support the Islamic revolution of Khomeini in Iran. They also demanded a fairer distribution of wealth within the kingdom and an end to discrimination against the Shi'is by the Sunni majority. They chanted slogans critical of the Saudi royal family. In a matter of hours the demonstrations and disturbances spread throughout Hasa and included such places as the oil-refinery town of Ra's Tanura, the oil towns of Abaqiq, Khafji and Sayhat, and the major towns of Qatif and Safwa. No violence was reported against the large American community in Dhaharan; but a British-Saudi bank in Qatif was reported to have been attacked and its windows broken. When the demonstrations threatened to get out of control in some of the towns north of Dhaharan, the nerve center of the oil region, the Saudi authorities rushed twenty thousand troops to deal with the demonstrators. Several people—seventeen, according to one source—were killed and dozens wounded, including women. To forestall further trouble, the Saudi forces sealed off the major towns of Hasa, most notably the area around Qatif which had the largest concentration of Shi'is in the region. According to persons who visited the Qatif area, the walls of the town had been covered with antigovernment slogans and exhortations to remember the "martyrs" of the clashes.

The Saudis initially denied these reports, stating that "the Kingdom's towns, cities and villages enjoy stability and security, thank God." Three days later, however, the interior minister told a Saudi paper that what had happened in the Eastern Province "was confined merely to limited demonstrations by a few groups."[27]

In early February 1980, the Shi'is took to the streets again. On February 1, the first anniversary (according to the Muslim calendar) of Khomeini's ascendance to power, a sermon in Qatif's main mosque inflamed many Shi'is to demonstrate in the market. Two banks were attacked and stoned: the kingdom's largest bank—the National Commercial Bank—and the largest money exchanger—al-Rajhi Company for Currency and Exchange. Fifty buses and cars as well as the local electricity office were burnt, and four people were killed. The demonstrators, car-

27. Accounts are based on *NYT, FT, Guardian* (London), December 4, 1979; *al-Safir* (Beirut), December 3, 1979; *Christian Science Monitor,* February 20, 1980; *FT,* March 12, 1980; Radio Riyadh, December 3—BBC, December 5, 1979; *al-Jazira* (Riyadh), December 6, 1979.

rying photographs of Ayatullah Khomeini, demanded the release of those arrested during the December clashes.[28]

More than being a reaction to religious discontent, the violent disturbances reflected growing social and economic unrest among the Shi'is. What disturbed them most of all was not their inability to hold the traditional mourning parade on Ashura but rather their status as second-class citizens in their own country. Had it been only a case of religious discontent (banning of the Ashura) with no social and economic discrimination, then the Shi'is might have, most probably, resigned themselves to the situation. Given the Wahhabi character of the state, the Shi'is might have accepted that Saudi rulers could not condone public religious rites that were anathema to the Wahhabi doctrine. But this should not have necessarily led to social and economic discrimination. Their second-class status became all the more striking and disturbing when the Shi'is realized that the sources of Saudi wealth were located right in the middle of their own region, but they were not afforded the opportunity to benefit from it equally with the majority of Saudis.

This social and economic unrest had remained subterranean until 1979 because the Shi'is were anxious not to alienate the Saudi regime. But the revolution in nearby Shi'i Iran provided the Shi'is in Hasa with a sense of power and self-confidence they had previously lacked. It also enabled them to sense an affiliation with a new, successful framework with which they could identify and in which they were considered equals and not second-class members. The victory of Khomeini and the success of the revolution gave the Shi'is the courage to stand up to their Saudi masters and voice publicly their grievances and demands. Thus, whereas the discontent created Shi'i antagonism and animosity toward the Saudi regime, the revolution transformed this hitherto-latent hostility into violence. The eruption of the disturbances was, thus, a spontaneous reaction by the discontented Shi'is in Saudi Arabia to the successful Shi'i revolution in Iran. Indeed, along the same lines of the Iranian Revolution, the disturbances in Hasa reflected previously concealed social and economic disaffection surfacing in the form of a religiously anchored protest against the regime. The religious Shi'i context of the protest served both as a symbol for the discrimination and discontent and as a cement, giving the Shi'is a sense of community cohesion and group solidarity. In addition, it seems that some organizational developments enabled the unrest to be translated into violence. The Shi'is apparently became more organized as

28. Accounts are based on *Wall Street Journal* (hereafter WSJ), February 5, 1980; *al-Ahram* (Cairo), February 21, 1980; *FT*, March 12, 1980.

they were integrated as laborers into the national market. These organizational networks, both lay and religious, must have played some role in mobilizing people into demonstrating their discontent with the Saudi regime.

From the Saudi vantage point, the disturbances in Hasa constituted the first political challenge posed by the Shi'i population to the Saudi regime since the establishment of the present kingdom in 1902 and the first known Shi'i riots in Saudi Arabia. In many respects, not the least being their proximity to Iran, the protest by so many members of the Shi'i community had graver implications for the regime than the fragmented rebels who had seized the Grand Mosque in Mecca on November 20, 1979, and were still in control of it when the disturbances broke out in Hasa in late November. The Saudi authorities, recognizing that the Shi'is were a dangerous, restive element, were alarmed by the disturbances on several counts.

For one thing, the eastern area is the oil region on which the whole economy rests. The danger of sabotage in the oil fields could not be excluded, especially as seven thousand of ARAMCO's Saudi workers (35 percent of the local work force) were Shi'is. The specter of disaffected Shi'is damaging the lifeblood of the kingdom by attacking vulnerable oil installations, perhaps aided and abetted by their fellow Shi'is in neighboring countries, was alarmingly conjured up by the demonstrations and riots. There was also concern that foreign elements might try to exploit the Shi'is' grievances for their own purposes and endanger the kingdom's stability. After all, the Shi'i community could prove fertile ground for the implantation of radical ideologies. And there was always the fear that the Hasa Shi'is might become an increasingly powerful lever in the hands of a radical, hostile Iranian leadership. The perception was that the Hasa Shi'is might be only the first target of an Iranian propaganda campaign, which would gather momentum and engulf the other Shi'i communities in the Gulf, primarily in Bahrain and Kuwait, and thus destabilize the whole Gulf region.

This danger became all the more tangible after the February 1980 riots when Iran stepped up its radio attacks against the Saudi regime. Criticizing the conduct of the royal family and challenging its very legitimacy by reiterating Khomeini's argument that Islam and a monarchy were incompatible, the Iranians called upon the Shi'is in Hasa to rebel against their Saudi masters. Illustrative of the Iranian campaign was the following broadcast:

> The ruling regime in Saudi Arabia wears Muslim clothing, but it

actually represents a luxurious, frivolous, shameless way of life, robbing funds from the people and squandering them, and engaging in gambling, drinking parties and orgies. Would it be surprising if people follow the path of the revolution, resort to violence and continue their struggle to regain their rights and resources?

Revolutionary masses, heroic people in Qatif . . . resist the government from the deserts where there is neither education, awareness nor culture. . . . Resist your oppressive enemies in the following ways: (1) continue writing slogans opposing the regime and its guards on walls, cars, and particularly government establishments; (2) distribute revolutionary leaflets and . . . encourage citizens to resist and stand fast; (3) challenge the authorities' forces by directing blows at them. Where are the arms? . . . Where are the Molotov cocktails prepared even by women and children? Where are the iron bars, staves, and stones?[29]

The Saudis could thus realize that Khomeini was going to be a consistent threat through his propaganda activities aimed at inciting the Hasa Shi'is. The Iranian influence forced them to conclude that if they did not act decisively and immediately, they were bound to face future troubles. Thus, in the aftermath of the disturbances, the Saudi regime decided to deal with the Shi'i problem in all its aspects by employing a carrot-and-stick approach to the Shi'i population. Large-scale investigations and arrests of Shi'is were carried out; scores of religious leaders and six hundred persons were imprisoned. The regime was said to have created an atmosphere of terror and fear among the Shi'is to prevent further demonstrations and violence.[30]

On the other hand, the government sought to devise a long-term approach to the problem, realizing that the outbursts also reflected deeply rooted grievances among the Shi'is arising from perceived social and economic discrimination. Indeed, immediately after the suppression of the violent demonstrations in February 1980, the government started to flourish the carrot. Entrusted with the task of restoring order and stability to Hasa and devising an overall strategy for the Shi'i problem, Deputy Interior Minister Prince Ahmad ibn 'Abd al-'Aziz visited the scene of the riots and held meetings with the townsmen. He admitted that the Shi'is had been neglected and that they had not prospered as much as others in Hasa. This was the first time any senior member of the royal family admitted that the Shi'is had been maltreated. Prince Ahmad promised reforms and improvements if only the Shi'is would offer their cooperation.

29. Radio Tehran (in Arabic) March 8 and 14—BBC, March 10 and 16, 1980, respectively.
30. *NYT,* January 3, 1980; *al-Safir,* December 22, 1979.

Under the leadership of Prince Ahmad, a comprehensive plan was launched, aimed at improving the living standards of the Shi'i population. It included an electricity project, the reasphalting of streets, new schools for boys and girls, a new hospital, the draining of large areas of swamps, and projects for additional street lighting, sewage, and communications. Perhaps most important, the government decided to provide loans, through the Real Estate Development Fund, to town residents to build new homes for themselves. All this activity received wide publicity and a high profile in the government-controlled Saudi Press Agency and the press. A week before the Ashura holiday in November 1980, the government announced a new development project for Qatif. On the same evening, Saudi television screened a newsreel on Qatif and its development. The timing of both was obviously significant, being a pointed reminder of how much had been done for the Shi'is in the preceding year. An even more conspicuous gesture was made by Crown Prince Fahd just days before Ashura when he ordered the release of more than one hundred Qatif Shi'is who had been arrested during the riots of November 1979 and February 1980.[31] Ashura of 1980 passed uneventfully.

As further proof of the government's care for the Shi'i population and in recognition of the tranquility that prevailed among them, King Khalid Ibn 'Abd al-'Aziz traveled to Hasa to visit major Shi'i areas, including first and foremost the town of Qatif. During his stay, which began only five days after Ashura, the king was accompanied everywhere by town elders from Qatif. The regime's new attitude was also reflected in the third Five-Year Plan, which included numerous projects in the fields of public health (clinics and hospitals), education (new schools, even in remote villages, for boys and girls), youth welfare, electricity, telephone, sewage, water, and so on. A large airport for the area was also being planned. In 1981, a special committee headed by Crown Prince Fahd was formed to plan the expenditure of 1 billion riyals for new development projects in the Eastern Province.[32]

It seemed that the desire to mend fences was mutual. While the government realized that it had to reassess its policies toward the Shi'i population, the Shi'is on their side felt that they had to reevaluate the situation, given the new Saudi attitude and developments in Iran. First, the swift Saudi repression of their demonstrations made the Shi'is very reluctant to stage such public protests in the future and run the danger of harsh Saudi reactions. Second, the new development plans did indicate a

31. *WSJ*, February 5, 1980; *FT*, May 5, 1981.
32. *al-Madina*, July 22, 1980; see also Quandt, *Saudi Arabia*, p. 97.

significant shift in the Saudi position, leading the Shi'is to believe that their economic and social conditions would improve. It would thus be counterproductive to alienate the Saudi regime by adopting an attitude of confrontation rather than one of cooperation. Last but not least important, the Shi'is were becoming increasingly disillusioned by the turmoil that continued to convulse Iran and by the ongoing, bloody Iran-Iraq War. They realized that although Ayatullah Khomeini might deliver fierce sermons, it was the Saudis who would, in the final analysis, control their lives and improve their standard of living. The result was that the unrest in Hasa subsided, soothed by the constant flow of money and attention that marked a shift in the regime's policies.

An overall assessment of the Saudi attitude toward the Shi'i minority points, thus, to a clear shift in the twentieth century and, more specifically, since 1930. Whereas previously the Saudi policy was anchored in religious-Wahhabi considerations, the new attitude is based on political-Saudi interests and guidelines. Instead of the religious differences being the crucial determinant, the political, social, and economic implications of these differences have become the critical factor. The Saudis are not anxious about the Shi'is forming a religious opposition, nor are they concerned so much about the Shi'is' religious identity; rather, they are apprehensive of the political significance of their identity and of the Shi'is' proximity to post-revolutionary Iran.

Viewed from the Shi'is' vantage point, it is clear that their primary concern has been their economic and social conditions, though some of the Shi'is might have been preoccupied with questions of religious freedom. Previously dormant and intimidated, the Shi'i minority was enabled by the revolution in Iran to rise and make explicit public demands. Once it became apparent, however, that they had scored significant economic gains, their basic motivation to challenge the Saudi regime disappeared. Under these circumstances, it is not surprising that there have been no outbursts of anger or protests among the Shi'is in Hasa since violent February 1980 and that the whole region has been quiet and stable. This is all the more remarkable given that throughout this period the Iranian regime has continued to broadcast its special radio programs in Arabic and to publish and distribute leaflets, calling upon the Shi'is in Hasa to rise against the royal family. It is further proof that the basic reasons underlying the Shi'is' discontent had to do with their social and economic conditions. Once these issues started to be dealt with, the Shi'is became satisfied and abandoned any idea of challenging or confronting the Saudi

regime. It is not to be ruled out, however, that changed future circumstances, both external—in Iran or the other Shi'i communities in the Gulf
states—and internal—in Saudi policies—or a combination of both, might
reactivate Shi'i discontent and opposition.

RUDI MATTHEE

Chapter Ten The Egyptian Opposition
on the Iranian Revolution

The Iranian Revolution and its leader Ayatullah Khomeini, in addition
to the impact they have had on Shi'is in the Muslim world, have also had
an important impact on Sunni Muslims, particularly the politically minded
revivalists among them. Nor is this strange, since Khomeini and his followers have never made a point of the differences between Shi'ism and
Sunnism but, on the contrary, have spoken of an all-Islamic revolution,
which they expect to spread as much in Sunni as in Shi'i countries. Even
Khomeini's earlier writings do not stress Shi'ism, and some have an almost
"Sunni" respect for the period of the first caliphs, who are traditionally
denounced by Shi'is.[1]

In their essential denial of the importance of Shi'i-Sunni differences
Khomeini and his followers are working within a century-old tradition of
militant Muslims who want to unite the Muslim world, regardless of sec-

1. In his *Vilayat-i Faqih,* Khomeini repudiates monarchical government and the hereditary principles it involves. His emphasis on the executive role and the nonhereditary
status of those who succeeded the Prophet, and their legitimacy on the basis of ability rather
than spiritual designation, leads him to deemphasize the hereditary rights of the imams to
succession and to take a mild position on the first two caliphs. See for this Mangol Bayat,
"The Iranian Revolution of 1978–79: Fundamentalist or Modern?" *Middle East Journal* 37,
no. 1 (Winter 1983): 30–42.

247

tarian differences, against the attacks and encroachments of the unbelieving West. Such was the message of pan-Islamist militants like Jamal al-Din al-Afghani and some of the young Ottomans. The militant Khilafat movement in post–World War I India similarly ignored Shi'i-Sunni differences; leading Shi'is there spoke in defense of the Sunni Ottoman caliph and against the British.

That Shi'is, worldwide, were more responsive to Khomeini than Sunnis, among whom positive response has become a minority phenomenon, must have been a disappointment to the Khomeinists, who like the early Russian revolutionaries expected to see a quick spread and implementation of their policies. Here we will study the response of those Sunni groups who chose to respond favorably to the Khomeinist revolution, despite their Sunnism, in one major country, Egypt.

In Egypt the response to the Iranian Revolution, from the very beginning of its occurrence, has set the government against those who oppose the present political structure. The regime is anti-Iran, though under Mubarak it is less outspoken than in Sadat's days. The opposition had been supporting the revolution, until the Gulf war seemed to demand an explicit choice between a pro-Iran stand and Arab solidarity. There were various motives for this support. The Egyptian secular nationalists were primarily moved by such aspects as the anti-imperialist struggle, social justice, and the mass movement character of the revolution. As for the religious opposition, it was the hoped-for materialization of a purely Islamic state that prompted its declarations of support. For those who opposed the Egyptian government, regardless of their ideals and ideology, the revolution in one way or another provided a useful means by which the domestic governmental structure could be attacked.

This essay is not concerned with the Egyptian secular leftist parties who saw a radical mass movement in the Iranian Revolution without giving due credit to the religious element.[2] It focuses rather on those opposition groups for whom Islam is, if not the exclusive, at least a fundamental ingredient of their vision of an ideal society. The religious or religiously inspired opposition consists of three movements or currents. The first one is composed of the broad and diffuse spectrum of contemporary radical Islamic groups known as Jama'at. These extremist groups, such as Takfir wa al-Hijra and al-Jihad, reject out of hand the present religious and political establishment on the basis that it leads and fosters a pagan and

2. For a discussion of the overall Egyptian press evaluation of the Iranian Revolution, see Mohga Machour and Alain Roussilon, *La révolution iranienne dans la presse égyptienne,* dossier 4 (Cairo: CEDEJ, 1982).

corrupt society. They vary in their analysis of the nature and extent of corruption—some of them regard only the state as evil, others extend their indictment to the whole of society—but they all see the armed struggle against the state as legitimate, indeed obligatory, for the attainment of a purely Islamic society. Being activist movements, the Jama'at have hardly expressed themselves in theoretical writing. As a result, an analysis of their stand vis-à-vis the Iranian Revolution based on written sources is next to impossible.

Of the two movements, then, that will be discussed here with regard to their appreciation of the Iranian Revolution, the first is the current version of the Egyptian Muslim Brotherhood. The present-day Brotherhood, though it is a continuation of the original Brotherhood, nevertheless shows different characteristics. For this reason it has been called the neo-Muslim Brotherhood.[3] However, as it continues to present itself as the Muslim Brotherhood and as we are not concerned here with its changed character, the movement will be simply referred to as Muslim Brotherhood or Muslim Brothers. It shares with the Jama'at a rejection of the present government structure and the Islam of the preeminent Muslim university and seminary, al-Azhar. It is, however, clearly distinct from the extremist factions in that it rejects, at least verbally, armed struggle against the state and indeed shows itself willing to cooperate with the authorities in certain domains.

The movement that will be considered in juxtaposition and comparison with the Muslim Brothers is the intellectual current that calls itself the Islamic Left (al-Yasar al-Islami). This loose confederation is made up of a number of Egyptian intellectuals, the most prominent of whom is Hasan Hanafi, a professor of philosophy at the University of Cairo and an erstwhile member of the original Muslim Brotherhood. Other members include Muhammad Ahmad Khalaf Allah, Muhammad Amara, and Tariq al-Bishri. Members vary in the extent to which they see a congruence between Islam and Arabism, that is, the degree to which they accept secular Arab nationalism. They agree, however, that the Islamic heritage, if stripped from its irrational and status quo–confirming attributes, can be revitalized so as to become a vital element in an authentic renaissance of the Muslim world. Like many Muslim reformist trends, al-Yasar al-Islami attaches great importance to reason as an indispensable tool for

3. This is a term used by Gilles Kepel in his excellent study of the contemporary Islamic movements in Egypt "Le mouvement islamiste dans l'Egypte de Sadate" (Ph.D. diss., Université de Paris, 1982).

adjusting Islam to the modern world in its attempt to reconcile religion and philosophy in shaping a progressive form of Islam.

There exist a few difficulties that seemingly would stand in the way of a meaningful comparison between the two movements with regard to their perception of the Iranian Revolution and the developments afterward. These difficulties primarily stem from the temporally uneven nature of publication of material. Unlike the radical Islamic movements, the Muslim Brothers have amply discussed revolutionary Iran in their publications. These mainly consist of the monthly magazines *al-Da'wah* (the Call) and *al-I'tisam* (Perseverance), and *al-Mukhtar al-Islami* (the Islamic Digest), a monthly modeled on *Reader's Digest* that presents the news in background articles and special dossiers.[4] As these magazines follow the course of events in Iran, one can discern an evolving perspective according to the sequence of events. This does not apply to the writings of al-Yasar al-Islami. Of its few writings that are relevant to the Iranian Revolution, the most important is the first, and only, volume of what was meant to become the magazine *al-Yasar al-Islami*. Permission to bring out subsequent volumes was never given, however. Aside from this, there are Hanafi's introductions to the Arabic translations of two of Khomeini's books, *al-Hukumah al-Islamiyah* (Islamic Government) and *Jihad al-Nafs au al-Jihad al-Akbar* (Jihad over Self or the Supreme Jihad), and two books on the roots and the ideological bases of the revolution, one by Ibrahim al-Disuqi Shita, a former professor of Persian at Cairo University, and the other by Muhammad Amara.[5] Because of their nonperiodic appearance, these publications lack a continuing perspective, but by providing a one-time exposure of the situation in Iran, they offer a more coherent analysis.

A further problem is that all periodical publications were suspended with Sadat's crackdown on the opposition in the fall of 1981. As a result, it is impossible to trace developments in viewpoints regarding Iran of the Egyptian Islamic opposition beyond that date. It would have been particularly interesting to see to what extent the Egyptian-Islamic appreciation

---

4. For a discussion of the history of the character of these journals, see Gilles Kepel, *Le Prophète et Pharaon: Les mouvements islamistes dans l'Egypte moderne* (Paris: la Découverte, 1984); and Saad Eddin Ibrahim, "An Islamic Alternative in Egypt: The Muslim Brotherhood and Sadat," *Arab Studies Quarterly* 4, nos. 1–2 (Spring 1980): 75–93.

5. *al-Hukumah al-Islamiyah* (Islamic Government), ed. and intr. Hasan Hanafi (N.p. [Cairo], 1979); *Jihad al-Nafs au al-Jihad al-Akhbar* (Jihad over Self or the Supreme Jihad), ed. and intr. Hasan Hanafi (N.p. [Cairo], n.d. [1979]); Ibrahim al-Disuqi Shita, *al-Thaurah al-Iraniyah: al-Judhur—al-Idilujiyah* (The Iranian Revolution: The Roots—the Ideology) (Beirut, 1979); Muhammad Amara, *al-Fikr al-Qa'id li'l-Thaurah al-Iraniyah* (The Dominant Thinking of the Iranian Revolution) (Cairo, 1982).

of Iran has been influenced by the violence Egypt itself underwent in October 1981 with Sadat's assassination. However, this does not make what material is available less valuable, nor does it preclude a meaningful discussion of two vantage points from which the Iranian Revolution has been observed in Egypt.

One last point should be made. It is not assumed that the writings quoted in the following discussion are absolutely sincere. Al-Yasar al-Islami calls itself a movement in the tradition of Jamal al-Din al-Afghani, and one suspects that, in the fashion of its illustrious precursor, politics and expediency play a role in the way its viewpoints are expressed. The circumspection with which Hanafi discusses the role of Islam when he addresses the domestic front reflects an attempt not to antagonize religious ranks. He displays a much more instrumentalist view of religion and seems less inhibited to express his politically leftist leanings when he says in an English-language article: "Nasserism without Islam will fall into secularism and will always be threatened by an Islamic movement. Islam is capable of serving as an umbrella for all political trends in the country: liberation, Marxism, and Arab nationalism."[6]

Similarly, a good deal of what the Muslim Brothers wrote under Sadat bears the imprint of an attempt to avoid censorship. This particularly applies to their avoidance of the question of the legitimacy of revolutionary violence, the caution with which the Iranian model is propounded as one that should be followed in Egypt, and the absence of any direct references to similarities between the shah and Sadat. However, except in the case of the Sunni-Shi'i question, where the expediency is too obvious to be ignored, the question of sincerity is often too moot to bring into an analysis of a variety of written works.

THE MUSLIM BROTHERHOOD

The Muslim Brothers were as slow as anyone in recognizing the true dimensions of the struggle that started to shake Iran in 1978. Iran had hardly been a topic of discussion for them prior to the revolution. But by the end of 1978 the Muslim Brothers were cautiously beginning to pay attention to the events that were taking place in the Muslim sister country. *Al-I'tisam,* after an earlier passing reference to the issue of female clothing, carried its first real coverage of Iran in September with an article in

6. Hasan Hanafi, "The Relevance of the Islamic Alternative in Egypt," *Arab Studies Quarterly* 4, nos. 1–2 (Spring 1980): 74.

which America was accused of duplicity because it allegedly started protesting the shah's regime only when the liberal movement was treated harshly.[7] *Al-Da'wah* started reporting in October with an article mentioning the closure of gambling casinos and the reinstitution of the Muslim calendar, and exhorting the Egyptian government to follow the example.[8] *Al-Mukhtar al-Islami* followed suit in 1979 with an interview with Imam Khomeini.[9] In August of that year, the magazine, which distinguishes itself from the other two by featuring in-depth background articles rather than following current events, came out with a six-page article in which the challenges to the new Islamic regime were discussed.[10] Also in 1979 a book appeared under the name *al-Khumaini: al-Hall al-Islami wa al-Badil* (Khomeini: The Islamic Solution and the Alternative).[11] This work, written in a tone unmistakably akin to that of the Muslim Brotherhood magazines, discussed the background of the revolution and put it in the perspective of the overall Islamic struggle.

From the last days of 1978 on, the events in Iran followed each other in rapid succession and the attention of the Muslim Brotherhood press increased accordingly, although it never reached the frequency and intensity that would have been justified by the importance of the revolution for the Islamic world.

Their slow recognition of the revolution's importance notwithstanding, the Muslim Brothers were quick to put the revolution in the context of a worldwide struggle between Islam and non-Islam and to raise it to the level of metahistory. This perception fits in with their overall view of the world, which is of an apparently clear-cut simplicity. To the Muslim Brothers, the world is divided into an Islamic and an un-Islamic sphere. World history is seen as the tale of an incessant struggle between Islam, that is, obedience to God, and the forces of ignorance and paganism, *jahiliyah*. The enemy is threefold; it is a Moloch composed of communism, neoimperialism (also called the Crusaders, that is, the West and its de-

---

7. "Hal huquq al-insan fi 'urf Karter . . . hiyya huquq al-insan al-salibiyin al-mawali li'l-gharb dun sawa?" (Are Human Rights as Practiced by Carter Merely the Human Rights of the Crusaders, the Clients of the West?), *al-I'tisam,* September 1978, 10.

8. "Iran tattajihu . . . nahwa al-Islam" (Iran Is Heading for Islam), *al-Da'wah,* October 1978, 11.

9. "Su'al wa jawab ma' al-Imam al-Khumayni" (Interview with the Imam Khomeini), *al-Mukhtar al-Islami,* July 1979, 58–61.

10. "Tahaddiyat amama al-thaurah al-iraniyah" (Challenges to the Iranian Revolution), *al-Mukhtar al-Islami,* August 1979, 30–36.

11. Fathi 'Abd al-'Aziz, *al-Khumaini: al-Hall al-Islami wa al-Badil* (Khomeini: The Islamic Solution and the Alternative) (Cairo: al-Mukhtar al-Islami, 1979).

pendents), and Zionism.[12] In the Muslim Brothers' conception, any phenomenon, temporal as well as spatial, can be reduced to the polarity between Islam and anti-Islam and thereby loses its historical and spatial perspective. As a result, the elements of the ever-present enemy are treated almost interchangeably and independent of time. Thus the Crusades, the abolition of the caliphate, the Russian invasion of Afghanistan, and Israel's settlement policy all become aspects of the continuing and relentless conspiracy that aims at the destruction of Islam.

This interchangeability is reflected in their analysis of the Iranian Revolution. To them the revolution can be explained as being the struggle of the Iranian people to regain their religion after a long period in which it had been humiliated, violated, and undermined. To underscore this, the Muslim Brotherhood press in innumerable articles reminds the reader of the inhuman nature of the shah's regime. The misery of the people and the impiety and depravity of the ruling classes figure prominently in their columns. The ferocious nature of the shah's rule is invariably described with reference to his attempts to destroy allegiance to Islam among the Iranian people. Thus *al-Da'wah,* in November 1978, wrote: "Thus began in Iran what is called the policy of modernization and 'Persification,' modernization being the introduction of all sorts of western phenomena in Iran, and 'Persification' equalling the elimination of the Islamic identity from Iran and the country's return to a Persian inclination."[13] Likewise, a great deal of attention is paid to Iran's dependence on the West and the role of imperialism under the shah. According to *al-Mukhtar al-Islami,* "the Iranian people suffered as much as any of the peoples of the Islamic fatherland from the practices of spiritual domination under the hands of imperialism, as well as from its extensive drive toward westernization in its attempt to destroy the Islamic identity and to remove active allegiance to this great religion from the heart of its adherents."[14]

The Muslim Brotherhood devotes little attention to finding religious justifications for the Iranian Revolution. The horrendous nature of the Pahlavi regime that trampled Islam, and the people's desire to retrieve their religion, seem to make discussions of that kind largely superfluous. Only occasionally does one come across an attempt to justify the over-

12. The Muslim Brothers see these forces as cooperating in a huge conspiracy against Islam. They emphasize in communism its Western essence as much as its atheist character. The Jews are alleged to be behind both Western imperialism and international communism.

13. "Al-tha'irun fi Iran: sud marksiyun am muslimun iraniyun?" (The Revolutionaries in Iran: Black Marxists or Iranian Muslims?), *al-Da'wah,* November 1978, 8–9.

14. "Iran: al-thaurah wa al-daulah" (Iran: The Revolution and the State), *al-Mukhtar al-Islami,* August 1980, 26–34.

throw of the Iranian order in religious terms. Thus *al-I'tisam*, in the section "The Question of the Month" of its February 1979 issue, referred to the verses "Thou art not charged to oversee them" and "Thou art not a tyrant over them" as Qur'anic injunctions that legitimize rebellion against tyranny. In addition, it mentioned the Tradition "For God the exalted the most perfidious title for a man is king of kings."[15]

If the Iranian people's choice of Islam over Western-style modernization explained the origin of the revolution, it also explained its successful outcome. Its success was indeed guaranteed, for in the Muslim Brothers' vision, Islam is the divinely led moving force of history, and there is no question that in the end it will triumph over its enemies. As a result, one of the most important aspects of the revolution was that it offered concrete evidence that God's party is the final winner. Thus in April 1979 *al-Da'wah* wrote: "The first lesson that the Islamic peoples . . . are able to draw is that God's party is victorious regardless of the power of tyrants and the forces that sustain and support them."[16] In fact, part of the heavy emphasis on the shah's reign in the Muslim Brotherhood press seems to have the aim of enhancing the luster of the revolutionary success. The fact that Islam defeated a king who commanded one of the most powerful armies in the world and who was backed by both the United States and the Soviet Union could not but invest the victory with a ring of miraculousness.

But there is more. If the revolution's success was due to the return to Islam, Islam also safeguards the continuation of its success. The absolute conviction that Islam holds a monopoly over truth leads to the equally obvious truth that the happenings in Iran are no passing phenomenon, the outcome of which is subject to arbitrary political circumstances.[17] On the contrary, these happenings form an irreversible, divinely sanctioned prelude to the definitive unification of religion and state power in Islam. Iran is only the beginning of this process. The temporary "absence" of Islam, the reversal of which is heralded by the Iranian Revolution, is to be seen not as indicative of a flaw in Islam itself but as a lack of awareness and commitment among the Muslims.[18] The idea that the

15. "Su'al al-shahr: ma huwwa mauqif al-muslim isa' ahdath Iran al-akhirah?" (Question of the Month: What Is the Position of the Muslim toward the Latest Happenings in Iran?), *al-I'tisam*, February 1979, 39. The Tradition is to be found in Bukhari, *al-Sahih*, 8:56.

16. "Ru'ya islamiyah" (An Islamic Vision), *al-Da'wah*, April 1979, 13.

17. "Qira'ah fi usul al-thaurah al-iraniyah" (Studying the Roots of the Iranian Revolution), *al-Mukhtar al-Islami*, April 1980, 44–60.

18. Ibid.

Iranian Revolution might be a temporary phenomenon can stem only from ignorance about the history and the nature of Islam.

It is in the nature of the Muslim Brothers' conception of Islam that they view the Iranian Revolution as neither limited to Iran as a country nor confined to the Iranian people. Iran's history is part and parcel of the collective history of the umma. Like all Islamic movements, the Muslim Brothers abhor the ideas of both territorial nationalism (*wataniyah*) and ethnic nationalism (*qaumiyah*). Nationalism is seen as a concept of foreign import, introduced by the West with the aim of dividing the Muslim world into separate national entities that would be easier to dominate. In their writings they incessantly denounce the principles of nationalism and secularism, the pernicious influence of which they consider to have begun with the forcible dissolution of the Islamic empires of the Ottomans and the Qajars. They analyze the history of the Islamic world since the disappearance of these last "truly Islamic states" as a tale of the continuous struggle between the forces of imperialism and secularism on the one hand and the forces of Islam on the other. The former, consisting of both the capitalist and the communist West, and Zionism, have always been intent on sowing discord and creating disunity among the Muslims. They managed to have the caliphate abolished through the Kemalist regime, the first of their regional clients. The forces of imperialism and secularism are thwarted in their aim—the separation of religion and politics in Islam— only by the indefatigable resistance offered by the Islamic movement (*al-Harakah al-Islamiyah*). The Islamic movement consists of many branches, ranging from the Islamic opposition against Kemalism to the Egyptian and Syrian Muslim Brotherhood, but their geographical and temporal position is hardly of any import, as they all fight for the same cause: the reinstitution of Islamic rule in a reunited Islamic community stretching from the Atlantic to the Indus and beyond.

In the light of the foregoing, it is not surprising that the Egyptian Muslim Brothers view the Iranian Revolution as a struggle with parallels with other Islamic resistance movements rather than as a continuation of a national Iranian or Shi'i tradition. Its role in the worldwide struggle between the Tangiers-Jakarta axis and the Washington-Moscow axis links it to a variety of movements, such as the Sudanese mahdist movement, the Sanusiyah movement in Libya, the Pakistani opposition to Zulfiqar Ali Bhutto, the Afghan resistance against the Soviet Union, and the struggle of the Muslim Brotherhood in Egypt and Syria. Thus Fathi 'Abd al-'Aziz writes: "The Islamic movements remained the center of gravitation in the region through their heroic resistance against imperialism, both before and after the fall of the Caliphate, beginning with the Islamic Mahdist movement in Sudan which, had it been given the time, would have altered the face of Africa and the Arab East, and ending with the latest Iranian revolution under the guidance of the Islamic leader Aya- tullah Khomeini."[19] Accordingly, any trace of nationalism, either territo- rial or ethnic, is vehemently denied in the Muslim Brothers' writings. It is argued that the revolution was a protest against the shah's policy of emphasizing the imperial Iranian heritage and the distinctiveness of Iran- ian civilization. Similarly, it is because of their adherence to nationalism and secularism that people such as Shahpur Bakhtiar, the last premier of the ancien régime, and the autonomist Kurdish leader Qassemlu are por- trayed as foreign-supported enemies of Islamic Iran.[20]

Concerning the history of the Islamic movement within Iran, it is interesting to see that the Egyptian Muslim Brothers incorporate the Con- stitutional Revolution of the early twentieth century, and even the short- lived Jangali movement of the 1920s, in their record of Islam's struggle in Iran. However, although both movements are presented as Islamic in character, they are on balance deemed unsuccessful for lack of Islamic leadership and lack of awareness of the nature of the enemies of Islam.[21] The ambivalence toward Iranian opposition movements prior to Kho- meini's revolution manifests itself most conspicuously in references to the Musaddiq period of the early 1950s. The Iranian struggle to gain control over national oil resources is frequently mentioned in enumerations of Islamic resistance against anti-Islamic forces, but the Muslim Brothers seem to acknowledge the merits of Musaddiq's struggle against imperi- alism only inasmuch as it runs parallel with the Islamic movement of Ayatullah Kashani. At no point is Mussadiq mentioned independently from his religious supporters. In fact, his policy is considered to have ultimately failed for want of Islamic leadership after his alienation of his clerical supporters. Most frequently mentioned of these is the name of Navvab Safavi, the founder of the militant Fida'iyan-i Islam who, together with Kashani, is hailed as the most important representative of the forces that challenged the shah and his foreign supporters.[22]

19. Fathi 'Abd al-'Aziz, 22.
20. "Thaurat Iran: bayn du'at al-ilhad wa du'at al-infisal" (Iran's Revolution: Between the Advocates of Apostasy and the Advocates of Secession), al-Da'wah, December 1979, 8–9.
21. "Qira'ah," al-Mukhtar al-Islami.
22. See, for example, "Al-tha'irun," al-Da'wah. Fathi 'Abd al-'Aziz (p. 35) also men- tions the meeting Kashani and Hasan al-Banna are said to have had in 1948 in Hijaz with the aim of coming to a better understanding between Sunnism and Shi'ism.

The Egyptian Muslim Brotherhood considers the Iranian Revolution the deathblow to the era of the shahs, the Ataturks and the Bhuttos, and the harbinger of the age of the Khomeinis and the Hasan al-Bannas (the founder of the Egyptian Muslim Brotherhood). This identification of the revolution with Islam *tout court* invests it with an unassailable halo and turns postrevolutionary Iran into a polity beyond criticism. Khomeinist Iran requires no justification, it only needs to be protected against slander and insinuation. This incorporation of the revolution into an exclusively Islamic framework and, hence, its equation with flawlessness make most Muslim Brotherhood discussions of it sound like discussions of the obvious. Instead of being a case study to be analyzed with the aim of assessing the extent to which postrevolutionary developments conform to the Islamic ideal, Iran acquires the status of a model, as fixed as it is abstract, by which foregone conclusions can be validated, a priori positions defined, and existing alliances reconfirmed. Iran, as the proclaimed embodiment of the Islamic ideal of the state ruled according to the divine laws, constantly reinforces the validity of the Islamic truth. Not the exploration of reality but the defense of the norm becomes then of paramount importance. It is here that the enemy, the combination of communism, neoimperialism, and Zionism, plays an indispensable role. As diffuse as it is self-explanatory, the enemy is at hand wherever explanations are sought and brought to the fore whenever exoneration and instant alleviation is needed. When apparent shortcomings and aberrations threaten to distort the ideal picture, a Muslim Brotherhood analysis invariably manages to lay the blame on the relentless machinations of the enemy. Used in this way the enemy is a double-edged sword. Discussions of the revolution invariably point to the anti-Islamic forces as being responsible for the misery, depravity, and impiety of prerevolutionary Iran. Their undermining influence continues to be invoked in order to explain postrevolutionary developments that seem out of line with the ideal. Thus the Iran-Iraq War becomes a conflict instigated by the Americans and the Russians;[23] the Baath regime is portrayed as a Christian-led gang;[24] the

23. See, for example, "Hawl al-harb al-iraqiyah al-iraniyah" (Concerning the Iraq-Iran War), *al-I'tisam*, September 1980, 3. 'Umar Tilmisani, in an interview with *al-Da'wah*, described the war as being the result of American and Russian machinations designed to divert attention from the Israeli usurpation of the rights of the Muslims. ("Harb al-'Iraq wa Iran, faji'at al-muslimin" [The Iraq-Iran War, a Muslim Calamity], *al-Da'wah*, October 1980, 4–6).

24. "Wa madha ba'd qadisiyyat Sadam?" (What after Saddam's [Battle of] Qadisiyya?), *al-Mukhtar al-Islami*, January 1981, 72–74. The reference "Christian-led gang" is because the founder of the Baath, Michel Aflaq, was a Christian.

explosion of June 1981 that killed Ayatullah Bihishti and many of his companions is attributed to American intrigue; and after the fall of President Bani Sadr America is accused of distorting the truth by portraying the Iranian domestic situation as a struggle between radical Muslims and enlightened Westernized intellectuals.[25]

The denial of the gravity of the Iranian situation involves a defensive as well as an offensive technique. In their defense of postrevolutionary Iran, the Muslim Brothers frequently refer to prerevolutionary conditions, the cruelty and arbitrariness of which they contrast with the justice that is said to characterize Islamic Iran. The execution of those who held authority under the shah is justified in this manner. Al-Da'wah, for instance, writes, "It is alleged that the difference between yesterday's and today's Iran is one between tranquillity and chaos, or between stability and unrest" and proceeds by saying, "Whatever the Shah and people of all sorts may claim cannot conceal the truth or wipe out the rivers that are filled with the Iranian people's blood, or obliterate from the historical record of Iran all those events during 35 years that were marked by the most outrageous forms of violence, oppression, tyranny, corruption and unrest."[26]

The offensive approach points at the distorted picture the West is said to give of the revolution. Whether or not deliberately employed with the aim of diverting attention from the less agreeable aspects of the Iranian scene, the approach serves its purpose in that it shifts the blame without the need for further investigation. A favorite theme in this regard is human rights "which were not mentioned by anyone when the Shah massacred 100,000 people"[27] and, more specifically, the reintroduction of Islamic punishments.

The Muslim Brothers also implicate the Arab press in the campaign that attempts to portray the new Iran as reactionary and obscurantist. The Egyptian press, for example, is accused of emphasizing the differences of leadership in Iran and the theme of Islamic punishment, and is criticized for advocating the separation of religion and politics and hailing the coming of the shah to Egypt. Amazement at the lack of Islamic solidarity with

25. See, for example, "Al-ahdath al-iraniyah al-akhirah wa sihafatuna al-qaumiyah al-shamitah" (The Latest Iranian Happenings and Our Gloating National Press), al-I'tisam, June–July 1981, 3.

26. "Al-Muslimun tajri dima'uhum 'ala al-mashaniq wa yuttahamuna bi al-qatl wa al-irhab" (While the Blood of Muslims Runs over the Gallows They Are Accused of Murder and Terrorism), al-Da'wah, April 1979, 8–10.

27. "Alladhina khayyabahum Allah yahqaduna Ayat Allah" (Those Who Are Thwarted by God Resent the Ayatullah), al-I'tisam, July 1979, 43.

Iran's case prevails. Although to *al-I'tisam* Western slander of the revolution is understandable, even self-evident, the magazine expresses astonishment at the media's approach in several Arab countries that "seem to be merely subordinate to the CIA."[28] Similarly, *al-Da'wah* shows surprise at the lack of solidarity shown by a member of the Islamic community when it comments on the attacks of "[Islamic] Egypt against the Islamic veil in Islamic Iran."[29]

The Egyptian Muslim Brotherhood press knew it was limited in the extent to which it could openly attack the ruling order under Sadat. It is probably for this reason that one finds no direct references to the violent stand Sadat took against the new Iranian regime. Nevertheless there can be little doubt that the remark in *al-I'tisam* that "many countries fear Iran because they themselves are ruled by oppressors" has, among others, the Egyptian leader in mind. A less general and, in fact, only thinly veiled reference to the Egyptian ruler is to be found in the same magazine when it says, "Every modern Muslim knows that the press of every Arab country attempts to turn its 'sultan' into the greatest sultan, the one who realizes miracles, the doer of heroic deeds."[30]

Much of the Muslim Brothers' view of the world in general, and of the revolution in particular, rests on the presupposition that the anti-Islamic forces constitute a monolithic bloc that, through the ages, has been intent on undermining Islam. This view necessarily runs parallel to a perception of Islam as forming a united and single-willed entity. The general Islamic tendency to emphasize the unity of the Islamic community reaches compelling heights for those Sunni Arabs whose sympathies lie with Shi'i Iran. How do the Muslim Brothers deal with the dilemma that results from the paradox between the postulate of an indivisible Islam and the existence of Shi'ism as a conspicuously divergent current within Islam? The response most frequently offered in answer to this problem is no response at all. That is, the Muslim Brothers in dealing with the problem of Shi'ism prefer silence above all. Instances of spontaneous discussion of the issue are rare and nowhere does a reference to the revolution as a Shi'i one occur. Indeed, an apparently conscious attempt to downplay the Shi'i aspects of the revolution is clearly visible. Thus, when the new

28. "Al-ikhwah al-a'da alladhina yuharibuna al-Khumaini yuriduna an ta'uda 'aqarib al-sa'ah ila al-warah" (The Inimical [Islamic] Brothers Who Fight Khomeini Want to Put the Clock Back), *al-I'tisam*, January 1980, 28–29.

29. "Al-qadayah al-Islamiyah fi ajhizat al-I'lam al-misriyah" (The Islamic Issues in the Egyptian News Media), *al-Da'wah*, December 1979, 30–31.

30. "al-Ikhwah," *al-I'tisam*.

Iranian Constitution is discussed in *al-Da'wah,* the explicit references to Shi'ism in this document are left out of consideration. The article does not mention the passages that refer to the hidden imam and, while emphasizing the fact that Islam as such is proclaimed the official religion, it concludes that the phrase "and the Twelver Ja'fari school of thought" does not preclude rights for the other schools. Instead, it calls attention to the (wholly theoretical) possibility created by the Constitution that a Sunni might become head of state.[31]

A different way of solving the problem is that of presenting Khomeini as a religious figure who preaches a nontraditional form of Shi'ism. A case in point is Fathi 'Abd al-'Aziz who says: "Khomeini takes an impressive and revolutionary stand when he stands up against those Shi'is who quietly wait for the Mahdi to establish the rule of Islam and to fill the earth with justice after it has been filled with injustice and oppression. . . . Khomeini oversteps many of the Shi'i interpretations of the Imamate by considering knowledge of the law and justice to be among its most important pillars."[32] Elsewhere he says:

> Talking about the Twelver Shi'is who today constitute the majority of the Shi'is, the conclusion is that they confess that there is no God but God, that He is the only one and without equal, and that Muhammad is the messenger of God—peace be upon him—who brought the truth and fulfilled prophethood, and likewise they believe in all the prophets of God and in everyone who has come from Him, and they also claim the Imamate for 'Ali and his eleven descendants whom they consider to be the most worthy of the Imamate and the best of creatures after the Prophet of God—peace be upon him—but their belief in the Imamate does not lead to their being unbelievers, for the Imamate of a person does not as such belong to the roots [usul] of Islam as seen by the Sunnis.[33]

In conclusion, the author approvingly cites the fatwa issued by the rector of al-Azhar in 1959, in which the Ja'fari branch of Shi'ism was proclaimed a legitimate school of Islam on a par with the Sunni schools.

Denying the existence of any fundamental points of difference between Sunnism and Shi'ism is indeed a generally used method of dealing with the issue and is mainly used as a means to defend the Iranian Revolution against its detractors. As a result, the most extended discussions of Shi'ism occur as a reaction to accusations against Shi'ism in the Egyptian press. Thus in August 1980 the Egyptian press printed a (false) story

31. "Dustur islami fi Iran" (An Islamic Constitution in Iran), *al-Da'wah,* December 1979, 54–55.
32. Fathi 'Abd al-'Aziz, 38–39.
33. Ibid., 59.

saying that Khomeini had insulted Islam by proclaiming that the hidden imam was a prophet after the Prophet of Islam, and even had presented himself as the awaited Mahdi. The angry reaction to this "distortion meant to sow discord" in *al-Mukhtar al-Islami* was a vehement denial of the possibility that Khomeini might have made such statements: "Khomeini has not said that the Mahdi—in whose coming Sunnism equally believes— is a prophet after Muhammad, nor that he [the Mahdi] will introduce a new faith, nor that he himself or any member of his family is the Mahdi."[34] Yet the same article concedes that mahdism is a principle in which Shi'ism distinguishes itself from Sunnism. Instead of further elaborating the issue, however, it concludes that the question of mahdism does not belong to the essential doctrines, or usul.

Elsewhere, *al-Mukhtar al-Islami* finds reason to attack the position taken on Shi'ism by *Majallat al-Azhar*. The latter magazine, in an article on the principle of mahdism in connection with Shi'ism, argues that mahdism is an undecided issue in Islam. The magazine manages to avoid a final verdict on the issue, noting that most Traditions referring to it are rather weak, and delegates it to a secondary (*far'i*) position. It uses the topic, however, to lash out at the Shi'i interpretation of mahdism as an absurd and heretical expectation of a superhuman imam at the end of time.[35] *Al-Mukhtar al-Islami,* in its reaction, rebukes the Azhar establishment for their shortsightedness on Shi'ism and Khomeinist Iran. It accuses the author of the article of making false comparisons and denies him the competence to judge the Shi'i faith.[36] But when the mahdist issue is up for discussion, the magazine becomes equally elusive, concluding that

34. "Khaybat al-dawafi' " (The Emasculation of Motives), *al-Mukhtar al-Islami,* October 1980, 8–12.

35. "Al-Mahdi wa al-Khumayni fi nazar al-Islam" (The Mahdi and Khomeini in the Opinion of Islam), *Majallat al-Azhar,* November 1980, 1635–48. After the revolution in Iran a flurry of booklets on Shi'ism started to appear in Egypt. Purporting to reveal the truth about Shi'ism and to show Khomeini's real intentions, these tracts address themselves above all to "those young members of the Islamic movement who, in their ignorance, are deluded by Khomeini's conciliatory tone toward Sunnism." In accordance with popular Sunni notions about Shi'i extremism and blasphemy, they accuse Shi'ism of putting the imams on a level superior to even that of the Prophet and of corrupting the Qur'an. They also claim that Khomeini, following the "established Shi'i tradition of *taqiyah,* " dissimulates his real anti-Sunni intentions behind spurious pan-Islamist rhetoric. The source of these vehemently anti-Shi'i tracts is not clear in all cases, but a number of them were published by the Saudi-sponsored al-Wa'i al-Islami press, and they all bear the stamp of government approval. See, for example, Mahmud Sa'd Nasih, *Mauqif al-Khumaini min al-Shi'ah wa al-Tashayyu'* (Khomeini's Position on Shi'ism) (Cairo, 1979); Muhammad Mal Allah, *Mauqif al-Khumaini min Ahl al-Sunna* (Khomeini's Position on the Sunnites) (Cairo: Maktabat al-Wa'i al-Islami, 1982); and idem, *al-Shi'ah wa tahrif al-Qur'an* (Shi'ism and the Corruption of the Qur'an) (Cairo: Maktabat al-Wa'i al-Islami, 1982).

36. "Mantiq al-Tair" (The Speech of the Birds), *al-Mukhtar al-Islami,* January 1981, 8–26.

"this is a controversial issue which it is not expedient to rake up at this moment (*la maslahah fi itharatiha al-an*)."

Yet, the same magazine, in an analysis of the role of the revolutionary intellectuals in Iran, concedes that people such as Bani Sadr and Qutbzadih show nationalist traits. This, *al-Mukhtar al-Islami* says, is forgivable, for the problem of qaumiyah in Iran has always been different from the situation in the Arab world, and the structure of Islam in Iran has always borne the strong imprint of Shi'ism.[37] Pursuing this issue, the magazine notes: "It remains important to realize that the Iranian revolution is not a complete alternative for the Islamic Movement for, apart from the fact that the Islamic Movement in one place is no alternative for the same movement in another place, the Iranian revolution shows a distinct pattern which seems impossible to be repeated, although use can be made of its experience."

One suspects that the defense of Shi'ism is dictated more by circumstances that call for a rigorous display of religious unity on the part of the Brotherhood protagonists than by inner conviction. A further indication of this is provided by a discussion of Shi'ism in *al-I'tisam* in 1977, a time when the revolution was not yet there to influence the evaluation.[38] In the article, one of the rare instances prior to the revolution in which Iran and Shi'ism are discussed in the Egyptian religious press, Shi'ism is charged with paying too much attention to "symbols that stand in the way between God and man." The conclusion is that Shi'i renunciation of "the excessive Shi'i veneration of others than the one and only Prophet" is a condition for the (unquestioned) future rapprochement with Sunnism.

Most interesting in this respect is finally the interview 'Umar Tilmisani, the present leader of the Brotherhood, gave to the weekly magazine *al-Musawwar* in January 1982, that is, after Egypt itself had been shaken by Islamic violence. Asked for his opinion on the events in Iran, he says:

> First of all, the Iranians adhere to the Shi'i school whereas we are Sunnis. The difference between the Shi'is and the Sunnis, the origin of which lies with the Shi'is and not the Sunnis, is very deep-rooted and serious. When Khomeini began his revolution we supported him and stood at his side despite the radical doctrinal differences that exist between the Shi'is and the Sunnis. . . . We supported him politically because an oppressed people had managed to get rid of an

37. "Iran, al-thaurah: al-quwwah al-fa'alah wa mustaqbal al-'alaqah ma' al-harakah al-islamiyah" (Iran, the Revolution: The Active Forces and the Future of the Link with the Islamic Movement), *al-Mukhtar al-Islami,* September 1979, 35–39.

38. "Mas'alat al-shi'ah" (The Question of Shi'ism), *al-I'tisam,* December 1977, 10–11.

oppressive ruler and to regain their freedom, but from the doctrinal point of view, Sunnism is one thing and Shi'ism is another.[39]

The wholesale manner in which the Muslim Brothers embraced the revolution, as well as their uncritical acceptance of both its means and goals, made it incumbent on them to raise the subject of its Shi'i aspects as little as possible.

The course taken by the revolution after its auspicious start made it increasingly difficult for even the most sympathetic observer to sustain their initial enthusiasm. The Egyptian Muslim Brothers, however, continued virtually unabatedly in their support of the events in Iran. Given their initial stance and the way in which they incorporated the revolution in their overall Weltanschauung, it would indeed have been virtually impossible to retreat. Nevertheless, a gradual shift in both the tone of discussion and the frequency with which Iran figures in the Brotherhood press is discernible. It seems in fact possible to distinguish three different stages in this respect. The first stage could be called the stage of unqualified enthusiasm and unconditional euphoria. This stage covers the period immediately preceding the triumph of the revolution, when the Muslim Brothers started to discuss developments in Iran, and the roughly one-and-a-half years after the inauguration of the Islamic regime. Aside from following the course of events, the attention given Iran in this period mostly revolves around denunciations of the shah's regime as barbaric and un-Islamic and a presentation of the revolution as the dawn of the restoration of true Islam in the world. The crimes of the Pahlavi regime are amply discussed, and other Islamic countries are exhorted to follow Iran's example of abolishing the separation of church and state.

The second stage could be called the defensive or apologetic stage. Defense was a corollary of the Muslim Brothers' adoption of the revolution as their foster child from the very beginning. The denunciation of the Western press, which "abounds in criticism of the alleged violation of human rights in Iran but kept silent when under the Shah 100,000 people were massacred," always figured prominently in the columns of their press. Indeed, a polemic tone is inherent in the nature of the Brotherhood's ideology, as it is in any dogmatic ideology. While attacks on the "maliciously distorted image the foreign press continues to present of the happenings in Iran," and the "ongoing attempts by the superpowers to undermine the revolution" continue, a gradual shift of tone toward discussions of an apologetic nature is nevertheless discernible in the course

39. *al-Musawwar,* January 22, 1982, 76.

of 1980. This shift of tone seems to have been primarily the result of increasing news reports about domestic problems in Iran, not all of which could be simply ignored or attributed to outside machinations. Growing terror, persecutions, the continuing power struggle, and some aspects of Iran's foreign policy could not but give the impression that the revolution was, if not deviating from its right course, at least having difficulty in implementing the ideal Islamic society overnight.

The apologetic tone becomes apparent in reactions to negative reports about the state of affairs in Iran. In a reaction to reports about the persisting chaos in the country, *al-Mukhtar al-Islami* says: "Nevertheless this revolution has not devoured its own children; one has even managed to hold elections. . . . a new constitution has been introduced. . . . Russia knew five years of chaos after its revolution, and in France the chaos persisted for eight years."[40] In the same article, *al-Mukhtar al-Islami* argues that the fact that leftist groups, who "pour out into the streets on the pretense that the Iranian people are against the government," are allowed to participate in the elections proves that Iran is not a dictatorship. The prominent role played by intellectuals of the Bani Sadr type is interpreted as proof of the Iranian attempt to reconcile with the modern world. Finally, accusations concerning the great number of executions are countered by saying that the number killed has been far less than in any other revolution and certainly less than during the shah's reign.

The second stage gradually merged into the third: that of decreasing attention. It is unclear to what extent the decline in attention paid to Iran in the Muslim Brotherhood press directly correlates to the persistent flow of negative reporting. There can be little doubt, however, that the outbreak of the war between Iran and Iraq in 1980 spurred a change of approach. The outbreak itself played in the hands of the Muslim Brotherhood observers, for had Iran launched the attack, a truly embarrassing situation would have arisen. As it happened, however, they were able to see the Iraqi aggression as being completely in line with the overall demeanor of the abject Baath regime. Nevertheless, the war itself could not but cause embarrassment in Islamic ranks. The various Brotherhood magazines, in their analysis of the hostilities, invariably referred to the war as a mark of disgrace (*wasmat 'ar*) for Islam, but were equally firm in trying to deny that this was a war between Persians and Arabs. Considering the war a triumph of jahiliyah and Iran its victim, the Muslim Brotherhood press was quick to decry the enemies of Islam as the originators of the war.

40. "Iran: al-thaurah wa al-daulah," *al-Mukhtar al-Islami*.

Another conspicuous example of an embarrassing situation is the growing cooperation between Iran and Syria. The apparently contradictory friendly attitude Iran displayed toward the Syrian Baath leadership—despised by the Muslim Brothers—seemed to puzzle them. Their reaction was that "the only conceivable explanation for these contacts is that America wants to destroy the Iranian revolution through its Arab client states," and they exhorted Khomeini to put an end to the situation, but the fact remained too glaringly contradictory for the explanation to seem convincing even to themselves.

The same holds for the growing dissension and splitting of ranks in Iran's domestic politics. The initial explanation of the existence of various political currents as proof of the "democratic" nature of revolutionary Iran started losing credibility with the growing persecution of those who deviated from the official line. Thus, whereas leftist "separatists" (*infisaliyun*) continue to be portrayed as the instigators of domestic trouble, the power struggle in the upper echelons is greeted with regret. Similarly, the infamous blast in June 1981, in which Ayatullah Bihishti was killed with about seventy companions, elicits anger and dismay. But, aside from a pointing finger at the "American and Russian hand in the tragedy" and a philippic against alleged official Egyptian gloating over the drama, no further analysis is provided.

Altogether, Iran in the last year before the roundup of oppositionists by Sadat received far less attention in the Egyptian Muslim Brotherhood press than during the first two years of the revolution, less than one would have expected even considering a natural decline after the world-shaking events at the beginning of the revolution. After a short inevitable upsurge following the outbreak of the war with Iraq, coverage of developments all but died out. Thus in 1981 *al-Da'wah* had four short comments on Iran, *al-I'tisam* mentioned Iran three times in insignificant statements, and *al-Mukhtar al-Islami,* after a last lengthy dossier in its January 1981 number, left the issue untouched until the closure of the magazine.

AL-YASAR AL-ISLAMI

The second movement to be discussed here represents an intellectual current rather than an organized movement. Its most prominent representative, as well as its spokesman par excellence, is the professor of philosophy Hasan Hanafi. An erstwhile member of the Muslim Brotherhood, Hanafi has never lost his sympathy for what he sees as the social revolutionary elements in the ideas of people such as Brotherhood leaders

Hasan al-Banna and Sayyid Qutb. His breaking away from the ranks of the Brotherhood resulted from his perception that the Muslim Brothers after the 1970 death of the socialist Egyptian president Gamel Abdel Nasser transformed these elements into a narrow-minded message that sees the solution to the ills of society in the mere reinstitution of the Islamic laws. On the lack of attention for the concrete problems of society shown by the Brotherhood in the 1970s, he says: "The themes of social justice in Islam, the battle between capitalism and Islam, world peace and Islam, were dropped from the Brethren's thought and were carried on by the revolution of the sixties. The more open and wide conception of Islam, that of the founder Hasan al-Banna, turned into a more closed and fanatic view of the world."[41]

Over the years, Hanafi has expressed himself in numerous articles and books on such issues as the role of religion in the modern world, the problem of Westernization, the need to make the Islamic heritage relevant to the modern world, and above all the role that the engagé intellectual should play in raising the consciousness of the masses and in laying the fundaments of real social, political, and economic change.

In the same article from which the quotation above was taken, Hanafi says: "The Islamic groups look more powerful than they are. Their voices are loud but they have no impact on the masses. Their slogans have no social content. 'Sovereignty of God' is one slogan. The question is: sovereignty of God for whom? For the rich or for the poor? For the oppressor or for the oppressed?"[42] In these words not only the dichotomy of al-Yasar al-Islami but also its fundamental difference with that of the Muslim Brotherhood becomes apparent. The dichotomy of al-Yasar al-Islami does not have the rigorous distinction between Islam and non-Islam as a point of departure. Whereas the Muslim Brothers value every phenomenon on its Islamic merits, thereby using an ahistoric, ideal-typical image of Islam as a yardstick, al-Yasar al-Islami sees justice as the main criterion. Al-Yasar al-Islami purports to be, in the words of Hanafi, the mouthpiece for the silent masses, sets itself as a goal the defense of the rights of the oppressed and the poor against the strong and the rich, wants to transform underdevelopment into progress, and supports the struggle of the Third World against imperialism.[43]

41. Hasan Hanafi, "The Relevance of the Islamic Alternative in Egypt," *Arab Studies Quarterly* 4, nos. 1–2 (Spring 1980): 61.

42. Ibid., 73.

43. Hasan Hanafi, "Madha ya'ni al-yasar al-islami?" (What Does Islamic Left Mean?), *al-Yasar al-Islami* 1 (1981): 5–6.

These ideals and goals al-Yasar al-Islami has in common with most liberal, leftist, and revolutionary movements. What distinguishes the movement from ordinary leftist parties, however, is that Islam plays an important role in its worldview—Islam and progressive thinking are inextricably intertwined. Islam, if rightly understood, is a guarantee of justice; liberation and progress are inherently part of the Islamic message. In the introductory article of the first issue of *al-Yasar al-Islami,* Hanafi, in explaining the title "Islamic Left," says:

> We know that critique will come from two sides: the Brothers in God [*al-ikhwah fi Allah*] will say that Islam does not know Left and Right, that Islam is one as the community [ummah] is one and God is one. This critique would be justified as far as the principles; it does not, however, pertain to reality, that is, it concerns Islam as belief but not as the reality of Muslims as they constitute societies, states, classes, and proprietors. We do not speak of Islam but of Muslims in a specific historic reality and a specific social setting. As long as we are part of history and time we will be confronted with struggle and movement, with contradictory interests, power struggle and income differences. On this level there is in fact a Left and a Right.[44]

After this introduction it is not surprising to learn that al-Yasar al-Islami considers the return of Islam to be neither the explanation of the origin of the revolution in Iran nor a guarantee for its success. Hanafi calls the revolution the "true indicator for the awakening of the Muslims," but at once concedes that its outbreak was unexpected "after Iran had seemed to the Arabs to be an oasis of tranquillity." Whereas the Muslim Brothers put the revolution in the perspective of the relentless struggle between Islam and non-Islam, al-Yasar al-Islami sees the happenings in Iran as part of the overall battle the Third World is fighting for its liberation from oppression. The jahiliyah to which the revolution has stood up is one of poverty, ignorance, and submission. There is no preordained guarantee that these will be beaten and conquered. The revolution is no divinely led struggle embodying static metahistory: it is part of a mundane war, a link in a laborious process leading toward a just and humane world. To al-Yasar al-Islami, not Islam as an abstract principle but the Iranian people triumphed in the revolution. It was, according to Hanafi, the people who, pouring out into the streets and withstanding violence and oppression with bare hands, were the fuel of the revolution, and it was thanks to their resistance that it was able to succeed. Islam played the

44. Ibid., 7–8.

role of popular ideology in this confrontation; it was a weapon in a process in which the Iranian people gained greater awareness of their situation.

It is this process of greater awareness that, Hanafi says, heralds the Islamic renaissance. Just as the Western world began with religious reform, so the new flourishing period of Islam at the threshold of the fifteenth century A.H. starts with a struggle within Islam itself. It is a struggle that must demolish the age-old domination of scholastic Ash'arite thinking and Sufi values before it will lead to a rediscovery of true Islam, which is leftist Islam. The Iranian Revolution is an Islamic revolution inasmuch as it plays a positive role in this struggle.

A different view of the role and the nature of the revolution leads to a different historic assessment of it—on a domestic level as well as in an international perspective. The Muslim Brothers put the revolution in a purely Islamic perspective. To Hanafi, too, the revolution stands in an Islamic tradition. He compares the overthrow of the shah to what he calls the first Islamic revolution against the Byzantine and Persian empires, against the nobility of Mecca and Arab tribalism. But as a "revolution of the mind" (*thaurat al-'aql*) the Iranian Revolution is not confined to a strictly Islamic framework: it is connected with any movement that aims at a fundamental change in the structure of society. It follows the tradition of the mahdist movement in the Sudan but it is equally related to the struggle of the progressive church in Latin America and the Vietnamese revolution of Ho Chi Minh. Whereas *al-Mukhtar al-Islami* regards the Iranian experiment as the "shattering of the heritage of Nasserism," Hanafi compares Khomeini to Nasser as a fighter against imperialism and for national independence, and recalls the good relations the two apparently had in the 1950s. Where, finally, the Muslim Brothers' stand toward that other popular hero, Musaddiq, is ambivalent, Hanafi says: "Just as the October war of 1973 kindled the sentiments of the Arab community in its eternal struggle with Zionism for the liberation of the occupied Arab territories, the great Islamic revolution in Iran was the realization of the national image that had begun with Musaddiq's oil nationalization in 1953 [*sic*; 1951]. And what is Khomeini but Musaddiq sent forth anew?"[45] Hanafi sees no contradiction between the Iranian and the Islamic aspects of the revolution. To him, the revolution as the hallmark of a revived Iranian identity does not thereby turn it into the expression of a narrow Iranian nationalism.

45. Hasan Hanafi, "Al-muslimun fi Asia fi matla' al-qarn al-khamis 'ashar al-hijri" (The Muslims in Asia at the Beginning of the Fifteenth Century A.H.), *al-Yasar al-Islami*, 165.

Just as, for Hanafi, the revolution, despite its Iranian nationalist aspects, is still an Islamic revolution, so its Shi'i elements do not detract
from its general Islamic character. His arguments are different from those
of the Muslim Brothers, but like them, he sees the revolution as an Islamic
one rather than as a Shi'i one. He compares Khomeini with Jamal al-Din
al-Afghani as a religious leader who transcends the limits of religious
particularism and who returns to the revolutionary roots contained in the
Qur'an. He concedes that differences do exist between Sunnism and
Shi'ism, but he considers sectarianism to be subordinated to the pressing
task of educating the masses and bringing about real change. Shi'ism
appeals to him because it knows two elements, *'aql* (reason) and *ijtihad*
(to Hanafi, the possibility to reinterpret religion in the light of changed
circumstances), that can guarantee a continued role for religion in the
accomplishment of these tasks and even bring about an Islamic renaissance
after ages of sloth and decline. He argues, however, against the existence
of fundamental points of divergence between the two main branches of
Islam. The two agree, he says, on the need to establish an Islamic government. In a discussion of principle of *Wilayat al-Faqih* (the Guardianship of the Jurisprudent)—a kind of discussion one looks for in vain in
the Muslim Brotherhood press—Hanafi explains this as a practical concept. Wilayat al-Faqih, he says, combines the caliphate and the imamate
in their functions of interpreting and executing religious precepts; it embodies the Qur'anic principle of authority and validates the position of
the *fuqaha* (jurists) as those who, rather than the imams, exercise authority in the real world. It is the Islamic alternative to kingship and
absolute rule and therefore necessary from both a religious and a political
point of view.

　While Hanafi pleads for an unbiased study of Shi'ism on the part of
Sunnism, other representatives of al-Yasar al-Islami are much more outspoken in their view of Shi'ism. In a book on the roots and the ideology
of the Iranian Revolution, Ibrahim al-Disuqi Shita, until recently a professor of Persian at Cairo University, not only expresses sympathy for
Shi'ism but presents it as Islam's revolutionary offshoot par excellence.[46]
He even tries to demonstrate that Shi'ism is the pure form of Islam. True
Shi'ism, he says, is not a response to the distorted image of 'Ali-deification
that Arabs commonly have in mind when thinking of it, nor is it the
accommodating and quietist religion of the Safavid period. Modeling himself on that ideologue of the Iranian Revolution, Ali Shariati, one of

46. Ibrahim al-Disuqi Shita.

whose pieces he translated for the first issue of *al-Yasar al-Islami,* Disuqi Shita traces the roots of genuine Shi'ism to its founder and symbol, 'Ali. 'Ali, he says, personified the leftist current of Islam, a revolutionary ideology that aims at liberating the oppressed classes and that has always withstood the rule of the unjust. It was only with the Umayyads that an accommodating and establishment-confirming form of Islam appeared. This trend later took over Shi'ism also and culminated in the Safavid period. With the Islamic revolution, Disuqi Shita concludes, the politically involved original Shi'ism was rediscovered and put into practice.

Disuqi Shita deals with the ideological background of the revolution. His book, which came out in 1979, does not discuss the event itself. As a result, any discussion of the extent to which the actual practice of the Islamic Republic conforms to his positive view of Shi'ism is absent. A third representative of al-Yasar al-Islami, Muhammad Amara, takes an opposing view when he discusses Shi'ism in his "The Dominant Thinking of the Iranian Revolution."[47] Writing when the Iranian Islamic Republic had already been in operation for a few years, Amara shows himself highly critical of Twelver Shi'ism, both as a doctrine and as it manifests itself in Khomeinist Iran. Amara recognizes the revolutionary element in early Shi'ism. He also hails the revolution itself as a rebellion of the downtrodden against an utterly tyrannical and corrupt regime supported by imperialism. He acknowledges Khomeini's role as a revolutionary leader who managed to move the Islamic masses as no one before him had. He argues, however, that the potentially progressive and liberating character of the revolution is greatly jeopardized by its exclusive Twelver Shi'i nature. Twelver Shi'ism, he says, gave up, with the quietist Imam Ja'far al-Sadiq, the revolutionary practice contained in original Shi'ism. After long ages in which Twelver Shi'ism led a dual existence, in theory claiming exclusive authority for the hidden imam but in practice acquiescing in worldly rule, it was in modern times and under the impact of imperialism that it started to advance the theory that, in the continued absence of the hidden imam, his practical authority devolved on the religious leaders. Thus the ulama became invested with Wilayat al-Faqih. What makes Khomeini new and innovative is that he turned the entitlement of the ulama to Wilayat al-Faqih from a theoretical idea into a practical concept, thereby enabling Shi'ism to overcome its political passivity and become a revolutionary doctrine. But, Amara says, as Khomeini's basic idea about the supremacy of the imam, on whose behalf the clerical ruler wields authority, remains thoroughly traditional Shi'i, the result is clerical authority deriving its legitimacy exclusively from the divine.

47. Muhammad Amara.

It is here that Amara shows himself much more skeptical than Hanafi when he discusses the political structure of the Iranian Islamic Republic and the role religion plays in it. Hanafi argues that the executive function of Wilayat al-Faqih has the revolutionary quality of making pious and passive waiting for the return of the hidden imam superfluous. Amara, speaking with the benefit of hindsight, emphasizes the dangers involved in clerical rule that is utterly detached from accountability to the community of believers. Hanafi hails the revolution as an Islamic affair, encompassing Shi'is as well as Sunnis. Amara, basing his argument on the new Iranian Constitution as well as on a three-year record of Khomeinist rule in practice, seriously doubts the universal Islamic character of the new Iran.

The fact that Hanafi wrote his comments on the Iranian Revolution quoted here in 1979 and was therefore unable to evaluate the actual performance of the Iranian Islamic Republic does not mean that he is uncritical of the Iranian experiment. Not so much the Shi'i aspects of Khomeini's thinking as his underlying conceptions about human society, its problems, and the way to solve them form Hanafi's points of critique. In order to understand on what grounds he criticizes Khomeini, it is necessary first to have a look at his own view on the role religion and philosophy can play in revolutionary change. What attracts Hanafi in the Iranian Revolution is that, to him, it seems an attempt to realize a real *tauhidi* system, an integrative society in which traditional modes of dualistic thinking have no place. The concept of oneness between theory and practice, the appeal for the demolition of the traditional dualism (*izdiwajiyah*) between thinking and acting, figures prominently in many of his writings prior to the revolution. In fact, these themes play the most fundamental role in his attempt to reconstruct the Islamic heritage (*turath*) so as to make it not just relevant to the modern world but indeed a constituting factor in a new outlook of the world and mankind. Thus he says:

> The vocation of philosophy is not the adherence to two different methods, a scientific one related to social phenomena, and a religious one related to faith and sacred history. Thinking knows only one method which applies to all phenomena. With many thinkers, however, we find this methodological dualism. . . . they have two methods, a progressive social-revolutionary one for the world and a reactionary private one for the Hereafter.[48]

48. Hasan Hanafi, "Risalat al-fikr," in *Fi Fikrina al-Mu'asir* (Beirut, 1981). The article originally appeared in the January 1971 issue of the journal *al-Katib*.

Hanafi's concern is to reconstruct the traditional Islamic belief system so as to turn it into a revolutionary ideology. It is, he says, the dead weight of Islamic tradition that, in its aloofness from reality, has obscured the real message of Islam and that has resulted in a disastrous gap between scientific and religious thinking. The differences between tradition and true religion he sums up as follows:

> All that is in tradition is not in religion, and all that is in religion is not in tradition. Thus, deification and anthropomorphism are part of tradition but do not appear in religion; predestination is part of tradition but not of religion; in tradition there appear calls for resignation, quietism, and contentedness and fear which do not appear in religion. . . . the "religion of revolution" exists in religion but not in tradition; the "religion of liberation" exists in religion and not in tradition, and the "leftist tendency" exists in religion and not in tradition.[49]

And in 1969 he wrote: "The old political thinking revolved around the qualities of the caliph—al-Farabi is an example—and formed the justification of his absolute authority. . . . Perhaps the reason why today we suffer from a pyramidical conception of the world and ruling systems that go from the top to the bottom, is to be found in this way of thinking."[50]

It is in this light that Hanafi's critique of Khomeini's thinking must be understood. Khomeini, he says, though rightly considering Wilayat al-Faqih a practical political duty, seems to attach a purely metaphysical basis to the concept. Furthermore, in his emphasis on Islamic government, he fails to pay sufficient attention to the Islamic peoples; in other words, he concentrates on the top rather than on the bottom. He seems to proceed from the pessimistic view that human nature is evil and therefore in constant need of the guidance of an imam. "It is as if, but for the Imam Khomeini, the people would turn into wild beasts, transgress the limits posed by God, strive only for personal pleasure, spread corruption in the world, and usurp the rights of the weak."[51] In his apparent conviction that real change comes with a change of government rather than with enlightenment and increased political awareness, Khomeini makes the same mistake that has made a failure of all the Arab revolutions to date.

A further, and related, point of criticism advanced by Hanafi concerns Khomeini's lack of concern for the real problems of society. Discussing Khomeini's conception of Jihad al-Nafs, the struggle with self, he con-

49. Hasan Hanafi, "Madha ya'ni al-turath wa al-tajdid?" in *al-Turath wa al-Tajdid* (Beirut, 1981), 11–29.

50. Hasan Hanafi, "Mauqifuna al-hadari," in *Fi Fikrina,* 58.

51. Introduction to *al-Hukumah al-Islamiyah,* 27.

cludes: "*Jihad al-Nafs* means the struggle of the self against its lusts, its whims and its desires, and withstanding all these with the aim of becoming free of the filth of the world and striving for the Hereafter."[52] He goes on to say:

> But the Imam Khomeini does not analyze the economic, social, and cultural reasons behind the expressions of imperialism, such as plunder, domination and discrimination, and the annihilation of the natural cultures of the colonized peoples, nor does he analyze the various forms of resistance, military, political, economic or cultural, but he limits himself to one subject, which is the reeducation of the 'ulama. . . . to the Imam Khomeini, the moral revolution is a condition for the political revolution, and must precede it. . . . To counter imperialist attempts to encapsulate the 'ulama of the Islamic community and to corrupt religion, the Imam Khomeini calls for purification of conduct, cleaning of the heart, and riddance from the self . . . as if resistance to imperialism is accomplished by noble morals and the education of the individual.[53]

Khomeini, Hanafi says, appears to be still entangled in the old way of reasoning which attributes the ills of society to bad moral conduct. Bad moral conduct, however, results from the ills of society and not the other way round. In its preoccupation with morality, finally, Khomeini's view of the world is directed to the hereafter more than to the actual world. But a mystical glorification of the world to come and the resulting withdrawal from the actual world is not the road to social and economic improvement. Islam, unlike Christianity and Buddhism, has always paid full attention to this world. If one did not know better, one would think that Khomeini was in accord with the wishes of the old colonialists, who were willing to let the ulama have their way as long as they did not touch on political matters.

CONCLUSION

The Iranian Revolution may have started in classical revolutionary fashion as a liberal opposition movement, and nonreligious groups may have fought in its front ranks, but its growth into a real mass movement and the resulting victory of bare hands over tanks must be largely ascribed to Khomeini and his fellows. Friend and foe cannot but admit that it was religious symbolism that gave the breakthrough its decisive power. If the

52. Introduction to *Jihad al-Nafs au al-Jihad al-Akbar,* 10.
53. Ibid., 15.

eventual clerical monopoly over the revolution has been largely the achievement of Khomeini, yet another, even greater achievement made him a real and indisputable revolutionary leader. Khomeini not only built a mass upheaval on the rigorous polarity between Islam and non-Islam, that is, good and evil, but also before his victory left the interpretation of both these terms so open that the broadest possible spectrum of oppositional forces were able to see their own ideology and ideals reflected and expressed in the struggle. A discussion of the position assigned to the revolution by, respectively, the Egyptian Muslim Brotherhood and al-Yasar al-Islami shows elements of the same convergence on Islam from opposite directions. Islam as an abstract moving force brought the two currents together as supporters of the revolution; the openness of Islam to interpretation, on the other hand, gave both movements the opportunity to recognize their own differing ideologies in the Iranian drama.

It seems warranted to conclude that the differences of approach and ideology that exist between these two Egyptian trends reflect the general discussion in contemporary Islamic ranks on the strategy that should be followed in dealing with a bewildering world that seems to drift further and further away from the professed Islamic ideal. The solutions proposed in this debate range from a narrow and self-contained reformism that excludes Western intellectual intrusion, via a call for a revival of the authentic Islamic tradition without, however, excluding the use of Western sources, to the militant approach that demands the rigorous overthrow of the existing order. Khomeini's thinking, despite his call for revolution, seems related to a reformist current that lacks a real analysis of the world and sees in moral rearmament and the return to what it considers to be pure Islam the solution to all problems of the modern world. The criticism Hanafi brings in against the facile and world-renouncing aspects of this thinking is of the kind that Shariati probably would have had against Khomeini's underlying conceptions; it is, mutatis mutandis, the same criticism that could be made against the narrow and closed perceptions of the world shown by the present-day Muslim Brothers in Egypt. But, whereas Khomeini's thinking has proven to be the antithesis of progressive development and whereas his limited and personalized theoretical framework hardly seems to guarantee the continuation of Khomeinist political leadership beyond his own charismatic lifetime, it is in part the very oversimplicity of his populist and uncompromising ideas that made a revolution possible at all. And a revolution is something neither the intellectual and analytical exhortations of the Shariati and Hanafi kind nor the reformist and accommodating ideology of the Muslim Brotherhood type is likely to succeed in effectuating.

MURIEL ATKIN

Chapter Eleven # Soviet Attitudes toward Shi'ism and Social Protest

Although Shi'is account for only slightly more than 1 percent of the Soviet population, the Soviets have developed a lively interest in Shi'ism and Islam in general.[1] Soviet views on the significance of Islam have changed considerably in recent years. Islam is no longer simply dismissed as a set of reactionary myths about supernatural forces used to distract the people from their proper goal of improving life in this world. While all religions are still considered fundamentally defective ways of understanding the world, a different aspect of Islam has lately been brought to the fore: its role as an effective vehicle, in certain settings, for the expression of social protest.

This change is the result of the interplay of pragmatic political considerations and the increased sophistication of Soviet scholarship on Islam. At work in Soviet perceptions of Islam are both questions of concepts, as embodied in scholarly interpretations and ideology, and practical politics, the judgment of how Soviet interests can best be served. Soviet pronouncements on Islam have occasionally identified developing trends but more frequently have rationalized developments after their occurrence.

1. This essay will deal only with Twelver and Isma'ili Shi'ism. Other religions that evolved from Shi'ism, such as the 'Alawi, 'Ali-Ilahi, Baha'i, and Druze faiths, are not discussed.

The Soviets have long appreciated the importance of Middle Eastern affairs to their own international interests; but they had underestimated the strength of Islam as a system of values that governs all aspects of life, the worldly as well as the spiritual, until events of the late 1970s challenged their assumptions. The most important of these events was Iran's Islamic revolution, which served as a catalyst in the Soviet reassessment of the functions of Shi'ism and Islam as a whole. At the same time, concern over the persistence of Islam among millions of Soviet citizens and the religious appeals of some opponents of communist rule in Afghanistan also affected the reconsideration of Islam's significance.

The 1970s saw the development of a new generation of Soviet Orientalists (a term not out of fashion in the Soviet Union), who are better informed and less doctrinaire than any of their predecessors since the 1920s. This bears directly on Soviet policy since Soviet academics who work on topical subjects are expected to do studies that can inform policymakers. There is no polarized debate on the significance of Shi'ism based on contending academic and political camps or other lines of division. Rather, the developments of the late 1970s and early 1980s have produced major shifts of interpretation that are reflected across the board in scholarly and political sources.

The Soviet center for the study of modern Islam in foreign countries is the Moscow headquarters of the Institute of Oriental Studies of the Academy of Sciences.[2] The Soviet leadership expects the institute to provide explanations of current events in Asian countries and to predict future developments.[3] Its director, E. M. Primakov, is an economist by training but has, in recent years, frequently discussed the role of Islam in the affairs of developing countries and distilled the arguments of the institute's specialists for the leadership. Most of the leading Soviet scholars in this field are based here. These include L. R. Polonskaia, who has worked on Islam first in Pakistan and then in Iran, and heads the Ideological Problems Section of the institute's Department of General Theoretical Problems; A. I. Ionova, a specialist on Islam in Indonesia and elsewhere in Southeast Asia; and E. A. Doroshenko, a specialist on the religions of Iran. Since the 1970s, all three of these historians have, through their many writings and addresses to conferences, played a prom-

2. Primakov, "Aktual'nye zadachi sovetskogo vostokovedeniia" (Timely Tasks of Soviet Oriental Studies), *Narody Azii i Afriki,* no. 5 (1983): 11.

3. B. N. Ponomarev, "Vysokaia nagrada Rodiny—krupneishemu tsentru sovetskogo vostokovedeniia" (High Award of the Motherland—to the Most Important Center of Soviet Oriental Studies), *Aziia i Afrika segodnia,* no. 12 (December 1980): 3, 5.

inent role in interpreting the upsurge of Islamic activism. The other member of the country's circle of leading experts on Islam abroad, M. T. Stepaniants, a specialist on nineteenth- and twentieth-century Islamic political and social thought, is based in another component of the Academy of Sciences, the Institute of Philosophy, where she directs one of its departments. All four of these prominent specialists are women.

Very little work on contemporary foreign Islam has been done at other institutions in the post–World War II era. The Leningrad branch of the Institute of Oriental Studies concentrates on ancient and medieval subjects and on languages and literatures. Academic institutions in the republics with large Muslim populations have virtually ignored the study of Islam abroad in the past two decades. This is true even of the Institute of the Peoples of the Near and Middle East of the Azerbaijan Academy of Sciences, the most important of the republic-level centers of Middle Eastern studies, which has produced many works on social, economic, and political topics regarding Iran and Turkey.[4] The same applies to Orientalists in other republican academies of sciences.[5] The only republic where there has lately been work on Shi'ism abroad, although so far very little, is Tajikistan.[6] The Tajik language is a dialect of Persian and the Tajik heritage is defined so as to overlap Iran's to a considerable degree. However, the Muslims of the Tajik S.S.R. are predominantly Sunni. For most of its existence, the Oriental Studies Institute of the Tajikistan Academy of Sciences has emphasized the study of literature, language, and ancient and medieval history. In 1980, in reaction to events in Iran and Afghanistan, a new department of the institute was established, the Department of Socioeconomic and Political-Religious Problems. It covers

4. Z. M. Buniatov, "Institut narodov Blizhnego i Srednego Vostoka Akademii nauk Azerbaidzhanskoi SSR" (Institute of the Peoples of the Near and Middle East of the Academy of Sciences of the Azerbaijan SSR), *Narody Azii i Afriki,* no. 6 (1982): 54–58.

5. M. B. Baratov, "Tsentr Vostokovednoi nauki v Uzbekistane" (The Center of Orientalist Science in Uzbekistan), *Narody Azii i Afriki,* no. 3 (1979): 149–50; Kh. A. Ataev, "Sektor istorii zarubezhnogo Vostoka pri Institut istorii im. Sh. Batyrova AN TurkmSSR" (The Sector of the History of the Foreign East of the Sh. Batyrov Institute of History of the Turkmen SSR Academy of Sciences), *Narody Azii i Afriki,* no. 1 (1984): 110–11.

6. Sh. Abdulloev, "Kul'turnaia ekspansiia Zapada i islam" (The Cultural Expansion of the West and Islam), in *Voprosy nauchnogo ateizma,* vol. 31 (Moscow: Mysl', 1983), 163–76; D. M. Anarkulova, "Mal'kom-khan i shiitskoe dukhovenstvo v Irane" (Malkum Khan and the Shi'ite Clergy in Iran), *Narody Azii i Afriki,* no. 4 (1983): 108–11; and the paper on Islam and nationalism in Iran presented to the Second All-Union Conference of Orientalists, May 25–28, 1983, as reported in A. E. Azarkh et al., "Vtoraia Vsesoiuznaia konferentsiia Vostokovedov" (The Second All-Union Conference of Orientalists), *Narody Azii i Afriki,* no. 6 (1983): 124.

such topics as the evolution of Islam and its social and political role in the contemporary world.[7]

In the postwar era, the Soviet assessment of Shi'ism remained negative until the recent changes in interpretation. E. A. Beliaev (1895–1964), the dean of the Soviet Islamicists molded by the Stalin era, in what is considered one of his major works, a slim 1957 study on Muslim sectarianism, portrayed Shi'ism as a failed social protest. All Muslim sects, he argued, combined the masses' protest against "feudal" oppression with leadership, usually from the elite, that almost always betrayed its followers. Even in the few cases when the leaders pursued the movement's original objectives, no social or political transformation resulted because religions are incapable of freeing the masses from oppression. In class societies, religion teaches people "total dependence on fantastic unearthly forces" to which all are enjoined to submit.[8]

According to Beliaev, Shi'ism spread in medieval Iran (he slighted its presence elsewhere) because Shi'i propagandists capitalized on the grievances of peasants and others oppressed by the Arab caliphate and Iranian "feudal" magnates by preaching that the victory of Shi'ism would better the masses' economic and social conditions. Yet Shi'ism's distinctive characteristics (not just the defects common to all religions) were an obstacle to just such changes. The legend of the hidden imam was used to make believers ignore the class struggle and put off the resolution of all problems until his return; it "deprived believers of the will to fight for the establishment of a just social order."[9] Beliaev treated Shi'ism's reverence for martyrs with heavy-handed contempt, stressing practices that would appear bizarre and fanatical, such as self-flagellation or not washing throughout the month of Muharram because being dirty was considered by some to be the best sign of mourning.[10]

Even though many of Iran's ulama participated in that country's Constitutional Revolution of 1905–11, that was not, in the Soviet view, an indication of a progressive function in a precapitalist society. There was nothing about Shi'ism that made it suitable as an ideology of protest. On the contrary, it sanctioned the status quo.[11] M. S. Ivanov, the leading

7. D. S. Saidmurodov, "Institut Vostokovedeniia Akademii Nauk Tadzhikskoi SSR" (The Oriental Studies Institute of the Academy of Sciences of the Tajik SSR), *Narody Azii i Afriki,* no. 5 (1981): 141.

8. Beliaev, *Musul'manskoe sektantstvo* (Muslim Sectarianism) (Moscow: Izdatel'stvo Vostochnoi Literatury, 1957), 4.

9. Ibid., 26.

10. Ibid., 28.

11. M. S. Ivanov, *Iranskaia revoliutsiia 1905–1911 godov* (The Iranian Revolution of 1905–1911) (Moscow: Institut Mezhdunarodnykh otnoshenii, 1957), 50.

specialist on modern Iran of the first postwar generation, argued that many of the ulama remained hostile to the revolution throughout its course. Those who supported it did so in order to increase their own influence in politics, undo the monarchy's limited secularization, combat its abuse of power, and block the growth of foreign influence. In any event, the masses were alleged to be increasingly unwilling to heed the ulama. The religious leaders eventually turned against the revolution as it moved toward more radical change. Only the lower clergy showed more empathy with the revolution. However, this had nothing to do with religion but rather reflected their economic position.[12]

The Soviet line became more sophisticated but hardly less antagonistic in the 1960s, even though by then Moscow had realized that Islam played a useful role in hostility toward the West in a number of Middle Eastern countries. Now Shi'ism was treated as a dynamic force that provided the ideology for numerous opposition movements but only in medieval, not modern, Iran.[13] This was the interpretation propounded by I. P. Petrushevskii (1898–1977), a historian of medieval and early modern Iran, who achieved international note in the 1950s and 1960s. In his interpretation, the return of the hidden imam was not, as Beliaev argued, a distraction from the struggle for social change but "the idea of social revolution put into religious form."[14] The cult of martyrs was not an expression of peculiar behavior but had meaning for the masses because of their own sufferings under the feudal yoke. Still, there remained strongly negative features to this assessment. Muhammad was not credited with preaching social equality or quasi-socialist ideas. Shi'ism had ceased to be an ideology of social protest centuries ago. In Iran the end came when the Safavid dynasty took power at the beginning of the sixteenth century and turned Shi'ism into an ideology of the "feudal" establishment. Popular, rebellious Shi'ism lasted for another century in Anatolia but ultimately was crushed by the Ottomans.[15]

12. Ibid., 50–52, 69, 75, 81, 85, 174–76, 509. A similar interpretation was presented in the *Bol'shaia Sovetskaia Entsiklopediia,* 2d ed. vol. 18 (1953), 413.

13. I. P. Petrushevskii, *Islam v Irane v VII–XV vekakh* (Islam in Iran in the VIIth–XVth Centuries) (Leningrad: Izdatel'stvo Leningradskogo universiteta, 1966), 3–4, 61, 241, 248. A number of Petrushevskii's works have been published in English and Persian.

14. Ibid., 267.

15. Ibid., 24, 267–68, 374. Ali Shariati (1933–77), the Iranian social theorist whose interpretation of Shi'ism and elements of Marxism influenced many in the younger generation of educated Iranian radicals, also distinguished between the socially just and the establishment forms of Shi'ism, in this case between the true Shi'ism of 'Ali and the succeeding imams and a distorted form presided over by the clergy in support of oppressive regimes. However, Shariati's ideas receive only infrequent attention in Soviet sources.

The opposition in the early 1960s by Iran's Shi'i ulama to the shah's White Revolution did not at the time or for many years thereafter encourage the Soviets to reconsider Shi'ism's potential as a vehicle for contemporary social protest movements. Moscow accepted the Iranian government's explanation that the Shi'i leadership opposed the White Revolution because it opposed land reform and other modernizing, secularizing changes.[16]

In the mid-1970s, the publication of two substantial scholarly works on Islam abroad signaled the transition toward a more nuanced, less polemical study of that religion. M. T. Stepaniants's *Islam in the Philosophical and Social Thought of the Foreign East (XIXth–XXth cents.)* extended Islam's progressive social function to modern times, albeit in a limited way. She argued that given the backwardness of Muslim countries and the consequent strength of Islam in the masses' social consciousness, Islam is a natural medium for the expression of ideologies of national liberation and the transition from feudal to capitalist society. It could even voice opposition to some aspects of capitalism and advocate an enlarged state sector of the economy. Therefore, where the transition to capitalism has not been completed, Islamic movements could be appropriate allies for Marxists and other progressives and should not be alienated by criticism of religion as a whole.[17] However, Stepaniants saw many negative factors intertwined with the positive. Wherever the transition to capitalism was far advanced, "religion fulfills an exclusively reactionary role."[18]

She divided Islamic reform movements into two categories: the synthesis of Islam and various Western bourgeois ideologies and the restoration of early Islamic values. The first strengthens Islam and therefore impedes the spread of socialist ideas. The second has broader support than the first but leads to irrationalism and exclusivism. There are limits to how far any Islamic reformer, even one who styles himself a socialist, will go, since acceptance of private property and social inequality as well as opposition to the class struggle and communism are inherent in all

16. A. I. Demin, "Obshchestvennye preobrazovaniia i osnovye tendentsii sotsial'no-ekonomicheskogo i vnutri-politicheskogo razvitiia Irana" (Social Change and the Fundamental Tendencies of the Socioeconomic and Internal Political Development of Iran), in A. Z. Arabadzhian, ed., *Iran. Ocherki noveishei istorii* (Moscow: Nauka, 1976), 321, 324; idem, "Sotsial'no-ekonomicheskii i politicheskii krizis kontza 50-kh—nachalo 60-kh godov" (The Socioeconomic and Political Crisis of the End of the Fifties—Beginning of the Sixties), ibid., 312.

17. M. T. Stepaniants, *Islam v filosofskoi i obshchestvennoi mysli zarubezhnogo Vostoka (XIX–XX vv)* (Islam in the Philosophical and Social Thought of the Foreign East [XIXth–XXth Centuries]) (Moscow: Nauka, 1974), 3–4, 16, 148–51, 159, 164–66, 174.

18. Ibid., 16.

shades of Islamic reform.[19] Overall, Islam, according to Stepaniants, "is a factor of social inertia, a brake on the path of socio-economic development."[20] In any event, she believed it to be a waning influence as development stimulates secularism.[21]

The year after the publication of the Stepaniants book came the publication of E. A. Doroshenko's *The Shi'ite Clergy in Contemporary Iran*. Like Stepaniants, she saw Islam playing a role in opposition ideology in modern times. She ascribed to Iran's ulama a role in various battles against foreign domination and the monarchy, although she noted the cooperation of many upper clerics with the government of Muhammad Reza Shah in the 1940s and 1950s because of a shared opposition to communism and fear of mass unrest. However, she also depicted the higher ranking ulama as economically privileged and closely linked to the "feudal aristocracy" and the upper middle class. She showed no sympathy for Ayatullah Kashani, whose prominent role in the political turmoil of the late 1940s and early 1950s set an influential example of Shi'i political activism. Although she acknowledged his conspicuous involvement, there was nothing positive about it since he was, in her estimate, a traditionalist theocrat who was motivated by opposition not only to the British but also to secularism, socialism, and the Soviet Union as well as by his lust for power. At the same time, he was well disposed toward the United States since he saw it as an opponent of the growth of communist influence. His support for nationalization of the Anglo-Iranian Oil Company stemmed from nothing more admirable than xenophobia.[22]

Although Doroshenko saw in the turmoil of 1963 active clerical opposition to the government couched in terms of opposition to imperialism and the shah's dictatorship, she presented this movement not as progressive but as the reactionary clergy's manipulation of the Muslim fanaticism of the petty bourgeoisie and urban lower classes to prevent land reform and the expansion of women's rights. She credited Ayatullah Khomeini with extensive influence as an opponent of the White Revolution and the monarchy itself and presented his views more positively than those of other religious leaders in that she portrayed him as heavily influenced by

19. Ibid., 14, 151–53, 157, 158–59, 161–63, 166, 168–69, 171–74.
20. Ibid., 4–5.
21. Ibid., 172.
22. E. A. Doroshenko, *Shiitskoe dukhovenstvo v sovremennem Irane* (Shi'i Clergy in Contemporary Iran) (Moscow: Nauka, 1975): 12–14, 33, 39–40, 42, 76, 79, 81, 84, 85, 91–92, 96–97.

Musaddiq's opinions and as having the support of more modern, educated elements of Iranian society. Yet she ascribed to the contemporary ulama, whether reformist or archconservative, a shared hostility toward class conflict and communism and support for the inviolability of private property. She judged that, as a consequence, most people considered the ulama hypocritical and self-seeking.[23]

Far from expecting the ulama to rally broad support for a revolutionary movement with a Shi'i ideology, Doroshenko expected the influence of both Shi'ism and the ulama to decline as Iran continued to modernize. She concluded that in recent years the growth of revolutionary movements and the rejection of religion drove the Iranian political elite and the Shi'i clergy into an alliance in which Islam is used to combat the spread of revolutionary and socialist ideas among the masses.[24]

In the second half of the 1970s, positive views of Islam received increased attention and became only slightly less important than the established negative arguments about Islam's anticommunism, its potential as a tool of the bourgeoisie or reactionaries, and its inadequacy as a program for solving the masses' problems. S. A. Tokarev touched off a heated controversy among those working on religion within the Soviet Union with his argument that since religions govern many aspects of the way people live, they can be studied as a social force, not just as a theology and, implicitly, without the invective associated with discussions of the strictly spiritual facets of religion.[25] Pronouncements now hailed in particular Islam's effectiveness as a means of mass mobilization when used by forward-looking politicians whose aims were fundamentally secular rather than religious. Other positive features were its strong association with nationalism, its extensive modernization, and the ability of Islamic socialism—for all its imperfections—to play a progressive role in societies at the particular stage of development many Muslim states had reached.[26] Still, one of the most positive conclusions the Soviets drew was that Islam's influence was declining, particularly in Turkey, Iraq, Lebanon, Iran,

23. Ibid., 17, 22–23, 62, 105–09, 116–17, 123–24.

24. Ibid., 157–61.

25. S. A. Tokarev, *Religiia v istorii norodov mira* (Religion in the History of the World's Peoples) (Moscow: Politizdat, 1976).

26. *Sovremennyi natsionalizm i obshchestvennoe razvitie zarubezhnogo Vostoka* (Contemporary Nationalism and the Social Development of the Foreign East) (Moscow: Nauka, Glavnaia redaktsiia vostochnoi literatury, 1978), 240–41, 243, 245, 247, 249–51, 255–56, 259–60; B. G. Gafurov, *Aktual'nye problemy sovremennogo natsional'no-osvoboditel'nogo dvizheniia* (Topical Problems of the Contemporary National Liberation Movement) (Moscow: Nauka, Glavnaia redaktsiia vostochnoi literatury, 1976), 185–89.

Afghanistan, Indonesia, and Malaysia. Iran's Shi'i opposition was still seen negatively, as a "semi-feudal ideological" trend.[27]

As late as October 1978, a conference of many of the Soviet Union's leading Orientalists conveyed the message that all varieties of Islam were inherently elitist and that Islam was in a state of crisis, with secularism advancing and belief declining rapidly among the young. Islamic activism represented the clergy's attempt to win back the young and combat the increasing influence of socialism. Although the Soviets could welcome Islam's influence among the masses as an expression of opposition to penetration by Western bourgeois culture, the negative corollary of this was opposition to the advance of science and technology.[28]

Since 1979, Soviet assessments of Islam have expanded upon and given more emphasis to existing arguments about the way it can serve as an agent of social, political, and economic change. Negative aspects are still perceived but the weight of these considerations in the overall discussion has declined. The balance between the positive and negative sides has shifted several times since 1979, as Moscow reacted to political developments in the Islamic world, but continues to favor the positive, although far more guardedly now than in 1980 and 1981.

The most important factor that contributed to the change was the Islamic revolution in Iran. The Soviets describe it as one of the most positive international developments in recent years, others being the revolutions in Vietnam, Afghanistan, and Ethiopia. The Iranian Revolution is frequently cited as a prime example of Islamic political activism in the cause of national liberation.[29] Initially the Soviets saw much to please

27. L. Polonskaia and A. Vafa, "Tipologiia nemarksistskikh ideinykh techenii v razvivaiushchikhsia stranakh" (Typology of Non-Marxist Ideological Trends in the Developing Countries), *Aziia i Afrika segodnia,* no. 9 (September 1977): 32.

28. Smilianskaia, " 'Islam i obshchestvo.' Chteniia pamiati E. A. Beliaeva" ('Islam and Society.' Lectures in Memory of E. A. Beliaev), *Narody Azii i Afriki,* no. 3 (1979): 158, 161–62.

29. G. F. Kim et al., *Zarubezhnyi Vostok i sovremennost'* (The Foreign East and the Contemporary Age), 3 vols. (Moscow: Nauka, Glavnaia redaktsiia vostochnoi literatury, 1980–81), 3:158, 166; R. A. Ul'ianovskii, "O natsional'noi osvobozhdenii i natsionalizme" (On National Liberation and Nationalism), *Aziia i Afrika segodnia,* no. 10 (October 1980): 5; idem, "Osvobodivshiesiia strany v mirovom revoliutsionnom protsesse: itogi poslednego desiatiletiia i perspektivy" (Liberated Countries in the World Revolutionary Process: Results of the Last Decade and Perspectives), *Problemy mirovogo revoliutsionnogo protsessa* (Moscow: Mysl', 1983), 3:78; B. M. Sviatskii, "Aktual'nye problemy sovremennoi Azii" (Topical Problems of Contemporary Asia), *Narody Azii i Afriki,* no. 1 (1983): 119–20; K. A. Merkulov, *Islam v mirovoi politike i mezhdunarodnykh otnosheniiakh* (Islam in World Politics and International Relations) (Moscow: Mezhdunarodnye otnosheniia, 1982), 5, 6, 13, 95, 104; *Pravda,* April 14, 1984, 6; L. Medvedkov, "Islam i osvoboditel'nye revoliutsii" (Islam

them about developments in Iran. The break of relations with the United States and the overthrow of the pro-American shah are changes Moscow has continued to laud even after expressing anger at other actions of the new regime in Tehran. Other early developments the Soviets regarded favorably included the opportunity for leftist forces, including the pro-Soviet communist party, the Tudeh, to function legally for the first time in a generation, and the prospect of far-reaching economic reforms, such as nationalizations and land redistribution. Even the condemnation of the Soviet invasion of Afghanistan by many Iranian leaders, though an irritant, was not in itself a serious obstacle to working relations between Moscow and Tehran. Simultaneously with the positive reaction to Iran's Islamic revolution, and perhaps as a result of it, the Soviets have increased their attention to the use of Islam in support of the radical policies of a number of Arab revolutionary regimes, especially in Algeria and Libya and to a lesser degree in Syria and the People's Democratic Republic of Yemen. The argument in each case is that these regimes have taken into account the continuing influence of Islam over many inhabitants of these countries and have successfully invoked religion to win public support for extensive social and economic changes.[30] The underlying theme of this new interpretation is that Islam is increasingly important as an ideological basis for rejecting close relations with the West and the capitalist development model.

The rallying cry of defending Islam used by Afghans fighting the communist government in Kabul and the Soviet troops in Afghanistan

and Liberating Revolutions) *Novoe vremia,* no. 43 (October 1979): 20; A. Germanovich and L. Medvedko, " 'Vozrozhdenie islama' ili probuzhdenie naroda" ('Renaissance of Islam' or Awakening of the People), *Nauka i religiia,* no.7 (July 1982): 56–57; I. Beliaev, "Islam i politika" (Islam and Politics), *Literaturnaia gazeta,* January 16, 1980, 14; L. S. Vasil'ev, *Istoriia religii Vostoka* (History of the Religions of the East) (Moscow: Vyshaia Shkola, 1983), 172–73.

30. Merkulov, *Islam,* 103–05; Vasil'ev, *Istoriia religii Vostoka,* 170; A. Vafa and S. Soboleva, "Religiia i ideino-politicheskaia bor'ba v razvivaiushchikhsia stranakh" (Religion and the Ideological-Political Struggle in the Developing Countries), *Aziia i Afrika segodnia,* no. 11 (November 1979): 36; L. R. Polonskaia, "Islam v gosudarstvennoi strukture i politicheskoi zhizni osvobodivshikhsia stran" (Islam in the State Structure and Political Life of Liberated Countries), *Voprosy nauchnogo ateizma,* vol. 31 (Moscow: Mysl', 1983), 48; I. L. Andreev, "Islam i ideinaia bor'ba v osvobodivshikhsia stranakh" (Islam and the Ideological Struggle in Liberated Countries), *Problemy mirovogo revoliutsionnogo protsessa,* vol. 2 (Moscow: Mysl', 1982), 211–12; S. Aliev, "Islam i politika" (Islam and Politics), *Aziia i Afrika segodnia,* no. 12 (December 1981): 7; I. Beliaev, "Islam i politika," 14; Malashenko, "Religioznaia traditsiia i politika revoliutsionnoi demokratii (na primere Alzhira)" (Religious Traditions and the Politics of Revolutionary Democracy [on the Example of Algeria]), *Aziia i Afrika segodnia,* no. 9 (September 1979): 21–22.

has had little impact on the positive Soviet assessment of Islam in other countries. The main consequence has been the Soviet stipulation that one must consider the particular context in which Islam operates. In some countries it aids progress, whereas in others it serves the cause of reaction. This is the official policy of the Soviet Communist party, as enunciated by Leonid Brezhnev at the Twenty-Sixth Party Congress in February 1981 and quoted in virtually everything since published by the Soviets on Islam abroad.[31] On occasion, the Soviets have tried to prevent Islam's role in opposing their objectives in Afghanistan from undermining their interpretation of its anti-imperialist, progressive functions elsewhere by arguing that the Afghan government follows policies consonant with Islam, whereas the guerrillas do not and attack mullas and mosques. However, other interpretations stress the use of Islam by Afghan reactionaries and imperialists bent on counterrevolution.[32]

On a more reflective level, the need to revise the assessment of Islam under the pressure of outside developments has caused some Soviet academicians to acknowledge that conceptual limitations distorted their understanding. Academician Primakov conceded that Soviet Orientalists had not anticipated the current "Islamic boom" because they had underestimated the influence of tradition on contemporary ideology and politics. Islam was the most important manifestation of tradition in this sense.[33] He directly addressed, without necessarily resolving, the question of how Marxist-Leninists, who were committed to atheism, could approve of Islamic activism and ascribe to it a revolutionary-democratic role in some cases. His answer was that religions and "mass religious movements" were two separate issues.[34] This built upon the argument made by various scholars in the 1970s that Islam was both a spiritual doctrine dealing with humanity's relation to the supernatural and a system of this-worldly values governing politics, economics, and social relations. An official of the Institute of World Economics and International Relations of the Academy of Sciences contended that in light of the revolutions in Iran, Afghanistan, and Ethiopia, Soviet experts needed, in essence, to redress the preoccupation with the economies of developing societies and pay more attention to religion, ideology, and culture. The root of the problem was a rigidly

31. *Pravda*, February 24, 1981, 3.
32. Merkulov, *Islam*, 39; Andreev, "Islam," 200; *Komsomolskaia pravda*, June 30, 1982, 2.
33. Primakov, "Aktual'nye zadachi," 11; Sviatskii, "Aktual'nye problemy," 117.
34. Primakov, "Islam i protsessy obshchestvennogo razvitiia stran zarubezhnogo Vostoka" (Islam and Processes of Social Development of the Countries of the Foreign East), *Voprosy filosofii*, no. 8 (1980): 70.

Eurocentric interpretation of Third World social and cultural developments, which stereotyped phenomena according to superficial resem-
blances so that their substance was obscured. The expectation that the
growth of capitalism and Westernization in developing countries would
eliminate traditions proved erroneous. In fact, these changes have
strengthened traditions in various ways.[35] However, there is opposition to
the quest for greater analytical flexibility. One of the party leadership's
foremost interpreters of Third World political trends, R. A. Ul'ianovskii,
has insisted that the Iranian Revolution is "nothing other than the expression of class struggle" even though the form is "blurred."[36]

The Soviets offer an additional explanation for the change in their
perception of Islam: that Islam itself changed, especially since the 1970s.
The issue, they contend, was not a revival of strictly religious values but
the expression in Islamic terms of solutions to political, social, and economic problems, which reached crisis proportions at this time in the Islamic world. Until roughly 1982, the Soviets frequently argued that Islam,
for all its limitations, could offer (although not all versions did so) a vision
of a more egalitarian society with values profoundly different from the
pursuit of wealth through exploitation associated with modern capitalism.
This outlook is said to resemble socialism in certain respects and is sometimes called Islamic socialism, and other times, simply Islamic economics.
However, there are too many capitalist, precapitalist, and utopian elements in Islam for it to be an authentic socialist doctrine. Although Islamic economic ideology can be merely a disguised form of bourgeois
ideology, it can, in some instances, be genuinely radical.[37] The Soviets

35. A. Gudymenko and V. Starostin, "Traditsii i obshchestvennyi progress v razvivaiushchikhsia stranakh" (Traditions and Social Progress in Developing Countries), *Mirovaia ekonomika i mezhdunarodnye otnosheniia*, no. 9 (1982): 119, 121, 126–27.

36. Ul'ianovskii, Predislovie (Introduction) to S. L. Agaev, *Iran: rozhdenie respubliki*
(Iran: Birth of the Republic) (Moscow: Politizdat, 1984), 8.

37. Kim et al., *Zarubezhnyi Vostok*, 3:137, 147–48, 152, 156–58; Polonskaia, "Islam v
gosudarstvennoi strukture," 34–35; idem, "Islam i politika na sovremennom Vostoke" (Is-
lam and Politics in the Contemporary East), *Nauka i religiia*, no. 4 (1983): 57–58; A. I.
Ionova, "Sotsial'noe razmezhevanie v musul'manskikh obshchinakh iugo-vostochnoi Azii"
(Social Differentiation in Muslim Societies of Southeast Asia), *Narody Azii i Afriki*, no. 4
(1981): 36; idem, "Musul'manskie dvizheniia sotsial'nogo protesta (na primere Iugo-
Vostochnoi Azii)" (Muslim Social Protest Movements [on the Example of Southeast Asia]),
Aziia i Afrika segodnia, no. 10 (October 1979): 36; G. Kerimov, "Islam i politika" (Islam
and Politics), *Molodoi Kommunist*, no. 12 (1982): 92, 93, 96–97; S. Aliev, "Islam i politika,"
6, 8; *Pravda*, April 14, 1980, 6; Vasil'ev, *Istoriia religii Vostoka*, 113, 163, 170; Merkulov,
Islam, 5–6, 8, 76, 96, 105, 166, 168, 170, 227–28, 299; Medvedko, "Islam i osvoboditel'nyi
revoliutsii," 20; Sviatskii, "Aktual'nye problemy," 122; Andreev, "Islam," 196, 202, 204,
205, 207, 211–12; Germanovich and Medvedko, "Vozrozhdenie islama," 56, 58; M. Atkin,
"Moscow's Disenchantment with Iran," *Survey* 27, nos. 118–19 (Autumn-Winter 1983):
255–56.

now argue that Islam remains a powerful influence, especially among the masses but also among the young and, in a cultural sense, among the educated, rather than declining as a consequence of modernization, as they formerly held.[38] Therefore, Islam can be used successfully to rally the masses and other diverse social elements in support of progressive revolutions, even when the leaders' aims are ultimately secular. This is all the more important because in such societies, secular leftists, including the communists, are weak and cannot themselves lead.[39] Therefore it is ideologically acceptable and tactically advisable for Communist parties and other progressives in Islamic countries to make common cause with those Islamic movements that expressed what were, in context, progressive ideologies.[40] That argument is still applied to Iran even after the Islamic Republic's suppression of the Tudeh party and increased criticism of the Soviet Union in 1983. However, the group that is deemed the proponent of progressive Islam is no longer Khomeini and his followers but rather the Mujahidin-i Khalq guerrillas, who are fighting the current Tehran government.[41]

From 1979 through 1982, the revised Soviet assessment of Islam held that Shi'ism was inherently more opposed to the status quo and more closely associated with the masses' grievances than Sunnism. This expanded upon the argument enunciated by Doroshenko earlier in the 1970s that Shi'ism began as a movement opposed to oppression and continued

---

38. Polonskaia, "Islam i politika," 60; idem, "Islam v gosudarstvennoi strukture," 35; Kim et al., *Zarubezhnyi Vostok*, 3:138, 157–58; Ionova, "Sotsial'noe razmezhevanie," 36; Primakov, "Islam," 61–62; *Pravda*, April 14, 1980, 6; Merkulov, *Islam*, 7, 10, 101–02; Andreev, "Islam," 194–95; Azarkh et al., "Vtoraia Vsesoiuznaia konferentsiia," 124; Vagabov, *Islam i voprosy nauchnogo ateisticheskogo vospitaniia* (Islam and Questions of Scientific Atheist Upbringing) (Moscow: Vysshaia shkola, 1984), 54; Vasil'ev, *Istoriia religii Vostoka*, 95, 171–72.

39. Andreev, "Islam," 199–200, 210–11; Germanovich and Medvedko, "Vozrozhdenie islama," 56, 59; Stepaniants, *Musul'manskie kontseptsii v filosofii i politike (XIX–XX vv.)* (Muslim Concepts in Philosophy and Politics [XIXth–XXth cents.]) (Moscow: Nauka, 1982), 6; Kim et al., *Zarubezhnyi Vostok*, 3:140; Vagabov, *Islam i voprosy*, 125; Ul'ianovskii, "Osvobodivshiesia strany," 81–82; *Pravda*, April 14, 1980, 6; Ionova, "Doktriny, dogmaty, zhizn'" (Doctrines, Dogmas, Life), *Nauka i religiia*, no. 4 (April 1981): 60; Merkulov, *Islam*, 7, 102, 105, 163, 168, 182–83, 300; Malashenko, "Religioznaia traditsiia," 20–22; Sviatskii, "Aktual'nye problemy," 122; Medvedko, "Islam i osvoboditel'nyi revoliutsii," 20; Aliev, "Islam i politika," 7; Atkin, "Moscow's Disenchantment," 258.

40. Andreev, "Islam," 197; Malashenko, "Religioznaia traditsiia," 22; Merkulov, *Islam*, 75–76; *Pravda*, April 14, 1980, 6; Medvedko, "Islam i osvoboditel'nyi revoliutsii," 21; *Kommunist Tadzhikistana*, November 13, 1980, 3.

41. S. L. Agaev, "Levyi radikalizm, revoliutsionnyi demokratizm i nauchnyi sotsializm v stranakh Vostoka" (Left Radicalism, Revolutionary Democracy, and Scientific Socialism in the Countries of the East), *Rabochii klass i sovremennyi mir*, no. 3 (May-June 1984): 144, 146.

to play that role in a host of struggles down to the present. The Shi'i clergy, including its upper levels, was portrayed as leading this opposition for a variety of motives, not least of which was the doctrinal one that legitimate authority resided solely in the hidden imam and that until his return any government other than a clerical stewardship was illegitimate. The crucial factor was the linking of the Shi'i ideal of government with Qur'anic quotations about social justice. That brought the masses, who were devout, into the revolutionary movement. The Soviets now credited the clergy's tradition of opposition in modern times with earning them a reputation for anti-imperialism.[42] In the hands of Ayatullah Khomeini, "the dogma and traditions of Shi'ite Islam . . . [became] an offensive weapon against the tyrant-shah and 'Westernization,' in the defense of 'Muslim spiritual values' and social order, which would serve the interests of . . . the oppressed majority."[43] Thus, "among all the Muslim clergy the Shi'ite clergy is distinguished by its socio-political activism," while "the Sunni clergy occupies more moderate and conservative positions," usually supporting the government of the state in which it lives.[44] Although there are indeed many examples of the Shi'i ulama's involvement in opposition politics, this argument glosses over the instances when the clergy did not challenge governments or was at least willing to compromise. The non-ideological motives for the ulama's opposition to Muhammad Reza Shah have at different times been described as the defense of powers and privileges threatened by reforms or the identification with the masses' antagonism toward an oppressive regime. The changing explanations have largely reflected the state of Soviet-Iranian relations.[45]

As long as the Soviets were optimistic about the course of the Iranian Revolution, they could explain away those less welcome aspects of clerical activism by stressing that opposition to the monarchy was in itself pro-

42. A. Fatulla-ogly, "Shiity segodnia" (Shi'ites Today), *Nauka i religiia*, no. 5 (1981): 37; Merkulov, *Islam*, 93, 154, 240–41; Vasil'ev, "Islam: napravleniia, techeniia, sekty. Opozitsionnyi islam. Shiity" (Islam: Orientations, Trends, Sects. Opposition Islam. Shi'ites), *Aziia i Afrika segodnia*, no. 2 (February 1980): 55; idem, *Istoriia religii Vostoka*, 152–53; Ul'ianovskii, "O natsional'noi osvobozhdenii," 5–6; Doroshenko, "Iran: musul'manskie (shiitskie) traditsii i sovremennost' " (Iran: Muslim [Shi'ite] Traditions and the Contemporary Age), *Aziia i Afrika segodnia*, no. 8 (August 1980): 60; Anarkulova, "Mal'komkhan," 108, 111; Medvedko, "Islam i osvoboditel'nyi revoliutsii," 19; I. Beliaev, "Islam i politika," 4; Germanovich and Medvedko, "Vozrozhdenie islama," 57; Polonskaia, "Islam i politika," 58; idem, "Islam v gosudarstvennoi strukture," 35; Kim et al., *Zarubezhnyi Vostok*, 3:143.

43. Doroshenko, "Iran," 59.

44. Merkulov, *Islam*, 301. A similar opinion was expressed in *Pravda*, April 14, 1980, 6.

45. Atkin, "Moscow's Disenchantment," 249–50.

gressive. As Stepaniants observed in the 1982 revision of her book, "regardless of the goals pursued by the Shi'i" clergy, their criticism roused many people against the shah's tyranny.[46]

When Moscow recovered from its initial surprise at the prominence of the ulama in the Iranian Revolution, it also came to see the Shi'i leadership as particularly well suited, in a functional as well as an ideological sense, to lead opposition politics. Given the strenuous efforts of the monarchy to suppress secular opponents and its fear of the consequences of applying similar methods to the clergy, Shi'i institutions became the only legal medium available for organized dissent. The Soviets noted that the Shi'i opposition had a network of personnel, in the form of many thousands of clerics throughout Iran, and a safe forum for disseminating its views, the mosque. Preaching in connection with holy days enabled the clergy to link current political activism with traditional Shi'i concerns over religious duty and sacrifice for a greater good. The threat to invoke a jihad against the monarchy was an important weapon in the psychological war during the closing stages of the revolution. The Soviets endowed the Shi'i tradition of *taqiyah,* the concealment of one's true beliefs in times of peril, with modern political usefulness, as an aid in forming a secret revolutionary organization.[47]

While the Soviets acknowledge the prominence of Shi'i rhetoric and clerical leadership in the Iranian Revolution of 1978–79 they disagree sharply on whether these were part of the essence of the revolutionary movement or merely attached themselves to it. This dispute is largely colored by practical considerations based on the state of Soviet-Iranian relations. The most favorable interpretation of clerical participation was widespread when those relations were at their best, in 1980 and 1981, although it did not disappear completely after that. According to this view, Shi'ism was an elemental component of Iran's revolution, which was "Islamicization on the basis of a movement from below."[48] The clergy was the driving force behind this movement, with Khomeini's ideas winning a

46. Stepaniants, *Musul'manskie kontseptsii,* 173.

47. Ul'ianovskii, "O natsional'noi osvobozhdenii," 6; Doroshenko, "Iran," 59–61; S. M. Aliev, "Antimonarkhicheskaia i antiimperialisticheskaia revoliutsiia v Irane" (The Antimonarchical and Antiimperialist Revolution in Iran), *Narody Azii i Afriki,* no. 3 (1979): 53; Merkulov, *Islam,* 254, 258–60, 264–66, 273, 285; G. I. Avdeev, "Prazdnovanie ramazana v sovremennom Irane" (The Celebration of Ramadan in Contemporary Iran), in *Iran: Istoriia i sovremennost'* (Moscow: Nauka, Glavnaia redaktsiia vostochnoi literatury, 1983), 132, 134, 136; D. Kasatkin and V. Ushakov, "Iran: osobennosti razvitiia revoliutsionnogo dvizheniia" (Iran: The Peculiar Development of the Revolutionary Movement), *Aziia i Afrika segodnia,* no. 4 (1979): 8.

48. Polonskaia, "Islam v gosudarstvennoi strukture," 35.

broad popular following. Among the clergy's valuable contributions was uniting the diverse opposition forces around the one goal they all shared, hostility toward the monarchy. Although there were drawbacks to the creation of an Islamic state rather than a secular one, the Soviets for a time emphasized what they considered the most positive features of the new order, the promise of equality and civil liberties and the perceived rejection of bourgeois democracy.[49]

The negative argument was heard in 1978 and to a lesser degree in 1979 as the Iranian Revolution was unfolding. It reflected the Soviets' assumption that a serious nationalist challenge to the monarchy could come only from the lay liberals and leftists. This view declined in importance from November 1978 and ceased to be heard after early 1979 as the Soviets came to appreciate Khomeini's strength and found that an accommodation could be reached with the new regime in Tehran. In 1983 that accommodation broke down. The diplomatic reversal was reflected in the return of the negative interpretation of the ulama's political activism, now couched in far harsher terms than before. The initiative for the breakdown came from Tehran, although Moscow's policies contributed to Tehran's antagonism. Soviet pursuit of good relations with both sides in the Iran-Iraq War while Iraq was on the offensive and, especially, support for Iraq once Iranian troops entered Iraqi territory in July 1982 stimulated increased criticism of the Soviet Union on that point and many others by the Tehran leadership. Moreover, those leaders sought a monopoly of power and social homogeneity, which led them to repressive measures against political rivals as well as ethnic and religious minorities. After this process was already far advanced, the Tudeh party was banned and some thousand of its members, including its leaders, arrested early in 1983. Although in some other countries the suppression of the local Communist party has not interfered with good diplomatic relations with the Soviet Union, in this case, the crackdown had a deliberate anti-Soviet message. In the much publicized confessions and trials of Tudeh members, the lesson conveyed was that the Soviet Union was just another superpower, which acted in typical superpower fashion against Iran's interests, that it conducted espionage in Iran through Tudeh members, that it sided with

49. S. Aliev, "Problemy politicheskogo razvitiia Irana" (Problems of the Political Development of Iran), *Aziia i Afrika segodnia*, no. 11 (November 1980): 15–17; Stepaniants, "Musul'manskoe vozrozhdenchestvo" (Muslim Renaissance), *Narody Azii i Afriki*, no. 3 (1983): 23–24; idem, *Musul'manskie kontseptsii*, 174; Kerimov, "Islam i politika," 92; Merkulov, *Islam*, 250, 256–57.

Iran's enemy in the continuing war, and that communist ideology was completely unsuited to the needs of the Iranian people. Although both Moscow and Tehran want to keep lines of communications open between them, Moscow's earlier hopes that the new Iranian regime would perceive a common interest with the USSR in foreign affairs and follow a leftist program domestically have for the present been dashed.

According to the revived negative interpretation, the Iranian Revolution was made by the left—the Tudeh party, the Fida'iyan-i Khalq, and the Mujahidin-i Khalq—and by the masses, acting on their own initiative because of secular social, economic, and political grievances. The clergy joined the revolutionary movement once it was far advanced and provided the leadership and the evocative rhetoric. In doing this the clergy was using the mass unrest for its own ends: to increase its power at the expense of the secular authorities.[50] The ultimate conclusion of this line of argument is that the clergy usurped power by riding the crest of the revolutionary movement and then breaking the genuinely revolutionary elements, the leftist political parties and mass institutions, such as popular militias and revolutionary committees and tribunals, which could have become the foundation for creating a new, genuinely revolutionary order. Instead, the clergy has created a despotic Shi'i theocracy with the form but not the substance of popular self-government.[51]

Soviet discussions of the Islamic Republic's social and economic program paralleled the shifting interpretation of the clergy's political leadership. At first the emphasis was on the progressive aspects of an imperfect approach to the creation of a new order. Although the Shi'i reformers' economic objective, the *tauhid* economy, was petty bourgeois rather than socialist, it was still an advance over the Western-style capitalism advocated by the shah. What appealed to the Soviets was its opposition to big business, economic ties to the major capitalist states, and ostentatious industrial projects that did not address Iran's pressing needs.

50. Aliev, "Antimonarkhicheskaia i antiimperialisticheskaia revoliutsiia," 53, 57; Merkulov, *Islam,* 256–58; Ul'ianovskii, "Moral'nye printsipy v politike i politika v oblasti morali" (Moral Principles in Politics and Politics in the Sphere of Morals), *Literaturnaia Gazeta,* June 22, 1983, 10.

51. Skliarov, "Stanovlenie novykh organov vlasti v Irane (1978–1981)" (The Formation of New Organs of Power in Iran [1978–1981]), in *Iran: Istoriia i sovremennost',* 197–201, 203, 206–08, 210–11; Ul'ianovskii, "Moral'nye printsipy," 10; Merkulov, *Islam,* 277–79; Atkin, "Moscow's Disenchantment," 254–55. Various Iranian revolutionaries opposed to the power of the clergy in the new regime criticize Khomeini and his clerical supporters in similar terms.

Instead, it promised income redistribution and welfare programs to aid the poor, attention to agricultural problems, and the encouragement of cooperatives and the state sector.[52] In sum, it advocated "the priority of collective interests over the individual."[53] This indulgent view of tauhid economics gave way to scathing criticism, in which the clergy and their supporters in the bourgeoisie and petty bourgeoisie were accused of wanting to preserve the essential features of the prerevolutionary economy. Talk about land reform and an end to exploitation was not accompanied by action. Attempts to create an Islamic economy in Iran—or elsewhere—could not possibly result in beneficial economic changes because the very concept was an attempt to apply irrelevant medieval concepts to a modern economy.[54] Similarly, the Islamic Republic's social and cultural policies were designed to impose the "antiquated moral-ethical norms of the Qur'an and the shari'ah."[55]

Soviet attitudes toward the foreign policy of Iran's Islamic Republic are beyond the scope of this essay, but it is apposite to note Soviet interest in the possibility that the revolution in Iran might encourage opposition to the status quo in other Muslim states. The Soviets believed Muslims in other countries, especially Shi'is in Lebanon, Iraq, Bahrain, and Saudi Arabia, were sympathetic to the Iranian Revolution. The Zia regime in Pakistan and some Arab governments were believed to feel threatened by international Shi'i loyalties to the Iranian clergy and by the Iranians' militant republicanism, domestic reform programs, and interest in exporting the revolution. At times the Soviets welcomed this as a chance to weaken rightist regimes. At other times they viewed it negatively as a power grab that threatened states the Soviets favored. Moscow particularly disliked the spillover of the Iranian Revolution into Iraq, where, in 1979, some Shi'is called for the creation of an Islamic republic modeled on Iran's, to which the government responded with a general political crackdown not only on the Shi'i leadership but also on the Iraqi Communist party. The main consequences of the Iranian influence were seen as the willingness of certain Muslim governments to be more vigorously anti-Israeli and cooler toward the United States and the increase in do-

52. Stepaniants, "Musul'manskoe vozrozhdenchestvo," 27; idem, Musul'manskie kontseptsii, 204–05; Aliev, "Problemy," 17; Merkulov, Islam, 256; Atkin, "Moscow's Disenchantment," 255–56.

53. Sviatskii, "Aktual'nye problemy," 122.

54. Ul'ianovskii, "Moral'nye printsipy," 10; Polonskaia, "Islam i politika," 58; Skliarov, "Stanovlenie novykh organov," 216–17; Merkulov, Islam, 171, 276, 278–79, 285–86; Ionova, "Doktriny," 61; Atkin, "Moscow's Disenchantment," 256–57.

55. Ul'ianovskii, "Moral'nye printsipy," 10.

mestic unrest in Saudi Arabia, Bahrain, and the United Arab Emirates. Yet the Soviets do not consider Saudi Arabia nearly as vulnerable to a Shi'i challenge as the Iranian monarchy. They see the Saudi regime as inherently stronger than the shah's because the former has a religious legitimation that the shah lacked, the Shi'is are a minority in a largely Wahhabi population, which approves of government policy, and the government has made some timely concessions to defuse Shi'i discontents. Whether this interpretation is sound time will tell, but it is worth recalling that Soviet estimates of the significance of Shi'i dissent in Iran were overtaken by events. In any case, the limited Soviet enthusiasm for the radicalizing effect of the Iranian Revolution on foreign Shi'is faded as the Iran-Iraq War increased the likelihood that inhabitants of other Gulf states would perceive Iran not as an inspiring revolutionary example but as a conventional expansionist power against which protection must be sought from the United States.[56] For a time, the Soviets also showed interest in the potential of the Mujahidin-i Khalq to encourage radicalism elsewhere in the Muslim world, but this waned as the Mujahidin's fortunes declined.[57]

The Soviets pay relatively less attention to Shi'is in Muslim countries other than Iran. There is a general recognition that Shi'is are often poorer but better organized than the Sunni communities which dominate them in various countries.[58] The Soviets are aware that this has led to instances of political unrest, but their attitude toward the unrest is ambivalent and the interest slight. In Lebanon, the political forces the Soviets find most to their liking and most interesting are the more familiar power brokers, the PLO and the Jumblatt family (as well as the Syrians). Moscow's experts are aware of Ayatullah Musa al-Sadr's transformation of the Shi'is' political role in the 1960s and 1970s through his assertive, radical organi-

56. Doroshenko, "Nekotorye aspekty shiitsko-sunnitskikh otnoshenii" (Some Aspects of Shi'i-Sunni Relations), in *Islam v stranakh Blizhnego i Srednego Vostoka* (Moscow: Nauka, Glavnaia redaktsiia vostochnoi literatury, 1982), 131–35, 139–41; Morozova, "Problemy shiitskoi obshchiny v Pakistane" (Problems of the Shi'ite Communities in Pakistan), in ibid., 155; Fadeeva, "Ob evoliutsii svetskikh tendentsii v sotsial'no-politicheskom razvitii Turtsii. K postanovke voprosa" (On the Evolution of Secular Tendencies in the Socio-Political Development of Turkey. Toward Posing the Question), in ibid., 76, 92; I. M. Kliamkin, "Islamskaia revoliutsiia: lozungi i soderzhanie" (The Islamic Revolution: Slogans and Content), in *Problemy mirovogo revoliutsionnogo protsessa*, vol. 3 (Moscow: Mysl', 1983), 275; Merkulov, *Islam*, 125–26, 146–47, 292–94, 298, 302; *Pravda*, April 14, 1984, 6.

57. I. Timofeev, "Rol' islama v obshchestvenno-politicheskoi zhizni stran zarubezhnogo Vostoka" (The Role of Islam in the Socio-Political Life of Countries of the Foreign East), *Mirovaia ekonomika i mezhdunarodnye otnosheniia*, no. 5 (1982): 55.

58. Doroshenko, "Nekotorye aspekty," 134–35.

zation, Amal, but have yet to treat that or any other Shi'i group as a critical force in Lebanese politics.[59] Given the acrimony of Soviet-Pakistani relations, the Soviets might have cause to look to the various Shi'i minorities there (including Twelvers and two principal Isma'ili sects) for welcome opposition to the government of Zia al-Haqq. The Soviets were intrigued by Twelver Shi'i protests against Zia's militantly Sunni Islamicization policy, which forced him to make some modest concessions in 1980. Yet this opposition has not been able to prevent further Islamicizing measures or to pose a serious challenge to Zia's authority. Moscow is inclined to dismiss the Isma'ilis in Pakistan and elsewhere as dominated by a prosperous middle class and unlikely to oppose the status quo.[60]

There is no reason for Moscow to look to Afghan Shi'i activism as an ally in the struggle for control of Afghanistan, even though the Shi'is there belong to non-Pashtun ethnic groups, which in the past have resented Pashtun-Sunni political dominance. Afghanistan's Shi'is as well as Sunnis have fought the communist government in Kabul and the Soviet invasion force, to Moscow's ire.[61]

The sometimes hostile relations between Shi'is and Sunnis is a subject that apparently perplexes the Soviets, since there is no consistent interpretation of it. Often it is dismissed as yet another example of imperialism's mistreatment of Muslims, in this case by turning them against each other to weaken them and thus facilitate their domination by imperialism.[62] However, some historians note that Sunni-Shi'i animosity has been deeply entrenched since early Islamic times, even if the particulars of the dispute have been political as much as religious.[63] This contradictory approach intertwines with the equally contradictory attitude toward the relation of Iran's revolutionary regime to the country's minorities, many of them Sunni. Imperialists and reactionaries are blamed for stirring up in-

59. Ibid., 137; A. B. Zubov, "Politicheskaia kul'tura Livana: proshloe i nastoiashchee konfessional'noi demokratii" (The Political Culture of Lebanon: Past and Present of the Confessional Democracy), *Narody Azii i Afriki*, no. 2 (1983): 173, 175–76.

60. Morozova, "Problema shiitskoi obshchiny," 144, 146–56; Polonskaia, "Islam i politika," 59; Merkulov, *Islam*, 89, 122–23; Andreev, "Islam," 206.

61. Merkulov, *Islam*, 113; Morozova, "Problema shiitskoi obshchiny," 155–56; Primakov, "Islam i protsessy obshchestvennogo razvitiia," 60.

62. Medvedko, "Islam i osvoboditel'nyi revoliutsii," 18; Kerimov, "Islam i politika," 94; Merkulov, *Islam*, 93–94.

63. Doroshenko, "Nekotorye aspekty," 142–43; Vasil'ev, *Istoriia religii Vostoka*, 110; V. V. Naumkin's introduction to the third Russian-language edition of H. Massé, *Islam* (Moscow: Nauka, 1982), 10; O. I. Zhigalina, "Rol' islama v razvitii ideologii kurdskogo natsional'nogo dvizheniia v Irane" (The Role of Islam in the Development of the Ideology of the Kurdish Nationalist Movement in Iran), in *Islam v stranakh Blizhnego i Srednego Vostoka*, 114–16.

cidents of Sunni-Shi'i conflict, but the Soviets have wavered on whether the central government seeks a fair accommodation with the minorities or wants to enforce the dominance of intolerant Shi'i-Persian nationalists.[64]

The Soviet Union has a large Muslim population of its own, which numbers between 45 and 50 million people, although the extent to which Islam is a factor in their lives is the subject of heated controversy. There are no official statistics published on the number of people who consider themselves Shi'is. The prevailing guess among outside observers is that there are slightly above 3 million Twelver Shi'is, the overwhelming majority of whom live in the Azerbaijan S.S.R., across Iran's northwestern border, and more than 100,000 Isma'ilis, most of whom live in remote villages in the Tajik S.S.R.'s Pamir Mountains. Since the broader question of the status of Islam in the Soviet Union is a vast subject that cannot be encompassed here, this essay will discuss Shi'ism in the Azerbaijan S.S.R. and the impact of Iranian Shi'i activism on that republic and the predominantly Sunni Turkoman and Tajik republics to the northeast of Iran. Some Western observers see postrevolutionary Iranian propaganda broadcasts to Turkoman as reaching a large audience with a message that emphasizes Islamic solidarity at the expense of Soviet patriotism.[65] Others see all Muslims of the Soviet Union, including Azerbaijanis, Turkomans, and Tajiks, as linked to one another and to foreign Muslims by the bond of Islam, which supersedes all other loyalties, whether to the Sunni or Shi'i sects or to the Soviet state. According to this argument, Soviet Azerbaijanis and Turkomans may well be powerfully attracted to Iran as an alternative to Soviet rule because their coethnics south of the border, although subject to linguistic discrimination, "are granted full religious freedom" and can participate in politics.[66] One could also look for Iran's Islamic revolution to have influenced the Soviet Union's nearly 3 million Tajiks, who have strong linguistic, cultural, and historical links to Iran's Persians.

64. Merkulov, *Islam*, 280, 295; "Khronikal'nye zametki," *Narody Azii i Afriki*, no. 1 (1983): 152–53; Aliev, "Problemy," 17–18; Zhigalina, "Rol' islama," 113–14, 119, 127; Kim et al., *Zarubezhnyi Vostok*, 2:252–53.

65. K. Dawisha and H. Carrere d'Encausse, "Islam in the Foreign Policy of the Soviet Union: A Double-Edged Sword?" in A. Dawisha, ed., *Islam in Foreign Policy* (Cambridge: Cambridge University Press, 1983), 174–75; Y. Ro'i, "The Impact of the Islamic Fundamentalist Revival of the Late 1970s on the Soviet View of Islam," in Y. Ro'i, ed., *The USSR and the Muslim World* (London: George Allen & Unwin, 1984), 177n64.

66. A. Bennigsen and M. Broxup, *The Islamic Threat to the Soviet State* (New York: St. Martin's Press, 1983), 109–12.

Soviet authorities acknowledge with dismay that some unspecified number of citizens in the Azerbaijan, Turkoman, and Tajik republics (and elsewhere in the USSR) still consider themselves Muslims, whether they observe religious rites to some degree or identify culturally with Islam. Islam is so deeply entrenched in the heritage of these people that they consider it intrinsic to their national identity.[67] The head of the Azerbaijan KGB, Z. Iusif-zade, complained about a "sectarian underground and the reactionary Muslim clergy, politically harmful occurrences among the intelligentsia and youths."[68] Hundreds of "clandestine mosques" are rumored to operate in the Azerbaijan S.S.R.[69] An Azerbaijani writing in one of the main atheist propaganda journals observed that Azerbaijani Shi'is also made pilgrimages to holy places and that among this community pilgrimage was an even more important practice than mosque attendance. He stated that the practices associated with the Muharram mourning remained important for Azerbaijani Shi'is, including the young, although self-flagellation is reportedly rare now. Shi'i marriage and funeral rites remain widespread, the latter even in the case of people who had not been observant in life.[70] The persistence of Shi'ism in Azerbaijan is strong enough to be considered worth a recent dissertation by an Azerbaijani graduate student.[71]

Iran's Shi'i militants have sought to spread their message north of the border. Radio and television broadcasts, some directed especially at Soviet Muslims, are heavily saturated with Islamic republican propaganda, including the importance of practicing Islam, criticism of the Soviet system, and calls for Muslim unity. There are reports that the message is spread further through the use of tape cassette recordings. Appeals to Islam are also broadcast to the Soviet Union from sources unrelated to Iran's Shi'i rulers, above all, the United States' Radio Liberty. The oc-

67. *Turkmenskaia iskra*, June 15, 1980, 3; Vagabov, *Islam i voprosy*, 3, 76, 103–04; M. Khalmukhamedov, "O chem govoriat musul'manskie propovedniki" (What Muslim Preachers Talk About), *Nauka i religiia*, no. 6 (June 1969): 59.

68. *Bakinskii rabochii*, December 19, 1980, 3.

69. Bennigsen and C. Lemercier-Quelquejay, "Muslim Religious Conservatism and Dissent in the USSR," *Religion in Communist Lands* 6, no. 3 (Autumn 1978): 157; Bennigsen, "Islam in the Soviet Union," in B. R. Bociurkiw and J. W. Strong, eds., *Religion and Atheism in the U.S.S.R. and Eastern Europe* (London: Macmillan, 1975), 95.

70. Fatulla-ogly, "Shiiti segodnia," 37–38.

71. In December 1981, Rabiiat Nurulla kyzy Aslanova defended her dissertation, "Shiizm, kharakter ego perezhitkov v Azerbaidzhane i nekotorye voprosy ateisticheskogo vospitaniia trudiashchikhsia" (Shi'ism, the Character of Its Survivals in Azerbaijan and Some Questions of the Atheist Upbringing of the Workers), for the degree of candidate in philosophy at Azerbaijan State University.

casional denunciations the broadcasting elicits from Soviet sources indicates that the leadership finds the practice at least irritating.[72]

What all this tells us about the level of Shi'i activism in the USSR or the impact of Shi'i propaganda from abroad is not clear. Outside observers of Soviet Islam must of necessity resort to speculation on the basis of fragmentary evidence. The overall tenor of Soviet official statements about Islam is that the great majority of Muslim citizens are loyal and productive members of Soviet society. Are these statements intended to disguise the seriousness of Muslim resistance to incorporation in Soviet society, or do they reflect an opinion among the Soviet leadership that the persistence of Islam applies mostly to the sphere of family matters and can be contained within acceptable limits? Soviet publications never extend to the USSR the observation made about the progressive relation of Islam to socialist-oriented policies in certain foreign Muslim countries. They could not do so publicly because their view of that function of Islam is predicated on the backwardness of a society not yet ready for socialism. Do authorities privately argue that if Islam has been demonstrated to be safe in Algeria and the People's Democratic Republic of Yemen it need not be an unmanageable problem for the Soviet system? Two of the most prominent Western experts on Soviet Islam consider its influence to be strongest among the Chechens and Ingushes of the Caucasus Mountains.[73] To what extent can one accurately extrapolate from reports of Islamic observance among these people, known mostly for their isolation, individuality, and frequently combative relations with others, to the broader status of Soviet Islam? Is Shi'ism in the Azerbaijan S.S.R. likely to contribute to increased political tensions there? The republic's economy has done extremely well by Soviet standards in recent years, in contrast to the abundant problems in Iran which contributed to the revolution there. We know so little about the causes of political strife that we anticipate unrest when economic conditions are bad but also look for revolutions of rising expectations.

The evidence tells us less than we would wish to know about the impact of Iranian Shi'i activism on Soviet Azerbaijanis, Turkomans, and

72. *Komsomolskaia pravda*, July 30, 1982, 2; *Turkmenskaia iskra*, June 15, 1980, 3; *Literaturnaia gazeta*, December 1, 1982, 10; Vagabov, *Islam i voprosy*, 112–13; Foreign Broadcast Information Service, *South Asia, Daily Report*, August 3, 1982, p. I 8; *Joint Publications Research Service*, no. 79497, p. 31; Ro'i, "The Impact of the Islamic Fundamentalist Revival," 177n64; Dawisha and Carrere d'Encausse, "Islam in the Foreign Policy of the Soviet Union," 174–75.

73. Bennigsen and Lemercier-Quelquejay, "L' 'Islam parallèle' en Union Soviétique," *Cahiers du Monde Russe et Soviétique* 21, no. 1 (January-March 1980): 53–54.

Tajiks. Reports of the strength of Islamic observance in the Soviet Union predate Iran's Islamic revolution. Soviet statements about religious propaganda from abroad are ambiguous about the role of broadcasts from Iran as opposed to other sources, especially Radio Liberty. Are complaints on this score a reflection of Soviet perceptions of a serious problem, or are they used for propaganda purposes: as yet another instance of hostile behavior to ascribe to countries with which the Soviets have troubled relations, and as part of the message long aimed at Soviet citizens that in so many ways there are foreign threats to the Soviet system? When the head of Azerbaijan's KGB relates that his agency has discovered foreign agents using Islam to stimulate antisocial activities, is he describing a serious problem, or is he voicing themes associated with the KGB's institutional interests: the existence of subversion and the KGB's success in thwarting it? Are Turkomans likely to be swayed by Islamic propaganda when it is associated with Shi'ism and Persians? Some Iranian Turkomans were not, as demonstrated by the unrest among them in the early months of the Islamic Republic. The Sunni Turkomans have a tradition of hostility toward Shi'i-Persian Iran, demonstrated most dramatically by the numerous devastating slave raids they conducted in Iran from the eighteenth century to the 1920s.

The press of the Tajik S.S.R. occasionally carries fairly explicit discussions of problems there but does not link them to Islamic activism in Iran. Many of the newspaper articles on events in Iran since 1978 were centrally produced and standardized, offering no special interpretation designed to deal with particular problems in the Tajiks' attitudes. Such articles are published not only in Tajikistan but also in other republics, some of which have negligible Muslim populations. In Tajik-language articles lamenting the persistence of Islam, the central issue is that Islamic views are an obstacle to the full development of the Soviet outlook, a problem that existed long before Iran's Islamic revolution. Furthermore, when official sources detail the particular manifestations they find troublesome, they do not refer directly or indirectly to the influence of developments in Iran but rather to the continuing observance of traditional rites and folk beliefs. These include marriage and funeral ceremonies, fasting, prayer at tombs, belief in amulets, fortune-telling, opposition to women's emancipation, relying on mullas instead of doctors, and supernatural explanations of earthquakes.[74]

74. M. Khojaev and Gh. Nu"monov, "Propagandai ateistiro ta"sirbakhsh menamoem" (We Are Effectively Conducting Atheist Propaganda), *Kommunisti Tojikiston* no. 10 (October 1982): 78–80; N. Boimurodov, "Sotsializm mutaraqqi va ozodi vijdon" (Developed

Islamic propaganda flows from the Soviet Union as well as to it. Soviet ulama, especially from Central Asia, have presided over Islamic conferences meeting in Tashkent in Uzbekistan, and Dushanbe in Tajikistan, to which foreign Muslims are invited, although foreign attendance is sometimes sparse and the visitors' reaction not always positive. The aim of such meetings is to rally support for a favorable picture of the status of Islam in the Soviet Union and to win endorsements for Soviet foreign policy, including its stance toward Afghanistan and the Arab-Israeli dispute, and also issues that are not particularly associated with Islam, like SALT II.[75] Soviet Muslims also travel to Muslim countries for religious purposes and as official emissaries to secular functions.

One of the most interesting examples of this is the highest ranking of the Soviet Shi'i ulama, Hajji Allahshukur Pashazada, who in 1980 was appointed head of the Muslim Spiritual Directorate for Transcaucasia (the government-sanctioned administrative body for Muslims in that region). His knowledge of languages reportedly includes fluency in Arabic, Persian, and Turkish. He has traveled to holy places abroad, including Qom, Mashhad, Karbala, Mecca, and Medina. A visit he made to Iran some time between 1980 and 1982 was not a public relations success since he and his delegation left the country in reaction to demonstrations of anti-Soviet feeling.[76] Radio Moscow's Persian-language broadcasts to Iran include favorable depictions of the status of Islam in the Soviet Union and indignant replies to Iranian pronouncements that dispute that image. The fact that these are recurring themes indicates the message has yet to find widespread acceptance.[77]

The long-term consequences of the current wave of Islamic activism is the weakest aspect of the Soviet discussion of the question. This reflects a fundamental problem the Soviets have in dealing with the role of Islam in the modern world. For all the growth of Soviet expertise in the field,

---

Socialism and Freedom of Conscience), ibid. no. 12 (December 1983): 75, 77; S. Ahmadov, "San"at va tashakkuli jahonbini ilmii ateistii mehnatkashon" (Art and the Formation of the Workers' Scientific Atheist Outlook), ibid. no. 8 (August 1983): 94, 95; *Gazetai Muallimon*, October 4, 1983, 2.

75. O. Volgin, "V preddverii XV veka khidzhry" (At the Threshold of the XVth Century of the Hijra), *Novoe vremia* no. 41 (October 5, 1979): 24; Dawisha and Carrere d'Encausse, "Islam in the Foreign Policy of the Soviet Union," 168, 173; Bennigsen, "Soviet Muslims and the World of Islam," *Problems of Communism* 29, no. 2 (March-April 1980): 44.

76. *Komsomolskaia pravda*, June 30, 1982, 2; A. Sheehy, "New Head of Soviet Shi'a Elected," *RFE/RL. Radio Liberty Research*, no. 213/80 (June 12, 1980): 23–25.

77. Foreign Broadcast Information Service, *Soviet Union. Daily Report*, September 1, 1982, H10; October 5, 1982, H10–11; March 9, 1983, H7–8.

ideology still restricts the permissible interpretations. Since Marxism-Leninism insists that all societies are evolving in the same direction, albeit at different rates, and that the most advanced stages of evolution must include the victory of atheism, materialism, and class consciousness, Soviet analysts of Islam must treat it as a transient phenomenon.[78]

Whatever the usefulness the Soviets see in Islamic activism for weakening Muslim countries' ties to the West, in the longer term it is at odds with Soviet goals. The smoothest projected transition from an Islamic to a more "advanced" outlook would come as the progressive petty bourgeois variety of Islamic revival is influenced by radical and democratic ideas and Muslims come to see the inadequacies of Islamic economic doctrine.[79] This argument is heard infrequently. The more widespread view stresses conflict. Since religious views are always to the right of their secular counterparts, Muslim petty bourgeois radicalism is less likely than the secular version to evolve into revolutionary democracy, a stage in the evolution toward socialism. Even radical Islamic movements oppose class consciousness and lack solutions to the problems of developing societies. Furthermore, not all varieties of Islamic activism nowadays are radical; some are reactionary. The Soviets see dangers in the fact that opposition to the West has contributed significantly to Islamic activism. What they fear is a sweeping rejection of everything produced by Western civilization, including elements admired by the Soviets, above all, Marxism and also industrial technology. The whole climate of the Islamic revival is conducive to making the religion resistant to voluntary adaptation and prone to virulent anticommunism.[80]

In some ways, the Soviet understanding of Islam as a force in contemporary society has grown considerably in the past decade. In addition to intelligence sources, which by their nature are concealed from public scrutiny, the Kremlin leadership has at its disposal a group of serious scholars of Islam. The sheer volume of information gathered is far greater than before. The emphasis on the classics of Marxism-Leninism as sources of information about Islam has declined, though it certainly has not disappeared. At the same time, Soviet scholars make extensive use of sources of evidence from various Asian and African countries as well as Western

78. Ionova, "Doktriny," 61.

79. Stepaniants, "Musul'manskoe vozrozhdenstvo," 26; Z. I. Levin and I. M. Smilianskaia, "Islam i problemy obshchestvennogo razvitiia arabskikh stran" (Islam and Problems of Social Development of the Arab Countries), *Narody Azii i Afriki*, no. 1 (1984): 106–07.

80. Kim et al., *Zarubezhnyi Vostok*, 3:156, 158; Vasil'ev, *Istoriia religii Vostoka*, 171; Merkulov, *Islam*, 104–05, 226, 300–01; Ionova, "Sotsial'noe razmezhevanie," 36–37; idem, "Doktriny," 60; Stepaniants, *Musul'manskie kontseptsii*, 6, 9.

scholarship. Polemical tirades still exist, especially in domestic propaganda, but even here some of the publications have been influenced by the more detached scholarly tone.[81]

Although Soviet experts are not alone in having difficulty anticipating the evolution of Islamic activism, they are subject to special constraints. The range of permissible analysis is determined by political considerations, which are reactive and tactical. Whatever knowledgeable experts on Islam might privately believe, their public utterances must not challenge the prevailing wisdom. Only after the pressure of events has displaced the old accepted opinion can experts argue against it and in favor of the new accepted opinion.

Although the Soviet leadership now knows more about Islam, even its short-term efforts to use Islamic movements for its own advantage have met with mixed results. It is unsure what the relation will be in the long term but has difficulty seeing Islam except as an adversary.

---

81. Prime examples of this are M. V. Vagabov's *Islam i voprosy ateisticheskogo vospitaniia,* a textbook intended for college students, graduate students, and teachers of atheism courses; L. S. Vasil'ev's *Istoriia religii Vostoka,* a textbook for a course given in the Oriental Department of the Ministry of Foreign Affairs' Moscow State Institute of International Affairs; and *Ateisticheskii slovar'* (Atheist Dictionary) (Moscow: Izdatel'stvo politicheskogo literatury, 1983).

Index

Abaqiq, Saudi Arabia, 240
'Abbas (half-brother of Imam Husain), 188
Abbasid dynasty, 5, 7
'Abd al-Rahman Khan, Amir (of Afghanistan), 203n, 205 and n, 206–07, 208, 221, 227, 229
'Abd al-'Aziz (Saudi ruler), 232
Abu Dharr al-Ghifari, 144
Abu'l-Qasim Rizavi, Sayyid, 16–17
'adl, 45, 53. See also Justice
Adloun, Lebanon, 173
al-Adwa' al-Islamiyah (journal), 191
Afghanistan, 2, 8, 11, 15, 107, 201–02, 283, 285; anticommunist resistance in, 201, 212, 221–24, 225–27, 228–29, 255, 276, 284–85, 294; Buddhism in, 201; communists of, 217, 219, 221, 222; Hazara War, 205–07, 227; Iran's policy toward, 97, 98 and n, 103–04, 224, 225–27, 229; late 1940s Shahristan revolt, 208–09, 214; 1949 attempted coup d'etat, 214–16, 220; 1964–73 parliamentary democracy, 216–19; 1973 coup d'etat, 216, 218n, 219; 1978 communist coup, 221, 228; political dissent in, 201–02, 203, 210–11, 219–21, 228; reign of 'Abd al-Rahman, 205–07, 227; reign of

Amanullah Khan, 207; Shi'ism in, 202–07, 204, 227–29; Shi'i disjuncture, 212 and n, 227–28; Shi'i grievances, 212–13; Shi'i politicization, 214–18, 228; Shi'i population estimate, 202; Shi'i protest, 203, 213, 214, 216–18, 221–24, 227–29; Shi'i resistance, factional conflicts since 1979, 224–27, 229; social banditry and political protest, 208–14, 227; Soviet occupation of, 15, 96, 98, 253, 255, 284–85, 294; Sunni party supported by Khomeini, 225–26; Sunnis of, 15, 202, 205 and n, 206, 212, 213, 215, 217n, 221, 227, 294; urban migration in, 212 and n. See also Hazarajat region, Afghanistan
Aflaq, Michel, 257n
Africa, 4, 62; Khomeini's influence in, 22, 27; West, Shi'i emigrants in, 145, 159, 161, 175
Agha Khans (Nizari leaders), 4–5
Ahl-i Haqq, 28n, 118
Ahmad ibn 'Abd al-'Aziz, Prince, 243–44
Ahmad Shah Durrani, 203
al-'Ain, Qurrat, 118
Aisha, 128
Ajami, Fouad, 158
akhbar (oral reports), 6

303

Contributors

MURIEL ATKIN, associate professor of history at George Washington University, is author of *Russia and Iran, 1780–1828* and of articles on recent Soviet-Iranian relations.

HANNA BATATU is professor of Arab studies at the School of Foreign Service, Georgetown University, and author of *The Old Social Classes and the Revolutionary Movements of Iraq*.

HELENA COBBAN, who works as a free-lance writer specializing in Middle East issues, is based in Washington, D.C. From 1976 to 1981 she was Beirut correspondent for the *Christian Science Monitor* and the London *Sunday Times*. She is the author of *The Palestine Liberation Organization: People, Power and Politics* and *The Making of Lebanon*.

JUAN R. I. COLE is assistant professor of history at the University of Michigan, Ann Arbor. His works include *From Iran East and West* (editor, with Moojan Momen) and the forthcoming *Roots of North Indian Shi'ism in Iran and Iraq: Religion and State in Nishapuri Awadh, 1722–1859*. He has published numerous academic translations and articles on the modern Middle East.

RICHARD W. COTTAM, university professor of political science, University of Pittsburgh, served in the U.S. embassy, Tehran, 1956–58. He is the author of *Nationalism in Iran, Competitive Interference and Twen-*

tieth Century Diplomacy, Foreign Policy Motivation, and *The Rehabilitation of Power in International Relations* (with G. Gallucci).

DAVID BUSBY EDWARDS is a doctoral candidate in anthropology at the University of Michigan, Ann Arbor. He recently spent two years doing fieldwork in Pakistan among Afghan refugees and has contributed chapters to the forthcoming *Afghanistan: The Politics of Survival* and *Islam and Ethnicity in Pakistan.*

JACOB GOLDBERG is permanently affiliated with the Shiloah (Dayan) Center for Middle East Studies and Department of Middle East History, Tel Aviv University, and has recently been visiting professor at Cornell University, George Washington University, University of California at San Diego, and San Diego State University. He has academic publications on Saudi Arabia.

FRED HALLIDAY is professor of international relations at the London School of Economics. He has written extensively on East-West relations and the politics of the Middle East, and his works include *Arabia without Sultans, Iran: Dictatorship and Development, The Ethiopian Revolution* (with Maxine Molyneux), and *The Making of the Second Cold War.* He is on the editorial boards of *Past and Present* and *MERIP Reports* and was for eight years a Fellow of the Transnational Institute (Amsterdam and Washington).

NIKKI R. KEDDIE is professor of history at the University of California at Los Angeles and past president of the Middle East Studies Association. Among her most recent books are *The Iranian Revolution and the Islamic Republic* (editor, with Eric Hooglund), *Religion and Politics in Iran* (editor), *Roots of Revolution: An Interpretive History of Modern Iran,* and *Modern Iran: The Dialectics of Continuity and Change* (editor, with Michael Bonine).

RUDI MATTHEE is pursuing a doctorate in Islamic Studies at the University of California at Los Angeles. He lived in Iran and Egypt for several years and has published scholarly articles on the Iranian Revolution and its wider impact in *Orient* and *Iranian Studies.*

AUGUSTUS RICHARD NORTON is associate professor of comparative politics in the Department of Social Sciences, United States Military Academy, West Point, New York. He conducted field research in Lebanon in 1980–81 and 1982. He has published widely in scholarly journals and the press on Lebanon and coauthored *The Emergence of a New Lebanon: Fantasy or Reality.* His book-length study on the Shi'is in Lebanon will be published in 1986.

R. K. RAMAZANI is Harry F. Byrd, Jr., professor of government and foreign affairs at the University of Virginia, where he has specialized in the Middle East for more than thirty years. His latest books include *The Persian Gulf and the Strait of Hormuz* and *The United States and Iran: The Patterns of Influence.*

NAHID YEGANEH is a doctoral candidate at the University of London and coauthored *In the Shadow of Islam: The Women's Movement in Iran.* She is a member of the editorial board of *Nimih-'i Digar,* a Persian-language feminist journal.